Y0-BZF-039

THE BLUE GUIDES

Albania
Austria
Belgium and Luxembourg
China
Cyprus
Czechoslovakia
Denmark
Egypt

FRANCE
France
Paris and Versailles
Burgundy
Loire Valley
Midi-Pyrénées
Normandy
South West France
Corsica

GERMANY
Berlin and Eastern Germany
Western Germany

GREECE
Greece
Athens and environs
Crete

HOLLAND
Holland
Amsterdam

Hungary
Ireland

ITALY
Northern Italy
Southern Italy
Florence
Rome and environs
Venice
Tuscany
Umbria
Sicily

Jerusalem
Malta and Gozo
Mexico
Morocco
Moscow and Leningrad
Portugal

SPAIN
Spain
Barcelona
Madrid

Sweden
Switzerland

TURKEY
Turkey
Istanbul

UK
England
Scotland
Wales
London
Museums and Galleries
   of London
Oxford and Cambridge
Country Houses of England
Gardens of England
Literary Britain and Ireland
Victorian Architecture in
   Britain
Churches and Chapels
   of Northern England
Churches and Chapels
   of Southern England
Channel Islands

USA
New York
Boston and Cambridge

Detail of the beautiful attentuated figure of the Prophet Jeremiah on the south portal of the Church of St-Pierre, Moissac

BLUE GUIDE

The Midi-Pyrénées

Albi, Toulouse, Conques, Moissac

Delia Evans

A&C Black
London

WW Norton
New York

1st edition May 1995

Published by A & C Black (Publishers) Limited
35 Bedford Row, London WC1R 4JH

A CIP catalogue record of this book is available from the British Library.

ISBN 0–7136–3853–2

Published in the United States of America by
WW Norton and Company, Inc
500 Fifth Avenue, New York, NY 10110

Published simultaneously in Canada by
Penguin Books Canada Limited
10 Alcorn Avenue, Toronto, Ontario M4V 3BE

ISBN 0–393–31269–0 USA

Maps and plans drawn by RJS Associates

Photographs by Delia Evans and the Comité Régional de Tourisme Midi-Pyrénées

The author and the publishers have done their best to ensure the accuracy of all the
information in Blue Guide Midi-Pyrénées; however, they can accept no responsibility
for any loss, injury or inconvenience sustained by any traveller as a result of information
or advice contained in the guide.

Delia Evans lives in Oxford and also has a home in the Midi-Pyrénées.
Educated at Reading University, she spent some years living and working
in Paris. She has translated a number of French art history publications and
contributed to the *Handbook of Modern British Painting 1900–1980* (1992).
For several years she has been involved with devising and leading cultural
tours in England and France.

Printed and bound in Great Britain by
Butler & Tanner Ltd, Frome and London

The publishers and the author welcome comments,
suggestions and corrections for the next edition of Blue
Guide Midi-Pyrénées. Writers of the most informative
letters will be awarded a free Blue Guide of their choice.

CONTENTS

Maps and Plans

Map of the Region **on the inside front and back covers**

INTRODUCTION

The *Région Midi-Pyrénées* is a huge, remote and largely unspoiled part of France between the Massif Central and the Spanish border covering some 45,382 square kilometres, an area greater than Switzerland. While the Midi evokes something southerly and the Pyrenees are self-explanatory, the majority of English-speaking travellers will be unfamiliar with the designation Midi-Pyrénées which was conjured up in 1972. Indeed, where its boundaries lie and what it encompasses is a mystery to much of the French population. The administrative outline, defined in 1960, draws together eight *départements*: the Ariège-Pyrénées, Aveyron, Gers, Haute-Garonne, Hautes-Pyrénées, Lot, and Tarn formed in 1790, and the Tarn-et-Garonne, created in 1808. With the exception of Hautes-Pyrénées, these are named after the rivers that run through them. The regional capital, Toulouse, some 686km from Paris, is far and away the largest town in the region. The regional identity is not based on one single coherent historic entity, and the heterogeneous nature of its culture is one of its charms. Before annexation to France in the 13C, the medieval territories consisted of a multitude of *comtés, viscomtés*, and *duchés* divided and sub-subdivided by continual conflict and therefore in constant flux. After annexation, provinces were governed by representatives of the king and the memory of the old *pays* lingers on, particularly in tourist publicity: for example, the Gers is described as the heart of Gascony; much of the Lot and the Tarn-et-Garonne is referred to as the Quercy, the *département* of the Aveyron is almost synonymous with the old Rouergue.

Two major pilgrimage roads crossed the region, through the Pyrenees and on to Spain: the Via Podiensis and the Via Tolosana (part of the Via Arelatensis). A third took a route across the Causses. The pilgrimages left in their wake a fine array of Romanesque art and architecture combining Mozarabic and Cluniac influences. Later, reaction to the problems of the Albigensian heresies produced a unique style of Gothic churches designed mainly for predication. And the styles of the Renaissance introduced directly from Italy or via the Loire valley, are represented by some charming châteaux and *hôtel particuliers*.

Midway between the Atlantic and the Mediterranean, no section of the Midi-Pyrénées touches the coast. The north-eastern border crosses the highlands of the Aubrac on the edge of the Massif Central, and the southern boundary runs along the jagged Pyrenean range on the Spanish frontier, with about 330km between them. Some 280km divides the plains and vineyards of Armagnac in the west from the more rugged Montagne Noire to the east. Contrasts of topography and climate combine with local traditions and raw materials, such as slate and schist, granite and basalt, brick and tiles, fragile limestone, red sandstone or grey marble, to determine the kaleidoscope of landscapes which provides the backdrop to every excurs-ion in the Midi-Pyrénées.

The climate is agreeably temperate, the summers long and sunny, the spring showery and the autumn magnificent. But while summer temperatures in Toulouse can beat all records in France, the Aubrac and the Pyrenees are high and cold enough to have winter skiing. Despite the lack of coastal attractions, the Midi-Pyrénées is refreshed by a multitude of beautiful river valleys: the Tarn, the Aveyron, the Garonne and the Dourbie; and lakes: Laouzas and La Ravièfe in the Lacaune, Pareloup and Pont de Salars in the Aveyron.

Acknowledgements

I wish to thank the Comité Régional du Tourisme Midi-Pyrénées and the eight Comités Départementaux for their practical assistance with travel, accommodation and the organisation of visits. I would also like to thank Brittany Ferries for their help with travel to and from the Region. I am especially grateful to Laurence Jay-Rayon of the Comité Régional who has dealt efficiently and cheerfully with all my queries and requests, as have her colleagues at the Comités Départementaux. Equally, the staff of tourist information offices and museums, châteaux owners and church officials throughout the Midi-Pyrénées showed infinite kindness and enthusiasm for opening doors and furnishing information; that they cannot all be mentioned individually in no way lessens my gratitude. A great debt is due to Maurice Scelles, and to Antoinette and Jacques Sangouard for all their excellent advice. I should also like to thank Gemma Davies of A & C Black for quietly keeping me on the right track. And special thanks to John, William and Siân for their constant encouragement and support.

How to Use the Guide

In adhering to the customary Blue Guide procedure of dividing the territory into a series of itineraries, this guide is aimed chiefly at motorists. The routes start, however, not at the edge but at the centre of the region, at Toulouse. With the main airport, and as the terminus for all public transport, it is the logical starting point for a fly-drive visitor. It is also good as a touring base, and ideally suited to the non-motorised traveller. The routes given in this guide follow a clockwise sequence around the region, some centred on a particular town with excursions, others as a journey between two points. Many of the tours concentrate on an historic *pays*. A visit could, for example, be planned around a river valley or valleys, concentrate on an historic region or have a topographical focus. The headnote to each route gives a summary of its major attractions and characteristics, and the cumulative distance where appropriate. The detailed route is included in the text. The telephone number of the local Tourist Information Centre is given for each centre. This guide is first and foremost an introduction to the art, architecture and history of the Midi-Pyrénées but, as far as space allows, includes information on points of local interest, such as the flora and regional cuisine, and on accommodation and restaurants.

To help plan your trip, there is a list of Highlights on page 18. Two stars indicate a point of outstanding interest; one star something of great merit. This does not, of course, suggest that un-starred sites are not worth visiting and an element of subjectivity is inevitable. The rest of the introductory section deals with such practical matters as how to get to Midi-Pyrénées, travelling around it, maps, accommodation, restaurants and food, and access to châteaux, museums and churches. There is also a list of Tourist Information Centres.

Getting There

By car and ferry

The most convenient ferry services are as follows: **Brittany Ferries** from Portsmouth to Caen (about 6 hours) or Poole–Cherbourg (about 4½ hours). Reservations: The Brittany Centre, Wharf Road, Portsmouth, PO2 8RU, tel: 01705 753033, or Millbay, Plymouth, PL1 3EQ, tel: 01752 229418.

P&O European Ferries from Portsmouth to Le Havre. Reservations: The Continental Ferry Port, Mile End, Portsmouth PO2 8QW, tel: 01705 827677.

These crossings avoid Paris, and link up with the A62 via Bordeaux to Montauban and Toulouse, the A68 Toulouse to Albi, the N20 via Limoges to Cahors and Toulouse, or the A75 from Clermont-Ferrand to Millau.

An alternative route is via northern Spain by **Brittany Ferries**—Plymouth/Portsmouth–Santander (23–24 hours), entering the Midi-Pyrénées via Tarbes or across the Pyrenees.

For those who prefer a shorter crossing but a longer drive, **Hoverspeed** have 12 daily flights by Hovercraft, from Dover to Calais (35 mins) and up to six crossings daily by **Seacat** from Folkestone to Bologne (55 mins). (City sprint coaches from London-Victoria to Paris run in conjunction with Hovercraft.) Information and reservations: Hoverspeed, International Hoverport, Marine Parade, Dover, Kent CT17 9TG, tel: 01304 240241

By train

Eurotunnel: passenger service only, from London-Waterloo to Paris-Gare du Nord, takes 3 hours. Information and reservations: Eurostar, tel: 01233 617575.

Le Shuttle, for passengers and cars, Folkestone to Calais, 35 mins platform-to-platform. Information and reservations: tel: 01303 271100.

TGVs Paris–Montparnasse to Toulouse via Montauban, run 3 times daily, (5 hours 10 mins); and to Tarbes, 3 or 4 times daily (5 hours 50 mins). There are frequent regular services from Paris-Austerlitz to Toulouse via Montauban; to Albi and Rodez via Capdenac; to Foix; to Luchon; and to Lourdes via Tarbes. Information from International British Rail Enquiries at Victoria Station, tel: 0171 834 2345, or the SNCF, 179 Piccadilly, London W1V 0BA, tel: 0171 409 3518.

Motorail runs regular services direct from Calais to Toulouse and to Brive, March–October, and from Paris to Toulouse all year. Information: 179 Piccadilly, London W1V 0BA, tel: 0171 409 3518.

By air

British Airways has two flights a day from London-Gatwick to Toulouse. **Air France** has one flight a day from London-Heathrow Mon–Fri, and one flight on Sundays. British Airways has one flight from London-Gatwick to Lourdes on Saturdays, from April to October. There are 19 flights daily from Paris to Toulouse from Paris-Orly, and from Paris-Charles de Gaulle. There are also flights from Paris to Tarbes-Lourdes, Rodez, Castres and Albi.

Travelling around the Midi-Pyrénées

Driving is the obvious and most convenient way to tour the region. If you arrive by train or by air there are a number of car-hire firms to choose from: Budget, Europcar, Avis, Hertz, Eurorent. Petrol prices are higher in France than in the UK and the most competitive prices are offered by garages attached to supermarkets.

There are good **train** links from Toulouse with the major centres—the region boasts 100 train stations—but travelling to smaller towns and cross-country needs detailed planning. Information: SNCF, 179 Piccadilly, London W1V 0BA, tel: 0171 742 6600.

Travelling by **coach or bus** (12 *gares routières*) is even more patchy and services vary from *département* to *département*. It is advisable to enquire at the main bus station in **Toulouse**: Gare Routière de Toulouse, 62 bd. Pierre Sémard, Toulouse, tel: 61 48 71 84; or at local bus stations or at train stations.

Cycling is a very popular pastime with the French and the variety of terrain in the Midi-Pyrénées offers something for the very fit and the less fit enthusiasts. Bicycles and mountains bikes can be hired from certain train stations, camp sites and Syndicats d'Initiative. For information and routes contact the *Fédération Française de Cyclotourisme*, 8 rue J-M. Jego, 75013-Paris, tel: 1 45 80 30 21; or the *Ligue des Pyrénées de Cyclotourisme*, Centre Léo Lagrange, 54 rue des 7 Troubadours, 31000-Toulouse, tel: 61 44 15 84; or the individual Comités Départementaux de Cyclotourisme.

Walking is very well catered for, with marked trails of every category from very strenuous to gentle amble. There are several GR (Grande Randonnée) trails, official long-distance footpaths, which cross or begin or end in the Region and include two main branches of the Pilgrim Route to Santiago de Compostela, GR10 and GR36. These are described in *Topoguides*, published by the Fédération Française de Randonnée Pédestre, 8 Avenue Marceau, 75008 Paris; or in information published by each of the eight *Comités Départementaux de la Randonnée Pédestre* and by *Randonnées Pyrénéennes*, Centre d'Information montagne et sentiers, 4 rue Maye-Lane—B.P. 24, 65420-Tarbes Ibos, tel: 62 90 09 92.

Boating as a means of getting around is possible on the Canal du Midi, the Canal Latéral à la Garonne and the Lot River. For information and reservations for boats on the Canal du Midi and River Lot: *Crown Blue Line*, Le Grand Bassin, 11401 Castelnaudary, tel: 68 23 17 51, and *Locaboat Plaisance*, Port-au-Bois, 89300-Joigny, tel: 86 9172 72; houseboats, *Les Chalandoux*, place de la République, 31290 Avignonet-Lauragais, tel: 61 27 82 95. For boats on the Canal Latéral à la Garonne: *Rive de France*, 172 bd. Berthier, 75017-Paris, tel: 42 22 10 86, and *Moissac Navigation Plaisance*, port de Plaisance, quai Charles de Gaulle, 82200-Moissac, tel: 63 04 48 28.

Maps

Michelin and *Institut Géographique National* (IGN) both produce good maps. The Michelin yellow regional map, number 235, scale 1:200,000 is easy to read but large and unwieldy. It cuts off the western and eastern extremities for which you need number 234 (Aquitaine) and number 240 (Languedoc-Roussillon). In the smaller version there are six maps to cover the region, numbers 79, 80, 82, 83, 85 and 86. In conjunction with the Région Midi-Pyrénées, IGN produces a Tourist map of the entire region, scale 1:250,000 (new edition 1995) available locally from certain bookshops. In the IGN Série Rouge, you need numbers 110, 111, 113, 114. Cyclists and hikers will find one or some of the following IGN maps useful: Série Verte, at 1:100,000; Série Orange, at 1:50,000; Série Bleue, at 1:25,000.

Tourist Information Centres

French Government Tourist Offices abroad

UK: 178 Piccadilly, London W1V 0AL, tel: 0891 244123, fax: 493 6594

USA, New York: 610 Fifth Avenue, Suite 222, New York, NY 10020-2452, tel: 315 0887, fax: 247 6468

USA, Mid-West: 654 North Michigan Avenue, Chicago, Illinois 60611-2836, tel: 337 6301, fax: 337 6339

USA, South: 2305 Cedar Springs Boulevard, Dallas, Texas 75201, tel: 720 4010, fax: 720 0250

USA, West Coast: 9454 Wilshire Boulevard, Beverley Hills, California 90212-2967, tel: 272 2661, fax: 276 2835

Canada, Montreal: 1981 Avenue MacGill College, Suite 490, Montreal, Quebec H3A 2W9, tel: 288 4264, fax: 845 4868

Canada, Toronto: 30 St. Patrick Street, Suite 700, Toronto, Ontario M5T 3A3, tel: 593 6427, fax: 979 7587

Région Midi-Pyrénées overall

Comité Régional de Tourisme Midi-Pyrénées, 54 bd. de l'Embouchure, B.P. 2166, 31200-Toulouse-Cédex, tel: 61 13 55 55, fax: 61 47 17 16

Departmental Tourist Boards

Ariège-Pyrénées, Hôtel du Département, BP 143, 09003-Foix Cédex, tel: 61 02 09 70, fax: 61 65 54 91

Aveyron, 33 avenue Victor Hugo, 12000-Rodez, tel: 65 73 63 15, fax: 65 73 63 29

Gers, 7 rue Diderot, BP 106, 32002-Auch Cédex, tel: 62 05 37 02, fax: 62 05 02 16

Haute-Garonne, 14 rue Bayard, 31000-Toulouse, tel: 61 99 44 00

Hautes-Pyrénées, 6 rue Eugène Ténot, 65000-Tarbes, tel: 62 93 03 30

Lot, 107 quai Cavaignac, BP 7, 46001-Cahors, tel: 65 35 07 09, fax: 65 23 92 76

Tarn, Hôtel du Département, 41 rue Porta, 81014-Albi, tel: 63 77 32 10, fax: 63 77 32 32

Tarn-et-Garonne, Hôtel des Intendants, place du Maréchal Foch, 82000-Montauban, tel: 63 63 31 40

Accommodation

Hotels in France are officially classified by a system of stars, running from one to four, indicating the range of amenities offered. There are also unstarred hotels which are perfectly adequate. The star system is only a rough guide to prices, which vary considerably within each category. Prices are usually quoted per room and not per person and do not normally include breakfast. Note, however, that half or full board rates are quoted per person. Tariffs are generally listed outside the hotel or in the reception area, and law requires that the price of a room is posted in the room itself. Garage parking, particularly in towns, is sometimes extra. Some establishments, especially smaller rural ones, expect guests to take dinner at the hotel, often to counterbalance the low cost of accommodation; it is tactful but not obligatory to comply, but a good idea to check out the situation when you make your reservation.

The *Comité Régional du Tourisme Midi-Pyrénées* publishes a brochure of hotels. It is advisable to book in advance for July and August and during the French national holidays (*jours fériés*) in May. In the Pyrenees the hotels are very busy from January to March.

Other sources of information are the *Michelin Red Guide*, the *Routiers Guide to France* (by post from Routiers, 25 Vanston Place, London SW16 1AZ, tel: 0171 385 6644) and, for the brochure *Logis de France-Pyrénées*, 14 rue Bayard, 31000 Toulouse (FF30), tel: 61 99 44 00. The French Government Tourist Office offers a computerised register of hotels.

Bienvenue au château. For something a little different, the eight local departmental Tourist Boards or the Comité Régional de Tourisme will provide information on Private Castles and Houses of Local Character which welcome paying guests.

Chambres d'Hôtes (the equivalent of Bed and Breakfast), and self-catering accommodation in **Gîtes Ruraux** are popular alternatives to hotels. The quality label and system of classification is by *épis* (ears of wheat). *Chambres d'Hôtes* cost from FF120–300 for two, *Gîtes* for up to four people, FF1000–2500 in season, less off season. Information and reservations for both can be obtained from the eight *départements*:

Ariège-Pyrénées, Service Tourisme-Chambre d'Agriculture, 32 avenue du Général-de-Gaulle, 09000-Foix, tel: 61 65 20 00, fax: 61 02 89 60; Relais des Gîtes Ruraux de l'Ariège, B.P.143-Hôtel du Département, 09004 Foix, tel: 61 02 09 73, fax: 61 65 54 91.

Aveyron, A.P.A.T.A.R. Loisirs Accueil de l'Aveyron, carrefour de l'Agriculture, 12006-Rodez, tel: 65 73 77 33, fax: 65 73 77 72.

Haute-Garonne, M.D.T.R.-Loisirs Acceuil Haute-Garonne, 14, rue Bayard, 31000-Toulouse, tel: 61 99 44 00, fax: 61 99 44 19.

Gers, Loisirs Acceuil Gers-'Découverte de la Gascogne', Chambre d'Agriculture-S.U.A.T., route de Tarbes, 32003-Auch, tel: 62 05 57 99/62 63 16 55, fax: 62 05 83 73.

Lot, Association du Tourisme Rural du Lot, Chambre d'Agriculture-B.P.162, 53, rue Bourseul, 46003-Cahors, tel: 65 22 32 83, fax: 65 30 06 11.

Hautes-Pyrénées, Relais du Tourisme vert, Maison de l'Agriculture, 22 place du Foirail, 65000-Tarbes, tel: 62 34 31 50/62 34 64 37, fax: 62 51 25 65; Loisirs Acceuil des Hautes-Pyrénées, 6 rue Eugène-Ténot-B.P.450, 65000-Tarbes, tel: 62 93 03 30, fax: 62 93 69 90.

Tarn, A.T.T.E.R.-Loisirs Acceuil Tarn, Chambre d'Agriculture-B.P.89, 81003-Albi, tel: 63 47 04 94/63 54 39 81, fax: 63 47 20 65.

Tarn-et-Garonne, Loisirs Acceuil du Tarn-et-Garonne, Hôtel des Intendants, Place Maréchal Foch, 82000-Montauban, tel: 63 63 31 40, fax: 63 66 80 36.

These services also cover **campings à la ferme** (farm camping) and **gîtes d'étape** (hostels for walkers).

Camping. For information on more than 100 camp sites designated Quality Plus in the Midi-Pyrénées contact: Fédération Régionale d'Hôtellerie de Plein Air, Capirot, 32700-Lectoure, tel: 62 68 84 47, fax: 62 68 88 82.

Mountain Refuges. Contact the Comités Départementaux for the Ariège, Hautes-Pyrénées and Haute-Garonne.

Restaurants and Food

The cuisine of the Midi-Pyrénées is as varied as its landscape and culture and it is possible to eat hearty, meaty and rustic meals at reasonable prices or *haute cuisine* at correspondingly high prices. There are restaurants of all categories throughout the Region and rural *fermes auberges* offer pre-booked meals. Restaurants are closed one day a week, often a Monday, so it is wise to check. Fixed price menus are a good formula for restricting the price of a meal, but the choice is also more restricted than à la carte. You can find lunch menus from FF50 upwards, dinners from FF80. FF120–150 is an average price for a good meal, but for a real gastronomic binge you can pay as much as FF600. In towns you may find restaurants and cafés offering lunch snacks, but out of town the midday meal is invariably considered the main one of the day and snacks do not exist.

Two restaurant guides are the *Michelin Red Guide* and the *Routiers Guide to France*. But it is also a good idea to ask locals—shop keepers, guides, car park attendants, and coach drivers—where they would eat. Eating is, after all, a national pastime.

In general the cooking of the region is based on the fat of the land: duck, goose, pork. But it is unwise to generalise because each *pays* has its own specialities. Excellent lamb is raised on the *causses* of the Quercy and the Rouergue, veal in the St-Gaudens area, beef in the Aubrac and freshwater fish in the Rouergue. Not only regional, but seasonal produce, plays an important part in the cuisine. Autumn is the time for dishes incorporating wild mushrooms, chestnuts, walnuts, and winter for truffles and *foie gras*.

Soup. *Garbure* is a Gascon soup of vegetables and meat; *tourin*, made with onions and garlic, and *moutairol*, are from the north of the region.

Fish. Freshwater fish such as *brochet* (pike), *truite* (trout) and *sandre* (perch). *Estofinado* is a traditional dish eaten in the Lot valley in the winter, made from dried haddock (stockfish), potatoes, garlic and parsley; dried fish from the Baltic became a lucrative cargo carried by boats on the Lot returning from the coastal port at Bordeaux.

Meat. Basic to the cooking of the Midi-Pyrénées are poultry, duck, goose and pork. The *foie gras* and *pâtés* of Gascony; the *charcuterie* (dried sausage) and *jambon cru* or *jambon de pays* (cured ham) from the Monts de Lacaune. The duck and geese fattened up for *foie gras* also produce *magrets* (breast fillets), *gésiers* (gizzards). *Confit* is poultry or pork preserved in its own fat and eaten hot or cold. *Saucisse de Toulouse* is fresh sausage sold by the kilo.

Cassoulet is a dish based on white haricot beans, goose fat, goose or duck and Toulouse sausage but with local variations. *Pistache* is a variety of cassoulet cooked in the Pyrenees. *Sanglier* (wild boar) and *marcassin* (young boar), game and venison can be eaten in certain regions, and *salmis palombe* is a dish made from wood pigeon.

Peteram is tripe as it is cooked around Luchon, in the Pyrenees; in the Quercy tripe is cooked with saffron (once an important crop here); and *tripoux de Naucelles*, in the Aveyron, is tripe cooked with ham and garlic in white wine.

Cheese. The greatest cheese in the Midi-Pyrénées is *Roquefort*, made from the milk of sheep raised on the *causses* of the Rouergue near Millau. Cow's milk is used for *Laguiole*, a smooth, yellow, fairly hard cheese produced in the Aubrac (Aveyron), and also for a number of Pyrenean varieties from Bethmale and the Couserans. The best known of the goats' cheeses are the *Cabecou* (from the Lot) and and the *Rieumes* (Haute-Garonne).

Vegetables. Truffles are used to flavour vegetables as well as meat dishes as, for example, leek and potato pie. Chestnuts from the Aveyron valley are used in a number of recipes. White garlic produced in and around Beaumont-de-Lomagne (Tarn-et-Garonne) and pink garlic around Lautrec (Tarn) are both of a superb quality.

Pastries and Sweets. *Croustade* is made with light-as-a-feather crisp flaky pastry called *pastis* and apples, sugar and butter plus Armagnac, in Gascony, or rum, in the Quercy. *Gâteau à la broche* is a conical shaped cake looking rather like a stalagmite, with a high fat content, cooked slowly on a revolving spit, found in the western part of the Pyrenees and in the Rouergue. *Fouace* is a semi-sweet cake with a little dried fruit to liven it up. Strawberries are grown in Saint-Geniès d'Olt and the Chasselas grape is special to the Moissac district, while melons, peaches, nectarines, plums, apples and pears are all cultivated in the southern Quercy. *Pruneaux fourrés* (stuffed prunes) and chocolate covered walnuts are found in the Quercy.

Wine

This is an ancient wine-producing area which has had its ups and downs since the phylloxera epidemic in the 19C. The best known wines are from Cahors and Gaillac. The Cahors vineyards are on the banks of the Lot to the west of Cahors. Gaillac is produced on the banks of the Tarn around the town of Gaillac. Lesser known wines are Madiran (red), Pacherenc-du-Vic-Bilh (white) and Frontonnais. Madiran and Pacherenc are produced where the *départements* of Hautes-Pyrénées, Gers and the Landes meet. The Frontonnais region is between Toulouse and Montauban.

Other smaller wine producing areas exist. In the Aveyron, terraced vineyards on the slopes around Marcillac are being revitalised, as well as at Estaing and Entraygues-et-Fel in the Lot Valley. In Tarn-et-Garonne are the wines of Côtes du Brulhois, Lavilledieu-du-Temple and Coteaux du Quercy.

Do not expect the great *crus* of Bordeaux or Burgundy, but good, reasonably-priced wines which can be consumed immediately or, in the case of Cahors or Gaillac, laid-down for a maximum of ten years. Production is on a small scale—many *domaines* are family businesses and produce *appellation contrôlée* as well as table wines. The range covers reds, whites and *rosés* (Gaillac *rosé* is a marvellous summer drink) and some sparkling wine (Gaillac for example). Most areas also have cooperatives. There is tremendous enthusiasm for local wine and a continual effort to improve the quality. The majority of producers and distillers, private or cooperatives, will be only too happy to give a *dégustation* (tasting) and talk about their wines.

The most familiar name connected with the region is undoubtedly Armagnac, a fiery brandy distilled in Armagnac country in the northern part of the *département* of the Gers around Condom and Eauze.

Visiting Châteaux, Museums and Churches

Opening times are given in this guide for most châteaux and museums and the major churches, but as these are subject to change, it is always advisable to check with local Tourist Information Offices. A few general rules should be remembered. Many châteaux and smaller museums are closed outside the tourist season, which stretches roughly from Easter to October and reaches its peak in July and August. Even during the high season many will be closed for two hours at midday and one day a week. Tuesday is the traditional closing day for state-owned museums but others may be closed on a Monday. However, there is an increasing trend amongst the more important museums and monuments to stay open continuously in high season. Some of the smaller churches may be manned during the peak months, but many are locked. When a key is available it is advisable not to interrupt the key-holder at lunchtime.

The annual *Journée des Portes Ouvertes*, on a Sunday in September, gives the public the opportunity to visit *Monuments Historiques* (listed buildings and sites) not normally open, and organises special events or reduced tariffs at those that are regularly open to the public. Details are available from the *Direction Régionale des Monuments Historiques*, 56 rue du Taur, B.P. 811, 31080-Toulouse, tel: 61 29 21 60. The *Monument Historique* signs indicate a listed building or site but this does not necessarily indicate that the monument can be visited. Visits to châteaux are usually accompanied by a guide, and where the château is privately owned the proprietor may conduct the visit, especially out of season. The standard of the commentary in châteaux is very variable, and occasionally you may find guides who speak English, especially in the high season.

Affiliated town guides attached to Tourist Information Offices are excellent and walking tours of most of the major towns are available. The larger towns have guides who speak English. Guided visits to major museums and churches are available at certain times. Enquire at local Tourist Information Offices.

Calendar of Events

Fêtes, foires and *festivals* abound in the Midi-Pyrénées. Every small village has a summer fair, and throughout the year there are special markets, regional produce competitions, local crafts displays, and the celebration of local traditions, as well as religious festivals. The individual *Comités Départementaux* or local Tourist Information Offices have up-to-date information on annual events and festivals, and on markets and fairs. The Regional Tourist Board will provide a comprehensive annual list on demand.

February
Albi (Tarn): Carnival

Palm Sunday and Easter
St-Félix-Lauragais (Haute-Garonne): Fairs 'à la cocagne'
Luz-St-Sauveur (Hautes-Pyrénées): 'Pâqu'à Luz' music festival

April
Albi (Tarn): Jazz festival
Fourcès (Gers): Flower market
Lourdes (Hautes-Pyrénées): International festival of religious music
Nogaro (Gers): Motor racing 'Coupes de Pâques'
Toulouse (Haute-Garonne): Street entertainment

May
Laguiole (Aveyron): Transhumance (seasonal moving of livestock to mountain pastures)
Condom (Gers): 'Bandas y Peñas'
Mirepoix (Ariège): Flower market
Montauban (Tarn-et-Garonne): 'Alors chante!' French song festival
Rieux-Volvestre (Haute-Garonne): The 'Papogay' fair

Whitsun
Vic-Fezensac (Gers): 'Féria de Vic', bull fighting

June
Ariège Trophy: The Ariège on foot, long-distance walk
Auch (Gers): Music festival
Ax-les-Thermes (Ariège): Festival of St-John
Cahors (Lot): Spring festival of photography
Montségur (Ariège): Summer solstice celebrations
Montauban (Tarn-et-Garonne): Occitan festival
Nailloux (Haute-Garonne): Messidor fair (giant cassoulet)
Pyrenees: Tour de France cycle race
Rodez (Aveyron): Music festival
Trébons (Hautes-Pyrénées): Onion fair
Villefranche-de-Rouergue (Aveyron): 'Festival Eurofanfare'
(festival for wind instruments)

July

Albi (Tarn): Festival of the theatre
Albi (Tarn): Film festival, 9.5mm film
Aveyron: Salt route, in the footsteps of the salt caravans; Stockfish route
Cahors (Lot): Blues festival
Castres (Tarn): Goya festival
Cazères-sur-Garonne (Haute-Garonne): Regatta
Condom (Gers): International folklore festival; Musical nights in Armagnac (Fleurance and Lectoure)
Cordes-sur-Ciel (Tarn): 'Fêtes du Grand Fauconnier'
Fleurance (Gers): Space festival
Gavarnie (Hautes-Pyrénées): Open-air theatre
Le Fousseret (Haute-Garonne): International art exhibition
Luz-St-Sauveur (Hautes-Pyrénées): Jazz festival
Mazamet (Tarn): Festival of music and folklore
Montauban (Tarn-et-Garonne): Jazz festival
Montréjeau (Haute-Garonne): Traditional market
Pamiers (Ariège): International festival of the theatre
St-Céré (Lot): Music festival
St-Eulalie-d'Olt (Aveyron): Festival of the Sainte-Epine
Souillac (Lot): Jazz festival
Toulouse (Haute-Garonne): Summer music festival—classical, jazz and folk
Trie-sur-Baise (Hautes-Pyrénées): 'Pourcailhade', pig fair

July-August

Conques (Aveyron): Musical evenings in the abbey-church
Cordes-sur-Ciel (Tarn): Music festival
Foix (Ariège): Medieval markets
Mirepoix (Ariège): Medieval fair
Moissac (Tarn-et-Garonne): Musical evenings
Quercy Blanc (Tarn-et-Garonne): Music festival
Sylvanès (Aveyron): International festival of religious music
St-Bertrand-de-Comminges (Haute-Garonne): Music festival
St-Lizier (Ariège): Classical music festival
Toulouse (Haute-Garonne): Summer music festival

August

Aulus les Bains (Ariège): Festival of the bear and the mountain
Gaillac (Tarn): Gaillac wine festival
Lautrec (Tarn): Festival of pink garlic; Bread and windmill festival
Luchon (Haute-Garonne): Flower festival
Madiran (Hautes-Pyrénées): Wine festival
Marciac (Gers): Jazz in Marciac
Montauban (Tarn-et-Garonne): Summer dance festival
Peyrusse-le-Roc (Aveyron): Medieval fair
Pont-de-Salars (Aveyron) Folklore festival
St-Céré (Lot): International Festival of sacred music
Vaour (Tarn): 'L'Eté de Vaour', International festival of laughter

September
Albi (Tarn): Grand Prix motor racing
Cordes-sur-Ciel (Tarn): Gastronomic Fair
Luz-St-Sauveur (Hautes-Pyrénées): 'Moutonades', transhumance of sheep
Moissac (Tarn-et-Garonne): Chasselas grape festival
Toulouse (Haute-Garonne): Piano Festival at the Jacobins; Jazz festival

October
Albi (Tarn): Antiques fair
Conques (Aveyron): Pilgrimage of St-Foy

November
Aurignac (Haute-Garonne): Gastronomic feast of St-Martin

Winter
Carbonne (Haute-Garonne): Foie-gras markets (second Thursday
of the month)
Gimont (Gers): Foie-gras markets (Wednesday)
Mirande (Gers): Foie-gras markets (Monday)
Samatan (Gers): Foie-gras markets (Monday)
Sauveterre-de-Rouergue (Aveyron): Chestnut and cider Fair

Markets

Smaller towns and villages hold a street market for produce once a week,
but in larger towns more frequently. Toulouse and Tarbes have a produce
market nearly every day. Trading usually starts at about 08.30 and ends
towards 13.00. However, there are dozens of special markets, depending
on the season or the region, and markets for things other than edibles.
Details of market days are given in the routes.

Highlights of the Region

** **Outstanding** * **Very good**
Cities and larger towns
**Albi; Toulouse; Cahors
*Auch; Castres; Montauban; Rodez

Smaller towns and villages
**Conques; Cordes-sur-Ciel; Figeac; St-Bertrand-de-Comminges;
St-Antonin-Noble-Val; Villefranche-de-Rouergue
*Ambialet; Arreau; Autoire; Belcastel; Bruniquel; Camon; Cauterets;
Condom; Estaing; Foix; Fourcès; La Couvertoirade; Laressingle;
Lauzerte; Lectoure; Lisle-sur-Tarn; Lourdes; Luz; Martel; Mirepoix;
Montjaux; Montricoux; Najac; Rieux-Volvestre; Rocamadour; St-Céré;
St-Cirq-Lapopie; St-Geniez-d'Olt; St-Lizier; Ste-Eulalie-de-Cernon;
Ste-Eulalie-d'Olt; Sauveterre-de-Rouergue

Carolingian, Romanesque and Cistercian churches and Romanesque sculpture
**Conques; Moissac; Toulouse (St-Sernin); Cahors (Cathedral)
*Carennac; Beaulieu-en-Rouergue; Escaladieu; Flaran; Loc-Dieu; Marcilhac-sur-Célé; Sylvanès; St-Gaudens; St-Just-de-Valcabrère; St-Lizier; St-Michel-de-Lescure; St-Mont; St-Savin; Souillac; Vals; Varen; and the Romanesque churches of the Oueil and Arboust valleys and Luchon

Gothic and later churches
**Albi (Cathedral); Toulouse (Jacobins)
*La Romieu; Rodez (Cathedral); Toulouse (Cathedral); Villefranche-de-Rouergue (Charterhouse)

Church furnishings
**Albi (choir enclosure); Auch (choir enclosure); Conques Treasures; St-Bertrand-de-Comminges (choir enclosure and organ)
*Montpezat-de-Quercy (16C tapestries in St-Martin); Notre-Dame-de-Garaison (17C murals)

Châteaux
*Assier; Bonaguil; Brousse-le-Château; Castelnau-Bretenoux; Foix; Monségur; Montal

Civic Buildings
**Burlats, Pavilion d'Adelaïde; St-Antonin-Noble-Val, Maison Romane; Toulouse, Hôtel d'Assezat
*Capitole, Toulouse

Caves, Archaeological finds, Sites and Museums
**Montmaurin, Roman Villa; Niaux, cave paintings; Padirac Caves; Toulouse, Musée St-Raymond
*Séviac, St-Bertrand-de-Comminges, Musée Archéologique de Lectoure; Musée Champollion, Figeac; Grottes de Pech Merle, Gouffre de Padirac

Collections of medieval sculptures
Monestiés, 15C Entombment group; Toulouse, Musée des Augustins

Paintings and collections of paintings
**Albi, Musée Toulouse-Lautrec; Castres, Musée Goya; Montauban, Musée Ingres; Toulouse, Musée des Augustins
*St-Céré, Atelier-Musée Jean Lurçat; Les Arques, Musée Zadkine, Rodez, Musée Denys-Puech

Ecomusées
*Cuzals, Musée de Plein Air du Quercy

Special Interest Museums
*Carla-Bayle, Musée Protestant; Cordes-Vindrac, Musée de l'Outil; Roquefort, cheese cellars; Souillac, Musée de l'Automate

Glossary

abrasion, a technique used in stained glass where the surface of an outer coloured layer of glass is ground away to reveal white glass beneath

ambo, early version of the pulpit, where the Epistle and Gospel were read aloud

annealing, the insertion of a jewel like piece of glass into a larger context without using leads

astragal, a small moulding around the top of a column, below a capital

bastide, medieval planned new towns, with a charter and economic and political advantages, whose inhabitants were free men. They were frequently built to a grid plan

bat, valley (Pyrenees)

bâtons écotés, a moulding resembling a branch whose off-shoots have been pruned

bolet, upper terrace or verandah reached by exterior steps leading to the entrance (Quercy)

cagots, group of outcasts, heretics or lepers in the Middle Ages of unknown origin

capitoul, the name given to the municipal administrators of Toulouse until the Revolution

castlenau, a community coming under the jurisdiction of, and protected by, a new castle and walls

causse, a limestone plateau

cazelle, rural stone refuge (Quercy)

chai, wine and spirit store

chemin de ronde, walkway around the battlements of a castle

chevet, the east end of a church, including the apse and ambulatory

chrism, chi rho monogram of Christ

cité, the oldest part of certain towns

corrida, bull fight

courses landaises, cattle running when cows (rather than bulls) from the Landes are used and not killed

dolmen, megalithic tomb of large flat stones

faïence, glazed earthernware

Floc, an aperitif based on either red or white wine (from the Gascon for 'flower')

four banal, a communal oven

Fronde, uprising against Cardinal Mazarin during the minority of Louis XIV (1648–52)

gariotte little hut (Quercy)

gave, river (in the Pyrenees)

Guyenne, the part of Aquitaine owned by the English

gypseries, a composition made from lime (gypsum) with powdered marble or plaster which could be modelled or stuccoed

halle couverte, covered marketplace

hôtel particulier, private town mansion

Huguenots, French Calvinists or Protestants

jubé, rood screen

lauze, stone roof tiles, pegged to the timbers with a single nail

lavoir, public wash house

mirande, a gallery, or small openings immediately under the roof to ventilate the roof timbers, which are found in many buildings in the Midi from the 13C onwards

neste, a pre-Celtic word for river used in the Pyrenees

paréage, the foundation of a bastide by a combination of local nobility, a representative of the King (seneshal) and the Church (abbeys or monasteries)

pastel, dyers' woad, cultivated in large quantities in parts of the Languedoc from the 14C to the 16C. The leaves were the basis of a high-quality blue dye. The industry was a source of great wealth

perron, an exterior platform with steps

pigeonnier, dovecote, common to Gascony and the Quercy. Pigeons were an important source of food and fertiliser until the 19C, and the size of the pigeonnier was a measure of the property of the owner. Pigeonniers are either integral with the farmhouse, or freestanding in a variety of forms

pontet or **pountet**, a construction joining two buildings, often spanning a public right-of-way

pousse rapière, a liqueur of orange and Armagnac with a sparkling wine served as aperitif

rinceau, low-relief frieze with foliate or floral motif

routier, a hired mercenary (or a sort of highwayman)

sauveterre/sauveté, a place of refuge under the protection of the Church

sigillated, impressed patterns applied with the aid of stamps or moulds

soleilho, open gallery on the top floor of a house, often used for drying crops

souillarde voûtée, outside scullery (Quercy)

stele, standing block

torchis, wattle and daub

vielle, the old word used in the Pyrenees meaning commune or rural district, expecially the Louron district, as a suffix and prefix (further north replaced by suffix ac)

vic, a subdivision or group of several villages (Pyrenees)

Chronology

35–20,000 BC	Aurignacian culture
15–9000 BC	Magdalenian culture
3C BC	Arrival of Celtic tribes. (Cadurcii, Tolosates, Volcae Tectosages)
2C BC	Installation of a Roman Garrison in Toulouse
6C BC	Fall of Uxellodunum
c AD 250	Martyrdom of St-Sernin in Toulouse
3C	Germanic invasions
412–419	Visigoth invasion
6C	Frankish domination of Toulouse; Vascons from the Iberian peninsula spread into future Gascony
7C	Duchy of Aquitaine created by the Merovingians
c 720	Arab invasions

778	First Count of Toulouse
800	Charlemagne crowned Emperor
843	Treaty of Verdun and breakup of the Carolingian Empire
9C	Norman invasions
10C	Creation of the Armagnac dynasty
1073	Ecclesiastic Reform
1095	First Crusade
1096	Consecration of the altar table at St-Sernin
1100	Moissac cloisters built
1144	Montauban, the first *bastide*, founded
1147	St-Bernard of Clairvaux in the Languedoc to preach against the heresies
1152	Marriage of Eleanor of Aquitaine to Henry of Anjou, later Henry II
1152	The first appearance of a Municipal Council in Toulouse
1159	Resistance by King Louis VII and Raymond V of Toulouse to Henry II Plantagenet
1206	Arrival of St-Dominic in Languedoc
1209–18	Albigensian Crusade
1211	First Siege of Toulouse by the Crusaders
1213	Battle of Muret, major victory for Simon de Montfort
1229	Treaty of Meaux (or Paris)
	Foundation of the University of Toulouse
1234	Introduction of the Inquisition
1259	Quercy ceded to the English by the Treaty of Paris
1271	Death of Alphonse de Poitiers (brother of St-Louis, son-in-law of the Count of Toulouse), resulting in the annexation of the County of Toulouse and Languedoc to the French Crown according to the Treaty of Meaux
c 1272	Choir of Toulouse Cathedral begun
1282	Albi Cathedral begun
1290	Counts of Foix inherit Béarn
1316	Jacques Duèze of Cahors elected second Pope at Avignon, John XXII
1337	Start of the Hundred Years War
1348–50	Black Death
1360	Treaty of Brétigny: Quercy and Rouergue made over to the English
1363	Gaston Fébus, Count of Foix, victorious over Jean I d'Armagnac
1369	Bertrand du Guesclin recaptures Quercy from the English
1453	End of the Hundred Years War and of English domination
1484	Battle of Lectoure marking the fall of the Armagnac dynasty
1527	Marriage of Henri II d'Albret to Marguerite d'Angoulême, Queen of Navarre, sister of François I
1539	Decree of Villars-Cotterets mandating French as legal language
1548	Jeanne d'Albret marries Antoine de Bourbon, parents of future Henri IV

1562–98	Religious Wars
1594	Croquants (peasants) Revolt
1598	Edict of Nantes grants freedom of worship and safe places to Protestants
1609	Henri IV unites his lands in the south-west with the French Kingdom
1629	Treaty of Alès: Protestants lose the right to places of safety
1681	Inauguration of the Canal du Midi
1685	Revocation of the Edict of Nantes
1789	French Revolution
1790	Creation of modern *départements*
1814	Battle of Toulouse between Wellington and Soult
1856	Toulouse railway station inaugurated
1864	Henri de Toulouse-Lautrec born in Albi
1875	Phylloxera attacks the vineyards
1944	Liberation of Toulouse
1969	First flight by Concorde from Toulouse

Further Reading

History
Christopher Allman, *The Hundred Years War*, Cambridge, 1994
John Ardagh, *Modern France*, Penguin, 1988
Anne Curry, *The Hundred Years War*, Macmillan, 1993
Maurice Keen, *Medieval Europe*, Penguin, 1991
Malcolm Lambert, *Medieval Heresy*, Blackwells, 1994
Emmanuel Le Roy Ladurie, *Montaillou*, Penguin, 1990

Art and Architecture
Kenneth John Conant, *Carolingian and Romanesque Architecture*: 800–1200, Yale/London, 1993
Hayward Gallery Exhibition Catalogue, *Toulouse-Lautrec*, 1991
Kathryn Horste, *Cloister Design and Monastic Reform in Toulouse*: the Romanesque Sculpture of La Daurade, OUP, 1992
Robert Rosenblum, *Jean-Auguste-Dominique Ingres*, Thames & Hudson, 1990
Meyer Schapiro, *RomanesqueArt—Selected Papers*, Thames & Hudson, 1993
Juliet Wilson, *Goya's Prints*, London, 1982

Travel Books in English
James Bentley, *Fort Towns of France*—The Bastides of the Dordogne and Aquitaine, 1993
Michael Brown, *South to Gascony*, Hamish Hamilton, 1989
Joy Law, *The Midi*, John Murray, 1991
Andrew Sanger, *South-West France*, Helm Guides, 1994
John Sturrock, *The French Pyrenees*, London 1988
Freda White, *Three Rivers of France*, Pavilion, 1992

Books In French

Guide Bleu Midi-Pyrénées published by Hachette, an extremely detailed guide to the region

Guide du routard Midi-Pyrénées, published by Hachette

Three Michelin Guides cover the region: *Pyrénées-Aquitaine-Côte Basque; Pyrénées-Roussillon-Albigeois; Dordogne-Périgord-Quercy* (the last one exists in English)

Sud Ouest Publications publish a series of regional guides and monographs. Specially recommended in the series is: Quitterie and Daniel Cazes' *Discovering Toulouse*, 1992 (also in English)

Editions du Rouergue publishes good quality books on the region covering all topics from art to cookery

Editions du Beffroi publishes small format guide books with colour photos on specific topics or monuments in the Aveyron. Some (including Conques) in English

The Collection Guides Tourisme et Patrimoine is a series of small format books on the Lot region. Two have been published, *Cahors et la Vallée du Lot* (1990), and in English, *The Valleys of the Lot and Célé* (1993)

In the series on Romanesque architecture and sculpture: Zodiaque, la nuit des temps: *Quercy Roman, Rouergue Roman, Gascogne Romane, Haut-Languedoc Roman* and *Pyrénées Romanes*

M. Beaulieu and V. Beyer, *Dictionnaire des Sculptures français du Moyen Age*, Picard, Paris 1992

Marcel Durliat, *La Sculpture Romane de la Route de Saint-Jacques*, CEHAG, 1990

Rene Mauriès, *The Midi-Pyrénées*, Nathan

Michel Roquebert, *Rues Tolosanes*, Privat, 1988

1

Toulouse

TOULOUSE (pop. 358,688, Tourist information tel: 61 11 02 22), the fourth city in France, is the capital of the vast region Midi-Pyrénées, its aeronautical industry contributing in large part to the prosperity of the metropolis and the surrounding area, while the 100,000 students of the university, now the second in France, add a youthful dynamism. A melting pot of many cultures, it is distinguished for its mellow brick buildings and the panoramas across the Garonne which have inspired many comparisons with Tuscany or Spain. The motorway network makes it all too easy to drive past but, for lovers of bustling cities, Toulouse's treasures are manifold.

History. The advantageous position of the fertile Garonne valley between the Atlantic, the Mediterranean and the Iberian peninsula attracted Celtic settlers, the Tectosages, in 3BC, followed about a century later by the Romans. Ancient Tolosa grew wealthy from the importation of wine, so that by the 2C it had acquired the status of colony, with 20,000 inhabitants. Only fragments of the 1C city walls remain in place, although the site of the ancient temple or Capitolium was discovered in 1992 during excavation work under Place Esquirol. The Capitolium was crucial to the history of the early Christian era and the martyrdom, in 250, of St-Saturnin (St-Sernin), the first Bishop of Toulouse, who refused to worship pagan idols and died after being roped to the half-crazed sacrificial bull by the crowds assembled on the steps of the Capitolium.

From 418 for a century the Visigoths made Toulouse their capital, after which came incursions from the Franks, Arabs and Normans. The history of the town and surrounding area as an almost autonomous principality begins in the 8C with the creation by Charlemagne of the *Comté de Toulouse*. In the feudal hierarchy this was part of the Kingdom of Aquitaine belonging to the French Monarchy, but allegiance to the French diminished to a purely nominal status as the Counts' power increased until they had dominion directly or indirectly over a vast territory where the language of Oc was spoken. By the 12C, the boundary of the Languedoc covered an area loosely contained by the Dordogne, the Gers, the Black Mountains, the Mediterranean and the Pyrenees, but was constantly in flux. The power of the princes and the Church developed side by side through the 11C and 12C, economic prosperity and civil liberties stimulating urban growth and Gregorian reforms adding to the authority of the ecclesiastics. A new Cathedral was begun in the 11C, in 1096 the altar table of the unfinished church of St-Sernin was consecrated and in the same year Raymond IV of Toulouse led the first crusade. In spite of this activity in the orthodox Church, a breakaway fundamentalist Christian movement, described then as a heresy and now as Catharism, took root in the Languedoc. It resulted in the only crusade by the French against their own people, beginning in 1209, and was popularly known as the **Albigensian Crusade**. Its hero and leader, Simon de Montfort (1165–1218) was killed during an assault on Toulouse. As much a political as a religious conflict, the power of the Counts of Toulouse was curtailed by the Treaty of Paris when fighting ended in 1229 which united the House of Toulouse to the French monarchy through the marriage of Raymond VII's only daughter, Jeanne, to Alphonse de Poitiers, the brother of St Louis (Louis IX). The Cathars, on the other hand, were not wiped out and harsh repression continued to be meted out by the Inquisition. The foundation of the University in 1229 was also a bid to counteract heretical beliefs with the teaching of theology and canon law. The destiny of the principality was irrevocably decided when Alphonse and Jeanne died on their return from the Eighth Crusade in 1271 without an heir. Adherents to the heresy were not totally eradicated until 1321.

The architectural style of the counter-heresy, generally referred to as **meridional** or **southern Gothic**, developed as religious orders created churches adapted to the liturgy and to preaching to the masses with one vast aisleless rib-vaulted space. The earliest extant model is the 13C nave of the Cathedral of St Etienne. The scarcity of stone in the alluvial basin of the Garonne contributed to the tradition of building in the elongated Roman-style brick which has become the hallmark of Toulousain architecture. Five serious conflagrations destroyed much of the town between 1463 and 1551 and the town imposed precise regulations in 1555 forbidding reconstruction in wood and stipulating brick or stone. The golden era of many towns in the region, not least Toulouse, began during a period of peace after the Hundred Years War (1337–1453) and ended with the start of the Wars of Religion in 1560.

A variety of factors contributed to the prosperity of Toulouse and the Toulousain: one was the definitive establishment in 1443 of the *Parlement*, a judiciary and a legislative institution, the second most important in France, elevating the status of the town to provincial capital; another was the commerce in indigo or *pastel* (woad) (see Lauragais and Gaillac). The *pasteliers* or **pastel merchants**, an élite of about a dozen families whose members often rose to eminent positions in the municipal hierarchy, were builders of Renaissance mansions. Renaissance Toulouse had close links with the humanists of Bologna university and also with the printing trade in Lyons, becoming, from 1476, the fourth town in France to have presses. However, until the beginning of the 16C documents were printed exclusively in Latin and Occitan. The introduction of maize to the region in the 17C and the means of transporting it by canal brought an era of renewed prosperity, and in the 18C the realisation of municipal schemes included dykes, ports, bridges and a canal. Hand in hand with this came the demolition of medieval buildings, including the once-great church of Notre-Dame de la Daurade. Toulouse, unlike other large towns in the Midi, adhered to the Revolution but after the suppression of Parlement in 1790 became simply *chef-lieu* (county town) of the *département* of Haute-Garonne, created in 1790. Napoléon's popularity gradually waned, largely because of the decline in corn prices due to the blockading of ports and war in Spain to the point where, in 1814, the French troops under Marshall Soult, retreating before Wellington's army, were not welcomed by the inhabitants of the town. On 10 April Soult was defeated and the Duke was received as liberator of Toulouse. (A pointless exercise, happening four days after Napoléon's abdication.)

The end of the 18C and 19C brought the destruction of many religious buildings and parts of the old *cité* to be replaced with new boulevards and public buildings. By the beginning of the Second Empire (1852) the population had increased to 100,000 but the industrial revolution had hardly touched this part of France. The building of the railway in 1856 linked Toulouse to the metropolitan north of France and helped to improve the economy. However, until the eve of the First World War Toulouse was still largely untouched by the developments in industry, its largest factory being the State-owned tobacco factory on the banks of the Garonne. The leap into the 20C was due, in the end, to its distance from the hub of activity and therefore of battle during the 1914–18 war, combined with plentiful supplies of manpower and energy (coal from Carmaux, hydroelectricity from the Pyrenees). P.G. Latécoère, a native of the region, established an aircraft factory here which was to become Aérospatiale, a major participant in the development of Concorde. In June 1993 a métro opened and the town is restoring many monuments and creating new art centres. Toulouse is the impulse which reverberates around a region whose furthest point north is some 200km away.

Walk 1: Place du Capitole and the Basilica of St-Sernin

The hub of Toulouse is the huge **Place du Capitole**. Beneath it is an underground car park. The square is a vast semi-pedestrianised area, created 1811–52, which springs to life on Wednesdays from 08.00 to 18.00 with a colourful market (there are smaller ones on Tuesdays and Saturdays). It has a good choice of pavement cafés, the most famous being the *belle époque* **Café Bibent**, and **Le Grand Café**. The space is dominated by the brick and marble façade of the **CAPITOLE** building (1750–60). The Capitole is an unusual title for what anywhere else in France would be known as the *Hôtel de Ville* (town hall). It stems from an historical and etymological mutation. By the 11C the elected council or Chapter of the municipality—Capitulum in Latin and Capitol in Occitan—enjoyed considerable autonomy. Capitulum, Capitol and Capitolium fused to become Capitole, meaning both the Chapter and the Maison Commune, and its officers were known as *capitouls*. The Maison Commune was established here in the 12C, deliberately distanced from the counts' palace at the other end of town (now Place Salin). The building which you see today—designed by Guillaume Cammas—was intended as a monumental screen for a disparate group of buildings which existed until 1873 when most were indiscriminately demolished. It now masks the town hall and the Théâtre du Capitole. The central pedimented portico is emphasised by eight columns in candy-pink marble from the Montagne Noire—to symbolise the eight *capitouls*—and there are large sculptures above the central portico by Marc Arcis, François Lucas and Louis Parant.

The central archway leads to **Cour Henri IV** (1602–06) with a **monumental gateway** begun in 1546 by Nicolas Bachelier (d. 1556–7), the most original and talented Toulousain architect of the Renaissance. Above the arch is a statue (1607) in polychrome marble of Henri IV. A marble plaque in the paving commemorates the execution of the Duke of Montmorency, Governor of Languedoc and godson of Henri IV, on 30 October 1632.

The Capitole can be visited during office hours and Saturdays and the entrance is in the north-east corner of the courtyard. The **Salle des mariages** has a light-hearted décor dedicated to themes of love (c 1916) by Paul Gervais. The next gallery has Impressionist-style murals by the local painter Henri Martin (1860–1943), including a frieze-like composition of a group strolling on the banks of the Garonne, among them Jean Jaurès, the socialist politician who came from the Tarn. The stuccoed and gilded gallery

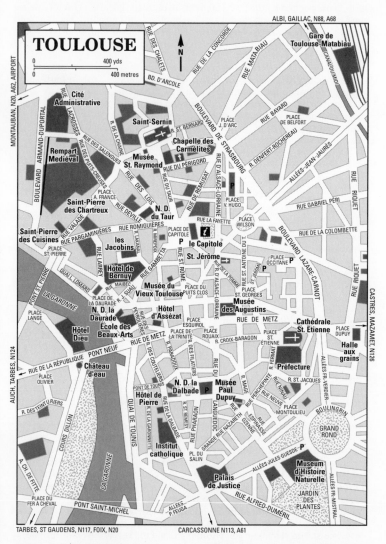

overlooking the Place du Capitole, the *Salle des illustres* (1892–98), inspired by the Villa Farnese in Rome and combined with turn-of-the-century excesses, was the creation of Paul Pujol. The statues represent illustrious citizens while the walls and ceiling carry historical and allegorical paintings of the great moments in the history of Toulouse.

The other side of the Bachelier gate is **Place Charles de Gaulle**, a pretty public garden with fountains and the **Tourist Office** housed in the **Tour des Archives** (1525–30). The tower, the only surviving part of the old Capitole, is more reminiscent of the Loire Valley than the Midi since its restoration in 1873 by Eugène-Emmanuel Viollet-le-Duc (1814–1879), chief architect of the *Monuments Historiques* created in 1830 to safeguard the national heritage.

Return to Place du Capitole and cross it to the north-west. You will see on the angle of Rue des Lois and Rue Romiguières, the **Hôtel du Grand Balcon**, a modest establishment but haunted by the memory of aviation pioneers such as Antoine de Saint-Exupéry (author of *Le Petit Prince*) and Jean Mérmoz. Take **Rue du Taur**, the old north–south route serving the bourg of Saint-Sernin. To the right above the rooftops appears the *clocher mur* (belfry gable), characteristic of the Toulousain, of the 14C brick **Church of Notre-Dame du Taur**. According to legend, the church of Notre-Dame stands on the site of Saturnin's first resting place. In the dingy interior of the aisleless building, begun c 1300, is a barely distinguishable painting of the genealogy of Jacob with 38 figures on the south wall.

The area west of Rue du Taur was the heart of the medieval university: Rue des Pénitents Gris leads to **Rue du Collège de Foix** where, behind a wall, stands the former college founded in the 15C by Cardinal Pierre de Foix; and in the same street are the steeple and the gateway, all that remain of the great 13/14C **Couvent des Cordeliers.** On the east side of Rue du Taur at the intersection with Rue du Perigord is **Tour Maurand**, a fragment of the oldest secular building in Toulouse. A pink façade and green door on the left of Rue du Périgord camouflages the small Counter-Reformation **Chapelle des Carmelites** (tel: 61 29 21 00, 10.00–13.00, 14.30–18.30, Jun–Oct). The chapel has recently been restored and its exceptional acoustics, due to the wooden roof, make it a perfect venue for musical performances. Between 1741 and 1751 the walls and ceiling of this simple building were decorated by the painters Jean-Pierre Rivalz (1625–1706) and Jean-Baptiste Despax (1710–73) with themes of theological and monastic virtues mixed with Old Testament prophets, scenes from the New Testament, and the Glorification of St-Theresa.

At No. 69 Rue du Taur is the monumental doorway designed by Bachelier c 1555 for the Collège de l'Esquile.

Rue du Taur leads to **Place St-Sernin** and the south flank of the most celebrated building in Toulouse, the **BASILICA OF SAINT-SERNIN**, the largest conserved Romanesque church in Europe. Small green gardens and mature trees soften the surrounds but most of the oval Place, created in the 19C to the detriment of the monastic buildings, is littered with cars. On Sundays (and to a lesser extent on Saturdays) the stalls of a **flea market** form a barricade around the basilica but these provide no barrier from pickpockets. Built in a combination of brick and stone, St-Sernin is emerging freshly pink and cream from a cloak of scaffolding enveloping parts of it since 1969 during a huge programme of repair, consolidation and derestoration undertaken to secure, clean and return it to its putative pre-1860/1872 profile. Viollet-le-Duc's restoration work in the mid-19C altered the profile of the upper part of the church but pollution has taken its toll on the fragile Carcassonne stone he used.

The first shrine on this site was planned by Bishop Silve but built by Bishop Exupère c 400 to shelter St-Saturnin's relics, translated in 402 or 403 from Bishop Hilaire's modest wooden oratory to the south. By the end of the 11C a larger building was needed—and a more beautiful one desirable—to accommodate hoards of pious travellers en route for Santiago de Compostela, and for the needs of the resident clergy. The Chapter was in pocket as a result of the Gregorian disciplinary reforms, and the new church was begun in the third quarter of the 11C. It took the form of a Latin cross with double aisles flanking the nave and radiating chapels around the apse and on the east side of the transepts. The altar table is inscribed with the date of its consecration by Pope Urban II, 24 May 1096, and is signed by the stonecarver, Bernard Gilduin. Raymond Gayrard, saintly canon and former builder of bridges, took charge of the building works at the end of the 11C when the chevet and the transept were already complete. By the time of his death in 1118 the three east bays of the nave were vaulted and the body of the church was finished up to the level of the tribune windows, the part in stone and brick visible from the exterior. The collegiate church was elevated to abbey in 1117 and attention then turned to the construction of the cloisters and the monastic buildings, leaving the church unfinished, although there was a surge of activity in the 13C under Abbot Bernard de Gensac (1243–64).

Exterior. The east end of the basilica is the most beautiful part of the building. The five semi-circular radiating chapels clustered around the apse and the four chapels of the transepts create an undulating rhythm, with a secondary rhythm of colour contrasts set up by the use of brick for the mass and stone for the structural elements. All the elements are repeated in different tempos resulting in a finely orchestrated yet powerful structure culminating in the 65m octagonal belfry. Recent restoration of the upper part, where there is an obvious lack of stone, has reinstated the *mirandes* under the eaves. The belfry was built in four stages: the first stage with blind arcades covers the crossing dome, then come two levels with double round-headed open bays. The last two stages with mitred bays were built in the second half of the 13C, and the stone spire was added in 1478.

On each transept is a portal in the form of a triumphal arch, but both are now closed, and only the **Porte des Comtes**, c 1082–83, on the south transept has kept its sculpted décor. Members of the noble family, the counts, were buried in the small funerary recess on the left in sarcophagi taken from the early Christian burial ground close to the first church. Above the portal is an aedicule inscribed *Sanctus Saturninus* suggesting it once contained the Saint's effigy. The eight storiated capitals address the contrasting themes of salvation and damnation through the parable of Lazarus on the right-hand side, his soul depicted as a little naked body departing to heaven, as distinct from the figures on the left, who are guilty of the sins of avarice and lust and punished by monsters devouring their sexual organs.

The delicately sculpted Renaissance archway, formerly part of the 16C enclosing walls, stands before **Porte Miègeville**, c 1110–15, opposite the middle street (*mièja vila*) on the south. A projecting bay with a single arch protects the carved tympanum, one of the first examples of its kind. Above is a heavily sculpted cornice. The **tympanum** deals in a literal manner with the theme of the Ascension, Christ assisted by angels who lift him physically by his waist. On the **lintel** below, the 12 disciples watch the act flanked by the two men cited by the Acts who explain that Christ will return. The stylised twisted postures emphasise the awe of the scene just as the deep carving of the folds emphasises the solidity of the bodies and the upward fluid movement of the whole composition. There are stylistic similarities with the altar-table carvings by Gilduin and by the master of Jaca, Spain.

Three of the four capitals flanking the door are storiated. On the right is the **Expulsion from the garden of Eden**, its counterpart left depicts the **Annunciation**, the antithesis to the Fall. Note that the Angel Gabriel has his legs crossed, one of the earliest appearances in sculpture in the

Languedoc of this convention for expressing movement. On the side face is a **Visitation** and the outer left capital graphically describes the **Massacre of the Innocents**. The fourth capital, two lions emprisoned in tendrils, suggests the influence of Santiago. Carved consoles support the lintel: on the left is **King David** the musician ancestor of Christ between two lions; on the right, two round-faced figures wearing Phyrigian bonnets sit astride lions, one foot bare and the other shod, an unexplained motif. In the right spandrel is **St-Peter**, holding the keys of heaven. The panel above, with two angels, was placed or replaced here in the 19C, whereas the panel below, representing **Simon the Magician**, has never been moved. In the left spandrel **St-James** is framed between bare tree-trunks, his name engraved in his halo, as it is at Santiago. Below him is a panel with two women astride lions with a male figure between them.

The **west portal**, begun after the Porte Miègeville, c 1115–18, although unfinished, shows a progression from the others in quality and wealth of decoration. Eight capitals are deeply and vigorously carved with intricate vegetal forms twined around human figures and animals which cling on to the astragals with fingers or claws. Sculpted reliefs have been moved to the Augustinian Museum. Above the double doorway is a gallery of five arches surmounted by a large rose window with no tracery. The narthex was not tampered with during the 19C and still has its original *mirandes*. The two incomplete towers were brought to their present state in 1929.

Interior. The interior is reassuringly harmonious and tranquil, unified by the regularity of the eleven bays of the nave and soft light from the aisles and the tribune. The barrel vaulted nave is 21m high, divided by transverse arches springing from engaged columns supported by square pillars. The double aisles take the thrust of the high nave, and also create beautiful diagonal views. The elegant tribune around the nave and transepts consists of a series of double openings, each pair divided by twin columns. The floor was lowered in the 19C.

In the 1970s, when the 19C plaster and paint were removed to reveal the alternating brick and masonry, several medieval **wall paintings** in the north transept were discovered. Among these on the last pillars of the north aisle are an angel seated on clouds and a Noli me Tangere. The largest fresco is on the west wall of the north transept, c 1180, using the arches to frame five scenes from the Resurrection, culminating with the Lamb of God in the vaults. There are other fragments in the north transept, and 14C murals in the south transept chapel dedicated to the Virgin. The 12C Christ on the Cross in wood and gilt was heavily restored in the 19C.

The finely carved choir stalls, 1670–74, were inspired by those at the Cathedral of St-Etienne. The famous **altar table** by Bernard Gilduin, carved on the chamfer, can be glimpsed through the 18C choir enclosure. The crossing has been subjected to many structural alterations and decorative additions. It received a painted decoration in the 16C, a reredos carved by Marc Arcis in 1720, and the final resting place of St-Sernin is beneath the ostentatious Baroque baldaquin, 1718–58, behind the altar. Etienne Rossat's sculpture of St-Sernin's was added in 1759.

The **carved capitals** are quite remarkable for their quality and quantity (some 268) carved over 50 years. Many are in the tribunes, and while the majority have vegetal designs of great skill, variety and beauty, some are storiated. They date from c 1080 in the east to c 1118 in the west. Many of them are difficult to see, and a full description would take another book, so it is a good idea to take binoculars.

Apse and crypt (10.00–11.30 and 14.00–17.00 except Sun am; 10.00–18.00 Jul–Sept). Enter from the north transept. The oldest storiated capital is of Daniel between some rather benevolent lions on the east capital of the south-east apsidal chapel. On the inner wall of the ambulatory are seven late 11C **marble reliefs** recalling carved ivories or metalwork on a monumental scale. The three smaller panels in the centre, attributed to Bernard Gilduin, may have been part of an altarpiece and are known to have been in this position since the 19C. The central panel portrays a fleshy, heavy jowled but dignified Christ framed in a mandorla, and surrounded by the symbols of the four Evangelists. On his right is a cherub, on his left a seraph. Flanking these are two angels and two apostles in a larger format and probably later. In 1258 the relics of St-Sernin were raised from the crypt and placed under a heavy canopy in the church, and the crypt was then rib vaulted. The lower crypt was vaulted in the 14C and its central pier is reputed to be the only surviving fragment of the previous church. There are a number of reliquaries on display but the most valuable have been transferred to the Paul Dupuy Museum.

In the 17C the ambulatory became the *Tour des Corps Saints* or the Circuit of the Holy Relics, where carved and gilded shrines of the CounterReformation were placed in the chapels and aedicules, demanding some considerable aesthetic adjustment. These were ripped out and dumped in the tribunes in the 19C but restored and replaced in 1980. There is also a 16C post-plague ex-voto offering suspended above the north ambulatory, and an altar table designed by Viollet-le-Duc in the main chapel. Sections of the **organ** case date from the 17C and the instrumental part was replaced in 1888 by an organ from the workshop of Aristide Cavaillé-Coll, adapted to the size of the building and to the sounds of the late 19C and early 20C using many of the earlier pipes.

West of St-Sernin is the **Musée St-Raymond** (temporarily closed; tel: 61 22 21 85, 10.00–17.00 summer, 14.00–18.00 winter), an important archaeological museum housed in the former college St-Raymond, an attractive brick building of 1523. It is an agreeable, go-ahead place with a wideranging collection from the Bronze Age to the early Middle Ages. Finds made in the Midi include Iron Age (3–2 BC) jewellery such as the splendid gold torques and bracelets from Lasgraïsses (Tarn), and from Fenouillet, near Toulouse; and from Toulouse come mosaics, trinkets, small bronzes and coins. The highlights of the collection are the antique **sculptures** discovered in the Villa Chiragan at Martres-Tolosane, notably portrait busts. The museum also owns such treasures as a replica by the Roman sculptor, Cnide, of Praxiteles' Venus, copies of Myron's Discobolus and Athena, and a series of vigorously sculpted reliefs of the Labours of Hercules.

From **Rue St-Bernard** to the east is a last glimpse of the Basilica, best in winter when the trees are bare. The faubourg of St-Sernin was incorporated within the *cité* walls rebuilt in 1346 at the time of the Hundred Years War. Turn right into **Boulevard de Strasbourg**, on the line of the medieval defences, where every morning except Monday **market-stalls** stretch along each side.

At the junction with **Rue de Remusat** is the department store built in 1908, now occupied by **Galeries Lafayette**, a vaguely Art Nouveau structure in exposed metal and yellow brick. The main north–south thoroughfare, **Rue d'Alsace Lorraine**, was carved through the medieval town in the late 19C. Rue Rivals leads to **Place Victor Hugo** and the combined car park and

Halles, closed Mondays and 13.00, which has interesting places to eat on the upper floor.

South-west of the market is **Place Wilson**, a charming 19C oval space with a garden, fountain and statue of Pierre Godolin, the most celebrated Occitan poet of the 17C, by d'A. Falguière (1831–1900). Around the square are cinemas, pavement cafés and the **Grand Hôtel Capoul** (tel: 61 10 70 70). Nearby in Rue Labéda is the **Hôtel-restaurant d'Occitanie** (tel: 61 21 15 92), popular with the locals who act as guinea-pigs for Catering School students; open only during term time, lunch tables need to be reserved some days ahead.

Place Wilson, with **Allées du President Roosevelt** and **Allées Jean Jaurès**, was part of a grand scheme opening out towards the Canal du Midi. Traces of distemper or *céruse*, in pale café-au-lait or other pastel shades, can still be seen on many 19C buildings. This was not simply a frivolous camouflage, but an attempt to brighten the streets at night to increase the safety of the public following an order of 1783 by the city fathers. Toulouse is one of the rare places where crystallised violets are still confected and sold in the quarter around **Rue la Fayette**.

On the corner of Rue Alsace-Lorraine is the first department store built in Toulouse, opened in 1899 and now occupied by Marks & Spencer. This brings you back to **Square de Gaulle** and the back of the Capitole building, an 1883–84 replica of the west elevation.

Walk 2: the Jacobins Church and the Quays of the Garonne

South-west of Place du Capitole, between the right bank of the Garonne and Rue St-Rome, is the former Dominican monastery of the Jacobins, the second most celebrated religious building of Toulouse.

Take **Rue Gambetta** and turn right into Rue Lakanal. In front of you is the cliff-like apse of the Dominican **CHURCH OF THE JACOBINS** (closed 12.00–14.30).

Dominic de Guzman (1170–1221), a Spaniard, settled in the south-west in 1206 with the express intention of turning people away from their heretical beliefs, and in 1215 he founded an order of preaching friars avowed to poverty. Recognised in 1217 by Pope Honorius III, the brotherhood grew and moved in 1229 to the present site where they began their first church in 1230. Dominic left Toulouse after less than six months but his followers grew ever more powerful and resolute, to the extent that in 1233 Pope Gregory IX confided to the Dominicans the task of General Inquisition. The Prior, Pons de Saint-Gilles, and four brothers were named Inquisitors. On 4 August 1234 the church was consecrated and in the same year the Inquisition began their persecution. In 1235 the brothers were expelled, to return a year later, and from then on the Dominican Inquisitors lived and worked from Place du Salin while the rest lived a monastic life at the Jacobins convent. The name Jacobins was acquired from their Parisian community in Rue St-Jacques. The church was requisitioned by the Artillery after the Revolution, altered and desecrated; and in the 1840s the Army deemed the building unworthy of attention. It survived thanks to Prosper Merimée and a lengthy programme of restoration. One of the tasks before restoration could begin was to remove 5000 cubic metres of soil used to raise the floor to street level.

Exterior. The church was built not to receive pilgrims but to preach to the masses. Its simple volumes, almost devoid of decoration, are a sober reminder of its predicative function and the avowed poverty of the Dominican order. Constructed entirely in warm russet-coloured brick and tiles, the articulation of the exterior is provided by tall angular buttress piers and narrow lancet windows in deep recesses creating a rhythm of deep shadows.

The only vestige of the church of 1234 is the late Romanesque-style arch and early Gothic capitals of the west façade, hidden until 1964 by 18C remodelling. A new campaign of building began in 1244 and continued for more than a century. The octagonal belfry of 1298, built to receive the great bell of the university, was undoubtedly inspired by the upper levels of the belfry of St-Sernin.

Interior. Enter by the south door, mainly a reconstruction of the 14C entrance, with the coat of arms of Cardinal Godin in the vault. The exterior does not totally prepare you for the unusual arrangement of the interior which is divided lengthwise by an enfilade of tall slender columns creating two equal sections, the south destined for the public, the north reserved for the clergy. On the ground of the first five bays, black marble slabs indicate the foundations of the earlier building which was extended eastwards with a five-sided apse 1244–53. This was raised and vaulted in 1275–92, and the first mass was celebrated on 2 February 1292 in the main chapel dedicated to the Virgin. The rest of the church was raised to the same height between 1324 and 1326 thanks to Cardinal Godin's bequest of 4000 florins. The glory of the Jacobins church is the elegant column at the east from which spring 22 ribs, like the branches of a palm tree, to support the vaults 28m above ground. The effect is enhanced by the use of alternate red and green to outline the ribs.

From the beginning this simple and austere edifice was held in such high esteem that in 1368 Pope Urban V, penultimate pope at Avignon and former student of Toulouse, selected it as the resting place for the relics of St-Thomas Aquinas (d. 1274), who was canonised in 1323. Returned in 1974 to their original 13C position at the centre of the north nave, the relics of the saint in a gilded wooden casket of 1827 lie beneath the main altar, a simple marble table. Of the 11 chapels, the four eastern ones were enlarged in the 16C, and in 1609 the axial chapel was converted into a rectangular shape with a four-sided brick dome and lantern. The painted wall and vault decoration, discovered under plaster, dates from the end-13C–early 14C, and is claimed to be 60 per cent original. Most of the medieval stained glass disappeared in the 19C. The new windows in the chevet were installed in 1923–30, and the modern glass in the nave was designed by Max Ingrand in 1951.

In the north-west corner of the nave a small door leads to the **cloisters** (pay to enter), a dark green oasis in the red-brick frame of the monastic buildings, with box hedges and cypresses. The cloister took shape between 1306 and 1310. It has brick arcades supported by 80 pairs of slender marble colonnettes with grey St-Béat marble capitals with foliate design and a tiled roof. Dreadfully damaged in the 19C to allow the horses stabled here to circulate, some of the original elements, which had been scattered throughout the region, were recovered and used in 1965–70 to return the cloister to its original form. The central well has a new coping and in the north-east corner is the cover of the piscina destroyed in an earthquake.

The **chapter house**, 1299–1301, has two slim hexagonal marble columns supporting the vaults on intersecting ribs, and traces of 17C mural paintings. The floor is reconstituted from fragments of old tiles and tombstones. The **St-Antonin Chapel**, wedged between the chapter house and refectory in the north-east angle, was built between 1337 and 1341 by the Dominican Bishop of Pamiers as a chantry chapel and burial place, and is dedicated to the patron of his diocese. Irreparable damage was inflicted in the 19C when it was transformed into the veterinary hospital for the Artillery, although the rich 14C painted décor of the Parousia and the legend of St-Antonin has survived on the upper walls and vault. The great **refectory**, which replaced an earlier, smaller one in 1303, was damaged in the 15C by the earthquake. It now houses exhibitions of modern and contemporary art. The entrance to the gallery is on Rue Pargaminières (tel: 61 21 34 50, 10.00–18.00 summer, 10.00–17.00 winter).

South of the Jacobins, the **Lycée Fermat**, Rue Lakanal, was named after the mathematician Pierre Fermat (1601–65) and founded by three *capitoul*s in 1566 as a Jesuit college. The great entrance gate on the diagonal dates from 1606. It occupies a building begun c 1502 by Jean de Bernuy, a Castillian who came to Toulouse to make his fortune in *pastel*. The **Hôtel de Bernuy** is a complete and delightful example of an early Renaissance *hôtel particulier*. The flat brick façade of 1504 on **Rue Gambetta** has a late Gothic doorway, sculpted by Aymeric Cayla in 1504, concealing the early 16C courtyard which can be visited during the academic year. The return of the façade and the right side of the courtyard, 1530, are the work of Louis Privat. In this small space is an abundance of Italianate motifs—busts in medallions, candelabra, deep cornices and a pierced balustrade. A perilously low coffered basket arch and vaulted passageway in the north-west leads to a second courtyard with a *tour capitulaire*, also by Aymeric Cayla, with angle windows and busts. Jean de Bernuy, who guaranteed François I's ransom, is said to have died in his own palace in 1556, when he organised a mini-corrida to celebrate the arrival of his nephew.

Rue J. Suau, named after the painter born at No. 8, has one of the rare Art Nouveau houses in Toulouse at No. 4. The street opens out into the **Place de la Daurade** and a garden beside the river. The area to the west of here is worth exploring, but beyond the scope of this book. It includes the churches of St-Pierre-des-Chartreux, St-Pierre-des-Cuisines, the Canal de Brienne and the mills of Bazacle, with some marvellous views of the river. Near the Canal de Brienne is the comfortable modern *Hôtel de Brienne* (tel: 61 23 60 60).

The riverbank, once the site of the gardens of the Benedictine **Monastery of La Daurade**, was pulled into shape from 1766–77 at the time of Lomenie de Brienne, Archbishop of Toulouse 1762–1788, to create the **Quai** and the **Port de la Daurade**. The loss of the gardens is regrettable, but even more so the gilded sanctuary *La dorée* which stood on the site of the parish church of **Notre-Dame de la Daurade** until 1759. The origins of this sacred precinct are a subject of debate. Usually cited as being of 5C origins, neglible documentation exists to record the splendour of the polygonal domed structure covered with gold leaf and mosaics illustrating the Life of the Virgin. It became a Benedictine priory in the 11C under the auspices of Cluny when a cloister was built. By 1759–61 the church was so insecure that it had to be demolished. The cloister went in 1811 but some of the magnificent 11C capitals were gathered up and are conserved in the Musée des Augustins. The present grandiose building was begun in 1772 and consecrated in 1838. The Marian tradition associated with this site is perpetuated in the Black Virgin and Child, an 1807 copy from memory of a 14C wood statue burned in 1799, venerated by pregnant women. The gloomy Neo-Classical interior is decorated with a series of seven episodes from the Life of the Virgin by J. Roques (1754–1847), and a late-19C enamelled ceramic composition by G. Virebent provides the background to the Black Virgin.

Immediately adjacent to the church of La Daurade is the jollier fin-de-siècle **Ecole des Beaux Arts**, by Pierre Esquié, inaugurated in 1895. The **Quai de la Daurade** provides a shady green quay for a hot dusty day, and for lunch try the pleasant *Brasserie des Beaux Arts* (tel: 61 21 12 12), on the corner opposite the **Pont Neuf**. The bridge was begun in 1544, in use by 1603 and completed in 1632. The seven low, almost semi-circular arches have gill-like openings outlined in stone in the massive brick piers, a practical embellishment to allow highwater to flow through. Now the oldest bridge across the Garonne, it once linked Languedoc, on the right bank, with Gascony on the left. From it you see the dignified brick elevation of the **Hôtel Dieu St-Jacques** and to the west the dome of the **Hospice de la Grave,** the successors to the plague hospitals and hospices for the poor founded in the suburb of St-Cyprien during the Middle Ages. Sheltering at the base of the Hôtel Dieu is the last remnant of the old 15C Pont Couvert at the narrowest part of the river.

Cross the Garonne for a magnificent panorama of the old town. At the end of the bridge is the photographic gallery, the **Château d'Eau** (tel: 61 42 61 72, 13.00–19.00, closed Tues and BH). Built in 1822, the year that Nicéphore Niepce invented photography, it is probably the only gallery anywhere installed in a circular watertower. Worth visiting simply for the building, it has excellent temporary exhibitions. Certain parts of the **Hôtel-Dieu Saint-Jacques** opposite can be visited, and nearby is the 14C **Church of St-Nicolas** which has one of the finest reredos in Toulouse, designed by J-B. Despax (1768). South of the Château d'Eau is **Cours Dillon** and a grassy area beside the river. Cross back to **Rue de Metz**, built in the 19C to join the Garonne to the Canal at the narrowest point and by-passing the ancient east–west route. During construction work the site of the Roman theatre was uncovered at the junction of Rue de Metz and Rue Peyrolières.

Follow the river along the **Quai de Tounis**, originally important commercial wharves but now a ship-shape recreation area. On the left is a street called **Pont de Tounis** because it was originally a bridge. It leads to Rue de la Dalbade and the eclectic west façade of the **Church of La Dalbade**. The brick mass of the 16C façade has a Flamboyant rose window above a stone portal with Renaissance motifs. In the tympanum is Gaston Virbent's eye-catching pastel-tinted ceramic copy of Fra Angelico's Coronation of the Virgin (1874). The church, the fourth on this spot, takes its name from the first, Notre-Dame de l'Eglise Blanche and was built c 1480–1550. Inside is a 17C polychromed processional statue of St Peter Walking on the Water, the patron of the *Confrérie des bateliers et pêcheurs de Tounis.*

The long and narrow **Rue de Dalbade** leading to Place du Parlement was the obvious place for wealthy parliamentarians to live. A discreet exploration of courtyards is often rewarding. Next to the church at No. 32 is the Hôtel des Chevaliers de Saint-Jean de Jerusalem, built in the 17C by Jean-Pierre Rivalz and inspired by the Chigi Palace in Rome. The **Hôtel de Pierre** at No. 25 is the most famous in the street. The house, built in 1538 for Jean de Bagis, bears the hallmarks of Bachelier's work in the arrangement of the window reveals around the courtyard as well as the tremendously powerful Atlantes supporting the pediment of the west doorway. François de Clary added antique marbles recuperated from the river bed in 1613 to the east and west wings of the courtyard and created the overpowering façade from stone originally intended for the Pont Neuf, to which were added huge sculpted motifs in 1857. Equally extravagant is the portal dated 1556 at No. 22, ironically bearing the motto '*sustine et abstine*', which marks the entrance to the fairly modest **Hôtel Gaspard Moliner**.

From the Church of La Dalbade, cut through from Square de Gorsse to **Rue Filatiers**, where linen spinners and tailors worked. Here are several timber-framed houses, some sympathetically modified and some modernised negligently. The triangular **Place de la Trinité**, refreshed by a fountain inaugurated in 1826, was one of the first of many projects designed by Urbain Vitry who became Chief Architect of the Town. There is a NeoClassical delight with a balcony, full-length statues and busts in niches at No. 57. **Rue des Marchands** has a specially fine selection of the many caryatids which prop up parts of Toulouse, the best at No. 28, made by Auguste Virebent in 1840. The Virebent dynasty capitalised on the properties of clay and new manufacturing techniques to produce for this stone-poor city every kind of decorative element in terracotta.

Cross **Place d'Assézat** to the **Hôtel d'Assézat**, the most famous of the *pastel* palaces and the finest Renaissance *hôtel particulier* in Toulouse. Pierre d'Assézat quit his native Rouergue seduced by the lure of the *pastel* industry, became a *capitoul* in 1552 and engaged the eminent architect, Nicolas Bachelier, in 1555 to build his mansion. Bachelier, who designed the north and west wings of the courtyard, came up with a very personal interpretation of the classical idiom using brick and stone. Pairs of superimposed orders on the façades isolate the windows. At the junction of the two wings is a square stairtower with a monumental entrance at the base. The tower extends upwards into a *tour capitulaire* topped with an elegant lantern. Pierre d'Assézat never saw the completion of his hotel. In 1561 his election as *capitoul* for the second time coincided with the collapse of the *pastel* industry and his exile because of his Protestant convictions. Bachelier's son, Antoine, completed the screen wall to the street c 1571. The extension to the east was never carried out and some of the original fenestration was altered in 1761. It became the home of the *Jeux Floraux*. In the portico on the reverse of the south façade is a statue of Clémence Isaure, the semi-mythical patroness of the *Académie des Jeux Floraux*, ancestor of the Académie Française, founded in 1323 to safeguard the language and poetry of *Oc* and organise an annual competition. In the 16C the story got about that the funds originated from a rich beauty, Dame Clémence, as the flowers distributed to the laureates were made of silver. Her statue is, in fact, the remodelled tomb statue of Bertrande Ysalguier, d. 1348. On 3 May each year, the winners of the competition are still presented with flowers blessed on the altar of the Black Virgin of la Daurade; among those honoured by the society have been Ronsard, Chateaubriand and Victor Hugo.

The Hôtel d'Assézat now houses the **Fondation Bemberg collection**. Among the works of art on display are over 40 European works, predominantly from the 16C and 17C, and more than 80 French paintings from the late 19C and 20C, including a large number by Pierre Bonnard. (Opening hours are 10.00–17.00, 10.00–18.00 June–Sept; closed Tue.)

Just past the Hôtel d'Assézat on the left in **Rue de la Bourse**, is the elegant 18C **Hôtel de Nupces**, and, almost opposite, the 15C **Maison Pierre Delfau**, also built by a *pastel* merchant, one of the few remaining houses of the late Middle Ages. Further along Rue du Metz is **Place Esquirol**, a large square where the recent discovery of the Roman Capitolium was made. (Close by is the Musée des Augustins, Walk 3).

To return to Place du Capitole, turn left into **Rue des Changes**. This street, with Rue des Filatiers and Rue Saint-Rome, was the medieval main artery between the Capitole and the Parlement. While the layout of the street and the plots have hardly changed, the fire of 1463 destroyed most of the houses and it was almost totally rebuilt by rich merchant families and *pastel* magnates. A lively, pedestrian street, since the beginning it has been full of boutiques, small tradesmen and general commerce. Look up at the variety of buildings huddled together with an occasional *tour capitulaire* showing above the façades. Parts of 15C or 16C houses remain at Nos 16 and 19.

Rue Saint-Rome—named after the Church Saint-Romain, the very first Dominican monastery in 1216, given by Bishop Foulques to Dominic de Guzman—starts at the junction with Rue Peyras. At one time the street was named after the fishmarket, Bancs Majous, where No. 14 now stands, and, although this market disappeared in 1550, there is still a distinctly fishy aroma in the courtyard. **No. 3** is one of the most beautiful Henri IV-style buildings in Toulouse, in alternating stone and brick with sculpted mullions, bossed door and arched boutiques partly uncovered, and the courtyard, opening on to Rue Tripière, was remarkably restored in 1974.

Tucked away in **Rue Tripière** are two interesting houses, built by *capitouls* in 1529 and 1617 and acquired in 1898 by *les Compagnons charpentiers*. In **Rue du May**, the **Musée du Vieux Toulouse** (tel: 61 23 32 80, 15.00–18.00, except Sun, Jun–Sept) is installed the 16C house of Antoine Dumay, doctor to Marguerite de Navarre, restored by Docteur Simeon Durand in 1914 before he made it over to the *Société des Toulousains de Toulouse*. In the dark rooms around an attractive courtyard in need of repair are many objects relating to the history of Toulouse.

Rue Saint-Rome leads back to Place du Capitole.

Walk 3: the Augustinian Museum and the Cathedral St-Etienne

Set off from the corner between the theatre and the luxury *Grand Hôtel de l'Opéra* (tel: 61 21 82 66), discreetly laid out around a small garden, the site of the 14C Collège St-Martial which became a convent in the 17C. South of **Rue Poids de l'Huile**, sandwiched between Rue saint-Rome and Rue d'Alsace, is a tangle of small streets radiating out from **Place Salengro** created in 1849, with a pretty fountain and some well-restored façades. The restaurant *Les Caves de la Maréchale* (tel: 61 23 89 88) in the courtyard of 3, Rue Chalande, uses typical brick vaults to advantage. **Place des Puits Clos** has four pink marble columns saved from the retable of the church of la Dalbade.

Turning east down Rue Baour-Lormian, cross Rue d'Alsace to **Rue Lt.-Col. Pélissier**. In 1576 the secular order of *Pénitents Bleus* made their base in this street and, in 1622, commissioned Pierre Levesville to build their church, **St-Jérôme**. This curious building exudes a secular atmosphere because the narthex is a passageway with display cabinets and is often used as a short-cut for shoppers. The church, all curves, stucco, and small loggias, decorated in the 18C by the painter J-P. Rivalz and sculptor Marc Acis, resembles a Baroque theatre. The corridor comes out into **Rue de la Pomme**, a pleasant shopping street which brings you to the most congenial square in Toulouse, **Place Saint-Georges**, with a small garden, pretty façades and a host of inviting restaurants and pavement cafés. Its ambience undoubtedly derives from the fact that it is one of the oldest squares and the main market for centuries.

Rue des Arts runs alongside the church and chapter house of the former Couvent des Grands Augustins begun in 1309, now the **MUSÉE DES AUGUSTINS** (tel: 61 22 21 82, 10.00–18.00, and Wed eve, closed Tues), the municipal Fine Arts collection. This is a very rich museum with a wide ranging collection and in an unexpectedly delightful setting. The religious community of the monastery was disbanded at the Revolution and part of the premises was occupied by the *Ecole des Arts* in 1804. It was partly demolished in the 19C, then given its definitive and dignified role as museum and art gallery. Viollet-le-Duc's project for the museum in 1873 was carried out by his pupil, Denis Darcy, who built the western galleries between 1880 and 1896.

Entering from Rue de Metz, a short flight of steps leads down to the large cloister completed in 1396, and a cloister garden has been recreated. On the left is a welcoming choir of upturned gargoyles from the old Cordeliers church. There are sarcophagi in the cloister aisles, and engraved medieval inscriptions (11C–16C) in a small gallery on the west. The museum has the most important collection of **Romanesque sculpture** anywhere in the world. The 350 pieces include capitals and other sculptures rescued from the cloisters of La Daurade, St-Sernin and St-Etienne. The eight oldest capitals, c 1100, are from the first workshop of La Daurade and show a great affinity to the Moissic cloister capitals but include themes not found there. Two famous and enigmatic sculptures from the west façade of St-Sernin, **Sign of Leo and of Aries**, first quarter of the 12C, are iconographically unique in Christian art. The St-Sernin cloister capitals (1118–25) show an advance in the technical skill of the 12C to create fluent carvings, mainly of animal and vegetal motifs. The cutting is deeper, more subtle, the detail more delicate and the plastic qualities of the carving enhanced. The group of capitals from the second Daurade workshop put more emphasis on narrative dynamism than the first. One of the most celebrated capitals from St-Etienne, **Herod's feast** (c 1120–40) has quite the most seductive of Salomés. Also from the cathedral are the very fine reliefs by Gilabertus of **St-Andrew** and **St-Thomas** and others from the same workshop.

Gothic sculpture can be found in the buildings east of the cloister, the sacristy, Chapelle Notre-Dame de Pitié (1341) and the chapter house (14C–15C). These include funerary objects such as the remarkable 14C recumbent **statue of Guillaume Durant**, 16 statues from the **Chapelle de Rieux**, including Jean Tissendier, the Bishop of Rieux, presenting the chapel which was part of the Cordeliers Church, and the exquisitely moving 15C **Notre-Dame de Grasse**. The youthful Virgin and her baby face outwards away from each other, suggesting they were originally part of a larger group. The 14C/15C church is used for a collection of **religious paintings** with local artists such as Antoine Rivalz (1667–1735), and Nicolas Tournier (1590–1639). Other European paintings include an early Murillo, one of three versions of the Legend of St-Anthony of Padua, c 1627–32, by Anthony van Dyck, Rubens' highly dramatic Christ between the Two

Thieves, c 1635, and a Perugino. The Bachelier reliefs from the Dalbade, 1544–45 are also here. A wide range of **secular paintings** from the 17C to the 19C are exhibited in the upper galleries of the west wing, rebuilt in the 19C. Local painters such as Chalette and Roques are represented among others. Outstanding is the charming portrait of **La Baronne de Crussol** by Elisabeth-Louise Vigée-Lebrun (1755–1842). The 19C is splendidly evoked by the *salon rouge* where *pompier* works are hung in the manner of the Salons, one atop the other against a red brocaded wall. Delacroix, Ingres and Toulouse-Lautrec are also represented. Overtly narcissistic are the 19C plastercasts echoed by duplicates on the staircase in the south-west corner.

Cross **Rue de Metz** at the junction with Rue d'Alsace-Lorraine and walk along **Rue de Languedoc** as far as **Place Rouaix**, so named since before 1180. There are still, in this part of town, some of the colour-coded street signs for the illiterate: yellow for streets running north–south, parallel with the Garonne, and white for east–west. Since 1913 the Chamber of Commerce has occupied the 18C Hôtel de Fumel at the start of **Rue Croix-Baragnon**, originally the residence of the Presidents of Parlement. An agreeably well-maintained street with some expensive boutiques, Croix-Baragnon is representative of the smart residential area this side of town. **No. 15**, called the Romanesque house, c 1300, is considered the oldest in Toulouse. Typical of the 18C, the **Hôtel de Castellane** is in brick and terracotta painted to imitate stone. Pause at the junction with **Rue des Arts** for an impressive double view which will help you understand the geography of the town: down Rue des Arts you see the belfry of the Augustins, and, at the end of Rue Croix-Baragnon, the strangely asymmetrical west front of the Cathedral St-Etienne. **No. 1** Rue des Arts is a rare example of a timbered house from before the blaze of 1463. Inside **No. 22** Rue Croix-Baragnon are the tastefully re-used and replicated arcades from the 16C Hôtel Jean des Pins, demolished at the beginning of the 20C. At **No. 41** is one of the best early Louis XVI façades, with superb ironwork by Bernard Ortet who worked at the Capitole and the Cathedral in the 18C.

The spacious triangular **Place St-Etienne**, the result of 19C and 20C remodelling, has many 17C and 18C houses. The **Griffoul** fountain in the centre of the square is the oldest in Toulouse. On the octagonal lower basin are spaces still awaiting the coats of arms of *capitouls*. The upper bowl, dated 1720, and the obelisk, 1593, by Antoine Bachelier supports four little figures spouting water, re-cast from four *mannikin pis* considered slightly improper in such a holy situation.

The **CATHEDRAL OF ST-ETIENNE** is set off to advantage by the Place but the building lacks the coherence of St-Sernin. The decidedly disturbing effect of the façade is due to a succession of modifications since the 11C. The cathedral is in fact made up of two incomplete churches, one dating from the early 13C and the other begun in c 1272. The first documented reference to a cathedral dedicated to St-Etienne (St-Stephen) is 844. At the time of Gregorian reform, Bishop Isarn, who was elected in 1071, stimulated moral and physical improvements including the rebuilding of the cathedral. The Romanesque church, transformed during the episcopates of a Cistercian, Foulques de Marseille (1205–31), and a Dominican, Raimond du Fauga (1232–70), is a prototype of the aisleless, rib vaulted meridional Gothic church.

Exterior. The earlier church seems to lean for support against the brick belfry, but is in fact supported by two enormous brick buttresses at right angles to the façade. Between these, under a slightly pointed relieving arch, is a large rose window inserted when the façade was almost complete. The Flamboyant portal, inserted c 1450, is decidedly off centre because the architect, Martin Baudry, was at pains to save the baptismal chapel north of the entrance. The belfry is composed of a Gothic portion on Romanesque foundations, capped by the 16C gable belfry. From the gardens on the north you see the large rectangular buttresses of the later Rayonnant building.

When Bertrand de l'Isle-Jourdain was elected to the episcopate he planned to build a catheral twice as large as the previous one to the east and north of the earlier nave. When work began in 1272, the Rayonnant cathedral of Narbonne was under way. Bertrand de l'Isle had been involved in settling a dispute in Narbonne over the site of the new cathedral, and was undoubtedly influenced by the work going on there. Continue round the chevet to the south courtyard where, until 1811, the Romanesque cloister and monastic buildings stood. The south buttresses are more elaborate than on the north. Enter by the south door and you are midway between the two different structures.

Interior. To your left is the rather dark and cavernous section known as **Raymond VI's nave** because of the east boss carved with 12 pearls in the shape of the Cross of Toulouse. A vast single space with wide rounded vaults, it is supported by powerful rectangular ribs which spring from Romanesque capitals salvaged from the 11C church. The only light falls from the rose window, containing some original glass. This part of the building was nearing completion during one of Simon de Montfort's sieges of Toulouse, in either 1211 or 1217–18. On the walls are **tapestries** woven in Toulouse in the 17C recounting the story of the Bishops of Toulouse.

Only three bays of the early 13C church remain and anything that previously existed further to the east has been consumed by the great late 13C choir. The effect of the interior is as disconcerting as the exterior because the two sections are not on the same axis and juxtapose two styles of Gothic architecture. The two sections were separated by a wall until the beginning of the 16C when Archbishop Jean d'Orléans attempted to begin the transept by building the massive **round pillar** now standing incongruously between the two parts. On it is a memorial to Pierre-Paul Riquet (1605–80) engineer of the Canal du Midi.

The vast proportions of the five-bay **choir**, with ambulatory and radiating chapels, dwarf the older nave. After Bertrand de l'Isle's death in 1286 the work was further slowed down when Pope John XXII reduced the size of the diocese, and came to a total halt at the end of the 14C due to lack of funds. By this time the choir up to the level of the triforium and 15 chapels had been completed, protected by a provisional wooden roof. The shafts are little more than undulations on the surfaces of the cylindrical cores, and the capitals minimal, but the triforium is ornate.

Work did not take off again seriously for over a century, and it was not until a fire in 1609 devoured the timber roof and all the choir furnishings that the stone vault was begun, in 1611, with money donated by Cardinal de Joyeuse, and carried out by Pierre Levesville. The height of the vaults at 28m is considerably lower than the planned 40m and the ribs spring from just above the triforium. The work was not completed until the 20C when the north door was built.

Of the 15 chapels, the oldest date from 1279 to 1286, but were mainly completed during the 14C, the time of some interesting carved bosses such as St-Louis enthroned, c 1300, in the St-Joseph chapel. The first chapel on the south is almost a church within a church, built in the 15C by Archbishop

Bernard du Rosier. The majority of the **stained glass** is 19C, but there is some earlier, including panels from the end of the 13C in the St-Vincent de Paul chapel. This is the oldest stained glass in Toulouse, created from windows salvaged from the Jacobins. These depict a Bishop and St-Etienne, St-Michael and a Virgin and Child. The glass in the St-Augustin chapel is also 14C, and that in the St-Louis Chapel is 15C with portraits of Charles VII, King of France and the Dauphin, the future Louis XI. There is some 17C glass which shows a similarity with the work of Arnaud de Mole in Auch.

The **furnishings** offer a series of interesting works, especially the double range of choir stalls carved in walnut between 1610 and 1613 by Pierre Monge of Narbonne. Their decoration includes pagan and mythological subjects which contrast with the little statue of the Virgin under the triumphal arch at the top of the episcopal throne. Also carved at the same time was the walnut case of the organ, perched some 17m above the floor. Restored in 1868 by Cavaillé-Col and again in 1976, it is often used for concerts. The tapestry hanging, c 1609, by Jean du Mazet from Castillon near Lombez, has scenes from the life of St-Etienne. The rather hectic Baroque retable of the main altar was designed by Pierre Mercier, and Gervais Drouet sculpted the central panel of the Lapidation of St-Stephen in 1667. The four Evangelists carved by Marc Arcis were added at the beginning of the 18C. The polychrome marble is from the Carcassonne region, carried to Toulouse on the Canal du Midi. The more restrained ironwork of the choir enclosure, 1766, is the work of Bernard Ortet, and the medallions were originally gilded. There are paintings by H. Pader and Nicolas Bollery (17C) and by Despax (18C) who delighted in the use of pastel colours. The 19C episcopal throne is by Auguste Virebent.

From the west door of St-Etienne you pass in front of the Préfecture, housed since 1800 in the former archipiscopal palace (17C). The area south-west of the cathedral is the nob-end of Toulouse, where the wealthy professionals and *haute bourgeoisie* have their homes. Most visitors do not get this far, but the old narrow streets lined with grand *hôtels particuliers* with courtyards and gardens make a very pleasant afternoon's wander.

Rue Fermat is a street rich in Louis XVI façades and elegant ironwork; the tiny **Place Saintes-Scarbes** has a modern fountain composed of six columns, a rather fine 18C balcony at No. 6 and an exclusive flower shop on the corner. **Rue St-Jacques** leads to a fragment of the 1C Gallo-Roman enclosure, uncovered in 1962, and the vast Palais du Maréchal-Niel built in the 19C for Napoléon III's War Minister in the style of a Parisian Palace. **Rue Ninau** contains the charming **Hôtel Ulmo**, purchased in 1526 by Jean d'Ulmo, first President of the *Parlement*, who had the house enlarged and embellished with a unique design for the main entrance consisting of a double flight of steps to a perron under a baldaquin.

Either Rue Ninau or Rue St-Jacques will take you to the green and pleasant spaces of the **Grand Rond** and the **Jardins des Plantes**. A former Carmelite property was used for natural history collections forming the basis of the Jardin des Plantes and the Faculté des Sciences, later to become the Medical School. In 1865 the **Musée d'Histoire Naturelle** (tel: 61 52 00 14, 10.00–17.00, closed Tues) opened its doors to the public. It boasts the second largest collection of stuffed monkeys in France, as well as the first Prehistoric gallery, thanks to historians E. Cartailhac and Abbot Breuil. Simon de Montfort met his death near here, killed by a missile from a catapult from the city walls on 25 June 1218. Not far from the Jardin des

Plantes is the **Musée Georges Labit** of non-European art and artefacts, 43 Rue des Martyrs-de-la-Libération (tel: 61 22 21 84, 10.00–17.00, closed Tues am & BH).

From Place St-Scarbes, take **Rue Perchepinte**, originally the main street of this aristocratic neighbourhood. The houses are modest but the overall effect is agreeably attractive with some pretty details and plenty of good ironwork. Where **Place Perchepinte** meets **Rue Espinasse** is what remains of the superb **Hôtel de Mansencal**, 1527–47, combining Gothic form with Renaissance decorative elements.

The **Musée Paul Dupuy** (tel: 61 22 21 83, 10.00–17.00, closed Tues am) is housed in the former Hôtel de Besson, 13 Rue de la Pleau, restored in a manner befitting this important decorative arts museum. Paul Dupuy, wealthy owner of the Toulousain department store Bon Marché, collected the items that others rejected and installed them here after purchasing the building in 1905. On the ground floor is the complete interior of the 17C Pharmacie du Collège des Jésuites with its jars and bottles. The museum contains a variety of religious artefacts and the famous *cor de Roland*, a 11C carved ivory oliphant from southern Italy described in the 15C as belonging to Roland, the legendary nephew of Charlemagne. Charmingly displayed on the first floor is porcelain and *faïence*, 17C Venetian glass and 19C and 20C glass by Baccarat and by Emile Gallé. The Salon de Musique has mainly 18C and 19C instruments, and a marvellous pink room displays an exotic automat called *La Leçon de Chant*, signed Robert Houdin, Paris 1844. The museum is probably most famous for its exceptional collection of clocks and watches of all kinds donated by Edouard Gelis, and it has recently added to this a series of magic lanterns and cinema apparatus. There are regular temporary exhibitions. This is a good district for restaurants, one of the nicest being *Au Gré du Vin* (tel: 61 25 03 51) just opposite the museum.

On **Rue Ozenne** is the Renaissance tower erected in 1533 by Guillaume de Tournoer or Tournier. When **Rue de Languedoc** was cut in the late 19C, **Hôtel Bérenguier-Maynier** or **Vieux-Raisin** was spared, although the neglect it has suffered since makes one wonder whether it will survive much longer. It has kept the Gothic wall on Rue d'Aussargues which was endowed with Renaissance windows after the *capitoul*, Bérenguier-Maynier, being a man of his time, acquired the house in 1515. He also added two wings to the principal dwelling. Jean Burnet became the owner in 1547 and, influenced by the work of architects such as Bachelier, built the front courtyard facing the Rue de Languedoc with a portico linking the two wings. All the façades are heavily adorned with caryatids, atlantes and fauns. Where Rue de Languedoc and Rue d'Ozenne meet is a classy confectioner and pastry shop, *R. Pillon*, selling a speciality cake called *Le Fénétra*, found only in Haute-Garonne and made with lemon and almonds.

Further along Rue de Languedoc is one early 16C façade of the sober **Hôtel de Pins**, the house of Jean de Pins, Bishop of Pamiers and Rieux, scholar of Bologna and Italian Ambassador to François I, who was condemned for his friendship with Erasmus. Rue d'Alsace Lorraine will take you back to Place Charles de Gaulle, or Rue des Changes to Place du Capitole (see Walk 2).

2

The Lauragais and the Canal du Midi

Total distance: 116km (73 miles).

The Lauragais, east of Toulouse, is part of the *département* of Haute-Garonne, a region that may be overlooked by the visitor who is heading for the Mediterranean or the mountains, yet it has a particular charm. Undulating and fertile, this wide exposed valley is frequently buffeted by the *vent d'autan*, the south-westerly wind which dries the land and reputedly drives its people mad. The wind was once harnessed and put to work through windmills, most now abandoned, usually sail-less, often headless, and sometimes just skeletons. The Lauragais had many Cathar communities in the 12C and 13C. In the next centuries, *pastel* (see Gaillac and Toulouse), was intensively cultivated in the valley and brought wealth to the region generally and huge fortunes to some individuals.

By the mid-16C imported indigo took the place of *pastel*, and by the 17C maize was extensively grown in the Lauragais. An overland trade route had crossed the valley for more than 1000 years carrying goods from the Mediterranean to Toulouse and on to the Atlantic via the Garonne. The problem of carrying increasing quantities of grain from the Toulousain to the Languedoc was solved by Pierre-Paul Riquet's great engineering feat in 1666, the Canal Royal du Languedoc, now called the Canal du Midi. Colbert obtained royal approval for Riquet's scheme in 1666, work began in 1667. In less than 14 years 240km of canal was dug. Over 60 locks, single, double and multiple, coped with the considerable slopes, and water was channelled from a reservoir at St-Ferréol in the Black Mountains to Naurouze, the highest point at 189m, from where it divided and flowed downhill in each direction. A workforce of 12,000 head (three women equalled two heads) dug the canal, but Riquet died, exhausted and penniless, in 1680, a year before the canal's completion. In 1856 le Canal Latéral à la Garonne (see Moissac) was realised and canal barges could make the entire journey to Bordeaux, instead of off-loading at Toulouse on to river craft. Shortly afterwards rail transport replaced the canal and in the 20C the Autoroute de Deux Mers follows the same route.

From Toulouse take the D4 south staying close to the right bank of the Garonne, for 17km, a reasonably pleasant way of leaving the metropolis, then join the N20 at Lacroix-Falgarde. As the road moves away from the Garonne basin, so it takes you out of the brick dominated region into an area where the main building material is stone. Take the N20 for 6.5km and come off at **Vernet**, past a pretty church with a regional-style belfry gable, and take the D74 across the river Ariège (1km). Of the Romanesque Benedictine abbey-church of St-Pierre in **Venerque**, only a part of the east end has survived. It was enlarged in brick in the 14C–15C to accommodate pilgrims who came to venerate the shrine of St-Phébarde and it has a 12C reliquary. The belfry was gradually transformed into a defensive tower or keep, and at the end of the 19C the upper part of the church was heavily restored and battlemented. There are some Romanesque capitals, but the lower sections of those of the St-Phébarde chapel and around the entrance are faithful 19C copies of the west door of St-Sernin in Toulouse. It is possible that the wrought iron around the font was originally part of the 18C screen dividing the choir and nave.

Take the D19, 19km to **Nailloux**, where a large fair, the *Foire de Messidor* is held each June involving, among other things, a giant *cassoulet*, a regional dish based on white haricot beans, goose fat, goose or duck and Toulouse sausage. Nailloux has a Gothic church in brick with a belfry gable of five bays between two polygonal towers; and in the centre of the town is a windmill.

Stay on the D19 for 2.5km to **Montgeard**, a small *bastide* founded in 1319 on a slope dominating the plains of the Lauragais. A *pastel* baron, Durand de Montgeard, was the principal benefactor of the brick **church** which was modelled on St-Cécile in Albi. The west tower with rounded buttresses was built in 1561, although the upper part is modern and the narthex has sculpted stone inserts. The interior is rendered and painted in splendid *trompe l'oeil* on a blue background, the ribs, tiercerons and bosses in gold, red and green. The elegant alabaster font is dated 1516, and there are four Renaissance alabaster reliefs (on the south-west wall, in the two chapels near the altar and above the pulpit) of the Assumption, St Catherine, the Coronation of the Virgin and the Mystical Throne.

In the village a small 16C château, undergoing restoration (tel: 61 81 52 75, 12.00–19.00, Sat, Sun, BH, 15 Apr–Oct, 12.00–19.00 Sun, rest of year), was built by the same Durand who bought his seigneurial rights from Catherine de Medici, Countess of Lauragais. A watchtower of the same period, on the angle of a wall at the end of a path alongside the grounds of a 17C house, was built to survey the precious fields of *pastel*.

Wind along the D25 past the small lake de la Thésauque, with a leisure area, and take the D622 towards Villefranche-de-Lauragais, 10km. At Gardouch a single lock interrupts the Canal du Midi as it goes on its straight and tranquil course. The road then takes you over the less tranquil autoroute, railway, and N113. The main, or only, reason to stop in **Villefranche-de-Lauragais** would be to eat *cassoulet*.

The fame of **Avignonet-Lauragais** (Tourist Information, tel: 61 81 63 67) 7km east on the N113, standing sentinel over the valley, rests on an incident on 28 May 1242, when a group of about 60 armed men commanded by Pierre Roger de Mirepoix descended from the Cathar stronghold of Montségur. Aided and abetted by the locals, they avenged the persecution of heretics by slaughtering all the members of the recently installed Inquisition including Inquisitors Guillaume Arnaud and Etienne de Saint Thibery. As a consequence the fate of Montségur, the last Cathar sanctuary, was sealed and early in 1243 the Council of Béziers decided to destroy the stronghold. There is a small, severe end-14C **church** in yellowy-pink stone dominating the little town. Its rectangular tower supports an octagonal belfry with simple two-light windows topped off by a small crocketted spire. There are fragments of the 13C and 15C ramparts, so-called Cathar crosses, and the narrow Tour de Ravelin, 1352, originally a prison, with the statue of a warrior.

Drop down into the valley and follow the signs Port-Lauragais (D43d). **Port-Lauragais**, at the intersection of the autoroute and the canal, is a pleasant Motorway Service Area as well as the Centre Pierre-Paul Riquet. The latter has a permanent exhibition and information on the Canal. South-east of Port-Lauragais (on the D80a) is the obelisk which indicates the highest point on the canal, the **Col de Naurouze**, 189m. Boat trips or canal cruises are popular ways of visiting the Lauragais, starting from Toulouse or Castelnaudary and other locks along the way (Crown Blue Line, boat hire, tel: 68 23 17 51).

Return towards Avignonet, turn left on the N113 and right on the D43 up to **Les Cassés** (10km) above the *rigole*, the channel which brings water from the dam at St-Ferréol to the Naurouze basin to feed the Canal. Like so many isolated villages in the region, Les Cassés harboured Cathars, 50 of whom were burned at the stake by Simon de Montfort in 1211. Contine a further 3km.

The high vantage point of the 13C *bastide* **St-Félix-Lauragais** (Tourist Information, tel: 61 83 01 71) offers a splendid view north to the *Montagne Noire*, the Black Mountains, and south to the Pyrenees. In the manner of most *bastides*, the focal point of the town is the central marketplace and St-Félix still possesses an *halle couverte* with a belltower. Around the square are timbered houses in various states of repair. There is a rare specimen of a *pastel* plant in front of the Tourist Office and the importance of the *pastel* tradition is celebrated around Easter-time with the *fêtes à la cocagne*. The 14C–19C church has a Flamboyant porch and an 18C organ. Next to it is the former canons' house with sculpted door and cross windows and further along, opposite the market, is the 17C–19C house where the composer, Déodate de Séverac (1873–1921) was born. On the north of the village, overlooking the plain, is the château (tel: 61 83 07 08, 10.00–12.00, 14.00–18.30 in summer)—around a square courtyard—dating from the 12C to the 18C, which hosted the first Cathar synod in 1167 in the presence of the Cathar Bishop Nicétas. Take the D622 east for 9.5km.

The largest town in the Lauragais is **Revel** (pop. 7704, Tourist Information, tel: 61 83 50 06), a *bastide* founded in 1342 by Philippe VI who laid down in the charter the dimensions of the houses and the length of time allowed to erect them. The huge 14C *halle* in Place Philippe-VI-de-Valois has ancient roof timbers around a central stone building with Serlian windows and a lantern belfry, now the Tourist Office. Market day is Saturday. The houses that surround the *place* are mainly 18C and 19C, and the result of constant remodelling. The *bastide* was originally contained within hexagonal walls and, although the walls were demolished after the Treaty of Alès in 1629, the exterior boulevards follow the same pattern. Revel has been the capital of quality reproduction furniture, marquetry and all associated crafts since the end of the 1889 when a specialist cabinetmaker from Versailles, Alexandre Monoury, settled here and opened a school. Samples can be seen at the Hall du Meuble. At St-Ferréol is the Musée du Canal du Midi (tel: 61 83 33 98, afternoons).

Leave Revel on the D1 stopping after 10km at **St-Julia**, also known as **Gras-Capou** (fat chick), a reference to the capons reared here since time immemorial and sold on the Sunday before Christmas. Part of the fortifications still stand with a 16C gateway, the Porte de Cers, and the Porte d'Autan, as well as the 14C church which was restored by Marguerite de Valois. Best of all is the beautfiul *clocher-pignon* on the church, with five arcades containing the oldest bell (1396) in Haute-Garonne. Perched on an escarpment protecting the border with the 13km on the D1 Albigeois, the little *cité* of **Caraman**, the ancient capital of the *pays de Cocagne*, has a small lake called the *Orme Blanc* with water sports facilities.

9km north of Caraman, by the D11/D20, at the pretty village of **Loubens-Lauragais**, is an interesting château (tel: 61 83 12 08, 14.30–18.30, Sun & BH, Easter, May–Nov; 14.30–18.30 Thurs–Sun, 14 July–31 Aug) owned by the same family since 1096 and remodelled in the 16C. South of Caraman on the D11 at Caragoudes (7km) are windmills.

3

The Volvestre: Valleys of the Garonne and the Lèze

Total distance: 79km (50 miles).

The Volvestre derives its name from a Celtic tribe, the Volques, who settled around Toulouse about 2000 years ago, and refers to the valleyed region south-west of Toulouse, lying midway between the plain and the mountains. The Garonne flows north-east through to the Toulousain and, on and off between 1259 and 1453, marked the border between Languedoc and English Guyenne.

Muret (Tourist Information, tel: 61 59 96 96), on the west bank of the Garonne, is now virtually part of greater Toulouse but was once the administrative capital of the Comminges. It is hard to believe that a decisive battle was fought here during the Albigensian Crusades between the combined forces of Raymond VI, Count of Toulouse and his opportunist brother-in-law Peter II of Aragon, against the crusading army of Simon de Montfort representing the French King and the Pope. On 12 September 1213 the defending army suffered a crushing defeat and Peter of Aragon was killed, giving de Montfort the opportunity to enter Toulouse. Muret was an important stage on the Pilgrim Route to Santiago, but the 12C Church of St-Jacques was remodelled in brick in the 14C and 16C and endowed with a two-tier Toulousain-style octagonal belfry. It has preserved the 12C Chapel of the Rosary where St-Dominic is said to have meditated on the eve of the battle, and it also contains some other good furnishings. The aviation pioneer, Clement Ader (1841–1925), was born in Muret and there is a museum dedicated to him in the Mairie. When the weather is clear there are fantastic views of the Pyrenees as you head south.

The main-roadphobe can avoid the N117 by meandering along the Garonne for a few kilometres. From Muret take the D15 to Lavernose Lacasse, cross the autoroute on the D53, and the D10 to the little town of **Noé** (14.5km), with the house of the Chevalier de Pardailhan, a rebuilt Romanesque church and one hotel, *L'Arche de Noé*, tel: 61 87 40 12.

Cross to the Lèze Valley on the D28/D4, 7km to **St-Sulpice-sur-Lèze**, one of many *bastides* founded by Alphonse de Poitiers. This stunning little town is entirely in brick, and the Place de l'Hôtel-de-Ville is one of the most impressive of its kind, surrounded by arcades and timber-framed houses. In the square is the good-looking *Restaurant La Commanderie* (tel: 61 97 33 61). A block away is the former Church of the Hospitallers, 1450–80, more interesting outside with an elaborate octagonal belfry with mitred two-bay windows and crocketed brick spire, than from the interior, reached by a long covered corridor running along the north wall. The south-west chapel off the aisleless nave does, however, have the remains of a late-15C/early 16C Last Judgement fresco.

Continue south on the D9 to **Lézat-sur-Lèze** (7km), also a pleasant market-town with small brick *halle*, 14C–16C timber-framed houses and a church with a weatherbeaten Romanesque west porch and some 15C and 16C frescoes.

Take the D626 to St-Ybars, a small town on a hill. From St-Ybars turn right on to the D25 and the D40, 17km, to **Montesquieu-Volvestre** (Tourist Information: 61 90 41 18) a *bastide* of 1246, founded by the counts of Toulouse near an existing château on the banks of the Arize. Protected by verdant slopes of the Plantaurel, it has been the most important town of the Volvestre since 1317. A brick town with a regular layout, its best features are the covered market on 20 octagonal pillars, and the Gothic (14C–16C) church opposite, with a massive, gabled west elevation. Dedicated to St-Victor whose relics it once claimed to own, it has a tall belfry, which is a 15C interpretation of the usual 13C/14C Toulousain belfry, on the south side. The tempo is doubled, so that it has 16 rather than the usual eight sides, each face with a narrow lancet window. The grand Renaissance portal in stone, 1552, inset into the blind central arch, is flanked by fluted Corinthian columns. Inside are a number of interesting pieces, including a 16C Entombment group in painted stone, a 15C wooden Crucifixion and, in the north-east, an Adoration of the Shepherds and the Magi painted on wood, 16C. There is a Baroque pulpit and a painting by Despax of the Martyrdom of St-Victor (18C). The crypt was rediscovered in 1983 and restored (light on left pillar). It was built c 1390 and blocked up in 1747, and contains four reliquary busts.

Detour. If you like caves and Protestant museums, make a larger loop between St-Ybars and Montesquieu. Continue south on the D9 from St-Ybars until the D14 (11km) to **Carla-Bayle**, a tidy little town with a wide view, which belies its stormy past.

Built on a ridge between the Lèze and Arize valleys, the medieval stronghold became a Huguenot bastion and suffered heavily during the Wars of Religion. In the 18C the community of Carla-le-Comte actively supported the Revolution and became Carla-Le-Peuple, acquiring its present suffix in 1879 in tribute to its most famous son Pierre Bayle, 1647–1706, Protestant philosopher, author of *Pensées sur la comète* and *Dictionnaire historique et critique* (1696–97). The birthplace houses the **Musée Pierre Bayle**, an excellent little museum retracing Bayle's life and work, and the best Protestant Museum in the region. Bayle, the victim of anti-Protestant persecution, settled with a French community in Rotterdam on 30 October 1681, where he published his works. His self-imposed exile saved him but not his brother who was imprisoned and executed because of Bayle's publications. His famous plea for freedom of conscience: '*C'est donc la tolérance qui est la source de la paix et l'intolérance qui est la source de la confusion et du grabuge*' (It is tolerance that is the source of peace and intolerance that is the source of confusion and mayhem) pre-empted Locke's ideas, and announced the spirit of the 18C, but his liberal ideas also led to conflict with fellow Protestants. The little house is arranged around an interior courtyard and the collection includes documents, engravings and acerbic cartoons. It also reconstructs Pierre Bayle's study and a kitchen of the period.

Round the corner from the museum is the Temple Protestant which can be visited (ask at the museum to be let in). Unrecognisable from the other houses from outside, it is a simple galleried hall with two spiral staircases, benches, an ancient stove, a piano and a wooden table. The pulpit in the centre is inscribed Gij zijt Gods tempel, I Cor. 3.16. The date over the porch of the Catholic church is 1687; the date of the Revocation of the Edict of Nantes was 1685. The village also has a small bar-restaurant, *Auberge Pierre Bayle*.

The D26/D119 takes you from Carla-Bayle about 14km to **Mas d'Azil** (Tourist Information, tel: 61 69 90 18), a pleasant *bastide* with a small Museum of Prehistory (tel: 61 69 97 22, June–Sept) next to the church (18C). In the vicinity are dolmens and megaliths.

The site is most famous, however, for the vast natural tunnel carved through the limestone range of the Plantaurel by the river Arize, the **Grotte de Mas d'Azil**, where primeval man, Cathars and Calvinists all apparently took refuge. Now the D119 disappears into the yawning black hole in the side of the hill (particularly disconcerting if arriving from the south). The caverns were inhabited by a succession of groups of early man which left reminders of their occupation—some of these are on display as part of the visit. There are tools and bones of the Magdalenian period and harpoons and coloured pebbles of the Azilien man (named after the location). The vast dark dry cavern, on three levels, is itself less interesting than the artefacts, as it has no fantastic mineral formations. Nevertheless the landscape is green and undulating.

Take the D116/D628 from Mas d'Azil through **Daumazan-sur-Arize**, which has a 12C church raised and enlarged in 16C and 17C (key at the Mairie) and a stone cross in the cemetery, to Montesquieu-Volvestre.

It is just 6km on the D627 to **Rieux-Volvestre** (Tourist Information, tel: 61 87 63 33), the best of the brick towns of the Volvestre, bordered by the meandering Arize. It belongs to the category *un des plus beaux villages de France* by virtue of its site, its stunning brick church and the picturesquely crumbling houses.

Rieux was given a diocese in 1317 by the beneficent Cadurcien Pope John XXII, and the Franciscan bishop Jean Tissendier rebuilt the **Cathedral of Ste-Marie** in brick in the second quarter of the 14C, incorporating the nave and chancel of earlier edifices. The refined, almost stark, elevations are mitigated by the use of brick and the surrounding water and greenery. The roof, resting on the *mirandes*, has a wide overhang to protect the walls. The sophisticated octagonal belfry, the pride and joy of Rieux, is a variation on the theme of the Jacobins in Toulouse, its tall lower level composed of blind arches surmounted with stone quatrefoils. Each angle of the octagon is outlined by an engaged column in pink marble, the three upper stages each set back from the level below, with traditional two-light bays under mitred arches, the whole crowned with a balustrade but no spire. There is a Flamboyant entrance portal on the south with the wooden Renaissance door still in place. The interior gives a feeling of space, but an unusual arrangement with three large chapels on the north and none on the south. The nave and choir of the older church were incorporated and more modifications were carried out in the 17C during the time of the three Bishops Bertier, when two chapels and the choir were rebuilt. There are some good 17C carved choir stalls, a gilded 15C Virgin, St-Sebastian carved in stone (16C), and an 18C polychrome marble retable. The most important treasure of Ste-Marie is the unique 17C **reliquary bust of St-Cizi** (to visit, enquire at the Tourist Office opposite the church). This effigy of the Roman fighter of Sarrasins and patron of the town was made in 1671/2 by Pierre

Desnos of Toulouse, in wood plated with five kilos of silver. The treasure also contains other reliquaries including a bust of St-Sebastian and a vast collection of richly embroidered chasubles in desperate need of restoration.

Rieux celebrates the Festival of Papogay (Occitan for 'Perroquet' or 'parrot'), held since the 14C, on the first Sunday of May. The archers of the Confraternity of Papogay take part in a competition to shoot a metal and wood bird, weighing 3 kilos, from a 40m post. Their patron, predictably, is St-Sebastian.

The village has a number of old streets and timber-framed houses as well as a covered market and is worth an extended visit.

Keep on the D627 for 6km to **Carbonne**, where the Arize meets the Garonne, a *bastide* founded c 1256 in *paréage* with Alphonse de Toulouse and the Abbey of Bonnefont. The principal monument is the 14C Church of St-Laurent, restored in the 19C, east of the town near the Garonne, with a three-stage belfry and huge porch with crocketed gable sheltering a fine 14C portal. It is usually closed. Near church is the Museum of sculptor André Abbal, d. 1953, whose works are exhibited in the very attractive gardens as well as inside (10.00–12.00, 15.00–19.00, closed Tues summer, Sat & Sun pm winter).

Follow the river on the D10 for 15.5km to **Cazères-sur-Garonne** (Tourist Information, tel: 61 90 06 51), a cheerful town on a wide expanse of the Garonne in the foothills of the Pyrenees. The Gallo-Roman town of St-Cizy developed on the road linking Toulouse and Dax and its position makes it a good point of departure today to explore the Comminges, the Gers and the Toulousain. It belonged to the Comminges in the 12C before coming under the control of the Counts of Toulouse and has always benefited from the rights of the passage to traders and pilgrims across the river between Languedoc and Foix and a long tradition of shipping on the Garonne. More recently, the construction of a dam has created a stretch of water where most aquatic activities can be enjoyed and a Regatta is held in mid-July.

From the D10 you arrive north of the old town, which is on a promontory above the left bank of the river, enclosed in modern boulevards. The Tourist Information is on the north-west of the old centre installed in La Case de Montserrat, a timber-framed house built in 1547. Purchased by the Benedictine Abbey of Montserrat in Spain, it was used by the Procurer General of Montserrat who travelled in France and beyond collecting donations to cover the costs, for three months, of pilgrims on the road to Montserrat and Santiago.

The Church of **Notre-Dame de Cazères** was built in the 14C and until 1795 had a very different west end from now, but the upper part was demolished by order of the Convention and the present unusual façade dates from 1885–96. The church has a long history as the centre of a Marian cult associated with a spring on the banks of the Garonne. It has a large and varied collection of furnishings and religious art, most of them exhibited in the Baptistry room. Most notable are the Romanesque font in stone, on a Gothic base, a superb 17C retable, from the Capucines Convent, with a Pietà attributed to François Lucas, and a number of reliquaries. The Chapelle de Notre-Dame contains a large retable with 18C paintings.

Opposite the church is the metal *halle* of 1904 with statues either end by Frédéric Tourte (who worked with Bourdelle) symbolising the principal agricultural activities of the region at the time. The road alongside the church, Rue Ste-Quitterie, marks the primitive *cité* and crosses the Hourride, where there is a fountain of 1562, to bring you via Rue Massenet to the Promenade du Campet overlooking the Garonne. At the foot of the church is the Grotte of Notre-Dame de Cazères, an oratory erected in 1630 following a plague epidemic. To the south, next to the bridge, is the old wooden boathouse. Cazères had an important boat-building industry, especially at the end of the 19C, and the last boat, a trawler, left this workshop in 1948 to go to Sète on the Mediterranean. The very attractive 19C bridge, rebuilt after the floods in 1875, has recently been restored.

Follow Bd. P. Gouzy away from the bridge, and in Rue des Capucins is the Capuchin monastery, 1612–19 with a cloister of 1717, which can be visited.

From here to Martres-Tolosane the D10 passes under an arch of the rampart of the 16C château of the splendid village of **Palaminy**. Even more celebrated than its picturesque 16C castle (private) is its reputation for *pétanque* (version of *boules* played in the Midi).

Continue on the D10 for 6km (or cross the river at Cazères and take the D62) to **Martres-Tolosane** (Tourist Information, tel. 61 98 80 02), a small pottery town with a circular centre and houses in old bulging pebbly walls. It is best known for its *faïenceries d'art*, hand-painted earthenware, and for the six Gallo-Roman villas in the area which have offered up the best antique statuary in the region, most of which is at the Musée St-Raymond in Toulouse. Martres has its own Archaeological Museum in the 13C keep in Rue du Donjon (open June–Sept), although many of its exhibits are copies of those in Toulouse.

The priory, c 1000, was replaced by the brick Church of **St-Vidian** (or Notre-Dame des Martyrs), consecrated in 1309, the belfry rebuilt in 1865. There are a number of pieces of ancient stone and marble re-employed in the walls, and two sarcophagi in Pyrenean marble at the west end of the nave. The portal from the Romanesque church is incorporated into the Chapel of St-Vidian inside which has a Flamboyant altar and the saint's relics. A colourful reminder of the battle between the Christians and the infidels, when virtuous Vidian was slayed, is re-enacted on the first Sunday after Whitsun. There is plenty of pottery on sale in the town and at the potteries: Le Matet (tel: 61 98 81 30), La Tolosane (tel: 61 98 81 17), Cabaré (tel: 61 98 81 24), Thomas Duran (tel: 61 98 84 44).

4

The Comminges: St-Bertrand-de-Comminges, St-Gaudens, Alan, Montmaurin

Total distance: 126km (78 miles).

This is a circular tour around St-Bertrand-de-Comminges, an idyllic spot in the Garonne valley midway between the plains of Gascony and the central Pyrenean chain, and crammed with history.

ST-BERTRAND-DE-COMMINGES (pop. 250, Tourist Information, Les Olivetains, tel: 61 95 44 44) is a major showpiece, the whole ensemble is spectacular. A wooded cliff is the backdrop to the Gothic cathedral which rises in overwhelming proportions above a medieval walled village set on a small mound. At its feet are more medieval buildings, Gallo-Roman sites and the Romanesque church of St-Just de Valcabrère, and in the distance are the mountains. Wherever you look, Gallo-Roman elements are re-used, or medieval stone is re-cycled. Despite its tiny population, St-Bertrand welcomes some 200,000 visitors a year, but like most small towns it is unlikely to be busy at either end of the day, so better to stay nearby than to come for the day. There is an annual Festival du Comminges in July and August with concerts in the Cathedral of St-Bertrand, at St-Just and at St-Gaudens. St-Bertrand is easily accessible from the major arterial routes. In the upper town are two hotels, *L'Oppidum* (tel: 61 88 33 50), and the *Hotel du Comminges* (tel: 61 88 31 43), and in the lower town, the *Vieille Auberge* (tel: 61 88 36 60) and plenty more in the surrounding area.

History. The **Comminges** was a semi-independent province in the Middle Ages, reaching the extent of its power towards the end 12C or early 13C under the first four counts Bernard. Evidence of prehistoric, Iron Age and Celtic man has been found in this *pays* which, according to a 4C text by St Jerome, was annexed by Pompey in 72 BC on his return from the Iberian peninsula, although this is not confirmed. The people who gathered here were known as the Convenae and by 15 BC their city, Lugdunum Convenarum, was the capital of a province of Aquitaine. This flourished until the arrival of the Visigoths in the 5C, became an episcopal see by the end of the 5C, but was devastated by the Franks in 585. It faded into obscurity until the 11C when Bertrand de l'Isle, the future St-Bertrand, put it back on the map. Modern Comminges refers to an administrative subdivision of the *département* of Haute-Garonne whose main town is St-Gaudens.

On Foot. Park in the large car park at the foot of the hill. To the north, either side of the D26, are three **Gallo-Roman sites** (to visit, enquire at the Information Office). The vestiges revealed by the excavations date from c 20 BC, the period of Augustus, to the 6C. When the settlement was elevated to the status of Colony in the 2C it expanded to cover some 60 hectares stretching from the foot of the hill to the banks of the Garonne and as far as the Romanesque church of St-Just-de-Valcabrère. The multitude of inscriptions, sculptures, domestic objects, artefacts, sarcophagi and the buildings themselves reveal the sophistication of this civilisation. The temple of the **forum** and its enclosure (west of the D26) built in the last years of the pre-Christian era, were abandoned by the 4C or 5C. The adjacent **thermae**, end-1C BC to end-1C AD, were rebuilt on a larger scale with hot and cold baths, piscina and hypocaust and decorated with mosaics. (A part reconstruction of this site is underway.) Part of the cardo (north–south axis) divided this from the vast **macellum** (east of the D26) on the site of an earlier basilica. The market had three monumental entrances and a large open space in the middle bordered by a double row of stalls to the south and one row on the north. A large porticoed square was a later addition to the market complex. Between it and the forum is a small round monument (reconstructed) whose precise function has not been identified but it may have marked the intersection of the Roman ways to Dax and to Toulouse. The **northern thermae** (north-west of the forum), begun at the beginning of the 2C and amended in the 3C, are the most complete, with piscina, natatio, frigidarium, tepidarium, praefurium, caldarium, etc., easily identifiable. Parts of just three terraces of the **amphitheatre** are visible on the hill behind the car park, the rest disappeared when the road was built in the 18C.

In the attractive lower town, near the little parish church of St-Julien, is the overgrown site of an **early Christian basilica** (5C); marble sarcophagi scattered around indicate its use as a burial ground. Take note of the magnificent example of a Comminges **barn** near the basilica, with hooped or semi-circular timbers in the upper part.

Take the steps from the lower town (continue along the road beside the basilica ruins) or walk up the road from the car park to the hill village, still confined within the medieval ramparts (in season, a little train runs from the car park to the Hyrisson Gate). Enter by the Cabirole Gate on the east which has Roman inscriptions on the outer wall. The little building opposite was built on to the remains of the barbican and re-uses some medieval masonry. A short way up the street on the left is the half-timbered Maison Bridaut, rebuilt 1577, with a Renaissance tower. Turn left at the Hôtel Oppidum—there is a 15C house with medallions under the eaves on the right—then right and past an 18C fountain to arrive at the centre of the *cité*. Suddenly, there is the great looming west front of the cathedral. On the left of the forecourt is the Neo-Gothic church of **Les Olivetains**, part of a former monastery attached to the Siennese branch of the Benedictine Order established here in the 19C. The buildings are occupied by the Tourist Information Office, bookshop, library, museum and art gallery (open Easter to All Saints). The 19C chapel is used as a museum to exhibit in rotation some of the 15,000 objects excavated from local sites. The most outstanding among these is part of an ensemble of statues and sculptures known as **the Trophy**, c 24 BC, an allegory of Augustus's conquest of Gaul and Spain. Some 115 fragments were discovered in 1926 and 1931 in ditches near the temple and have been pieced together. Opposite is a small covered market.

CATHEDRAL OF ST-MARY. Bertrand de L'Isle, great Church reformer and builder, Bishop of Comminges from 1083 to 1123, was responsible for the first cathedral, consecrated in 1200. In 1218 Bertrand was canonised and in tribute Lugdunum Convenarum became St-Bertrand-de-Comminges. Such was the veneration of St-Bertrand that a later Bishop, Bertrand de Got, 1294–99 (who became the first Pope at Avignon, Clement V), initiated, supervised and financed, the transformation of the cathedral to accommodate the influx of pilgrims through his intermediary Canon Adhémar de

St-Pastou. The building was completed at the time of Bishop Hugues de Châtillon (1336–52).

Exterior. Work started at the east c 1307 with the chevet. The Romanesque nave was incorporated into an aisleless Gothic structure and 14 gabled and pinnacled buttresses support the walls which were extended upwards. At the west, under the Gothic carapace, elements of the old church are visible in the narthex and the first three bays with simple lancets. The austere façade was enlarged and the belfry raised in the 14C. The west portal, approached by marble steps, submerged in a deep recess, has a richly sculpted décor. On the marble Romanesque tympanum is the theme of the Epiphany watched by St-Bertrand, and the lintel carries a relief of the twelve apostles. The five capitals of the porch carry figures and animal motifs with stylistic similarities to the west porch of St-Sernin in Toulouse.

Interior. Open 09.00–19.00, you pay to visit the choir, mausoleum, cloister and treasure. The massive narthex conserves capitals and half-barrel vaults from the 11C–12C church. Built in silvery-grey local stone, the fairly small cathedral (55m x 16m and 28m high), with five radiating chapels and no transept, has simple quadripartite vaults and little integral decoration except painted bosses bearing the coats of arms of the bishop-builders. The beautiful calm greyness of the Gothic church is disrupted by the heavily ornate 16C **choir** enclosure of burnished oak whose *jubé* is at the level of the second bay of the nave. The screen consists of a gallery with pendant bosses and above are 20 figures including God the Father, Ecce Homo, Apostles and Virgins and on the two lower panels are polychromed statues including the Virgin and Child.

Placed on the diagonal on the north of the first bay, to serve both the choir and the nave, is the equally ornate three-tier Renaissance organ, supported on a coffered platform by five fluted columns which was donated by Bishop Jean de Mauléon (1523–55). Stripped of its lead pipes at the Revolution, it has undergone three restorations and was returned to its original sounds in 1975. Incorporated in it is the 16C pulpit which faces the parish altar in the Saint-Sacrement chapel added in 1621. The chapel contains the famous crocodile ex voto.

The choir enclosure. The closed partitions of the wooden church-within-a-church separate the choir from the body of the cathedral. The bequest of Jean de Mauléon, inaugurated at Christmas 1535, this is one of the rare complete choir enclosures left in France, and one of three in the Midi-Pyrénées with Albi and Auch. The enclosure provided an area where the clergy could perform mass unobserved and undisturbed by the public who would, nevertheless, hear it from the ambulatory.

The exterior is relatively sober, whereas the full glory of the carved oak is reserved for the inner sanctum. Arranged in two tiers around three sides of the choir are the 66 stalls assigned, according to status, to canons and church dignatories—the 38 in the upper row, with sculpted backs and canopies, reserved for higher ranks. The tribune, on the reverse of the *jubé*, has at its centre the ambo from where the Deacon read aloud the Epistle and Gospel.

The **iconographic programme** leads the faithful, via saints, prophets, sibyls, virtues and various biblical characters, towards salvation. The carving is profuse and harmonious using a variety of woodcarving and marquetry techniques: the large figures on the back of the upper stalls are in relief; on the stall ends the images carved in the round take the form of little scenes such as the Tree of Jesse, the Temptation of Adam and Eve, the Virgin and

Child, the Four Evangelists, and the Temptation of Christ in the Desert; and marquetry on the episcopal throne as well as the seats of the celebrant and his acolytes for the images of St-Bertrand, St-John the Baptist and St-John the Evangelist. Added to the religious, mythological and allegorical mix typical of the 16C, are animal motifs on the carved armrests, and the traditionally mundane and profane subjects of the famous misericords which are executed with exuberance and humour. Throughout the carvings of the choirstalls are versions of foliate heads or 'green men'.

The decorative wooden **retable**, which received a garish coating of paint and gilt in the 18C, has an extraordinary frieze of 27 animated paintings of the Life of Christ and the Virgin. The main altar, in Sarrancolin marble, dates from 1737 and the lectern is 18C. At the east end of the choir enclosure is the 15C stone **Mausoleum of St-Bertrand**, erected at the time of Bishop Pierre de Foix in the form of a large casket. The side facing the east is covered with scenes of the life of the saint painted in the 17C with a silver reliquary bust containing St-Bertrand's head on the altar. The other side forms a small passageway and in the central cavity is the large silver and ebony casket containing the body of the saint.

Of the 15 windows of the cathedral, three in the east contain **16C stained glass**. In the centre window is the kneeling figure of the donor, Jean de Mauléon, with scenes of the Nativity and the Baptism of Christ; in the north the Annunciation, and, south, the Presentation at the Temple. The Flamboyant **Chapel Notre-Dame**, late 14C–15C, contains the 15C marble tomb of Hugues de Châtillon who was responsible for the chapel.

The **St-Marguerite Chapel**, or **Chapelle Haute**, was built above the north gallery of the cloister in the 14C, and has the entrance to the Chapter House and **Treasury** which contains, among other things, two medieval embroidered copes, with scenes of the Passion and the Virgin and Child, given by Clement V to celebrate the translation of St-Bertrand's relics on 16 January 1309, brilliant embroideries of the *opus anglicanum*, produced by workshops in London.

On the south flank of the cathedral is the only **Romanesque cloister** still standing in the Comminges, albeit much remodelled. Built above the ramparts, since the 19C the south gallery arcades have been open towards the countryside, bringing a garden-like gaiety to what is normally an enclosed contemplative space. The layout is unavoidably lopsided with three 12C aisles, west, south and east, with eight, twelve and five bays respectively. Pairs of slender columns and double capitals support round arches and a light timber and tile roof. The central western pier is made from the drum of a Roman column carved with figures heavily inspired by antiquity, and on the capital above are the Labours of the Months and the Signs of the Zodiac. The best capitals are on the west and include an elegant foliate design, Adam and Eve, the Sacrifice of Abraham, and four with decorative motifs. The only indication of the former monastic buildings is the trefoil entrance and walled-up Romanesque window of the chapter house. The cloister served for a time as a burial place, and in recesses in the vaulted late-Gothic north gallery, known as the *Galerie des Tombeaux*, there are sarcophagi with epitaphs of seven canons and benefactors.

Leave the village by the **Majou Gate**, the main entrance to the medieval town, which was rebuilt in the 18C and used as a prison. On the inside is a Roman funerary stele, and, outside, the arms of Cardinal de Foix (15C).

Leave St-Bertrand by the D26 to **Valcabrère** (1.5km) and turn right in the village. The basilica of **ST-JUST-DE-VALCABRÈRE** (tel: 61 95 49 06, 09.00–

12.00, 14.00–19.00, June–Sept, rest of year check) is an outstanding Roman-esque building in a pastoral setting. To enjoy the famous view of St-Just surrounded by cypresses with the casket-like cathedral in the distance, take the narrow road before the church, park on the incline and take the unmade track on the right-hand side.

Incorporated in the gateway are 1C inscriptions and a medieval chrism. The exact dates of the basilica are not known, but it is likely a church was begun in the 11C, slightly before the first church of St-Bertrand, on the site of an early Christian necropolis near the ruins of the Gallo-Roman town plundered for its stone. Numerous antique carvings and early-Christian funerary monuments were used in the construction of this church which has a simple, well-proportioned belfry. On the tympanum of the 12C north entrance is a relief of Christ enthroned, framed in a mandorla, with two censer angels and four rounded Evangelists. Either side of the entrance are marble **statue-columns** with traces of colour similar to the cathedral cloister pier; a little scene on each capital identifies the main figure. From left to right: the decapitation of St-Just; the lapidation of St-Etienne (Stephen); probably St-Helen; a man invites a woman to mount a horse watched by an angel, a possible allusion to the pilgrimage of the mother of Constantine; and the arrest and flagellation of St-Pasteur.

On the south side of the church are fragments of pre-Romanesque walls, and embedded in the wall of the church is an engaging antique carving of a theatrical mask. The splendid east end is a complex structure progressing from rectangle to polygon via a round arch and squinches.

Interior. The variety of textures and colours in the interior is very beautiful. It consists of four uneven barrel-vaulted bays, half-barrel vaults in the aisles, and a trilobed east end less complicated inside than out. Massive pillars separate nave and aisles. Behind the basin-shaped table covering the altar is a facsimile of a document found in 1886 recording the dedication of the altar to St-Etienne, St-Just and St-Pasteur in October 1200. A sarcophagus supported on a vaulted passage behind the altar contained the relics of St-Just and St-Pasteur, and pilgrims could either pray below it or climb the steps to touch it. The richest decoration in the east bay includes paired marble columns standing against the piers on antique bases, and two inverted antique friezes as well as a frieze of acanthus leaves. On the south wall a tombstone dated 347, and another in the pier to the right of the entrance, testify to the introduction of Christianity by the 4C. Two hollowed-out Roman capitals standing on columns against the two north-west pillars are used as holy-water stoups.

Trading on the antique reputation of the district is a restaurant between Valcabrère and Sarp, just off the N125, called *Le Lugdunum* (tel: 61 95 88 22) specialising in the gastronomy of ancient Rome.

Cross the Garonne and take the D26 to the attractive spa of **Barbazan** (2km), where the waters were taken during the colonial era as a cure for malaria but are now used to combat stress. Like all spa towns, it has several hotels and amenities as well as gardens and a small thermal establishment. From here the D26 is a pretty wooded 5km to **Sauveterre-de-Comminges**. A few kilometres south of Sauveterre is the comfortable *Hostellerie des Sept-Molles* (tel: 61 88 30 87).

Turn north on the D9 to the *bastide* of **Valentine** (7.5km). A large 4C **Gallo-Roman villa** site existed near here next to the D8 (1.5km, direction Luchon) at Arnesp. Several Christian churches were built on the ruins of a 4C temple, the last becoming part of a Benedictine priory in the 13C, destroyed in the 18C by the Protestants. The town was famous for its blue faïence in the 19C (see the museum in St-Gaudens). A small museum in the Mairie has finds from the Roman villa although the major pieces are in St-Bertrand or Toulouse.

Cross the Garonne again (2km) to **St-Gaudens** (pop. 12,000, Tourist Information tel: 61 94 77 61), sub-préfecture of Haute-Garonne, main industrial centre in the Comminges and important market town. The farmers' market on Thursdays has been held on the same site for 700 years and there are numerous fairs as well as a large cattle market serving a region famous for its veal. St-Gaudens is on a high ridge above the Garonne with what would be a marvellous panorama of the Pyrenees if it were not marred by the unfortunate situation of the steaming factories of Cellulose du Rhône et d'Aquitaine in the valley below. Medieval pilgrimage routes to Santiago from St-Giles, St-Girons and St-Bertrand once converged here; today the N117 carries traffic between Toulouse and Tarbes. St-Gaudens is not a place to linger very long, but the **church** is of interest.

The persecution of a Christian community which developed in this region between the 6C and 8C is traditionally associated with La Caoue, on the Luchon road, where a tiny oratory was erected and rebuilt last century. According to legend, the decapitated Gaudens, whose mother was Quitterie, set off with his head under his arm to the site of the present church. The cult was officially recognised and drew numerous pilgrims in the Middle Ages. After the destruction of Lugdunum Convenarum (St-Bertrand) its Bishops took refuge at St-Gaudens and established a Chapter of Canons here until the Revolution. A church was begun during the period of ecclesiastical reform between 1056 and 1063 by Bishop Bernard II of the family of the Counts of Toulouse. At the end of the 11C and beginning of the 12C—the time of the great pilgrimages and of the Chapter's increasing fortune—a grander church was begun, inspired by St-Sernin in Toulouse. Bernard II's unfinished church was incorporated into the new one, and for a short period stone-carvers of remarkable skill worked in the Collegiate Church.

Exterior. Part of the building of c 1059 is conserved in the walls of the three east bays, and a large portion forms the lower part of the apse but much of the decoration was lost in the 19C when the building was profoundly altered. The cloister on the south, begun towards the end of the 12C, was destroyed c 1810 but has been recreated in golden stone. Here the new capitals modelled on seven originals prove the influence of the Toulousain cloister workshop. The 13C chapter house contains a small museum of religious art from the Comminges. The west door of the church is 19C as are the belfry (1874) and the two-level roof (1887). The north entrance is 17C although the marble relief in the tympanum was probably salvaged from the 12C doorway portal destroyed in the 16C. This is an elaborate and elegant version of a chrism in a circle decorated with lozenges and supported by four angels emerging from clouds.

Interior. The barrel-vaulted interior has five unequal bays with galleries in the two east bays. When the decision was taken in the late 11C to build a church with a gallery, the east bay was already complete. To minimise disruption to worship, work began in the second bay with the construction of a tribune or gallery, after which an adjacent tribune and the existing vault was raised. Lack of funds then put paid to the ambitious scheme for a galleried nave and the remainder of the church is closer to the one envisaged by Bernard II. From this brief period date the eight finest **capitals**

(once attributed to the 19C) influenced by the Spanish workshops of the Jaca-Frómista group.

The interior is rather obscure, so go armed with a 1Fr piece for the lights (box at the west end and a 10-second delay to get in place). The iconography of the capitals principally addresses morality and original sin. Their execution is vigorous and the carving crisp. On the capitals of the **north pier** are lions in foliage (west) and monkeys in obscene positions attached with ropes around their necks to men who seem to be leading them (east); on the **south pier**, a man is devoured by a lion while his companions try to save him (south) and in the Temptation (east) Adam and Eve flank the serpent, and the **west capital** has a man leading an animal by a rope. The oldest capital (**south chapel**) has a horseman among foliage and interlacings. The **tribune carvings**, including the scene of a baptism, were carried out slightly later and do not show the same virtuosity as the Spanish-influenced ones. Virtually all the Romanesque décor of the chevet has been replaced by 19C paintings by Lamothe (1858) of the religious history of Comminges. The stalls are 17C but were damaged during the Revolution. In the aisles are late-18C Aubusson tapestries of the Triumph of Faith and the Transfiguration. In the background of the tapestry of the Martyrdom of St-Gaudens, made for the church, is a panorama of the town c 1760. The 17C organ was restored in 1981 and the church is used for concerts during the Comminges Music Festival.

To the east of Place Jean-Jaurès is the Information Centre, and in Place du Mas-St-Pierre the **Museum of Local History and Traditions** which has a collection of blue porcelain from Valentine. The town has a number of parks and gardens and west of the old town, on Bd. E. Azémar, in the public gardens, is part of the cloister of the Abbey of Bonnefont.

Take the N117 in the direction of Toulouse. Straight, busy and boring it may be, but the tedium is always alleviated by the view of the mountains to the south (provided the weather is good). After 9km turn off to Labarthe-Inard (D88) and then left after the Garonne (D21) to Mane on the Salat (10km). 3km north on the D117 is **Salies-du-Salat**, the second most important spa town in the Comminges.

2km from Salies is **Monsaunès**, the site of an important Templar Commandery founded in 1156. The Romanesque chapel in stone and brick still stands, its west doorway decorated with scenes of the Crucifixion of St-Peter, the Stoning of St-Stephen, the Raising of Lazarus and Christ and the Apostles, and inside are murals of the same period.

To visit what little remains in situ of the former **Abbey of Notre-Dame**, **Bonnefont-en-Comminges**, turn left on the D81 and follow the signs to Bonnefont (5km). A remote place, good for picnics, an effort is being made to revitalise the abbey. Founded in 1136, it was the most important Cistercian abbey in the Comminges and became the burial place of the Counts of Comminges. Still standing is the wing reserved for the lay brothers.

St-Martory, 4km on the D117, spans the Garonne at the crossroads between St-Lizier and St-Bertrand. It once used its natural resources to manufacture paper. St-Martory was the birthplace of Norbert Casteret (1897–1987) speleologist and co-pioneer in the techniques of pot-holing in France. In 1931 he confirmed the source of the Garonne as the Pic d'Aneto in Spain. Among his important discoveries in the vicinity, an area riddled with grottoes, were drawings and the oldest statues in the world at Montespan, south-west of St-Martory (closed to the public) in 1923. The church on the north of the river is difficult to visit because the traffic hurtles through on the main road, so park on the south and cross the three-arched bridge, built in 1724, which has preserved its monumental toll gate decorated with the French cockerel and Louis XIV's sun emblem. A menhir and Gallo-Roman funerary stele are erected near the remodelled church of 1387, which has a 12C marble font, a Romanesque door from Bonnefont and a 16C terracotta Pietà.

Leave the Garonne valley on the D52 for **Aurignac** (Tourist Information, tel: 61 98 70 06), 12km, a pretty village on the ridge of a hill. Over the town gate is a Flamboyant belfry and the 15C **church porch** has rare cabled columns from the Chapelle du Crucifix demolished in 1791. The capitals are cubic inside and hexagonal outside. Discoveries of bones and other objects in nearby caves (1.2km on the D635) made in 1860–61 by Edouard Lartet marked an important advance in research on Cro-Magnon man. The Aurignacian period, 30–27,000 BC, marked the appearance of figurative art and the small, modern **museum** (tel: 61 98 90 08, 10.00–12.00, 15.00–18.00 July–Aug, check rest of year) devotes a section to the subject and includes a copy of the Venus of Lespugue.

A sign on the road between Aurignac and Alan leads you to the unique experience of an extraordinarily well-conserved **Gallo-Roman piscina** in a bucolic farmyard. Call at the farm house.

Alan, 5.5km east of Aurignac (D8, D10), midway between St-Bertrand-de-Comminges and Toulouse, was the excellent choice in 1270 of the Bishops of Comminges as the site of a **residence** (tel: 61 98 71 12, 10.00–12.00, 15.00–19.00, 15 June–15 Oct). Successive bishops left their mark on the buildings over five centuries, and time has taken its toll, but there are some reminders of past glories. Jean-Baptiste de Foix-Grailly, elected in 1470, undertook major revisions including a monumental Flamboyant porch adorned with the Béarn cow from his coat of arms. The palace was saved in 1969 by the opera singer Richard Gaillan, and is used for concerts and exhibitions. On the large square is a 13C–15C church and the *halle* which has been restored.

1km south-west of Alan is the **Hôpital Notre-Dame de Lorette**, built by Bishop du Bouchet in 1734 to care for the sick. Privately owned and lovingly restored, the pharmacy, cloister and chapel can be visited on Sunday afternoons. It is also an unusual place to stay in a *gîte* or a guest room (tel: 61 98 98 84).

From Aurignac take the D635 west to **Ciadoux** (14.5km) where the church has some interesting fittings.

Continue on the D635, then the D9e and D98a (9km) to **Lespugue**, and the ruins of a 13C château overlooking the Gorges de la Save. The village is famous for the discovery in 1922 of the so-called Lespugue Venus, a rare prehistoric female figure carved in mammoth ivory. The original is at the Musée des Antiquités Nationales at St-Germaine-en-Laye, but there are faithful copies in the museums at Montmaurin and Aurignac. The caves, including the one where the statue was found, are visible from the D9d through the **Gorges de la Save**, and can be visited.

At the end of the gorges (5km), is the important **archaeological site of Montmaurin**, the largest excavated Roman villa in France (tel: 61 88 74 73, 09.30–12.00, 14.00–18.00 Apr–Sept, closes 17.15 rest of year). The ancient routes from Agen to Lugdunum Convenarum and Toulouse to Spain crossed this pleasant alluvial plain, where in the mid-1C a large villa was constructed at the centre of cultivated land. The site was abandoned towards the end of the 2C or early 3C, when the Save burst its banks, until the mid-3C. Around 330 AD the main building of the earlier construction was transformed into a luxurious residence, and c 350 more buildings were added, arranged around successive inner spaces to create a unified architectural ensemble of great beauty. Although consumed by fires in the 4C, the parts excavated evoke the harmonious layout of the villa. The setting is enhanced by well-maintained hedges and a scattering of dark cypress trees.

The visit begins at the point furthest away from the public entrance at the hemispherical main courtyard which was the ancient entrance and reception area. Contained within the hemisphere is a temple. Following on is a large courtyard with peristyle flanked by living accommodation on the north-west (the south-east has not been excavated) and beyond is a second courtyard with fishponds surrounded by the summer quarters with some fragments of mosaic still in place. To the north-west of the large courtyard is the thermal wing, the most complete section, comprising nymphaeum, piscina, hypocaust, hot and cold baths, garden surrounded by slender columns, and a pergola facing out towards the landscape.

In the village, the very modest **Museum of Montmaurin** next to the Mairie is devoted to the prehistory and Gallo-Roman history of the area. As well as the replica of the small (14.7cm) but curvaceous Lespugue Venus, there is the 30,000-year-old Mandibule de Montmaurin, the jawbone of palaeolithic man of the Aurignacian period found near Aurignac in 1949 by R. Cammas.

Hidden among cypresses in the cemetery just before the village of **St-Plancard** (8km) is the delightful 11C chapel of **St-Jean-des-Vignes** (key at the café/tabac on the D633 entering the village). A perfectly simple shape, with an apse each end and one chapel on the south, the roof timbers rest directly on the walls, which are pierced by three small windows in the east, and the walls carry some precious 11C murals discovered in 1943. The features are stylised, the colours delicate, and images faint, but it is possible to decipher a Christ in Majesty surrounded by the Evangelists, and a Crucifixion on the east wall; and in the south chapel, Christ enclosed in a double mandorla surrounded by numerous figures, with the Hand of God above and the Temptation of Adam and Eve to the right. On the arch of the chapel is a decorative frieze.

The D633 continues to **Montréjeau**, founded as a *bastide* in 1272, a small commercial town with an important Monday market which holds a Folk Festival in August and hosts some concerts during the Comminges Music Festival.

The N117, N125 bring you back to St-Bertrand (about 25km).

The Pyrenees

The highest section of the Pyrenees lies in the south of three *départements* of the Midi-Pyrénées: Hautes-Pyrénées, Haute-Garonne and Ariège-Pyrénées. The next six itineraries cover this area of varied and breathtaking natural beauty offering a great choice of outdoor activities.

The Pyrenees are in fact two ranges running more or less east–west, but with a tiny break in the middle—the Vallée d'Aran, south of Luchon in the Central Pyrenees—and form a huge natural barrier between France and the Iberian Peninsula. The highest peak in the French Pyrenees is Vignemale (3298m) south of Cauterets, and many peaks are over 3000m, but the highest of all, the Pic d'Aneto at 3404m, is in Spain. Although there are not such high peaks in the Pyrenees as in the Alps, there are Pyrenean valleys at a higher altitude than the Alpine ones. A multitude of rivers rising in the mountains flow south–north carving out valleys and gorges.

As in all mountains, the weather is very changeable, even in the summer when mists or rain suddenly descend; snow can close the high passes from November to March. From west to east (about 150km) there are cultural and scenic differences. The west is greener, more lush, influenced climatically by the Atlantic and culturally by Gascony and Aquitaine, while the eastern part, more Mediterranean and arid, is historically part of the Languedoc.

History. The frontier between France and Spain, which runs more or less along the crests, was determined by the Treaty of the Pyrenees in 1659. There are distinct historic, cultural, linguistic, climatic and geographic differences either side of the divide. The southern slopes, turned towards the Iberian peninsula and Africa, can guarantee more hours of sunshine, while the French Pyrenees, which rise more suddenly and steeply from the plain, have more dramatic panoramas and a greater variety of landscape. Conversely there are traditional and cultural similarities binding all the mountain people together. In the 5C BC Iberian tribes settled north as far as the Garonne; the Romans crossed the mountains and colonised the region at the beginning of this era, and capitalised on the spas and the marble quarries. The Visigoth and Carolingian Empires extended either side of the range as did the territories of the Kingdom of Aragon. The great pilgrim route which crossed the Pyrenees at several points carried artistic and architectural influences in both directions. Both licit and illicit trade across the border continued for centuries and, closer to the present, during the Spanish Wars and the Occupation of France in World War II the mountains provided refuge to many.

Three main routes cross the border from the Midi-Pyrénées into Spain: the N20 from the Ariège into Andorra through the new Tunnel de Puymorens; the N230, or the D618, near Luchon in the central Pyrenees, cross the border and go through the Vielha tunnel; and the D929/D173 from St-Lary-Soulan in the Hautes-Pyrénées goes through the Tunnel de Bielsa.

The Pyrenees thrived during the 18C but suffered hugely in the 19C when local industries such as mineral extraction, marble quarries, farming, forestry and weaving went into severe decline, precipitating a huge depopulation which left many of the more remote villages with tiny permanent communities. The main industry today, apart from tourism, is *la houille blanche*, hydro-electric power generated by seven power stations. The energy potential of mountain torrents was recognised by Aristide Bergès (1833–1904) born near St-Lizier, and first harnessed in 1869. Iron ore is still extracted in the Ariège, where there is also a talc quarry, a cigarette paper works and the only tungsten mine in France. There are plenty of cattle and sheep, and cheese is made in the mountains, but the major industry today is summer and winter tourism.

The **spas** are the oldest resorts and of the 17 spa towns in the Région Midi-Pyrénées 13 are in the Pyrenees. Different spas offer different *cures*—the range is astounding—the French *curistes* combine treatment and holiday with the help of the French Social Security and the latest fad is a fitness programme. The water acquires its curative properties by rumbling around underground, picking up minerals, and sometimes heat, for anything between a few to several hundred or even millions of years.

Some spas double up as ski resorts, which total 21, and many of the cable-cars and lifts run in the summer to carry walkers (or non-walkers) to the higher places and an opportunity to get closer to nature. The Tourist Centres have a vast range of information on *Promenades et Randonnées*, categorising walks into different levels from very easy, taking up to three hours, to those taking several days, with details of guides and lists of mountain refuges. A series entitled *Les Sentiers d'Emilie*, published by Milan, has easy walks for children (of all ages) in various parts of the region.

The **Parc National des Pyrénées** west of the range is a protected area created in 1967, covering 45,700 ha, 60 per cent of it in the Hautes-Pyrénées, the rest in the Pyrénées-Atlantiques. On the other side of the border is the Spanish equivalent, the Parque Nacional de Ordesa, 15,000 ha, reached on foot through the Brèche de Roland at Gavarnie. The park stretches from the Upper Valley of the Aspe to the Upper Valley of the Aure, from an altitude of 1067m to its highest point, the Pic du Vignemale. There are 230 lakes, many rivers and torrents, and no habitation, although 50 per cent of its surface is used for grazing and the flora and fauna of the whole park are protected. Much of the park can be driven through, and there are 350 kilometres of paths, refuges for long-distance walkers and picnic areas, while campsites and *gîtes* are confined to the periphery, as is skiing. Five *Maisons du Parc*, one for each valley, provide documentation, information on ways of exploring the park such as organised walks, exhibitions of flora and fauna, etc. The Réserve Naturelle de Néovielle, 2300ha, also comes under the protection of the National Park.

Not confined to the park, although in it they are protected, are vast quantities and numerous species of plants and wildlife. Flowering plants include lilies, valerians, orchids, fritilaries, asphodels, gentians, saxifrages, edelweiss and rhododendron with 150 plants endemic to the Pyrenees. Also indigenous are two types of butterfly and a curious little animal that has survived in small numbers, the Desman, a sort of aquatic mole with an extended snout. Tragically the Pyrenean brown bear has been hunted to near extinction and it is estimated that only about a dozen survive who steadfastly refuse to take refuge in the park. Birds, especially birds of prey, are frequent, and there are grouse, izards (Pyrenean antelope), marmots and so on.

5

The Basse Ariège: Vals, Mirepoix, Montségur

Total distance: 138km (86 miles).

The Valley of the Hers in the Basse Ariège crosses the Pré-Pyrénées, a lower (1000m) parallel range to the Pyrenees proper, consisting of the Plantaurel hills and the Monts d'Olmes which, without the obvious attractions of the high ranges, have many vistas of great beauty enhanced by fields of golden sunflowers in July, and a number of interesting towns and villages, such as Mirepoix and Camon, alternatives to Foix as a base for touring the eastern Pyrenees. Close to Carcassonne, the area harboured some large and tenacious Cathar communities, including Montségur, and consequently suffered extensively from persecution and the crusade led by Simon de Montfort.

Start south of Toulouse, just off the N20 at Cintegabelle, to avoid the main route south to Spain, joining it again at Ax-les-Thermes.

From Cintegabelle, on the banks of the Ariège, take the D35 which follows the Hers valley, past Calmont, and becomes the D11 at the departmental boundary between Haute-Garonne and Ariège. After 15km you come to **Mazères**, founded in 1253 by the nearby Abbey of Boulbonne. It was one of the main *bastides* in the Basse Ariège in the territory of the medieval Counts of Foix, powerful vassals of and contenders to the Counts of Toulouse. The château of Mazères was the favourite residence of Gaston Fébus (1331–91), most legendary of all the Counts of Foix, and where he grandiosely entertained the French King Charles VI in 1390. There is nothing left of the palace, which was destroyed by the Protestants during the Religious Wars in the 16C, as was the nearby Abbey of Boulbonne. Consequently Mazères presents a post-Reformation face, the 17C and 18C houses and market influenced by the brick buildings of Toulouse. The Gothic church has a Neo-Classical façade. The one notable exception is the Renaissance hôtel d'Ardoyn, built c 1580 for a *pastel* merchant.

Take the cross-country route via the D11/D502 to Belpech, and the D525 to the mainly 17C **Château de Gaudiès**, D430 to La Bastide-de-Lordat, and D6, passing close to **St-Félix-de-Tournegat**, a fortified village whose rebuilt Romanesque church has an extraordinary *clocher-peigne*.

The D6 meets the D40, and turn right to Vals, about 30km in all. **Vals**, a tiny hamlet in a rural setting, has a small but sensational *église rupestre*. One of the most ancient churches in the Midi, **Sainte-Marie** was erected at the site of a Celtic oppidum and pagan temple. Using a small mound of puddingstone for its foundations, at the west end is a tower-keep and, adding to the drama, the entrance to the sanctuary is through a natural cleft in the rock. Twenty-three steps lead down to the crypt-like nave of a 10C sanctuary, part-troglodite, part-manmade. To the east, on a slightly higher level, is the flat-ended barrel-vaulted 11C apse. This is decorated with 12C **paintings** discovered in 1956 (light switch to left of steps). Influenced stylistically by Catalonia, the paintings are executed predominantly in red and black pigment, complemented by grey, yellow and white. The theme of Christ's birth, in the east bay, is represented by the Annunciation, the Nativity (where the Virgin is covered by a cloth decorated with circular medallions), the bathing of Jesus and, only a fragment left on the east wall, the Adoration of the Magi. In the vaults is the Christ of the Last Judgement, accompanied by the tetramorphe, and the Apostles two by two. On the north is the figure of Christ his hand raised in blessing. The next level of the church is much modified, and has 19C plastered vaults. On the third level is a 12C chapel dedicated to St Michael which was transformed into a tower in the 14C. The large arch was opened later and outside on the north wall is a discoidal cross probably from the cemetery. An upper floor of one of the houses in the village has become a small archaeological **museum** of the area from prehistory to the 20C, exhibiting finds from the immediate vicinity (tel: 61 68 83 76, church and museum open 15 May–15 Sept, or telephone).

Take the D40/D6 or the D119, 13.5km to Mirepoix.

The main town in the Pays d'Olmes, **MIREPOIX** (pop. 4000, Tourist Information, tel: 61 68 83 76), is a *bastide* with a particular character and some exceptional characteristics. True to *bastide* format, it is laid out on a grid system around a central *Place* unusually planted with grass and rose bushes. This is just the place to relax with a glass of *Blanquette de Limoux*—sparkling wine from neighbouring Aude—in remarkably luxurious café chairs.

The first *bastide* was founded in 1207 by Raymond-Roger of Foix, but it harboured a great many Cathars, and two years later it was taken by Simon de Montfort who dispossessed Pierre-Roger de Mirepoix and installed his own man, Guy de Lévis. In 1229 Guy became the King's representative for the region, a sensitive area between Toulouse and pockets of Cathar resistance in the mountains. The original *bastide* was on the right bank of the Hers, but obviously too close to the river because in 1279, when the dam broke at Puivert 28km away, it was completely washed away. Ten years later Guy de Lévis decided to rebuild in a safer place on the left bank, near the castle and a Benedictine chapel. The layout of the town centre has not altered since the 13C, although a fire in 1380 destroyed many buildings and the houses date from the 14C onwards. The first floors extend over the public right of way around the square, supported by timber posts and lintels, creating an arcade or *couvert*; several are decorated. Outstanding is the 15C or 16C **Maison des Consuls** on the north, its 25 joists sculpted at the extremities with a variety of strange animals and human heads. To the south side of the square is the **covered market**, an elegant turn-of-thecentury wrought-iron construction on slender columns.

The **Cathedral of St-Maurice**, in a large, shady square created in the 15C, is the third church on the site. The post-flood town encompassed a small Benedictine chapel which was rebuilt as a parish church in 1298, itself considered too modest when the Cadurcien Pope, John XXII, raised the status of Mirepoix to diocese in 1317. The originality of the Gothic cathedral is its enormously wide nave, the second widest Gothic nave in Europe after Gerona in Spain. However, the problem of vaulting the 22m span was not resolved until the 19C when the church was finally completed. The first two bishops raised the funds to build the chevet between 1343 and 1349, determining the ambitious dimensions of the nave, but work was interrupted from the mid-14C by the Hundred Years War. Building started again with the eighth bishop, Guillaume de Puy, 1394–1433, and surged ahead from 1493 during the episcopate of Philippe de Lévis who was responsible for four main constructions: the octagonal belfry with its crocketed spire, the Episcopal Palace contiguous with the church, the new west wall, and the Renaissance door on the south. He also built the Episcopal Chapel above the north entrance dedicated to Ste-Agatha, and opened the three Flamboyant windows. When Philippe de Lévis died in 1537, activity ground to a halt until a long time after the suppression of the diocese. Only in 1858 were the walls of the chevet raised and the choir vaulted. Viollet-le-Duc advised on the second campaign of work 1861–67, when the chapels were pushed back to enlarge the nave by about 3.30m in order to line it up with the choir, and the later walls were raised. The strange arrangement of gables above each face of the apse, as well as the flying buttresses and slate roof—both atypical of the region—are all 19C. The Flamboyant north entrance has sculpted capitals but has lost its statues. The wide aisleless nave is disproportionate to the height (24m) and length (48m), making the vaults appear to bear down on the space.

The interior décor is mainly neo-Gothic and little is left of the earlier furnishings except a funerary statue of Constance de Foix, wife of Jean de Lévis; the 14C bosses of the choir chapels sculpted by the Master of Rieux; and a 14C polychrome wooden crucifix of Catalan origin. The pulpit is all that remains of the 15C wooden fittings made locally. Next to it is a gilded retable presenting the fifteen mysteries of the Rosary. The Crucifixion by the Flemish painter Larivière Viscontius in the St-Maurice chapel is the only surviving example from a series of seven works by this painter, heavily influenced by Velasquez. The Episcopal Chapel above the porch has a fine painted tile floor of 1530, the most precious part being the labyrinth, the last to be placed on the floor of a Western church. The cabled columns, part of the altar of this chapel, have been moved to the Chapel of the Virgin. The glass is 19C, as is the organ, built in Munich, and inaugurated in 1891.

On the west of the town is the Porte d'Arval, the last gate of the city defences left standing. There is a pleasant walk along **Les Cours**, a tree lined avenue on the old city ditch filled with water from the Cantirrou, and a magnificent 18C **bridge** over the Hers.

Take the D626 east and turn south on the D28, 9km, to the ruined **Château de Lagarde** (tel: 61 68 24 86 to visit), one of the most picturesque ruins in the Ariège, evocative of its past splendour. The property passed to the Lévis family in 1215 and was rebuilt in 1330 by François de Lévis. Their descendants, the Lévis-Mirepoix, lived in it continuously, making frequent modifications as fashion or needs dictated. Its fate was sealed at the Revolution when it was confiscated and badly damaged.

Continue south for 6km on the D7 to **Camon**, an extraordinarily pleasant and peaceful golden stone village on the Mediterranean side of the Ariège, dozing in the green valley of the Hers, with a more welcoming air than some of the villages further into the mountains. It merits a visit or even a stopover in one of the stylish *chambres d'hôtes* of the 16C abbaye-château (tel: 61 68 28 28).

Entrance to the village is through an elegant archway of 1684 with a clock, and an ancient bronze bell (1342) placed above it. As so often, legend attributes the beginnings of the village to Charlemagne, but more certain is that a Benedictine abbey existed here in 923, coming under the protection of the Abbey of Lagrasse in the Aude in 943, and designated priory in 1068. The village developed as a *sauveté* or safe place around the abbey but this gave it no protection against devastation by the flood of 1279. It was rebuilt as a fortress at the end of the 13C, and was enclosed in fortifications 1360–85 during the Hundred Years War, although in 1494 the abbey and church were again destroyed. The village took its present form between 1503 and 1535 when the Bishop of Mirepoix, Philippe de Lévis, began another campaign of reconstruction improving the living quarters in the great rectangular tower, which then became known as the château, and enclosing the village in an enceinte. During the Religious Wars the defences were amended between 1560–70 by Cardinal Georges d'Armagnac, Prior of Camon. After the dissolution of the priory at the end of the 18C the château became private property. Today, as well as guest rooms, it has a restaurant and snack bar and is used for temporary exhibitions. In the small garden is a medieval well and a 14C cross sculpted on both sides. The interior, still being restored, has some good features such as 16C tiles, 16C murals of mythological scenes in the former prelate's study, and a guest bedroom with a 20C painted décor by a local artist, Mady de la Giraudière. The church was rebuilt by Philippe de Lévis and its embellishment was continued by successive priors in the 17C and 18C.

Head 6km south-east of Camon to Chalabre. The D18 leads to the **lake of Montbel**, covering 70ha, a welcome oasis in the summer for visitors and for migratory birds.

From Chalabre, it is 8km on the D12 to the ruined **Château de Puivert** in the Aude, beseiged by the Crusaders in 1210. On flat ground, this is one of the easiest Cathar castles to visit, with parts of its defences and the keep still standing.

West of Lavalenet (D117/D9, 29km), the very ruined château of **Roquefixade** stands on a rocky outcrop above the valley. Argued over by the Counts of Toulouse and Foix, it became a French garrison, only to be dismantled in 1632 after the Wars of Religion. It is possible to visit the little that is left. The church of the *bastide* below has a notable gilded Baroque (1727) altarpiece.

The D9 in the opposite direction goes through the village of Montferrier to bring you in 10km to the most celebrated of all the Cathar citadels, **MONTSÉGUR**, vertiginously perched at 1207m on a granite outcrop in the St-Barthélemy range and visible from all around; it is impressively forbidding in winter. There is a car park at the foot of the hill. The site is one of the most stunning and the story the most legendary and moving of the whole saga of Cathar persecution.

History. For about forty years the rock had an exclusively Cathar population but first the Cathars, who were never builders, had to persuade Raymond de Péreille, a local member of the lesser nobility sympathetic to their cause, to rebuild his ruined château around 1204. During the Albigensian Crusade, 1209–29, the family of Raymond de Péreille occupied the château keep and the Cathar population lived there in safety. With the annexation of Languedoc to France at the end of the Crusades, the region was put under the protection of a French Governor, Guy de Lévis. In 1232 Guilhabert de Castres, the Cathar Bishop, chose Montségur as a place of safety, bringing with him the elders of the Cathar church, consequently elevating the site to the spiritual centre of the Cathar faith. The community grew to about 400 to 500 grouped around the château in a terraced village clinging to the rocky outcrop, probably with a complicated and extensive defensive system. The site was not challenged until after 1240 when Raymond VII of Toulouse, reminded by the King of his undertaking to fight the Cathars, made a derisory attempt to take Montségur. The task was then assigned to the more resolute Seneschal of Carcassonne, Hugues des Arcis. The mounting crisis was compounded when, in 1242, Cathar knights slaughtered the Inquisitors at Avignonet in the Lauragais. The fate of Montségur was sealed. In 1243 an army of some 1500 men was raised and, with the blessing of the Archbishop of Narbonne, Pierre Amiel, laid siege to Montségur in May. The defence of the refuge was commanded by Pierre Roger de Mirepoix, one of Raymond de Péreille's henchmen, and the defenders, supported by their faith, by a continuous stream of supplies made possible by weaknesses in the blockade, and above all by the difficulties posed by the steep mountain, held out for ten months. Gradually, however, conditions deteriorated for the Cathars and by Wednesday 2 March 1244, a surrender was agreed and a 15-day truce negotiated giving the faithful time to prepare for death by taking the *consolamentum* or last rites. On 16 March the château was evacuated and over 200 who refused to convert to Catholicism were burned at the stake for their heretical beliefs. Guy II de Lévis became seigneur of the fiefdom of Monségur sometime after July 1245 and rebuilt most of the fortress where a small garrison was installed until the end of the 15C. The village on the hill was demolished or left to decay. Mentioned once in 1510, the château and its story lay forgotten until in 1862 the ruins were classified as an Historic Monument and Napoléon Peyrat published his *Histoire des Albigeois* (1872), a romanticised version of the drama embellishing the legends of the site. A monument to those who were massacred was erected in 1960 at the foot of the mountain, and today the site attracts a huge number of visitors.

The **climb to the top** by a well-trodden track takes about half-an-hour and is not too difficult but fairly steep in places. The **château** is an irregular shape, the longest of the five sides on the north, with the main entrance on the south-west and a smaller one opposite. The interior space, about 700 square metres, is enclosed by high walls built into the natural rock with no openings, only regularly spaced hollows to receive wooden building supports. In the centre is the sign of a small triangular paved patio. There are three flights of stone steps up to the *chemin de ronde* and at the north-west extremity the keep, originally accessed from the upper floor by a wooden ladder, has a spiral in the south-east angle to the lower level. There are a few signs of rudimentary comfort, such as a fireplace, vaulted ceilings and windows, and in the western part of the ground floor was the cistern. The east wall is very thick, about 4.2m, with grooves made to contain beams to support the platform of a catapult.

The **village** (Tourist Information, tel: 61 03 03 03) is south-east of the citadel. (Do use the car park as the streets are very narrow.) It has a hotel and some eating places as well as the small **Musée de Montségur**. This contains explanations and information about the site, a model of Montségur at the time of the Cathars, and some of the best archaeological finds from local sites plus plenty of literature.

The **D9/D5 to Bélesta** passes after 13km the intermittent waterfall of **Fontestorbes**, an eccentric torrent with a singularly fascinating habit of gushing for 35 mins then, once the reserve is empty, slowing down to a trickle for 25 mins.

From Bélesta the D16/D29 climbs through pine woods over the Col de la Croix des Morts. Turn right on to the D613 towards the wide Hers valley through Belcaire (16km), and about 8km later the small D105 on the left leads to the universally famous but almost abandoned village (12 residents) of **Montaillou**. The Cathar community of this place was the subject of

Emmanuel Le Roy Ladurie's book Montaillou based on information contained in the Inquisition Register by Jacques Fournier, Bishop of Pamiers, 1318–25, and kept in the Vatican archives. A few houses, a rebuilt church and the ruined medieval château are, sadly, all that are left. The road climbs up over the Col de Chioula to Ax-les-Thermes.

6

The Ariège Valley: Pamiers, Foix, Niaux

The Ariège-Pyrénées, in the south-east corner of the Région Midi-Pyrénées, from which the *département* takes its name, flows northwards from its source in Andorra to join the Garonne south of Toulouse. The N20 follows this wide valley connecting the Toulousain with the Pyrenees, Andorra and ultimately Catalonia, with a brand-new tunnel under Puymorens. Here the climate is influenced by the Mediterranean and the landscape is of extremes: mountains and caves, Cathar castles and Romanesque churches.

PAMIERS (pop. 15,000, Tourist Information, tel: 61 67 52 52), on the N20, mainly in brick like the towns of the Toulousain, is the largest town of the *département* of the Ariège but not the *préfecture*, that honour going to Foix in 1790. Not an immediately appealing town, it probably has fewer tourists and as many facilities as Foix, with markets on Tuesday, Thursday and Saturday and a fair the second and fourth Tuesday of each month.

An abbey, first mentioned in 961, was built at the site of the martyrdom in 507 of Antonin, Christian grandson of the Visigoth King Theodoric I. In 1111 the Counts of Foix came to a partnership agreement with the powerful abbots when Roger II, Count of Foix, returning from the first Crusade, built a château named Apamie after a town in Asia Minor. During the Cathar crisis in the 12C and 13C the town remained orthodox and was rewarded for its constancy by elevation to episcopal see in 1295, and Jacques Fournier, Bishop of Pamiers and of Mirepoix, became third Pope at Avignon, Benoit XII.

Most of Pamiers' medieval buildings were destroyed during the Wars of Religion in the 16C. The Ariège was navigable from Pamiers to the Garonne during the Middle Ages when canals were created for the dual purpose of defence and to run the mills. A canal still delineates the old town. On its banks is a small public garden around a former mansion, now the Municipal Library, and the **Tourist Office** on Bd. Delcasse. West of the gardens, in Rue du Collège, is a **Carmelite chapel**, founded in 1648 and rebuilt in the 18C, arranged internally to correspond to a mystical ascension by successive levels to a high altar. The square tower outside was built as a keep by Count Roger-Bernard III in 1285.

The **Cathedral St-Antonin**, in the middle of Place Mercadal, the old town centre at the foot of the hill where the Counts' castle stood, was formerly the parish church of St-Mary of the Mercadal but rededicated when it became the cathedral in the 16C. Apart from the octagonal belfry modelled on the Jacobins in Toulouse in the 14C, which served as a watchtower, the building was demolished by the Protestants in 1577 to be reconstructed 1657–89. Only the Romanesque portal, badly mutilated, has survived from the earlier church. The already crude carvings of the capitals have suffered with time but it is just possible to make out a Martyrdom of St John the Baptist, Adam and Eve, Cain and Abel, Daniel in the Lions' Den, Samson Slaying the Lion, and opposite the door, a Martyrdom of St John the Evangelist, the two St Johns being the patron saints of the very first church. The furnishings include a 16C wooden statue of Mary Magadalene, and five 19C paintings of the legend of St-Antonin.

On the perimeter of the square are the 18C Palais de Justice, the 17C seminary now the Lycée, and the Mairie in the 17C Episcopal Palace; the present Bishop's Palace is on the south. Near the Mairie, on the west, the Porte de Nerviau is a fragment of the fortified enclosure separating two quarters, altered in the 15C. There is a bust of the composer Gabriel Fauré (1845–1924), who was born in Pamiers, in the gardens at the foot of the castella plateau.

The **Tour de la Monnaie**, Rue Charles de Gaulle, was originally adjacent to a building of 1419 in which Count Jean I of Foix established a mint to make copper coins called *Guilhems*, to pay the troops who fought against William of Orange. This street leads to the present lively commercial centre and the **Church of Notre-Dame du Camp**, rebuilt in the 17C except for the massive 14C rectangular façade flanked by two small towers. The portal was rebuilt in 1870 and the gloomy interior has nothing to retain the visitor. Further north is the belfry of the old Cordeliers church, 1512.

About 6km **north of Foix**, the small Romanesque **Church of St-Jean-de-Verges** (where the N20 and D919 converge) was part of a priory attached to the abbey of Foix, and is one of the most sophisticated in the Ariège, inspired by the Toulousain. The influences are manifested in the quality of the materials, the architectural ensemble and the finesse of the decoration around the windows as well as on the capitals both inside and out which are reminiscent of the transept of St-Sernin in Toulouse.

The **Underground River of Labouiche** (tel: 61 65 04 11) on the D1 south-west of St-Jean-de-Verges, is the opportunity for a 1500m subterranean boat trip.

Some 18km **south of Pamiers** on the N20 is **FOIX** (Tourist Information, tel: 61 65 12 12). With a population of 10,000, it is one of the smallest *préfectures* in France. Midway between Toulouse and Spain, with road links east to Perpignan and west to St-Gaudens, and rail connections with Toulouse, it is an obvious centre for visiting the Ariège but it is disappointing for hotels and eating places, the best being the *Hôtel-Restaurant d'Audoye Lons* (tel: 61 65 52 44). It has a market on Fridays and Wednesdays and a Fair on the first, third and fifth Monday of the month and during the summer a Medieval Market in the old town with entertainments and parades.

Its landmark is the castle on a rocky outcrop above the old town, inextricably bound up with its Counts and its history. The first Count, in the 11C, was Bernard, the second son of the Count of Carcassonne and the dynasty, which established a *paréage* with the abbots of St-Volusien in 1168, ended in 1391 with **Gaston Fébus**. Neighbours of the counts of Toulouse whose dominance they challenged, the Counts showed Cathar sympathies during the Albigensian crisis. After the annexation of Languedoc to France in 1229, they extended their domain southwards to Andorra and in 1290, when Roger Bernard III inherited the Viscounty of Béarn, the most splendid period in their history began. The legendary blond warrior Gaston III

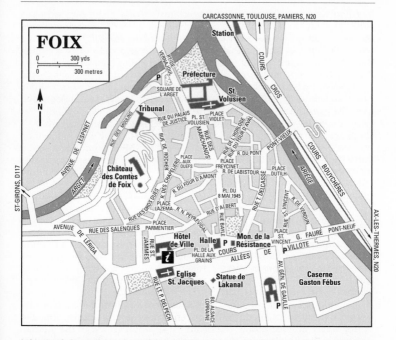

inherited these lands in 1343 and, consummate self-publicist, he poetically chose the surname Fébus, Occitan for Phoebus. His vast inheritance was fraught with political and military problems but he defended it on all sides: against the English in Aquitaine, the French in the east and against the armies of Armagnac to the north-west, and he managed to add the Bigorre to his territory. He controlled an important east–west route between the Mediterranean and Bayonne with a chain of castles from Mazères to Pau in Aquitaine. The line ended with his death in 1391, as he himself had killed in 1380 his only son who had tried to poison him. The Bigorre was added to the huge county of Foix-Béarn in 1425 under Jean I, and that passed eventually to Henri III of Foix-Béarn, King of Navarre, who acceded to the throne of France as Henri IV in 1589.

Begin the visit from behind the **Hôtel de Ville**, built where the old pilgrimage hostel of St-Jammes stood. Place Parmentier, the potato market in the 19C, has some 16C half-timbered houses. Take Rue des Salenques, then Rue des Grand-Ducs and Rue Rocher de Foix, old streets leading up to the **Château des Comtes de Foix** (tel: 61 65 56 05, every day, times vary), high above the town, with three towers linked by battlemented walls, silhouetted against the mountains. In the rock beneath the castle are caves which were inhabited in prehistoric times. Nothing is known about the first fort on the site, mentioned in the 11C. The castle was besieged by Simon de Montfort during the Albigensian Crusade—but he finally took it by cunning rather than force in 1214—and then by the King of France, Philippe the Hardy, in 1272. Gaston Fébus frequently stayed here at the beginning of his reign but after 1364 more rarely, preferring Mazères. The square towers linked by a two-storey building seem to have been built by the end of the

13C, the Arget tower to the north probably the oldest; but the round Fébus tower was added in the 15C. The castle was saved in the 17C when many others were destroyed at Richelieu's orders, and was used as a prison until 1862. The castle was given its 19C look during restoration and modification in 1885–97 by Paul Boeswilwald, pupil of Viollet-le-Duc, including the bell tower of the Arget tower.

Six rooms in the castle are devoted to the **Musée de l'Ariège** which has exhibits ranging from local archaeological finds to displays of rural life and 19C building materials. It also has seven Romanesque capitals from the abbey cloisters, one recalling the martyrdom of St-Volusien in 507, a collection of armoury and a Henri IV (16C) bed.

In the 10C–11C the town grew at the foot of the castle in the quarter around Rue du Palais de Justice and the ancient church of St-Nazaire. **No. 30** Rue des Chapeliers was the house of Monsieur de Tréville, a descendant of the Captain of the Musketeers at the time of Louis XIII.

The **Préfecture**, opposite the church, has a grandiose but crumbling 19C stone and brick façade with caryatids. The **Church of St-Volusien**, which used to shelter the body of the saint, is open afternoons only. The 12C sanctuary was rebuilt two centuries later, then damaged during the Religious Wars, and the Romanesque portal, with four sculpted capitals, was salvaged from the first church. The belfry was rebuilt in the 16C and the choir raised and vaulted in the 17C. The church was restored in the 1960s. Inside there is a band of Gothic-style polychrome carvings around the choir, a 16C polychromed terracotta Entombment and the stalls from St-Sernin in Toulouse.

The little **Place St-Volusien** is the ancient commercial centre of Foix. Rue des Marchands, leading out of it, was one of the grandest of the old city, containing the buildings of government and administration of the former province of Foix.

East of the church, **No. 34** Rue du Rival has a fine door dated 1617, and at the end of this street is the old bridge over the Ariège. There are several small squares with fountains in the old town: **Place Dutilh**, **Place St-Vincent**, and **Place de Labistour**, where one of the old city bastions stood, and in **Place du 8 Mai 1845** is an 18C portal. **Allées de Villotte**, a wide tree-lined avenue at right angles to the river, built on the old ramparts outside the medieval enceinte, is now the main road of the town with a large grain market built in 1870. The hospital opposite the town hall was the former Capuchin church of St-Jacques. To the west of the roundabout there is a fine view of the castle from Pont de St-Girons.

Route des Corniches, Ax-les-Thermes

Total distance: 49km (31 miles).

Take the N20 from Foix for 16km until Bompas, then turn left on to the D20, a winding route above the valley which runs parallel with the N20 and avoids the hurly burly of the main road. There are several Romanesque churches and a château strung out along it. Just outside **Arnave** (3.5km), is the pre-Romanesque pilgrimage church of St-Paul, reached by a half-hour walk up a narrow footpath into the hills. After 7.5km, take the D120 to the right for 4km to the little church of St-Blaise at **Verdun**, with a belfry-porch and gable, the only building to survive a flood in 1875 which destroyed the village.

Return to the D20, and after about 7.5km at **Axiat**, overlooking the valley, is a small 12C church with a square belfry with triple openings on two levels. The date of the portal is contested but could be as early as 1075, and unfortunately the interior decoration has been badly multilated. Structural changes were made at the end of the 17C when the nave was lengthened.

1km on **Lordat**, at 900m, is a small village dominated by the proud ruins of what was one of the largest medieval castles in the County of Foix, possibly built in the 10C. The ten minute walk up is worthwhile for the splendid views, explained by three *tables d'orientation*, as well as for the military architecture. Three successive elliptical enceintes defended the castle keep from the east and south. One wall of the keep is perhaps from the first construction, but as the castle was rebuilt in 1295 it is difficult to date accurately because of its state of delapidation. It served as refuge to Cathars after the fall of Montségur in 1244. It was dismantled in 1582.

A more prosaic curiosity 12km north is the great white **talc quarry** at **Trimouns**, at 1800m. It can be visited (guided tours by coach from the car park, May–October) but it is recommended to book in advance (tel: 61 64 60 60).

One of the best Romanesque churches on this route is **St-Martin d'Unac** on the D2, about 4km south-west of Bestiac. Built at the end of the 11C at the time of Roger II of Foix, it was a dependency of the Abbey of Foix. Part of the nave and the belfry with double openings on three levels are survivors of the first church which was enlarged in the 12C when the three apses were added. Its main features are the decorations inside and out: the three east windows—outlined with billets, zig-zags, rosettes and stars—and the capitals are all in marble. Inside, around the choir, are some good capitals and their quality suggests a link to the workshop of St-Sernin in Toulouse. On the south wall is a 15C mural depicting St Michael in the role of a knight, a pilgrim kneeling before him, an open book in his hands.

A farm in **Unac** offers an ecologically sound way of getting to grips with the mountains for a couple of days or even a week, by renting a donkey or taking an accompanied trek from the *Ferme aux Anes*, tel: 61 64 44 22.

The D44 brings you down to Ax-les-Thermes (see below) or from Bestiac stay on the D2 east to join the D613 at the Col de Chioula leading to Cathar country (see Basse Ariège).

The Valleys of the Southern Ariège

A whole gamut of valleys radiate out from the Ariège.

Tarascon-sur-Ariège, strategically situated where five valleys converge, is an obvious starting place for exploring the southern Ariège. Once an important town, there are only a few reminders of its illustrious past. The château was demolished in 1632 and survivors of the old town on the hill, destroyed by a conflagration in 1702, are the Tour de l'Horloge, Place Garrigou, the 14C St-Michel tower and one of the town gates, the Porte d'Espagne. The 16C church of La Daurade has a rich and dramatic décor.

The **Saurat Valley**, D618, goes west across the Col de Port from the bare slopes of the Ariège to the greener valleys of the Couserans. At the head of the valley, the vast **Bédeilhac Caves**, of both geological and prehistoric interest, were requisitioned during World War II by the French army, then by the Germans who contemplated using them as an aircraft factory and even, whimsically, as an underground runway! Remarkably the Magdalenian paintings, engravings and animals modelled in clay are still in place. The main village, Saurat, is stretched out along the old road and the valley offers a variety of scenic walks.

The **Valley of the Vicdessos**, south-west of Tarascon on the D8, carves its way through the enclosed valley to the village of Vicdessos and then divides to climb to the multitude of lakes which are the beauty of this part of the High Pyrenees, most of them accessible only on foot. At the junction of the N20 and the D8 in the direction of Vicdessos, the Romanesque **Church of Notre-Dame de Sabart** has an unmistakably 19C face, its façade, designed by Viollet-le-Duc, rebuilt in 1842. The church was badly damaged during the Wars of Religion but the pillars and arches (11C) survived. The Black Virgin dates from the Renaissance, but only the hands and head are sculpted, the rest is dressed. There is some 13C glass—rare for the region—with an image of St Peter. The rest of the decoration is 17C or later.

The Région Midi-Pyrénées has innumerable caves and grottoes, caverns and underground rivers, all fascinating, different and tremendously popular with children, but for the sheer beauty of the prehistoric paintings, the **CAVES OF NIAUX** are singled out.

The entrance is up a winding road off the D8 (tel: 61 05 88 37, 08.30–17.30, every day July–Sept, 11.00, 15.00 and 16.30, Oct–June). Numbers are strictly limited for conservation reasons and it is essential to book in advance. The visit is a round trip of 1.5km over broken ground so good walking shoes and a warm sweater are recommended; lamps are supplied. The first tourists started to come in the 17C, but, undisciplined and unsupervised, they carried off pieces of the calcite formations as souvenirs and left graffiti in exchange. The majority of the paintings accessible to the public are concentrated in what is called the **Salon Noir**, a huge cavern about 700m into the cave. They date from the Magdalenian period, between 10,900 BC and 10,590 BC, the last and most brilliant, in artistic terms, of the Upper Paleolithic era (35,000–9,800 BC). In 1925 a new gallery with a number of paintings was found beyond an underground lake, and discoveries continued to be made up to 1975. In total there are **104 animal paintings**, three-quarters in the Salon Noir, most frequently of bison but also of horses, ibex, and a few aurochs, fish and deer, and many undeciphered signs and symbols. The animals are always represented in profile and most are painted, either in red pigment (iron ore) or black (manganese oxide or finely ground charcoal) over an outline sketch drawn first in charcoal or occasionally engraved. The motivation for these inspired creations can only be hypothesised. The effect of the paintings, especially in lamplight, is quite magical. They are profoundly moving images, skilfully executed, sensitive to individual characteristics of texture and expression, yet drawn with an economy of line that has no temporal boundaries.

All the paintings at Niaux, from the Salon Noir and other galleries, are exhibited in the form of facsimiles in the Parc Pyrénéen de l'Art Préhistorique near Tarascon-sur-Ariège (tel: 61 05 01 10, 10.00–19.00 Apr–Oct).

At **Alliat** in the valley almost opposite Niaux are the caves of **La Vache** which also have paintings. The **Musée Paysan de Niaux**, beside the D8, is a collection of over 2000 artefacts which show life in the Ariège from prehistoric times to the end of the last century.

The Renaissance house at **Siguer**, a charming village on the D24, was the hunting lodge of the Counts of Foix. Slate was mined here at one time, but there are still red-tiled roofs as far south as Tarascon, and at the beginning of the 19C iron ore mines at Rancie supplied 74 wood-fired *forges catalanes* in the Ariège. However these activities have been replaced by tourism and skiing.

The D8 goes through the wild and rugged scenery of the Vicdessos region, dominated by the Montcalm (3078m), Canalbonne (2914m) and la Rouge (2902m) peaks, the landscape becoming even more lunaresque over the Port de Lers (1517m), to the popular lake, the Etang de Lers.

Ussat-les-Bains, on the N20 south of Tarascon-sur-Ariège, is a small spa on the banks of the Ariège with a shady park, where the waters are used to treat psychosomatic and neurological problems. The **Grotte de Lombrives**, opposite Ussat, is reputedly the largest underground grotto in the European Union. A panoramic ride in a little train takes visitors up to the entrance at 640m. There are plenty of concretions and some of the best stalagmites in fairylike grottoes. For Verdun, see above.

Running south from **Les Cabannes** the **Aston Valley** is considered one of the most beautiful, with a cross-country ski centre at Plateau de Beille. **Luzenac** links up with the **Route des Corniches** (see above).

Ax-les-Thermes (Tourist Information, tel: 61 64 20 64) at 720m, the last town of any significance before Andorra, is, as its name would imply, a spa town. Archaeological evidence suggests that the curative properties of the waters were appreciated even before the Romans arrived. Three valleys, the Ariège, the Lauze and the Oriège meet here, and it has more facilities, hotels and camp sites than most other centres in the Ariège, catering both for those in their dressing gowns coming for a *cure*, and for more hardy specimens in their boots intent on an outdoor activity holiday or skiing in the winter 8km away at Ax Bonascre.

The most entertaining and novel feature of Ax is the **Bassin des Ladres** in the town centre where anyone can strip off their boots or shoes and dangle their aching, or even non-aching, feet in the hot (77°C) sulphurous water. According to tradition, St-Louis (Louis IX) founded the neighbouring hospital to treat leprous soldiers returning from the Crusades. Of the medieval town there is only one gate, the Porte d'Espagne to the south.

Three major routes lead out of Ax

One route is the N20 which climbs up to l'**Hospitalet** (1436m) at the border with Andorra passing through the **Valley of Mérens** which boasts the oldest Romanesque church of the Haute Ariège (10C and 11C), although all that is left is the Catalan style belfry with three levels of double openings, the walls of the apse and one apsidal chapel. This beautiful valley is also famous for its small black horses, descendants of those captured in the paintings of Niaux, well adapted to mountainous terrain. It is possible to explore the region by pony (tel: 61 64 03 92, 61 64 36 10).

The second option is the D22 which follows the **Orlu Valley** on the Oriège, through Orgeix with its lake, and Orlu, crosses the Réserve Nationale d'Orlu, inhabited by herds of izard, and finally peters out to become a footpath after less than 10km with walks up to the lakes at around 2000m.

The third alternative is the D613 and D25 via Ascou, with a ski centre at Pailhères, and the **Valley of the Lauze**, a route running alongside the Lake of Goulours and over the Col de Pailhères (2002m), rich in woodland and flowers, to the ruined castles of Usson and Quérigut in the canton of Donezan, a high plateau surrounded by summits of over 2000m. This is the last outpost of the Ariège on the border with the Aude, ultimately linking up with the D118 and D117 north and east to Perpignan, or south on the D118 and D618 to Font-Romieu and Spain.

7

The Couserans: St-Lizier

Total distance: 133km (83 miles).

The **Couserans** was an ancient viscounty, tucked in between the land of the Counts of Foix and the province of Bigorre, ruled by vassals of the counts of Comminges. The designation is still used to describe part of the *département* of the Ariège. Despite the barrier formed by the Pyrenees, there were close links between the Couserans and Catalonia and Aragon during the Middle Ages. The Spanish participated in pilgrimages to Notre-Dame-du-Marsan, near St-Lizier, and St-Lizier was a stage on the route to Santiago crossing the Pyrenees at the Col d'Aula. However, there is no modern route from the Couserans into Spain.

Many rivers rise in the mountains forming a network of valleys which divide and sub-divide and divide again, making eighteen in all. The main ones are the Valleys of Bellongue, Biros and Bethmale plus three which join the upper Salat, the Ustou, Garbet and Arac. The smaller valleys can be entered by car but often they just peter out in a track leading to the border. This is a walkers' paradise with well indicated and documented routes with an abundance of sub-alpine and alpine flowers above the forest line as well as animals. St-Lizier-St-Girons, twin towns which complement each other, are the main centres in the Couserans.

ST-LIZIER (pop. 1800, Tourist Information, tel: 61 96 77 77) on a hill beside the Salat, is the architectural high-spot of the Couserans. The *cité* of the ancient Consorani people and capital of the Couserans, a Roman settlement, it was elevated to episcopal see in the 5C and maintained this status until 1801. Bishop Glycerius, of Spanish or Portuguese origin, who died c 540, was reputed to have defended his city from Visigoths and Vandals. Canonised he became St-Lizier.

The small town has the distinction of having co-cathedrals, both founded in the 11C, in the two separate quarters of the town. Notre-Dame-de-la-Sède, inside the *cité* walls, from *la Séda*, Occitan for episcopal see, was the original cathedral. The sanctuary in the *bourg*, built by Bishop Jourdain I in the late 11C, was consecrated in 1117 by St-Raymond, Bishop of Barbastro in Spain, probably on the site of a sepulchre. Today this is known as the Cathedral of St-Lizier.

From the D117 drive across the 16C bridge to the base of the town which descends in tiers to the riverbank. The square tower to the right was built to protect three mills. There is parking at the top in the square by the Cathedral.

Cathedral of St-Lizier. Many stages of reconstruction of the cathedral are all too evident from the exterior. The only remaining part of the 11C building is the south wall of the nave, visible from the cloister. The church was extended east with a transept and five-sided apse before the consecration in 1117. Gallo-Roman friezes and columns were haphazardly incorporated into the ashlar. A little later the walls were raised to take vaults. The apse with its heavy cornice dwarfs the two earlier low undecorated chapels with hugely thick walls flanking it. The church was badly damaged in the 12C when the Counts of Comminges attempted to take control of St-Lizier and the nave was enlarged and modified in the 14C. Above the crossing are two levels of a c 1300 Toulousain-style octagonal belfry in brick with mitred bays, crowned by ugly modern crenellations. The 15C entrance on the north has recessed brick arches and marble columns. On the right-hand wall is the scallop-shell symbol of St James.

Inside, the stylistic juxtapositions and strangely irregular shape are quite endearing. The north wall of the aisleless nave is not straight so that the pillars, heightened in the 15C when the nave was rib vaulted, are not opposite each other. The nave is out of alignment with the choir, and the transept, enlarged in the 14C, is also uneven. The most ancient parts are the massive walls of the apsidal chapels, the rest taking its basic form at the end of the 11C or beginning of the 12C when two large semi-engaged columns were added to support the chancel arch. While the exterior of the main apse is angled, the interior is semi-circular.

The greatest glory of the cathedral is the **Romanesque murals**. The paintings in the **choir**, discovered in 1960, are on two levels and date from two different periods. The walls, erected and painted in the late 11C, were tampered with when the choir vaults were reconstructed in the 12C. Part of the original decorative scheme, in muted colours, has survived in the bays either side of the windows. This consists of friezes, heads and, framed by the architectural setting of blind arcades which are also painted, pairs of standing figures, the Apostles in the apse, and Kings and Prophets to the side. Below are images of the Three Magi in the house of Herod, the Adoration of the Magi, the Annunciation, Visitation and Nativity. The elongated figures are strikingly beautiful, the most moving being the Visitation, with Elizabeth and Mary cheek to cheek, their haloes fused. The work is attributed to a painter who worked in the Catalonian Pyrenees and in the Val d'Aran, identified as the Master of Pedret. The vault paintings, containing the arms of the Bishop Auger de Montfaucon, which place them at the end of the13C or early 14C, are in a rather less eloquent style and a rosy-cheeked Christ in Majesty surrounded by the symbols of the Evangelists beams down.

The 12C murals in the **north chapel**, discovered in 1980 under a thick layer of plaster, are interesting for their unusual iconography based on the Revelation of St John at Patmos. Two groups of three figures with haloes stand before the six gates of Heavenly Jerusalem, their arms outstretched towards the kings of the earth who carry treasures. Beneath them are the symbols of the Evangelists and the figure of St John at the moment he receives his vision from an angel. The words *Sanctus Andreas* can be deciphered on the north, and the east wall has a Virgin suckling the Infant Jesus, c 1300. The shadow of an inscription below the Virgin indicates that there was also an image of St John in the east end.

The large capitals of the transept are simply carved and the column bases have human feet, both bare and shod. A vaulted recess in the south transept, discovered in 1958, was the sepulchure of the bishops, including St Lizier before his relics were placed under the altar. It now contains a sarcophagus with the relics of 13C and 14C bishops. The stalls are 17C and the 18C black marble altar incorporates part of the original altar. The Gothic painted décor of the nave was uncovered during restoration in 1978–83 and in the window opposite the door is 15C stained glass. There are a number of post-Reformation pieces in the nave including the 17C organ with rather curious little angels at the top, restored in 1983.

The other great feature of St-Lizier is the fine **Romanesque cloister**, the only one in the Ariège, the result of two building campaigns, the first from 1150–80 and the second in the 13C, accounting for a variety of styles of capitals and different types of vaulting. In the 14C the cloister was shortened by two bays when the transept was built, and the upper level was added in the 16C. The 32 bays are supported by alternate single and double marble columns with a cluster of four in the west gallery. The **capitals** are decorated with allegorical, geometric and vegetal designs, the most accomplished in the north gallery. The rare figurative images include Adam and Eve, in the north gallery, and Daniel in the Lions' Den with Habbakuk in the east. Round the cloisters are several medieval tombs and in the **sacristy** a remarkable collection of treasures from the 11C to the 19C of diverse origins. The best is the very elegant Renaissance **reliquary bust of St-Lizier**, made by Antoine Favier of Toulouse, in embossed and gilded silver studded with gems.

On foot from here, take the road to the east of the square which takes a sinuous route up to the old *cité* at the top of the hill enclosed in about 740m of ramparts. Gallo-Roman walls, erected in the late-3C or early-4C, punctuated by six semi-circular towers and two gates, have been rebuilt. Inside it is strangely empty except for the square tower and the episcopal buildings. This part of St-Lizier is lifted above the gardens and tiled roofs of the houses clustered around the Cathedral, carrying the eye beyond the fields and wooded slopes of the St-Gironnais to the distant Pyrenees and the dome of Mont Valier, 2838m. The **Cathedral of Notre-Dame-de-la-Sède**, of fairly modest proportions, was begun in the 11C adjacent to the south ramparts and there is not a great deal left to visit. The apse, of the end 11C, is the oldest part, and in the Romanesque chevet are re-used Roman friezes, while the three-bay nave dates from the late 15C. The choir stalls and altars are 17C and the wood-panelling is late 18C. There is nothing left of the cloister to the north, but the 13C chapter house with brick vaults has survived.

To the west is the **Bishops' Palace**, built c 1660 into the Roman constructions, a sober building with towers at each extremity. It has recently been renovated and now houses a **museum** with a well-displayed local history collection from the Valley of Bethmale.

Return by the Porte de l'Horloge west of the Bishops' Palace. Also to see in the village is the **Pharmacy of the Hospice** (now a Retired Peoples' Home) (May–30 Oct 10.00–12.00, 14.00–18.00), built in 1771 adjacent to the Cathedral cloister, complete with all the wooden cabinets and locally made jars, an operating table and a dictionary of pharmaceutical prescriptions. One of the oldest and most prestigious music festivals in the Region takes place at St-Lizier in July and August when concerts are performed in the Cathedral.

2km south of St-Lizier is **St-Girons** (pop. 7700, Tourist Information, tel: 61 66 14 11), the largest town in this part of the Ariège and *sous-préfecture*. It makes a good base for excursions into the Couserans. Apart from being a small dynamic commercial centre with a lively Saturday market, it is not of any particular architectural interest. Originally called Bourg-sous-Vic or Bourg-sous-Ville, in acknowledgement of its subordinate role to St-Lizier, it was called St-Girons when the remains of the Christian martyr Gerontius were brought here after the sack of St-Lizier by the Counts of Comminges in 1130.

The advantages of its position in the wide valley where the three rivers Salat, Baup and Lez converge are obvious and the riverbanks are still St-Girons' strong point, with tree-lined walks and pleasant gardens surrounding the remodelled Château of the Viscounts of the Couserans, now municipal offices. The parish church, rebuilt in the 19C, has conserved its 15C belfry, and in the south-east of the town, the much-restored 12C Church of St-Vallier still has its Romanesque portal.

St-Girons has hotels of most categories, while on the D117 at Lorp Sentaraille (north) the *Hôtel Horizon* 117 (tel: 61 66 26 80) has an excellent restaurant. The *chambres d'hôtes* (guest rooms) at the *Relais d'Encausse* (tel: 61 66 05 80) just outside St-Girons, offers a warm welcome and a good *table d'hôte*.

From St-Girons, follow the D618 on the left bank of the Salat through the enclosed and densely wooded Gorges de Ribaouto. After 25km, at Biert, the D18 veers off to the Col de la Crouzette towards Rimont. A further 3km is **Massat** (Tourist Information, tel: 61 96 92 76), between the Col de Port and the Gorges de l'Arac, which was the medieval capital of the Viscounts of the Couserans. Hints of 18C affluence are evident in doorways and wrought iron balconies, particularly the Hôtel de Ville. The Baroque façade of the collegiate **church** (1700–50) is surprisingly splendid for such a small place, replacing the church of 1290 destroyed and pillaged in the 16C by the Huguenots of Mas d'Azil. Standing free beside it is the 15C octagonal belfry tower, in yellow-gold stone, the tallest in the Couserans. All that was salvaged from the 13C church is a statue of a nude child draped with the shawl of Abraham on the baldaquin of the pulpit. Otherwise, 18C and 19C statues and paintings, including a copy of Leonardo's Last Supper (1849) signed Scurruité and two paintings given by Napoléon III in 1866, adorn the interior. The widespread devotion and veneration of the cult of the Virgin in these mountain communities is exemplified by the simple chapel dedicated to the Virgin at the west of the town.

Roads lead out of Massat to the **Col de Port** and to the **Etang de Lers**, through bucolic mountain landscapes, with the occasional auberge or *chambres d'hôte*, and scattered buildings in traditional style, the roofs covered with beautiful silver schist cut in fishscale shapes. The journey follows the D17 for about 15km, a narrow road with a few tiny hamlets to start with, through chestnuts and acacias, then beech forests to the **Col de Saraillé** (942m) when the scenery changes and the trees are mainly silver birch. Gradually the landscape expands into a wide deforested valley scattered, in the summer, with harebells, clover, candytuft and some modest cottages. Especially precious are the rare examples of **shepherds' huts** with stepped gables (*à pas d'oiseau*), designed to withstand winter snow, and originally thatched but now sadly mainly patched up with corrugated iron.

Detour. The D32 takes you either south-east 19km to **Aulus-les-Bains**, arguably the most out-of-the-way spa town in the whole of France (very

friendly *Hôtel de la Terrasse*, tel: 61 96 00 98), or you can c
north-west to **Oust** whose church has a strange bulbous belfry and C ~~....~~
Reformation retable. **Vic d'Oust** (2.5km) has an 11C church with gable
belfry (church is closed). This has been a cheese producing region since
Roman times and at **Seix**, south on the D3 for 3km, the **Fromagerie
Artisanale Julien Coumes** can be visited. This village is the most important
of the Haut-Salat with three hotel restaurants and an auberge. Above the
village is the Château du Roi, and houses with wooden balconies overhang
the river, a veritable mountain torrent at this point and a popular centre for
canoeists. The Baroque church has a strange neo-Romanesque belfry, 1897,
and inserted in the façade buttress and base of the belfry are carvings from
an older building.

3km from Seix, the D17 from Sentenac d'Oust follows for 23km the **Valley
of Bethmale**, considered the most beautiful of all the Couserans valleys,
scattered with purples, pinks, mauves, blues, of the flowers of the
meadows—wild orchids, wild thyme and bilberries—on the way up to the
Col de la Core, 1395m. This is such a popular place for walkers and
motorists (and hang-gliders who add a dash of primary colours) that it is
almost crowded in the summer. On the descent from the Col is the equally
popular (because it is so accessible and beautiful) **Lac de Bethmale**, in a
glade abundant with bees, berries and butterflies, raspberries and wild
strawberries. There are small communities strung out along the valley with
several old *lavoirs*, but poverty and abandon is all too evident and has
necessitated more creative use of corrugated iron.

In **Samortein** there is a *sabotier* who makes wooden clogs with long
curved pointed toes which look quite impossible to wear but are part of the
traditional costume of Bethmale. At **Borde-sur-Lez** cross the lovely old
bridge to the hamlet of Ourjout and the 12C Church of St-Pierre (key at the
last house up the lane past the church) and the Chapel of Aulignac (follow
the river and ask for the key at the farm). The **Valley de Biros** begins here
(D4) and about 8.5km into the wooded valley **Sentein** is the grandest of
several little churches in this remote valley. It has a reddish sandstone
belfry, the third highest in the Couserans. The octagonal section of the
belfry is 14C and the spire was added in 1749. Its Romanesque base is the
baptistry whose entrance has an unusual arrangement of simple capitals
on the outside supporting the arch and four columns inside. The body of
the church was amended in the 14C and has late-15C–early-16C **paintings**
in the east bay of the nave of Apostles, Prophets, and Doctors of the Church,
and in the west bay 12 figures in contemporary dress. The choir paintings
are 18C and in the south chapel is a 12C chrism. Two very rustic towers
with witches' hat roofs were part of the fortifications.

Return on the same road (D4) to **Castillon** (10.5km), where the Chapel
St-Pierre, perched above the village, has an impressive belfry and a statue
of St-Pierre. 1km further brings you to the D618 which to the west follows
the **Bellongue Valley** then crosses the Col de Portet d'Aspet (1069m) and
drops down into the Comminges. **Audressein** is a pretty village at the start
of the valley with a lovely 14C church, **Notre-Dame-de-Tramesaygues**
(open Sundays 09.00–18.00) beside the river. The deep porch has a series
of ex-voto scenes in true fresco technique, restored 1987–88. The large
figures of angels, St James and St John the Baptist are more sophisticated
than the anecdotal scenes presenting individuals in some sort of trouble
or danger—sick, imprisoned, tumbling from a tree, departing on a
crusade—who are all subsequently saved and are shown giving thanks to
Notre-Dame. There is a *sabotier* in this village.

Detour. Deeper into the valley (10km) at **Galey** the church shelters a Renaissance retable in wood with 13 painted panels.

It is 12km on the D618 from Audressein to St-Girons.

8

Pyrénées Centrales: Luchon and the Nestes

Total distance: 69km (43 miles).

The central Pyrenees is dependent on its natural resources, the celebrated mountain scenery, the properties of the waters and the Pyrenean National Park, to attract both summer and winter visitors. This is an area where there are no major monuments but many small ones of great charm. Rural communities, built in schist and slate, have ancient but modest churches, decorated with murals or frescoes at some point from the 12C through to the 16C. They do sometimes take a bit of finding, and are frequently closed for protection, but visits are arranged through the local Tourist Information Centres as indicated below. A visit to the Romanesque churches of the Val d'Aran could be combined with this itinerary by following the Garonne by way of the N125 across the Spanish border at Pont du Roi, then taking the D618 over the Col du Portillon (1293m) to Luchon.

The tour starts at St-Béat and ends in the next major valley to the west, the Vallée d'Aure.

St-Béat (pop. 542, Tourist Information, tel: 61 79 45 98), built on both banks of the still narrow defile of the Garonne, is grandly called the Key to France, a title it acquired in the Middle Ages because of its position close to the Spanish border, yet it is a modest town. In the southern part of the old province of Comminges, now part of the *département* of Haute-Garonne, on the N125, it is easily reached from N117. It is famous for the marble quarried here during Roman times and used all over the south-west but there was a break in production during the Middle Ages. The quarries were reactivated (when fashions changed) in the late 17C and 18C and the marble was used in such prestigious palaces as Versailles as well as in many more modest locations including the houses of St-Béat, and for many a Baroque retable or altarpiece in the region.

North of the village are the ruins of an 11C château with 12C and 15C walls; its keep, rebuilt in the 19C, stands sentinel over the valley. The church was built in 1132 and has been tastefully restored. On the tympanum is a fairly standard Christ in Majesty and the symbols of the four Evangelists and the four decorated capitals include an Annunciation and Visitation. It has a collection of mainly 16C to 18C furnishings. Also of note is the Consuls House (1553). Maréchal Galliéni was born in St-Béat in 1849.

From St-Béat to Luchon take the D44 passing the Lake de Géry and the marble quarries at Marignac and the D125, 20km; alternatively go south on the N125, through a corner of the Spanish Pyrenees and the D618 over the Col du Portillon (1293m), (44km).

LUCHON (pop. 3000, Tourist Information, tel: 61 79 21 21), full name Bagnères-de-Luchon, the Gallo-Roman city of Ilixon, is sometimes described as La Reine des Pyrénées. In a minor way it is the region's answer to a coastal resort, a typically bourgeois spa town and is, in fact, the third thermal station in France. It is advertised as the leading French seasonal thermal resort (emphasis on the seasonal) offering all the facilities of a **spa town** in the summer and **skiing** in the winter, and a huge number of hotels. Enclosed in deep wooded valley about as far south as one can go in France (not quite as southerly as Ax-les-Thermes in the Ariège), the properties of its sulphurous sodic waters were already recognised in 25 BC and appreciated for six centuries until it returned to obscurity between the 5C and 10C. Its rebirth in the 18C was due mainly to Antoine Mégret de Sérilly, better known as Baron d'Etigny, the King's Intendant at Auch, who visited the town for the first time in 1759. He was responsible for a new access route from Montréjeau and for instigating a programme of works to link the old town with the baths, a radical exercise in Haussmanism before his notorious successor's time. By 1827 the town owned 78 springs and this heralded the beginning of a fashionable period for the spa patronised by the rich and famous from all over Europe (Flaubert, Mata Hari, Lamartine, Alexander Dumas Jnr., Bismarck, Leopold II of Belgium) until the beginning of this century. Both Luchon and St-Béat claim the balcony that inspired Edmond Rostand's (1868–1918) duplicitous scenes in *Cyrano de Bergerac.*

To learn more about Luchon, the 10 rooms of the **Musée du Pays de Luchon** (tel: 61 79 29 87, closed Nov and Mar) cover such subjects as local archaeology, the mountains, winter sports, local history and architecture. The grander buildings along the dead-straight **Allées d'Etigny** date from the mid-19C and near the end of this linden-lined avenue there is the faint but distinct aroma of sulphur. The **Parc des Quinconces**, with its catalpas and tulip trees, bandstand, pond, pony rides, and a statue of d'Etigny by G. Crauk (1889) surveying it all, was created in 1849 after the Etablissement Chambert was built in 1848 to replace the baths destroyed by fire in 1841, its elegant colonnade in St-Béat marble. The **Pavilion du Prince Impérial** was built in 1960 and in 1970 the glass, steel and grey marble Vaporarium, with natural saunas, was the first in Europe. In this near equivalent to a health farm, most of the 28,000 French *curistes* are subsidised by Social Security although private treatments are available, as is a fitness programme (Vitaline tel: 61 79 22 97).

To the east of Allées d'Etigny is the Casino surrounded by another park of four hectares with pond and grotto and exotic plants, but the casino only has croupiers of the one-armed variety.

In 1993, a new cablecar was opened from the centre of town to the ski-resort **Superbagnères** (1797m), and there are plans afoot to bottle the local mineral water.

There is a market on Wednesdays and a flower festival the last Sunday in August and accommodation in the town is provided by 60 hotels and 3000 furnished apartments.

In the vicinity of Luchon are **31 Romanesque churches**, but to protect precious furnishings and decoration the only way to see the interiors is through visits organised by the **Bibliothèque Pour Tous**, 9 avenue Jean-Boularan, 31110-Luchon (no telephone). If organising that is too much of a hassle, so integrated are these little mountain churches with the landscape that most views are enhanced simply by the fact that they are there, their characteristic rusticity set off by bell-towers with slate spires.

Leave Luchon on the D618 west in the direction of the Col de Peyresourde and turn right after 4.5km on to the D51.

The **Vallée d'Oueil** is a pastoral valley running north–south leading to two rural 12C churches built in schist, **Benque-Dessus** and **Benque-Dessous**—the latter has slightly better conserved Romanesque characteristics while the former has Gothic murals. The little church at **St-Paul d'Oueil** has a sculpted tympanum, and the quite miniscule St-Barthélemy at **Saccourvielle** is endowed with one of the loveliest bell-towers in the area (about 8km).

Return to the D618, and 1km on the right at **ST-AVENTIN**, at the start of the Vallée de Larboust (park at the bottom and walk up the 100m slope), is the most outstanding of these **small churches**, the presence of venerated relics of the local saint accounting for its importance. The structure is typical of the first Romanesque style in the Midi (early 11C): bare walls, small windows and a blind arcade around the east end. The eastern of the two towers is the older, and a simple gable was replaced by a taller tower with double, triple and quadruple openings in ascending order above the stepped west façade. Apart from some Gallo-Roman stones embedded in the south wall, most of the **sculptures** date from the second half of the12C. Above the porch, Christ in a mandorla, supported by angels, is surrounded by the four Evangelists holding their symbols. On the capital to the right is the martyrdom of St Aventin, who reputedly met his death in the hands of the Muslims, and on the left the Massacre of the Innocents and Mary Magdalene anointing Christ's feet. A pillar faced in marble east of the portal is carved with a somewhat chunky Virgin and Child, Mary's hair centrally parted, with animals around her and under her feet, and on the east face is Isaiah, similar stylistically with the sculptures at St-Just at Valcabrère. On the buttress to the right is a relief showing the legend of St Aventin's relics being discovered by a bull.

The pilasters in the nave and aisles are proof that the original building was designed to be vaulted, but not the vaults we see now. The surprisingly high nave is flanked by narrow aisles and the interior is decorated with a series of **paintings** from the end of the 12C through to the end of the 13C or 14C. Some are faded and difficult to decipher as they were hidden under plaster until the end of the 19C. On the apse walls St-Sernin and St-Aventin are in the place of honour, their names written in the banderoles. In the dome are visions of glory, with a cycle of the Life of Jesus in the upper register. In the nave Christ's image is represented in a medallion supported by six angels, and the hand of God between Cain and Abel framed in another, while on the intrados of the large arcades are Adam and Eve, probably painted in the 14C. There are several Romanesque pieces such as a holy-water stoup carved out of a capital, another stoup with strange reliefs, a wrought iron screen and a crudely executed marble crucifix.

A further 1km on the D618 and another valley (D76) runs south along the **Neste d'Oô** leading to a series of natural lakes at 1504m or more reached only on foot. Almost opposite this turning is the little church at **Billière** with an apse at each end. At 2km from Billière, the 11C church of **Cazaux-de-Larboust** has a typical bell-tower but its main attractions are the 15C **frescoes** which include a Christ in Majesty and the four Evangelists, Mary and the Apostles, Adam and Eve, the Birth of Eve, the Temptation and the Expulsion, and the Last Judgement. Another 2km west on the D618 is a charming little 9C–10C church isolated in the middle of a field at the foot of the Col de Peyresourde, with a multitude of names: **St-Pé-de-la-Moraine**, **Moraine de Garin**, or **Sants-Tristous**, and other variations on these themes. A simple belfry-wall with antique bells, a staircase to the roof, and tiny windows, it has a number of Gallo-Roman **marbles** with pagan imagery incorporated into the construction both inside and out. It also has a **mosaic** stone floor with a rare early representation of the Christian sign, the fish. Somewhat anachronistic but not unusual is an 18C retable with wooden statuettes of Christ, St Peter and St James.

The **Col de Peyresourde** (1569m) marks the departmental boundary with the Hautes-Pyrénées, after which the road drops down into the Louron Valley. There is a series of **Romanesque chapels** with **16C murals** on the old pilgrim route. To protect these fragile works, visits are arranged on Thursday afternoons in the summer from the Maison du Tourisme at Bordères-Louron (tel: 62 98 64 12, in winter, by prior arrangement). The Renaissance decorations, either tempera on wood or fresco on plaster, were added to these simple structures after the Council of Trent in 1563, coinciding with increased prosperity in the valley resulting from a growth in trade with Spain, particularly in wool, following the discovery of the New World in 1492, and from the integration of the region into France.

Before the junction with the D25, at **Mont**, **St-Barthélemy** is exceptional as some of the **painted decoration** is outside. In an oratory in the cemetery are frescoes relating to the life of St Catherine of Alexandria, signed by Bona. Under the church porch is a Crucifixion and there is a large Last Judgement on the wall between the buttresses. The nave paintings, dated 1574, attributed to Melchior Rodigis, have scenes from the Passion, Christ before Pilate and Christ with the four Evangelists as well as Isaiah announcing the birth of Christ. The north chapel contains scenes from the Life of John the Baptist and a Visitation, Annunciation and Nativity. The two painters' styles are quite distinctive, but both use contemporary dress for their figures.

St-Blaise at **Estarvielle**, a Romanesque church remodelled in the 16C, has a Baroque retable which partly obscures the paintings. On the north side is Christ carrying the Cross, and on the south a Descent from the Cross. Framed by the central part of the retable is a Crucifixion representing the moment when Christ's side is pierced by Longinus's lance and a scene of the soldiers playing cards on Christ's tunic. After 16km you come to the junction with the D25.

Turn left and go a further 1km to **Vielle-Louron**. The plain exterior of **St-Mercurial** gives no clue to the stunning **interior decoration** painted in intense colours. Several themes cover the walls: an Annunciation; scenes from the Passion, from the Flagellation to the Entombment; a vivid Last Supper; and St-Mercurial fighting the infidels. On the vaults are The Tree of Jesse, a Tetramorphe, and a Christ surrounded by the Apostles. In the lateral chapel, now the Sacristy, is a Last Judgement with a very explicit image of the Jaws of Leviathan.

The **Vallée de Louron** is a beautiful valley, gentle and restful, perhaps too beautiful for its own good. The tiny community of **Génos** has about 150 residents, but the château ruins, lake, swimming pool, hotels and other facilities, as well as two ski resorts, attract 30,000 visitors in the summer. It also has one small quaint rustic attraction that cannot go unmentioned, the **Source Thermal de Saoussas**, open in July and August (tel: 62 99 65 50) where, for just a few francs, you can take a relaxing sulphurous dip in one of the four old-fashioned black marble tubs in the thermal bathing establishment of 1923. May this never be modernised.

Return on the same road to the D618 and Arreau (16km).

ARREAU (Tourist Information, tel: 62 98 63 15), at 730m, has the typical steep slate roofs with attic windows and subdued silver-grey colours of all the mountain towns. It used to be the capital of the Four Valleys: Aure, Magnoac, Barousse and Neste, and is well placed between the mountains, the plain, and Spain via the Tunnel de Bielsa. A visit to the town, built between the Nestes d'Aure (Robinson Crusoe's route through the Pyrenees) and de Louron, is accompanied by the sound of water rushing into the valley.

Park on the right bank near the cream and grey **Château des Nestes** on the water's edge which was a Commandery protecting the sanctuary of St-Exupère in the 11C, a judiciary building in the 17C, a mill and grand residence in the 18C, and now shelters the Museum of the Year 1000. The **Chapelle St-Exupère** opposite is dedicated to the 5C Bishop of Toulouse who was born in Arreau. His story is told on one of the six archaically decorated Romanesque capitals of the portal which is flanked by pink marble columns and outlined by three carved voussoirs. On the tympanum is a chrism typical of the high valleys of the Nestes and Bigorre, and the octagonal tower has triple windows. Inside the porch is a wooden coffer for offerings. Most of the chapel is Flamboyant Gothic style and a 16C wrought iron screen protects a Romanesque stoup. Next door is the fine building known as **Maison St-Exupère** of 1554 and overhanging the river is the balcony of the 18C Maison de la Molie with marble columns.

On the other side of the bridge are the covered market with a little belfry (Thursday market) and the famous 16C **Maison aux Lys**, on Grande Rue, its façade timbers carved in a fleur-de-lys pattern as a reminder of the moment when, at the end of 14C, the inhabitants opted for allegiance to Louis XI and the Crown of France rather than to the successor of the Count of Armagnac, Jean V. Note the rounded, flower-like swastika of the Pyrenees used liberally to decorate doors and façades.

Further up the slope, on the left bank (the same side as the market) in the old quarter, is the parish church of Notre-Dame, basically Romanesque with Gothic aisles and a 16C tower with two-light bays. The *Hôtel d'Angleterre* (tel: 62 98 63 30), on the Luchon road, boasts a long tradition and a mention by the English mountaineer, Henry Russell, in Souvenirs d'un montagnard, 1889.

The tiny hill village of **Jézeau**, a stone's throw (2km) east of Arreau on the D112, has a proportionally tiny church, basically Romanesque with Gothic extensions, and a monogram of Christ from the portal is reused in the cemetery wall. Its east end, painted white and gold, looks positively anthropomorphic from the cemetery gate. Inside are Renaissance (16C) paintings on wood.

Excursions from Arreau

Round trip: 50km.

Heading **south from Arreau** along the Neste, lined with scattered clumps of buildings, the D929 takes you through Cadéac, which has a 16C church, and where the Chapelle de Pène-Tailhade straddles the road, past Guchen and Ancizan, their slate roofs glinting in the sun, to the neat silver-grey village of **Vielle-Aure**. In a beautiful setting, its pleasant 16C, 17C and 18C buildings are in striking contrast to the jarringly modern ski resort of Soulan above it. Just off centre, the small Church of **St-Barthélemy** has a Lombardy style east end, massive piers, and a Romanesque altar, but has been modified since the 12C. Murals were added in the 15C and a Flamboyant door in the 17C. Scallop shells and a statue of St James testify to this alternative pilgrimage route into Spain via the Rioumajou Valley.

At 12km from Arreau, Vielle-Aure's far more dynamic neighbour, **St-Lary-Soulan** (836m, Tourist Information, tel: 62 39 50 81), which has a much-restored 12C **church** to the north of the town near the baths, was on the same route. Two Romanesque carvings, a Christ and a chrism, are reused on the exterior of Ste-Marie and the church preserves an eyecatching Baroque retable from the now-demolished Church of St-Hilaire. St-Lary-Soulan is quite a buzzing little centre for walkers and skiers, a mixture of old and new, with a number of hotels. As one of the six gateways to the **Pyrenean National Park**, the Maison du Parc, installed in a 16C building, supplies all the information you need to know about this protected area. The Maison de l'Ours is dedicated to the safeguard of three bears and unravels the facts and myths attached to the plight of this unfortunate creature in the Pyrenees.

St-Lary is on the doorstep of the 2300ha of the **Réserve Naturelle du Néouvielle**, containing the Lac d'Orédon. This is a wondrous Garden of Eden with carmine wild roses and lilac asters, thistles, dianthus, saxifrages in all varieties, dark-blue gentians, and so on. Some 1250 plants have been identified flowering above all in June and July—not much appears before May but many plants flower through August and September. The 15 lakes of the Réserve also have an exceptional number of animals and vegetation. The road, quite winding in places, is closed in the winter.

The last monument this side of the Spanish border is in the **Plan d'Aragnouet**, on the right of the D118 (13km). The so-called Templar Chapel is a little gem, its two stages of belfry wall silhouetted against the mountains. If the weather is inclement in France you may fare better the other end of the Tunnel de Bielsa in sunny Spain.

Returning to Arreau from St-Lary, take the D25/D116 on the right bank of the Neste through such villages as Bourisp, Sailhan and Bazus-Aure.

7km north of Arreau on the D929 on the Neste at **Sarrancolin** is an interesting and original **church** in the shape of a Greek cross. It is crowned by an admirable belfry with triple round arches on small columns on the upper level and a candle-snuffer spire with spirelets. The first church was built here by Benedictines from Simorre in 952 and was replaced in the 12C and 13C. Dedicated to a local martyr, St-Ebons, by some miracle the superb 13C **reliquary** made to contain the saintly remains is still in the church despite being thrown in the Neste at the time of the Revolution and being carried off by thieves in 1911. This is a wooden casket covered with gilded and enamelled copper and is one of the finest in France. On one face are Christ, a King (possibly St-Louis), St-Ebons, Apostles and Saints; on the other scenes from the Birth of Christ; and on the gables at each end are St Peter and St Paul. Following a fire c 1570, the choir has been enclosed by a wrought iron screen and contains the late 16C choir stalls and misericords and the altar and retable of 1651. In the north transept is a 17C gilded polychrome relief with the Annunciation, Visitation, Martyrdom of St Laurence and Jesus Preaching at the Synagogue.

In the village, all that is left of the protective walls is the old door called the Prison Tower and there are some fine 15C and 16C jettied houses. From antiquity until an earthquake in 1749 caused the collapse of the quarry, red marble was extracted here.

9

Bagnères-de-Bigorre: two excursions

The **Bigorre** was an ancient county between the Pyrenees and the plain created in the mid-9C, its name derived from the ancient people, the Bigerri or Bigerriones, who populated the region during the 1C BC at the time of Julius Caesar. The pic du Midi de Bigorre is one of the best known peaks in the Pyrenees and the Cirque de Gavarnie is the most spectacular of many natural sites of great beauty. Bigorre, except for the Neste Valley, now corresponds roughly to the *département* of Hautes-Pyrénées. The main arterial road, the D935, follows the Adour valley which has been the main route to the mountains since ancient times. This itinerary is centred on Bagnères-de-Bigorre.

BAGNÈRES-DE-BIGORRE (pop. 9500, Tourist Information, tel: 62 95 50 71) is a pleasant watering hole in the wide Campan Valley on the banks of the Adour with all the usual characteristics of a spa town. Its mineral waters are used in the treatment of rheumatoid, psychosomatic and respiratory problems. All this, the proximity of the mountains, numerous hotels and campsites in the surrounding area make Bagnères a popular French family holiday centre.

The old town is bordered by Allées des Coustous (the site of a bustling market on Saturdays) to the east and Place des Thermes on the south-west. Conserved in a small garden at the angle of Rue des Thermes and Rue St-Jean are the Gothic portal of the Church of St-Jean, and the remains of the cloister of the Jacobins convent destroyed at the Revolution. Also in the area are the 15C tower of the Jacobins, **Tour de l'Horlorge**, and the **Maison de Jeanne-d'Albret**, 1539. The Church of **St-Vincent** (c 1366), north-east of the old quarter, has a 14C belfry gable and the remains of a fine Renaissance porch (1557), but the belfry and lateral chapels to the choir were not added until the 19C. There is a Baroque pulpit, and 20C Scenes of the Passion decorate the east end. The organ, rebuilt in 1708, has been entirely restored.

The extensive **gardens** on the slope on the west side of Place des Thermes colourfully frame the **spa buildings** which consist of the Neo-Classical marble façade of the thermal baths of 1823, added to in 1860, and the **Musée Salies**, built in 1930. The museum contains a modest collection of paintings organised thematically with works by Daubigny, Chasseriau, Isabey and Jonkind, the Orientalists against a bright-red background. There are also floral works by a local painter, Blanche Odin (1865–1957), and ceramics and sculptures. Look out for the open work wooden balconies, typical of the domestic architecture of Bagnères known as *style thermal*.

Excursions north-east of Bagnères: Escaladieu, Château de Mauvezin, Grottes de Gargas

Total distance: 38km (25 miles).

The **Baronnies** is an unspoilt section of the foothills of the Pyrenees spanning the area between the Adour and Nestes Valleys east of Bagnères, and defined by the D938 to the north. A Daedelian confusion of narrow routes links small communities built on the wooded slopes along the valleys of the Arros and the Luz. The point where these two rivers meet (10km east of Bagnères on the D938) was, c 1140, the site chosen by Cistercian monks originally from Morimond in Burgundy, for the **ABBEY OF ESCALADIEU**, on the D938, (tel: 62 39 13 13, every day in summer, weekends and holidays at other times). Although wilfully damaged and wasted from the 14C to the 16C and again in the late 18C, it still evokes the majestic tranquillity of all Cistercian abbeys. The restored buildings are used for concerts, conferences and exhibitions and part has been converted into the *Hostellerie de l'Abbaye de l'Escaladieu*, with moderately priced rooms and a gastronomic restaurant.

Enter through the 17C gatehouse to the west of the church. All that remains of the **cloister**, partly enclosed by buildings but completely devoid of galleries, is the ghost of its physical presence and an aura of claustral peace enhanced by swallows, a catalpa tree, some fragments of masonry and an 18C fountain.

To the south, bordering the road, the impressively simple **abbey church** (1143–63) has also retained its grace and harmony despite mutilation. A Latin cross of 44m long, the nave was reduced to six bays in the 14C when the apse was also destroyed. The pointed barrel-vaulted nave is flanked by interconnecting chapels which form rhythmically satisfying aisles when viewed along their length. The truncated east end was closed by a flat wall in the 16C and two flat-ended chapels built into each transept. In the 17C the south transept received the distinctive octagonal belfry which dominates the street elevation of the abbey church. The pillars of the nave show traces of the original 12C stone stalls which were replaced by wooden ones at the end of the 16C. Immediately next to the north door are the three round arched bays of the *armarium claustri*, the cloister library, and the sacristy, its original doorway and window almost intact. The layout of the **chapter house** is unusual, comprising six full and three half bays. The ribbed vaults are supported by four marble columns while a stone bench runs round the edge. It opens on to the cloister through a triple arched round headed doorway flanked by double windows. On the floor above, the narrow lancets with brick surrounds indicate the monks' dormitory, and under the blocked off staircase leading to it is the 14C prison.

After the *auditorium* or parlour is a corridor to the garden bounded by the river. A doorway in the north wing opens into an entrance with a 17C/18C staircase leading to the 17C rooms now used for exhibitions. The *scriptorium* or common room below makes a very attractive setting for the restaurant—a medieval menu can be ordered in advance. West of the entrance is the warming room, with a marvellous flagstone floor, the only room with a fireplace.

The ruins of the **Château de Mauvezin**, 2.5km away, are a very different kettle of fish. This grassy hillock, the site of an ancient oppidum and a Roman castrum above the village of Mauvezin, dominates the Arros valley, the Baronnies and the Tarbes–Toulouse route. The strategic advantages of the castle were not lost to the Counts of Bigorre in the 12C nor to the English when Aquitaine, including the Bigorre, came under the control of the Black Prince in 1360. After a long siege in 1373, the fortress capitulated. The golden boy of Foix, Gaston Fébus, took advantage of his power and the weakened circumstances of others to buy the seigniory in 1377, and rebuilt the château as a link in the chain of forts controlling traffic across the Midi.

The castle is a classic medieval stronghold with a square keep 34m high in the south side and a square courtyard of 30m square with powerfully buttressed walls enclosing a 12C cistern. It is now the headquarters of the *Escole Gastou Fébus*, a Gascon language society which saved Mauvezin from complete desuetude. It is an interesting site for the medieval fortification enthusiast, and a magnificent view from the top of the keep for everybody.

Stay on the D938 through La Barthe-de-Neste, until the D26 at St-Laurent to **Nestier**, 21km, then follow the signposts to **La Calvaire**, a curious enfilade of 12 bare stone oratories, the first one more-or-less underground, built up the grassy slope of Mont-Ares. Constructed in stages during the mid-19C they had almost disappeared under the brambles until a cleaning up operation was embarked on in 1984. At the summit is a simple altar in the ruins of a chapel. During the summer open-air plays are performed in the small modern amphitheatre outside the restored monastery, now a *gîte rural*, alongside the Calvary.

It is 4km on the D26 to the **Grottes de Gargas** at Aventignan (tel: 62 39 72 07/62 39 72 39, guided visit of 45 mins), 600m. While these caves do not have the overall appeal of, say, Pech Merle, nor paintings as outstanding as Niaux's, they are of considerable interest. The caves are in two parts and lit by electric light making the visit relatively easy. Along with the best, Gargas contains both geological concretions and a large number of prehistoric decorations but is most famous for the unusual and baffling series of more than **200 hands represented in silhouette**.

Prehistoric man used the caves over a long period during the last Ice Age, but the decoration is the work of late-Palaeolithic Cro-Magnon man, between 25,000 and 30,000 years ago. The hands, mainly in red or black, are in ten clusters of up to 43 silhouettes in the first gallery of the lower cave, but there are others further on, including the *Sanctuaire des Mains*. The silhouettes were created by projecting pigment from the mouth, but it is unclear whether the intention was to colour the hand or leave the imprint and the interpretation of these images remains enigmatic. A frequent feature of the hands is that one, sometimes two, fingers are incomplete or deformed although the thumb is never missing. In different parts of the caves are the **148 animal images** probably executed over a long period, but due to difficulty of access and their fragility only a few can be seen and the visitor has to make do with a number of reproductions. Some of the drawings, the majority of which represent oxen, bison and horses, are easy to decipher, whereas others are unfinished or piled up on each other like a tangled skein of thread.

Gargas is only 6km from St-Bertrand-de-Comminges on the D26.

South of Bagnères: Campan Valley, Col du Tourmalet, Barèges, Luz-St-Sauveur and Gavarnie

Total distance: 67km (49 miles).

Setting out southwards from Bagnères, the D935 follows the Adour valley past the **Grottes de Médous** (tel: 62 91 78 46/62 95 02 03, April to October), rich in exotic stalactites and stalagmites. The visit includes 200m by boat on an underground section of the Adour.

Beaudéan was the birthplace of Baron Dominique Larrey (1766–1842), surgeon to Napoléon and the Grande Armée, who invented the mobile hospital otherwise known as an ambulance. On the banks of a tributary of the Adour, the village is dominated by the 16C church with a distinctive slate-covered spire with pinnacles, typical of the region, and near the river is an old *lavoir*. The recently refurbished *Hôtel le Catala* (tel: 62 91 75 20) has comfortable and reasonable accommodation and a good restaurant even if the décor is somewhat idiosyncratic.

Campan (Tourist Information, tel: 62 91 70 36) is a pleasant village on the D935 with a fine 16C covered market and fountain, and a 16C/17C church. A pretty valley, with occasional houses with stepped gables, it opens out as it climbs up to **St-Marie-de-Campan** (857m), 12km from Bagnères, at the foot of the Col du Tourmalet, well-known to participants in the Tour de France cycle race. Here the road becomes the D918 and a right fork takes you over the Col de Tourmalet linking the valley of Haut Adour with the Vallée des Gaves. (The left fork crosses the Col d'Aspin, and the ski resort of Payolle, dropping down into the Aure Valley). The distant views are, as one would expect, spectacular and the pastures in the foreground are inhabited by grazing cattle and sheep, and a profusion of flowers including, in July, vast patches of dark blue Pyrenean iris.

La Mongie, on the very edge of the road, is a graceless modern ski resort with all the ironmongery and criss-crossing cables that the sport necessitates. The bright colours of the drifting parachutes of numerous parascenders and hang-gliders are far more acceptable. After 17km you reach the **Col du Tourmalet** (2115m). The **Pic du Midi-de-Bigorre** (2865m) dominates the landscape for miles around and is easily recognisable by the television mast and Observatory and makes an interesting visit, reached by a toll road (5.5km) from the Col.

Barèges (1250m, pop. 260, Tourist Information, tel: 62 92 68 19), 11km from the Col de Tourmalet, is a small, essentially modern, resort with plenty of modest hotels. It is the highest spa town in France and the oldest winter sports centre in the Pyrenees, established as such in 1921. Until the 18C it was difficult to reach because of poor roads but by the 18C Colbert exploited the potential of the spa waters for treating the military. The route over the Col was improved in 1730 and some years later the route through the gorges was built. The **thermal baths**, an elegant building in shades of grey, were built in 1861 around the time that the spa became fashionable, and in 1879 the young Toulouse Lautrec came here with his mother to recuperate from his first accident. It did him little benefit as he fell again resulting in the fracture of his right femur. Barèges is in the Valley of the Toÿ, giving rise to inevitable jokes about Toy Boys.

Continuing west, the villages of **Betpouey** (*pouey* means viewpoint and comes from the Toÿ-patois) and **Viey** have picturesque churches. At **Viella** the part-Romanesque **church** of St-Michel (if locked ask for the key at the *auberge*) has a recently restored retable, dated 1730, executed by father and son Soustre, sculptor-carpenters from Asté. Incorporating a profusion of putti and gilded grapevines, it is one of the richest in the Hautes-Pyrénées with no space left undecorated.

The main town in the Barèges Valley, 7km on, is **LUZ-ST-SAUVEUR** (pop. 5000, 711m, Tourist Information, tel: 62 92 81 60, Maison du Parc et de la Vallée, tel: 62 92 87 05). It is really two towns: Luz, and the spa of St-Sauveur to the south which benefited from the patronage of Napoléon III. He and the Empress Eugénie both suffered bad health, and spent some months at St-Sauveur. They endowed the town with a spectacular bridge completed in 1861, its single arch suspended 65m above the Gave de Pau.

Luz is a charming medieval town, with houses embellished with pearl-grey marble and slate roofs around the remarkable fortified **Church of St-André**. A primitive sanctuary, built here at the end of the 11C by the St-André family, was handed over to the Hospitallers of St-John of Jerusalem in the 14C. The Hospitallers fortified the church and dug a ditch around it to protect the inhabitants of the town from the *Miquelets*, Aragonese bandits. Amazingly this little church has retained many of its medieval characteristics including the battlemented wall, each merlon protected by a piece of schist held down with a large stone, completely surrounding the church and its graveyard. The arsenal tower to the north was built to defend the original entrance and in the vault of the passageway is a 14C fresco restored in 1867. The stepped gable belfry is typical of the Luz valley with two open arcades containing the bells, and at the angle of the nave and right transept is the high clock tower. Over the south porch is a high relief of Christ surrounded by the four Evangelists, badly damaged in 1793. Above is the monogram of Christ and the Hand of God painted on the voussoir above that; the capitals and bases of the columns supporting the tympanum are also decorated.

The mainly Romanesque church was tampered with during the 19C when a new church was mooted but the work never really got under way due to lack of funds. The most interesting things inside are the 12C font with a cover, the splendid 18C pulpit and confessionals not dissimilar to good-quality wardrobes. To the left of the entrance to the St-Joseph chapel a 13C child's tomb was for a long time used as a holy-water stoup. The 17C Chapel of Notre-Dame de la Pitié contains a collection of paintings and sculptures including a 12C Virgin and Child and a 15C Pietà.

Luz still commemorates the traditional transhumance of sheep from the high summer pastures with the *Foire aux Cotelettes* in September. This is a colourful festival originally arranged to coincide with a livestock market on St Michael's Day (29 September).

The D921 bifurcates after 19.5km at the village of **Gèdre** (1000m); the right fork after passing the rocky disorder of the Chaos de Coumély continues climbing to **Gavarnie** (Tourist Information, tel: 62 92 49 10), another 10.5km, which at 1365m is the highest village in the Pyrenees. The crowds do not, however, come for the village but for its deservedly famous natural site, the great **CIRQUE DE GAVARNIE**. A sheer wall of snow-capped rock, it is a vast natural amphitheatre averaging 1676m in depth, 890m wide at the base and fanning out in three stages to 11km between Pic de Pinède and Pics Gabiétous, it was created some 20,000 years ago when an immense

glacier slid down the valley towards Lourdes scooping out t
limestone rocks. Its crest is the border between Spain and Franc
it are a group of peaks over 3000m and across the border in Spain is **Mont Perdu** (3355m).

Gavarnie developed the time of the pilgrimages to Santiago when a Commandery was established for the protection of travellers. The mainly 14C church, originally the hospice chapel, stands on the old pilgrim route. The village, also a ski resort, has eight hotels and two campsites and was an important centre for Pyreneanism in the 18C and 19C. It is an easy walk from the village to the Hostellerie du Cirque (1570m)—but there is alternative transport on donkey or horseback—to view at closer quarters the amphitheatre and the Grande Cascade, the highest waterfall in Europe, crashing out from the back of the cirque to drop some 423m. There is a vast choice of walks, some more demanding than others, and a ten hour trek into Spain and back through the gap known as the Brèche de Roland, supposedly carved out of the rock by Roland's faithful sword Durandal.

Just south of the cirque at 1400m are the **Botanic Gardens** of the **Parc National**, at their best in June and July when the 400 or so species of flora of the High Valley of the Gave de Pau are in flower. Also in July the cirque provides the backdrop to a music and drama spectacular.

10

Lourdes and the Lavedan Valleys

The wide valley of the Gave de Pau flows through one of the most beautiful and thriving areas of the Pyrenees, the Lavedan, between Lourdes and Spain in the western part of the Bigorre. The Lavedan consists of seven valleys: Barèges is the largest, then four on the left bank of the Gave de Paul, Cauterets, Estrem de Salles, Bats-Surguère, and Azun. Two lesser valleys are the Néez and Davant-Aygue on the right bank. The lower Lavedan is pleasantly green, with pastures and wide-leafed trees but further into the higher terrain after Soulom, where the valley divides, the scenery becomes more rugged, the vegetation changes and there are spectacular waterfalls, culminating in the best known natural site in the whole range, the Cirque de Gavarnie on the Spanish border, described in Route 9.

LOURDES (pop. 18,000, Tourist Information, tel: 62 94 25 64) is the principal place of pilgrimage in Europe, the product of an intense veneration of the Virgin in the Pyrenees, and an impressive promotional exercise in much the same way that elevated Santiago de Compostela in Spain to the most important European shrine in the Middle Ages.

The history of Lourdes began on the limestone promontory dominating the Gave de Pau where in the 11C the Counts of Bigorre built a stronghold. It was subsequently occupied by the English and then by Gaston Fébus, Count of Foix, before the region reverted to the French by the Treaty of the Pyrenees in 1659. Lourdes would probably have remained a fairly insignificant town but in 1858 its fortunes were completely reversed when

Bernadette Soubirous, a poor and devout child of 14, out collecting fire-wood, received 18 visions of the Virgin of the Immaculate Conception in the Grotto of Massabielle beside the Gave. The statistics concerning Lourdes since then are, to say the least, miraculous. Over five million pilgrims, many sick or disabled, from 130 countries pour into the valley from the Sunday before Easter to mid-October, by plane (to Tarbes), by specially adapted trains, or by road.

There are more hotels in Lourdes than any other town in France after Paris (18,000 rooms in 350 hotels and guesthouses), ranging from very reason-able to luxurious, plus 30 camp sites; even the sheer organisation of such numbers is quite a feat. The extent of the facilities makes it an excellent centre for touring; conversely, it can be a difficult place for the non-pilgrim observer. The material exploitation, from the tacky souvenir shops to the risk of pickpocketing, is probably little different from pilgrimage towns through the ages, although the McDonalds and the waxworks add a purely 20C dimension. Nevertheless, even as a non-participating observer, the experience of the youth Mass on a Saturday evening or the torch-light procession every evening at 20.45h, and the overwhelming atmosphere of solidarity of people with a common cause, is contagiously moving.

The town is divided by the Gave de Pau. The old town, clustered at the foot of the medieval castle, is to the east, and the Marian City, built around the Grotto of Massabielle, to the west. A visit to the **old town** is centred around the castle and the sites connected with the Soubirous family. The latter include the 19C parish church of Sacré-Coeur in Rue Lafitte, which shelters the Romanesque font used for Bernadette's baptism on 9 January 1844; the **Cachot de Bernadette**, Rue des Petits-Fossés, where she had her first vision in 1888; in **Rue Bernadette-Soubirous** the **Moulin de Boly**, birthplace of the saint on 7 January 1844 and her home from 1858 until she entered the convent in 1863; and also the **Moulin Lacadé**, which her father ran, and which Bernadette visited until 1866 when she left for the Convent of St-Gildard at Nevers where she died in 1879.

The **Château-Fort de Lourdes** is home to the **Musée Pyrénéen** (tel: 62 94 02 04, open all year), entrances on Rue du Bourg and Rue le Bondidier, the latter has a lift. The museum constitutes an interesting resumé of the prehistory and palaeontology of the Pyrenees, its natural history and local traditions, and is, therefore, a good introduction to the mountain culture. From the terrace of the château the whole of the Marian City is clearly laid out before you with the fast-moving Gave below.

The castle dates from after 1407 and was modified in 1590. It subsequently became a prison and was damaged at the beginning of the 19C but restoration work began in 1828 and the museum was installed in 1922. An eclectic collection, it has 18 rooms around a courtyard attractively laid out with a rock garden and models of regional houses. The Ramon de Carbon-nières room is dedicated to Pyreneeists who conquered the high peaks from 1796 to 1956, including Count Henry Russell who made 33 ascents of Vignemale (3298m) between 1861 and 1904. The rural life section has curious *cires de deuil*, spaghetti-like coiled candles still used in some villages at funerals to represent the dead and to protect the living; and there are elements of medieval architecture.

Boulevard de la Grotte is the main route to the sanctuaries. The Esplanade des Processions was built in 1875 to accommodate the vast numbers who gather here, bifurcating into raised walkways which sweep up to the two superimposed basilicas at the apex. The neo-Gothic Church of the Immaculate Conception, consecrated in 1876, is built immediately above the **Massabielle Grotto** where the Virgin of the Immaculate Conception appeared to Bernadette. On the lower level is the neo-Byzantine Basilica of the Rosary designed by Durand-Hardy, 1883–89. In the grotto a sentimental 19C marble statue of the Virgin by Carrate watches over the continuous file of the faithful. Two further basilicas, cavernous, concrete, and functional were designed this century to accommodate thousands of worshippers, wheelchairs and stretchers. The oval underground Saint Pius X Basilica, consecrated in 1958 by Cardinal Roncalli, later Pope John XXIII, resembles a vast fallout shelter and can hold nearly 30,000 pilgrims. A desultory attempt to cheer it up are *Gemmail, art de lumière* decorations, an impasto stained glass technique, by Jean-Paul and Germaine Sala-Malherbe. More recent is the Church of St-Bernadette opposite the grotto, inaugurated in 1988, made up of two adjacent amphitheatres.

Probably worse than seeing Lourdes heaving with pilgrims and onlookers, helpers and the merely curious, is to see it empty. Without the emotional content it is very jaded indeed. A way to distance yourself from Lourdes without using a car is to take the **Petit Train** to the funicular station of the **Pic du Jer**, on the N21 south of Lourdes.

Excursion to Lestelle-Bétharram, Arrens, Aucun, St-Savin, Cauterets

Total distance: 102km (64 miles).

Follow the Gave de Pau 10km west from Lourdes on the D937. **St-Pé** has a pretty square with arcades. The remains of a Romanesque abbey were incorporated into the parish church. The nearby (2.5km) **Grottes de Bétharram** (Easter–Oct), a spectacular five-level network of caverns, are visited partly by boat and partly by little train.

In another 2.5km is the village of **Lestelle-Bétharram**, *département* of Pyrénées-Atlantiques, a site of pilgrimage for 700 or 800 years and, like Lourdes, dedicated to the Virgin. It was frequently visited by Bernadette Soubirous. The **chapel** was badly damaged by Protestant troops in 1569 and rebuilt between 1614 and 1710 at a period when an increasing number of miracles revitalised the site. The exterior is grey marble decorated with white marble statues of the Virgin and Child and the four Evangelists. In contrast the interior is heavily ornate, every surface decorated with gilt and paintings, 1690–1710. On the front panels of the tribune above the west entrance are scenes of the early miracles performed in the chapel, below are depictions of the ancestors of Christ. The organ case is 1710 but the organ itself was replaced by Napoléon III as the original was damaged in 1793. The 19C statue of Notre-Dame de Beau-Rameau by Alexandre Renoir on the main altar evokes the miracle of a drowning girl saved by the Virgin who holds a branch out to her. Another apparition of the Virgin to local shepherds is the subject of the retable (1620–30) in the south aisle chapel. In contrast to all the Baroque flamboyance is the Second-Empire mausoleum of St-Michel Garicoïts, Bernadette Soubirous' mentor. Covered by a glass dome, it was designed by the architect Gabriel Andral and consecrated in 1928. There is also a small local history museum, and on the hill outside a Calvary 1840–45.

The old bridge near the chapel is dated 1687 and the D226 alongside is a pleasant drive through woods and open countryside to join the D126. Follow this south towards Ferrières, arriving after 42km at the **Col du Soulor** (1474m) to enjoy, weather permitting, splendid views particularly at the Col itself, a favourite stopping place with a rustic chalet-café and local cheese for sale. The D918 from the higher Col d'Aubisque (1870m) joins the D126 here and wiggles its way 8km down into the Val d'Azun.

The **Church of St-Pierre** at **Arrens** probably dates from the 13C, the end of the Romanesque period in this region. The porch has a Romanesque tympanum with Christ surrounded by the symbols of the four Evangelists and some Gothic decoration. In the graveyard wall to the right of the entrance are the remains of a Gothic window protecting the *bénitier des cagots*, the font or stoup used by a group of medieval outcasts, who existed on the fringes of society participating at Mass only from a distance. Also in the surrounding wall is an elegant Renaissance window. The church furnishings include a large polychromed wooden statue of Christ, possibly 13C, above the Romanesque altar in the north chapel, and a Renaissance consuls' bench.

More spectacular, but tricky to find as it is surrounded by buildings on the hillock at the junction of the D105, 800m south of the village, is the 18C **chapel of Notre-Dame-de-Pouey-Laün**. It was erected on the site of a pilgrim hospice built into the solid granite of the hill. The exterior of the domed chapel is soberly classical, but the interior is something else. Not surprisingly, it is known as the **Chapelle Dorée** (gilded chapel) because of the abundance of gold leaf used on the ornate Baroque interior, the work of the Ferrère brothers from Asté. The retable of the main altar is resplendent with vine-entwined cabled columns and an Assumption on the pediment above a statue of Our Lady of Pouey-Laün. The retables of the chapels, dedicated to St Anne and St Joseph, are slightly less emphatic but nevertheless very splendid. The overall effect, including the woodwork of the choir and other furnishings, is joyously over-the-top.

The D105 follows the Arrens valley, entering the **Parc National des Pyrénées** at **Porte d'Arrens**, a region of romantic mountain lakes where in springtime the valley becomes a multi-coloured flowered carpet.

The much-modified 12C–13C church of **Marsous** contains a large 16C polychrome Christ on the Cross, some 17C and 18C woodwork, retables and paintings.

Still on the D918, at **Aucun** (3km) is Monsieur André Fourcade, a local personality, who owns the village shop-cum-bar and created the **Musée Montagnard du Lavedan** in 1963 (visits at 17.00, but best to telephone: 62 97 12 03). Dressed in plus-fours, he will regale you (in French) with tales of local history, traditions and wildlife, using his vast collection of tools and implements as visual aids including a *tour solaire*, or miniature sundial, of 1649, used by shepherds. Next to the museum is the little **Church of St-Félix**, part 11C and part Gothic. Above the south door is an 11C monogram of Christ with a bird and a lamb, possibly relocated when the church altered in the 15C. The apse, with billeted cornice and simple carvings, is also 11C. On the west is the entrance to the old cemetery and a porch used by the *coussous*, municipal authorities, for meetings, and the doorway and font once reserved for the *cagots*. On the north are two baptismal vats used for the immersion of ailing newborn babies. The most interesting pieces are the 16C baptismal **font** and holy-water **stoup**, both in granite. The former is decorated with curious mundane scenes, such as a goat chewing a tree, and an acrobat on his hands;

the latter has even stranger primitive carvings of animals and figures. Another 2km, at **Arcizans-dessus**, is an extraordinary concentration of tiny, rustic mills, some restored and fitted out (tel: 62 97 52 54, for guided visit). Continue for 6.5km on the D918.

Argelès-Gazost (Tourist Information, tel: 62 97 00 25), Sub-Préfecture of the Hautes-Pyrénées, at the junction of three valleys (and the D918, D921 and N21) capitalised on its potential as a spa in the late 19C and is now crowded out on market day (Tuesday). The old town, built on the flank of the hill, has some interesting streets and 16C and 17C houses, and near the 17C Tour Mendaigne (next to the Tourist Office) is a sunny terrace overlooking the Gave de Pau with a *table d'orientation*.

3km south of Argelès is **Saint-Savin**: well-kept houses and *embans* or *couverts* (arcades) and three hotels around the irregular *Place* look down to the valley some 580m below. The **abbey** was a victim of the Revolution but the comfortingly solid Romanesque church still stands guard at the north, although it was never a fortress. Its proportions were altered in the 14C when the walls were raised, making it more elegant, less squat. It is enlivened by the play of light and shade on the *mirandes*, the buttresses and the octagonal drum of the belfry and the distinctive candle-snuffer roof.

The Romanesque **church** (1140–60), a regular Latin cross with a main apse and two absidal chapels, sturdy pillars and buttresses, was covered with a timber and slate roof in the 14C and the belfry was raised at the same period. On the **tympanum** of the main west doorway is a rare image of Christ in Majesty dressed in priestly garments, surrounded by the symbols of the four Evangelists. The south door (19C) is decorated with a Romanesque chrism, and on the cornice of the south apsidal is a tetramorph.

The church has a remarkable number of interesting **furnishings**. Inside the west door is a ten-sided Aragonese stoup, 1140, and font (10C and 18C). Further into the nave, opposite the 17C pulpit, is an impressive 14C Spanish-style Crucifixion carved in wood and polychromed wood. The nave is dominated by the Renaissance organ (1557) with 16C and 18C decoration including three mechanised wooden masks below it activated by the organ pedals. In the south transept is a Romanesque font called the *Bénitier des Cagots* carved in granite and supported by two little figures back to back. The St-Catherine altar has a 12C table and Renaissance retable of the Descent from the Cross, and in the chapel of St-Peter there are an 8C table and 19C tabernacle. The main altar is the 11C black marble tomb of St-Savin and behind it stands part of a 14C gilded Tower of the Eucharist. Either side of the choir are two large 15C panels with paintings on wood of scenes from the life of St-Savin and his miracles. The 28 choir stalls are walnut, and the arms of Mgr de Foix, Abbot 1540–1606, are on the officiate's stall. There are also 15C and 17C paintings. The north apsidal chapel, dedicated to the Virgin, has two Renaissance retables, and a Virgin and Child in wood, the altar and paintings are all 17C, and the frescoes are 19C.

A door from the north transept leads to the sacristy and the 12C **chapter house**, the only part of the monastic buildings still intact, with simply carved capitals and bases. The window capitals have shallow reliefs of bearded heads facing inwards and masks towards the cloister, and a variety of symbolic images. There is a small museum of treasures including a 15C reliquary in the form of a château with turrets at the angles, three outstanding 12C statues of the Virgin and Child and masonry from the former cloister. What remains of the cloister and monastic buildings are mainly reconstructions providing rooms and offices for the Mairie.

South of St-Savin on the D13 is the **Chapelle de Piétat**, 11C–14C and 18C, which contains a 15C painted wooden statue of Notre-Dame de l'Espérance, fragments of 14C murals, and 18C murals, *le Jardin de la Vièrge*.

The D13 drops down into the **Pierrefitte-Nestalas** where the road divides, the left fork, the D921, continuing to Luz-St-Sauveur and the Vallée de Barèges (see Route 9). The right, the D920, leads in 13.5km to **CAUTERETS** (pop. 1100, Tourist Information, tel: 62 92 50 27), the best known spa town in the Pyrenees for many centuries with a formidable array of **thermal springs**. It can also claim the longest list of illustrious visitors, particularly of the literary variety: Jeanne de Navarre and Gaston Fébus in the 14C; Rabelais in the 16C; and Marguerite de Navarre, sister of François I, reputedly wrote part of her *Heptaméron* (1559) here. A new influx of the late and great, such as J-J. Rousseau, benefited from a new road in 1763; but the greatest era was the 19C when Romantic fervour for nature and the picturesque, combined with the patronage of King Louis of Holland and Queen Hortense, drew about 25,000 *curistes* a year, helped by improved transport, monumental hotels and the exploitation of further thermal springs. Victor Hugo wrote about Cauterets in 1843. By 1882 the community reached nearly 2000 and the first tarmacked road in France was built between the Raillère and the Griffons Baths in 1903. Baudelaire, Alfred Lord Tennyson, Chateaubriand, George Sand, Edward VII, Gabriel Fauré and Claude Debussy all came. After a decline the town is again thriving and a **ski resort** was established in 1964 in the cirque du Lys (1850–1250m) reached from Cauterets by cable car.

On the edge of the Pyrenean National Park, Cauterets has one of the five **Maisons du Parc des Pyrénées** opened in 1974. At 1000m and on the river, this is a bright and lively centre. The old train station, a delightful wooden building (1897) in a combination of alpine and western styles, can be visited but no longer functions as a station. There are numerous public **gardens**, the most famous of them the Esplanade des Oeufs; many **thermal baths**; a memorial to Marguerite de Navarre, 1492–1549, near the Neo-Classical gold and grey Thermes de César in the older part of town; Belle Epoque grandeur on Boulevard Latapie-Flurin; and to top it all is Princess Galitzine's villa in avenue du Mamelon-Vert.

There is a vast choice of **walks** either from Cauterets centre or by using the cable-cars, and more further along the D920. Eight kilometres, several hairpins, and numerous cascades later, through alpine scenery and rocks, highlighted by masses of wild flowers, is **Pont d'Espagne**, the start of more walks in the National Park and the country of the legendary Lac de Gaube and Henry Russell.

11

Tarbes and the Lannemezan

TARBES (pop. 50,000, Tourist Information, 3 Cours Gambetta, tel: 62 51 30 31) the capital of the Bigorre and the second largest agglomeration in the Midi-Pyrénées, is a somewhat characterless garrison town relieved by fountains and green areas. A Roman settlement developed here in the

Adour valley on the important Bayonne–Toulouse route, and after the usual changes of fortune, it is now the most dynamic industrial centre in the region well served by road (A64, N117, D935, N21), rail and air connections. Its Thursday market is particularly lively and it is worth visiting for its parks, the best being Jardin Massey, and for the Haras National (National Stud Farm) founded in the 18C.

On Foot. From Place de Verdun (parking) go west on Rue Abbé Torné. The characteristic building material of the Tarbes plain is smooth round pebbles, with stone or brick chaining, often arranged in herring-bone pattern. The **Cathédrale de la Sède**, begun at the end of the 12C or early 13C, and extensively restored, is an interesting combination of brick, stone and pebble, and a mixture of styles from Romanesque at the east with a massive octagonal belfry, to Neo-Classical at the west. On the south flank are the remains of a Romanesque cloister. The interior décor is predominantly 18C, its main features are the wooden stalls and

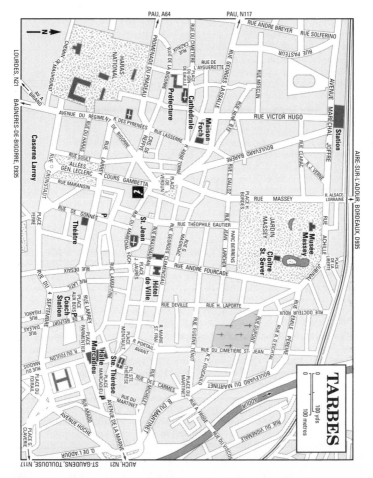

panelling, the wrought iron and chequered floor, and the altar and baldaquin by Marc Arcis using coloured Pyrenean marble. Above the crossing is a an octagonal lantern on pendentives. The restoration of the 17C organ was completed in 1993.

One block north of Rue Abbé Torné at 2, Rue de la Victoire, is the birthplace of Field-Marshall Foch (1851–1929), Commander of the Allied Forces in 1918, now a museum (tel: 62 93 19 02).

North of Place de Verdun, the **Jardin Massey** is a 14ha green oasis bequeathed to the town by Placide Massey (1777–1853), naturalist and director of the Orangerie at Versailles. The park has a collection of exotic trees, a Wallace fountain and several sculptures, including the bust of the writer Théophile Gautier (1811–72, born in Tarbes), by his daughter Judith, and of the poet Jules Laforgue (1860–87) by Michelet. It also contains four galleries of a 14C **cloister** salvaged from the former Benedictine Abbey of St-Sever-de-Rustan destroyed by Protestant troops in 1573 and sold at the Revolution. There does not appear to be a logical explanation to the order of the capitals which was probably upset when they were moved. The iconography includes scenes from the Old Testament, the Creation of Adam and Eve and original sin, the Birth of Christ, the Passion and martyrdoms, as well as allegorical themes and foliate capitals.

Massey's house, designed by Jean-Jacques Latour, was begun in 1852 at a time when Hispanic styles were in vogue, and is now a museum with two distinct sections. The **Fine Arts Museum** (tel: 62 36 31 49), a rather dusty affair, has an archaeological section in the first room with a remarkable Bronze Age mask of the local god Ergé. The collection of European paintings from the 16C to the present is arranged by school and chronologically, with pride of place being given to a painting by Utrillo (1883–1955) *La Préfecture des Hautes-Pyrénées à Tarbes en 1935*. Also of note are *Adoration of the Magi*, School of Jan Scorel, 1475–1562, some pleasing 16/17C Dutch and French portraits, and landscapes by William Didier-Pouget (1864–1959). The other half is made over to the **International Museum of the Hussars**: a dashing array of arms, uniforms and models of the history of the Hussars conveys the glamour of this élite regiment.

The main commercial quarter of Tarbes is east of Place de Verdun. **Rue Brauhauban** is a pleasant pedestrian street lined with some good 18C and 19C houses among them Gautier's birthplace at No. 2. The Collegiate Church of St-Jean was first mentioned in 1268 but the church as it stands dates from the 15C, with a massive tower built later and 19C additions. **Place Montault** has an imposing fountain (1874). **Place du Marcadieu**, dominated by the grand Duvignau fountain, 1896, evoking the four valleys of Bigorre—Aure, Bagnères, Argelès and Tarbes—is at the heart of the market quarter with its the splendid *halle*, a typical construction of the 1880s in iron.

The **Haras National** (tel: 62 34 44 59/62 51 30 31, open weekday pm, July–Sept, end Oct and Christmas) is south-west of Place de Verdun, the entrance on the south side. The cavalry stud was established in Tarbes at the order of Napoléon I. This is a refreshing place even for the non-horse lover as it is graced with a beautiful group of Empire buildings designed by the architects Devèze, Larrieu and Ratouin in 1881. The light and airy stables, for pampered horses, have recently been restored using original materials: pebbles and cobblestones for the floor, marble for the troughs, loose-boxes (some of the first examples) in solid oak, and a curved ceiling in chestnut, with false-marbling reproduced inside and out. Equestrian events are held here regularly.

Excursion to St-Sever-de-Rustan and Notre-Dame de Garaison

Total distance: 76km (48 miles).

This is a gentle, unsensational route, far from the madding crowds at any time, with superb examples of rural architecture in traditional building materials. In the summer it is green and peaceful but in the winter, when the fields have been ploughed, the farm buildings of mud brick and plaster become one again with the raw siennas and ochres of the soil. A fascinating contrast is the wholehearted enthusiasm for the use of paint and gilt in post-Reformation church décor.

Leave Tarbes on the D21 east, via Séméac, through quiet countryside, fields of maize, pebble walls against a mountainous backdrop, and after 16km turn right on the D20 to the hamlet of **Moulédous**. Here resides a listed Baroque **retable** of traditional style, returned to its original glitzy splendour in 1982–86, issuing perhaps from either or both the workshops of the two families of artists, Ferrère and Soustre, from Asté (south of Bagnères). The central panel represents the Assumption of the Virgin with a Saint-Bishop and St John the Baptist either side, and God the Father above flanked by St John and St Matthew (if locked, enquire at the house opposite or at the café, tel: 62 35 73 19).

Return to the D14, and go 7.5km north, through **Chelle-Debat** where there are examples of rough textured pebble walls and wooden lattice-work haylofts, and on, 5km, to the former **Abbey of St-Sever-de-Rustan** (tel: 62 96 63 93, every pm, summer; Sun & BH pm winter) on the banks of the Arros River. A Benedictine community existed here early in the 11C and seems to have flourished until the 14C when it was overtaken by the Hundred Years War, then abused by secular abbots, and finally overrun by Protestant troops in 1573. The restoration was begun in 1646 by the Congregation of St-Maur, and in the 18C the abbey received temporal decoration typical of the period and of the St-Maur abbots; but the Revolution brought everything to a halt and parts of the abbey were sold off.

The cloister ended up in Jardin Massey in Tarbes and the organ in the church of Castelnau-Magnoac, but there are still the church, the sacristy and monastic buildings to visit. The Romanesque portal in the south wall of the abbey church has been in this position since the 18C. Part of the nave is also Romanesque with a round-arched window curiously inserted in the south buttress. The carved capitals, like the storiated capitals of the nave, have stylistic links with the late 11C carvings at St-Sernin, Toulouse. A Gothic-style east end seems to have been hastily and clumsily added during rebuilding in the 16C, and the church bears the traces of several stages of modification or adaptation. The major legacies of the 18C are the monastic buildings, some beautiful wood panelling in the sacristy, the monumental staircase in the south-west of the former cloister and some fine stucco-work.

14km south-west on the D6 is **Trie-sur-Baïse** where one of the largest pork markets in France takes place every Tuesday and which is also notorious for the annual competition to find the person who can utter a sound most like a pig! This *bastide* was founded in 1323 by Jean de Trie and has kept its original layout despite pillage by the English in 1356 and destruction in 1569 during the Religious Wars. The cloister of the oldest church belonging to a Carmelite Monastery has been reconstructed in the Cloisters Museum,

New York. The very large central square has a graceful 19C iron **halle** encompassing the stone Mairie. On the south side the parish church, **Notre-Dame des Neiges**, was begun in 1444, the date of the peace treaty between the English and the Counts of Foix and Bigorre. The massive porch-belfry of the church has a stair tower with arrow slits, part of the town defences, a Flamboyant doorway on the north, and 19C spire.

Look out for examples of buildings using adobe (sun-baked brick) some-times in conjunction with fired brick or pebbles around **Castelnau-Magnoac** (D632 going east, 16km), an appealing market town (Saturday) with half-timbered houses and a Gothic collegiate church (there is a light switch in the choir). In the church the 18C wooden stalls with carved ends and misericords have acquired a rich patina, and the 18C organ is from St-Sever-de-Rustan. It also contains a rare late-15C sculpture of the Virgin suckling the Infant Jesus.

Head **south** on the D929 (direction Lannemezan) and turn off after 5km on the D8 through **Monléon-Magnoac**, where against the wall of the church stands one of the old town gates and inside are wood carvings from Notre-Dame de Garaison. The sanctuary of **Notre-Dame de Garaison** (usually open, tel: 62 99 41 55/62 99 40 26) belongs to the long tradition of Marian devotion practised throughout the Pyrenees, notably along the pilgrim route from Notre-Dame de Rocamadour in the Lot to Montserrat in Catalonia, passing by St-Savin, Aragnouet, Luz, Bourisp and Gavarnie. Garaison was the site of a cult dedicated to Notre-Dame de Septembre in the Middle Ages which was destroyed in 1623. In 1520 a young shepherd-ess, Anglèze de Sagasan, received visions of the Virgin near the fountain of Garaison telling her to create a new chapel and this was indeed under-taken in the 16C to become an important centre of veneration in the 18C and 19C.

The Gothic-style sanctuary, built in brick with rib vaults, is entirely decorated with 16C and 17C **murals** and has furnishings from the 15C to the 18C. It is part of a stunning group of buildings—now used as a Catholic boys' school—and built around a semi-formal garden. The 17C main door, graciously painted in shades of blues, is a foretaste of the unusual but colourful decoration of the church. The narthex has paintings dated 1699 inspired by a popular book about Garaison published in 1646, and naïve paintings of the appearance of the Virgin, dressed in white, to Anglèze de Sagasan, which anticipated by some 200 years the apparitions of the Virgin at Lourdes to Bernadette de Soubirous. There are also scenes of the history of the sanctuary including a file of the devout across the ribs of the vault, and medallions added in the 18C. The tempera ex voto paintings on the walls of the nave are reminders of some of the many miracles and cures associated with the site and represented on the vaults is the local martyr, St-Sabin. The paintings (c 1560–80) of the chapels represent St John the Baptist and St Catherine, and on the vault of the first chapel north are medallions of the prophets including Isaiah and Ezekiel. The sacristy, through the door to the left of the choir (there is a light switch on the right before the steps), is also completely covered with paintings in tempera. Built c 1612, the paintings were carried out in 1618.

Return to the D929 via the D34 and Lassales through woods which smell of wild mint in July. Here there is another superb barn, with star and diamond shaped timbers. The road takes you south across the plain to **Lannemezan** (13km), the old name for the middle land, with the Pyrenees in the distance.

12

Mirande and the bastides of the Astarac

Total distance: 119km (74 miles).

This tour takes you to a sample of the many Gascon *bastides* south and west of Mirande accessible from, or on, the N21, as well as a couple of small, rustic churches.

MIRANDE (pop. 4150, Tourist Information tel: 62 66 68 10), on the banks of the Baïse, one of the largest and best preserved of the *bastides*, would make a good touring centre for the southern Gers. It has a church with a massive porch-tower straddling the street, and a modest museum-art gallery. There is a market on Monday and a *marché aux gras* (foie gras) in the winter. It was conceived in 1281 as a *paréage* between the Counts of Astarac and the Abbots of Berdoues, and was the old capital of the Astarac a small medieval fiefdom between the provinces of Armagnac, Fezensac and Bigorre, from the 10C to the 15C. Mirande was a garrison town and Alain-Fournier (1886–1914), author of *Le Grand Meaulnes*, did his officer training here. The large square is surrounded by arcades in warm yellowish stone and has a pretty bandstand in the middle.

The small and refreshingly well presented **Musée des Beaux-Arts et Arts Décoratifs** (10.00–12.00, 15.00–18.00) in a purpose-built gallery of 1983 next to the Tourist Information Office, was created in 1832 from the private collection of Joseph Delort. It has Italian, Flemish and French paintings (15C–19C), including a number of charming portraits and works attributed to Largillière and J.B. van Loo; and among the landscapes are one or two from the School of Barbizon. There is an important group of faïence from the main French producers and from the south-west and a few pieces of medieval scuplture.

The hope that Mirande would be raised to the status of episcopal see accounts for the **church** of grandiose proportions begun in 1409 and dedicated to Ste-Marie. The most original part of the building, which had to be fitted into an area surrounded by already existing streets and houses, is the west tower and porch. The road runs under the porch, above which flying buttresses support the four-level belfry with turrets and a complex roof. Flying buttresses are used on the north and south elevations, unusual in this part of the world, and although the church gives an impression of homogeneity, only the openings on the southern façade are original. In each façade is an identical portal with a statue of St Anthony on the north and St John the Baptist on the south. The Flamboyant west portal, now closed, was heavily restored in 1877–80. The church contains some 15C glass, the Virgin and Child and St Michael slaying the Dragon, with the arms of the town, in the St-Sacrament chapel. The remainder of the glass was made by Thibault of Clermont-Ferrand in 1860–61.

Go south on the D939 through **Berdoues** past the remains of the ancient abbey (now privately owned) that helped found Mirande, and after about 6km turn left towards **Belloc** and almost immediately right. After a short distance you see isolated in a field the tiny rustic **chapel of St-Clamens**. Ask for the key at the farmhouse surrounded by trees down the lane opposite the path to the chapel. This remarkably unaltered 11C chapel was built on the foundations of a Gallo-Roman temple and, to prove it, under the makeshift porch on the south is a white marble pagan funerary monument, discovered in 1886, decorated with reliefs and an inscription to Arulianus, possibly the owner of a Gallo-Roman villa. The miniscule windows of the apse are flanked inside and out by 8C or 9C capitals and columns and inside are 12C and 16C wall paintings in a perilous state.

In front of the altar is an outstandingly beautiful white antique marble **sarcophagus**, probably 4C, found on the site c 1820. The carving on the lid is a possible allegory of the passing of life represented by a wheel pushed by four winged figures with a winged head at each corner. The base is more deeply engraved with a portrait of the defunct in a medallion supported by four figures, and either side of it are scenes representing the seasons. The weatherbeaten Gothic font was formerly kept outside, and there are two 18C statues.

Continue to St-Michel on the D939, turn left on the D127 and right at the sign after about 7.5km to the remote 16C **chapel** of **Theux**, principally for its marvellous site on a ridge between the Baïsole and the Petite Baïse. There are some superb **farm buildings** around here, built in chequerboard patterns using adobe bricks and pebbles.

The D127 **west from St-Michel** leads to **Miélan** (10km), another *bastide*, founded in 1284, which was destroyed by the English in 1362, but benefited from the 18C route from Paris to Bagnères-de-Bigorre. It has an attractive arcaded square with some 14C jettied houses.

The range of the Pyrenees unfolds before you on a clear day from the **Puntous de Laguian**, 6km west on the N21. At around 400m it is the highest point in the Gers. Clear day or not, take the D156/D16 from Miélan (8km) to **Tillac**, an absolute gem of a 13C *castelnau* with a narrow arcaded street bordered with timber-framed houses, two ancient town gateways with towers, and a 14C church with, if you are unwise enough to press the button, a recorded message and guided visit. The **church**, c 1334, which succeeded the chapel of the château, was badly damaged by fire in 19C destroying the 17C timber roof. The choir stalls on the left are 18C but the rest are neo-Gothic. There is a gilded retable (1741) from the famous Ferrère workshop in the Asté (Pyrenees) and behind it a ciborium with Renaissance décor.

Rather than take the main road, return to the D156 via **St-Christaud** (11.5km) where, on a knoll, a great Gothic (c 1250) brick heap with diamond openings was built to watch over the pilgrim route. From here take the D159/D943 (9km) to **Marciac** (pop. 1119, Tourist Information tel: 62 09 30 55/62 08 21 04) where, unlikely as it may seem in this conventional, sleepy *bastide*, crowds have gathered every August since 1979 for the annual **jazz festival**. The main concerts are held under a zebra-striped marquee on the rugby pitch, and the effervescence bubbles over into the arcaded *place* and streets during the day. The idea is contagious and other towns in the Midi-Pyrénées—Montauban, Albi, Souillac and Villefranche-deRouergue—have their jazzy moments. Marciac has a large lake with hotel and campsite, and numerous other amenities.

The crocketed spire of **Notre-Dame de Marciac** marks one of the loveliest churches in the Gers, built in yellow stone in the 14C to the east of the main square. The spire, which stands on a square tower, was completed in 1865 to a height of approximately 90m, making it the highest in the Gers. There are matching early Flamboyant portals on the north and south and a narthex was added in the 15C and closed by a wrought iron grille in the 18C. The entrance is through the south door. The church has a four-bay nave with aisles with large screened chapels flanking the choir. There is a shallow pentagonal apse and two smaller chapels in the east. The western part of the nave was partly rebuilt after suffering in the hands of Protestant iconoclasts in the 16C when the original octagonal piers and pointed arches were replaced by cylindrical pillars and round arches. The church was vaulted in 1869 when some restoration was accomplished. The nave is lit by a series of rose windows in the clerestory.

There is some rich and interesting **sculpture** in the east of the church which shows a curious nostalgia for the archaic forms and iconography of Romanesque art. The capitals at the entrance to the main apse present Daniel in the Lions' Den and Samson and the Lion, and in the south apsidal chapel are various episodes from the life of St-Eloi, patron saint of blacksmiths. Note also the carvings at the bases of the clustered shafts in the choir. The Flamboyant west porch, enclosed in the 15C when the two chapels either side were added, has some decorative sculpture of varying quality. There are large sculpted bosses in the narthex vaults.

Continue along the D3 past the lake in the direction of Plaisance for 10.5km. **Plaisance** (pop. 1575, Tourist Information, tel: 62 69 44 69), on the Arros, is an alternative to Marciac for accommodation or restaurants.

Before Plaisance, a right turn on to the D946 leads to the pretty village of **Beaumarchés**. This *bastide*, founded in 1292, was named after its founder Eustache de Beaumarchais. A small village, perched up high, it is dominated by a Flamboyant church with a massive west porch supporting an incomplete belfry.

The D946 follows an east–west ridge with some good views. After 12km make an 8km **detour** north on to the D102 to visit the villages of **Baccarisse**, with a 17C church and six-level belfry, and **Gazax** with a part-13C church and house in sun-baked brick (adobe), and then to **Peyrusse-Grande** which has a Romanesque church, altered in the 16C, with some fine carvings.

Back on the D946 you will see the massive keep of the village of **Bassoues** (4km). This *bastide*, founded by the Archbishops of Auch in 1279 not far from a monastery they had acquired in the 13C, is well worth a visit. The huge square **tower** with angle buttresses and machicolations built in 1368 and financed by Archbishop Arnaud Aubert, is a magnificent piece of military architecture completing the military fortifications to protect the community. It contains a permanent exhibition on *sauvetés, castelnaux* and *bastides* in Gascony. Next to the keep is the former archbishops' residence which was altered in the 16C and 17C. The other major curiosity is the beautiful 16C timber-framed **halle** which straddles the road (like Gimont only smaller) with some pretty houses either side. The 15C aisleless Gothic rather empty parish church near the market is built into the slope of the hill. In the cemetery on the western edge of the village, past the keep, is the 15C and 19C basilica containing the tomb of the legendary local hero St-Fris, nephew of Charles Martel, who died in mortal combat against the infidels near Bassoues in the 8C. The legend of his death is remembered over the south and west doors.

A picturesque village with an aristocratic name, **Montesquiou** (D943, 8km), home of the maternal family of d'Artagnan, is a small *castelnau* on a hill with a medieval fortified gate. Every 22 July there is an important cattle fair here called La Madeleine. **St-Arailles**, north on the D34 (6km), is also a picturesque village.

Return to the D943 by the D179 and cross the Baïse at L'Isle de Noé to arrive at **Barran** (12.5km), a well-kept *bastide*—perhaps because it is close to Auch—with golden stone houses and a good market square. It also has a strangely contorted church spire, covered in grey slate which, although very celebrated, is slightly unsatisfying as it twists irregularly and looks suspiciously like a case of warped timbers.

The D943 joins the N124 to bring you to Auch, 21km, or return via l'Isle de Noé and the D929 to Mirande, 14km.

13

Central Gascony: Fleurance and the vineyards of Armagnac and Madiran

Total distance: 23km (14 miles).

FLEURANCE (pop. 6089, Tourist Information tel: 62 06 10 01/62 06 27 80), conveniently located on the N21 between Agen and Auch, is one of the main commercial centres of the Gers today; but it is not quite as great as its Tuscan namesake. Situated on the Gers river, with plenty of amenities, including a lake, it is an excellent base for touring the area. The co-founder, Eustache de Beaumarchais, instrumental in the creation of many *bastides* in Gascony and the Toulousain, had a penchant for naming his *bastides* after foreign towns. The buildings that surround the 60m-square *place* with acarded *couverts* are 18C but undoubtedly laid out to the plan of the original *bastide* founded c 1272. The houses on the west and east are the best conserved, and many have good wrought iron. The wonderful Neo-Classical **halle**, 1834–37, is a serious work on two floors designed by an architect from Auch called Ardenne. At the exterior angles of the *halle* are fountains with graceful statues in bronze, by A. Durenne, representing the four seasons.

The amply proportioned **Church of Notre-Dame and St-John the Baptist** was begun during the last third of the 13C. Three successive campaigns of building from the 14C to the 16C, and a difference in the level of the site from west to east of about 4m, contributed to the mixture of materials and the unevenness of the exterior elevations as well as to the varying heights and arrangement of the roofs. To absorb the thrust of the high nave, small flying buttresses in brick were used for the first time in the region. The west elevation, entirely in stone, was deprived of much of its decoration during the attacks on the town by the Huguenots. Twelve corbels above the portal signify the existence of a covered gallery at one time, and the outline of arches on the north are all that remain of a chapel. The lower part of the belfry is said to be an ancient Gallo-Roman tower and the octagonal Toulousain-style belfry, in stone, was completed at the beginning of the 15C.

The **interior** is dark as there are only small clerestory windows and, typical of Midi, there is little integral decoration. The three earlier east bays of the nave have quadripartite vaults and the west bays tierceron ribs. The discrepancy in floor levels was dealt with in the 18C resulting in the disappearance of the bases of the eastern piers under the floor. The showpiece of the church is undoubtedly the three windows of the east end with Rayonnant **tracery** and **stained glass** by Arnaud de Moles and his workshop. Arbitrarily dated 1500 by E. Hirsch who restored them in 1877, they are thought to have been executed between 1506 and 1520. On the left in the main panels are St Laurence, Mary Magdalene, and St Augustine; above is a Pietà and below the martyrdom of St Laurence, Noli me Tangere, and St Augustine's conversion. The central window has a large Trinity flanked by Christ Resurrected and the Virgin, with a choir of angels and the Crucifixion. The third is a Jesse window crowned by the Virgin enthroned in a large flower. Among the furnishings is a 15C statue of the Virgin and Child (Notre-Dame de Fleurance) in the St-Jean Chapel, the source of numerous miracles during the Religious Wars; and in the St-Jean chapel three paintings by J-B. Smets, one of a family of Flemish painters living in Auch in the 18C. The 19C organ has been restored and is used for concerts during the summer.

Take the D103 to **Lavardens**, a picturesque Gascon village clinging to a rocky bluff, a stonghold of the Counts of Armagnac in the 13C and inherited in 1496 by Marguerite d'Angoulême, mother of Jeanne d'Albret. The streets are too narrow and steep for motor vehicles, but who would want to drive through it anyway? Five of the old towers of the enceinte still survive but the huge **château** which dominates the village was dismantled by Henri de Navarre's troops in 1577. Rebuilding began in 1620 under the direction of the architect Pierre de Levesville but was interrupted by a plague epidemic in 1653. It changed hands twice in the 18C and after 1820 it was more or less abandoned until 1970 when restoration work was undertaken. The west part of the château is the most elegant, standing proud above the valley. It can be visited (tel: 62 64 51 20, 14.00–19.30 Jul–Aug) and although it has few rooms there are some quite outstanding tiled floors.

Still on the D103, continue to **Jegun**, an attractively restored village *perché* strung out along the ridge, with a variety of 15C and 16C houses and an *halle* with a Neo-Classical building above it. The church SteCandide, part 12C, was altered in the 15C and two aisles were added in the 19C to support the nave.

Bas Armagnac and the Madiran

Total distance: 79km (49 miles).

The **Bas Armagnac**, also known as Armagnac Noir, is the north-western part of the Gers and the heartland of Armagnac brandy (see Condom), where vast stretches of vines overlap with forests.

The **Madiran** is a small wine-producing region between the towns of Maubourguet, Riscle and Lembeye, straddling the border between the Midi-Pyrénées and Aquitaine in the valleys of small rivers which flow north into the Adour. Although its history is long, the region went into crisis at the beginning of the century and was reduced to only 6ha in 1953, but vines again cover over 1000ha and the wines are gaining recognition. The wine, introduced and perfected by the Benedictines of the Abbey at Madiran in the 11C and 12C, was used as communion wine and was appreciated by pilgrims on the Santiago road. It was awarded *appellation controllée* status in 1948 but its first official recognition was the *lettres de noblesse* (letters patent) issued by François I and the court of England in the 16C. The wines used in the production of the exclusively red wines of Madiran are the Tannat, a local variety of black grape, Cabernet Franc and a small amount of Cabernet Sauvignon. The most recent appellation in the region was the Côtes de St-Mont in 1981. The delicious white wine Pacherenc of the Vic-Bilh, the old name of the region around St-Mont, is produced from local grape varieties with curious names: Arrufiac, Gros Manseng, Courbu and Petit Manseng; plus a little Sémillon and Sauvignon.

Vic-Fézensac (pop. 4000, Tourist Information, tel: 62 06 30 08/62 06 34 90), a popular centre for tourism, is best known for the Whitsun *corrida*. Twice monthly on a Wednesday during July and August there are late-night illuminated markets (regular market Friday). The medieval town was divided between the counts of Armagnac and the archbishops of Auch which held it in a state of constant tension. In the 18C the town was physically cut in two when Baron d'Etigny drove the main road through the middle of the old *place*. It lost its market in 1866. The most interesting part of the church, founded in 1190 by the bishops, is the Romanesque chevet with some of its original decoration and some 15C paintings in the south. The 15C nave was repaired and covered with a timber roof in the 17C. The altar and font are 18C and the octagonal belfry is a 19C confection. The 15C tower of the canons' residence and the 14C–15C square tower of the former Cordeliers Convent founded by Count Jean III d'Armagnac in 1382, are original, but most of the Cordeliers had to be rebuilt after the Reformation.

Take the D35 south through the **Roquebrune**, with its ancient well, and D174/D37 west to **Lupiac** (16.5km), a modest village with a large square and timber arcades, described as the *Berceau d'Artagnan*. The villages in this district, around here called the *Pays d'Artagnan*, have capitalised on Alexandre Dumas' hero because the real man behind the myth, Charles de Batz-Castelmore, was born between 1610 and 1620 at the Château of Castelmore (privately owned), about 4km north of Lupiac on the D102. Although Dumas tidied up the facts, Charles de Batz, who adopted his mother's name, had an illustrious career in the service of Louis XIV. He died during the siege of Maastricht in 1673 and legend has it that he is buried at Lupiac, but of this there is no proof. The St-James chapel (or Notre-Dame de la Pitié) was founded by Charles de Batz, uncle of the Musketeer, in 1605.

When in these parts, a rural setting and traditional food can be found at the *Ferme-Auberge de Ruat*, near Lupiac, tel: 62 09 26 33, the first of its kind in the Gers.

The D174 across rolling countryside brings you after 9km to **Aignan** (pop. 940, Tourist Information, tel: 62 09 22 57), the first residence of the counts and therefore first capital of Armagnac, and now an important commercial centre for Armagnac brandy with a cooperative *chai* which can be visited. Aignan suffered badly in the hands of the English in 1355 but the church has conserved several 12C carved elements around the portal and some good capitals inside around the two apses. It was modified in the late 13C when the massive square belfry was topped by a distinctive roof and lantern. Traditional houses and an arcaded square (Monday market) and the start of a *route touristique* of the forest, which has a lake and other facilities, make this a popular centre.

Just 3km along the pretty road, the D48, from Aignan is the attractive village of **Sabazan**, with a 17C château-domaine producing Armagnac and a dear little church with an 11C–12C apse with simple carvings and an overhanging timber gallery on the tower, added in the 13C.

Stay on the D48 to **Termes d'Armagnac** (7.5km), which is not difficult to track down because of the splendidly massive 13C keep towering over the valley of the Adour, the only part still intact of the castle built on the border (*terminis*) between the ancient territories of Armagnac and Béarn. This was the château of Tibault d'Armagnac who, alongside several hundred other Gascons, fought with Joan of Arc. The spectacular vantage point of this lofty edifice (36m) will be appreciated by those who can cope both with the climb to the top and the six levels of reconstructed history in the form of thematic tableaux called the *Musée du Panache Gascogne* (tel: 62 69 25 12, 14.00–18.00, all day Jun–Aug). The church next door, with a belfry-porch and distinctive roof, has been subjected to many alterations but proudly displays a magnificent 18C gilded retable (light switch to right of door).

Take the D3/D935, 7.5km, through **Riscle**, busy on Fridays, market day, but probably not at any other time, with tidy 17C/18C houses and a church with a Flamboyant portal overlooking the main square.

Go 5.5km west on the D946. **St-Mont** is the most interesting village of the Madiran, with a cooperative winery, the Union des Producteurs Plaimont (tel: 62 69 62 87). The village, as the name suggests, is perched on a hill and overlooks the Adour valley. There are pretty pebble and brick houses lining the street up to the tall but sturdy stone church at the summit which has conserved a small number of remarkable Romanesque capitals. The key is with Mme. Nadaud, at the house just below the church. The area in front of the church is landscaped but next to it are the abandoned buildings of the 18C priory.

The **abbey** of St-Mont, dedicated to St John the Baptist, was founded in 1045 by Bernard II of Armagnac with the unlikely name of Tumapaler and was attached to Cluny in 1055. The abbey's history is obscure, but it was ransacked by the Protestant troops of Montgomery in 1569 and then rebuilt. After the Revolution all the buildings except the church were sold. The interior is wonderfully light and spacious, and the aisleless nave not quite lined up with the apse. All that remains of the 11C building are the south transept and apsidiole and part of the south wall of the nave. The vaults were added and the north side of the church altered at a later date, around the late 12C or early 13C. The oldest and finest **capitals** from the first building campaign at the entrance to the south apsidiole—vegetal on the left and lions in tendrils on the right—show an affinity to the work at St-Gaudens. There are stylistic similarities to Jaca (Spain) in the next two slightly later capitals on the south-west, one with a double Corinthian motif, and the other with the theme of David and his Musicians, as well as a re-used capital in the south-east of the main apse with the story of Balaam's Ass. There are more carved capitals in the south transept and on the south side of the nave.

Return to Riscle and take the D935/D25 12km to **Nogaro** (pop. 2209, Tourist Information, tel: 62 09 13 30/62 69 07 10), the small rural capital of Bas-Armagnac with a market on Wednesday and Saturday. It has two specific attractions: motor racing in April and October at the Circuit Paul Armagnac, and an interesting church. This was a *sauveté* created by the Archbishop of Auch in 1060 and has one of the largest Romanesque churches in the Gers, although it was much modified in the 17C, and again in the 19C. There are Romanesque elements around the north door, including Christ and tetramorph. The vault of the three bay nave was rebuilt in brick in the 17C but the arches with ovolo moulding between the nave and aisles date from the end 11C. The capitals in the east end are sculpted with, from left to right: acanthus leaves, a centaur between two horsemen, Daniel in the lions' den, musicians, Christ with Zacchaeus in a sycamore tree trying to get a better view of Jesus, and Jesus in a boat with the two sinners. The sacristy was a 16C addition. The collegiate buildings which, with the church, once contributed to the protection of the town, now protect what is left of the cloister. Transformed into a garden, just one bay of the outer wall of the old cloister gives a clue to the beauty of the original carvings.

It is a village with plenty of half-timbered houses and boasts the oldest producer of Armagnac. It is well equipped with hotels and sports facilities and the *courses landaises* championships are held here every three years.

Leaving Nogaro to the north-east, it is 18km on the N124 and D931 to **Eauze** (pop. 4293, Tourist Information, tel: 62 09 85 62). Ancient city of the Elusates people, Elusa became one of the three main political, administrative and commercial centres, with Auch and Lectoure, during Roman occupation. Buildings and treasure have been excavated and in 1985 an extraordinary collection of jewels and 28,000 coins was discovered. This is on display in a new **archaeological museum** on Place de la Liberté. Eauze is now the Armagnac Capital, a busy commercial town with a market created by Charles IX in the 16C (market Thursday) and an Armagnac Fair in Ascension week (May).

Its most famous house, on the central arcaded square, Place d'Armagnac, is the timber-framed **Maison Jeanne d'Albret**. The King of Navarre (future Henri IV) was taken ill here on the 15 June 1579, and was cared for by Queen Margot (Marguerite de Valois) for 17 days. There are small streets with timber-framed houses in varying degrees of dilapidation, and the octagonal belfry tower in stone and yellowish brick with a distinctive roof, indicates the 15C–16C **Church of St-Luperc**. Long, narrow and aisleless with a three-sided apse, the interior is enlivened by the fact that the walls are not rendered, adding colour and texture to an otherwise plain church (except for the 1977 murals in the apse) with little fenestration. The painted bosses contain the coats of arms of France and Eauze and of Jean Marre, prior of Luperc and Bishop of Condom in the 16C.

Eauze is one of several towns in Bas Armagnac which hold *corridas*.

14

Auch

AUCH (pop. 25,000, Tourist Information Office, 1 Rue Dessoles, 32003 Auch, tel: 62 05 22 89). The first glimpse you are likely to get of Auch is the mass of the cathedral rising above the old *Ville Haute* on the bluff above the Gers. Auch is midway between Aquitaine and Languedoc, 77km west of Toulouse, and is the Préfecture of the *département* of the Gers. The **Gers** (the 's' is pronounced) is the heart of old Gascony, the land of swashbuckling Gascon swordsmen and musketeers, but these days 37 per cent of the

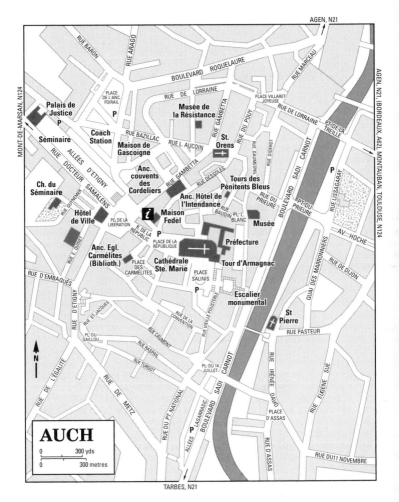

AGEN, N21

AUCH

0 ——— 300 yds
0 ——— 300 metres

sparse population of the Gers is concerned with agriculture. The Gers, the most westerly of the eight *départements* of the Midi-Pyrénées, turns historically and culturally to Aquitaine rather than to the Languedoc, and the Gascon language, which you may chance to hear in a market place, differs slightly from Occitan.

The landscape is characterised by shallow valleys and softly undulating ridges determined by the Gers and other small rivers which rise in the foothills of the Pyrenees and fan on their way north. Vines are cultivated on the slopes in the north and west of the *département*, while sweeping fields of wheat and maize cover the plains. The Gers may not have the sharp contrasts of landscape of the other departments of the Midi-Pyrénées but it does offer such contrasting experiences as *corridas*, motor racing and jazz, flower festivals and the June music festival in Auch. It is also synonymous with Armagnac brandy, and a hearty gastronomy, dishes based on goose fat, rustic dishes such as *touren*, *garbure*, *grattons*, *foie gras*, *magret*, *confit* and *croustade*, a dessert using Armagnac. The local wines are Madiran and Buzet, and an aperitif called *floc de gascogne* blends grape juice and Armagnac.

Auch has all that is needed to make an excellent base for touring. Roads converge on it from Toulouse, Agen, Mont-de-Marsan and Tarbes and there are good rail links. The received expert of Gascon cooking is André Daguin, who owns the superb hotel and restaurant, *Hôtel de France*, Place de la Libération, Auch, tel: 62 61 71 71.

History. The first settlers of the oppidum Elimberris were a Celtic tribe, the Auscii. After their defeat by the Romans in 56 BC the hill fort was abandoned and Augusta Auscorum, one of the main cities of Roman Aquitaine, developed on the right bank of the river. From the 9C the population returned to the hill, established the core of the medieval *cité* and built a simple oratory. The Duchy of Gascony was formed in 852 with the division of Carolingian Aquitaine, defined by the wide arc of the Garonne to north and east and the Pyrenees to the south. As the town of Auch expanded it came under the shared authority of the consuls, the Count of Armagnac, the Archbishop of Auch and the Prior of Saint-Orens. Gascony was joined to Aquitaine in 1036 and in 1152 the marriage of Eleanor of Aquitaine to Henry Plantaganet introduced English domination, resolved only in the 15C at the end of the Hundred Years War. The proliferation of *castelnaux*, *sauvetés* and *bastides* that sprang up between the 11C and 14C are an integral part of the Gers. Gradually Gascony-Aquitaine was controlled by three main feudal dynasties: Foix-Béarn, Armagnac, and Albret. In the 15C the Armagnac dynasty was extinguished and Auch was occupied by Louis XI's troops. Marriages and successions favoured the Albrets towards the end-15C and into the 16C. In 1527 Henri II d'Albret married Marguerite d'Angoulème, sister of François I, and inherited the House of Armagnac. Their daughter Jeanne d'Albret inherited all three great Gascon domains and at her death in 1572 these passed to her son, Henri de Navarre, who was to become king of France in 1589 through his father, Antoine de Bourbon. In 1607 Henri IV united his fiefdoms with the Crown of France (with the exception of Basse-Navarre and the Béarn, incorporated in 1620). Auch grew into a separate *généralité* or administrative centre in 1715, representing a huge region which until 1768 comprised nearly all the territory between the Garonne and the line along the crest of the Pyrenees. The 18C was the high point for Auch, largely due to its Intendant from 1731 to 1767, Baron Antoine Megret d'Etigny, who invigorated the economy of the town and the region with a huge road-building programme linking Auch with the mountains and the Canal du Midi. The Province of Gascony disappeared in 1789 and the larger part of it became the Gers.

On Foot. Start the visit from **Place de la République**, in front of the cathedral, where markets are held on Wednesday, Thursday and Saturday. The Tourist Information Office is in the pretty timber-framed house, **Maison Fedel**, on the north side of the *place*.

The **CATHEDRAL SAINTE-MARIE** (closed midday), was one of the last Gothic cathedrals in the south-west, begun at the end of the 15C, just after Albi Cathedral was completed. It replaced a Romanesque church consecrated in 1121. At about the same time a canons' residence had appeared on the south and an episcopal residence on the north and these, as well as the steep escarpment to the east, restricted the spread of the new cathedral designed by Jean Marre, Bishop and architect of Condom cathedral. However, it was to the south and east that the cathedral was extended, the east supported by a crypt built into the rock. The first stone was laid on 4 July 1489 and the unfinished building was consecrated in 1548. It was not fully completed until 1680.

Exterior. The exterior more than the interior shows the evolution of styles over the 200 years of construction. Viewed from the north or south, it appears to be a fairly standard Flamboyant construction with flying buttresses and a non-salient transept. It is impossible to walk around the east end of the cathedral and for a decent view you have to be in the lower town on the other side of the river (with your binoculars).

The three entrances, begun in 1560, were the work of the architect Jean de Beaujeu. The north and south portals and the four buttress-towers flanking them had risen to the height of the aisles by 1567 and were completed c 1635. Above each portal is a Flamboyant rose window beneath a triangular pediment. The decoration of each doorway is transitional, juxtaposing Flamboyant aedicules with pinnacles and crockets and delicately carved Italianate friezes. The massive but elegant west elevation, completed by 1680, uses an exclusively classical idiom. The three round-arched entrances correspond to the nave and aisles and lead to an open portico, closed by railings in the 18C. The square towers above are on two levels and the Corinthian order is applied throughout. The niches have always been empty.

Interior. The interior is regular and harmonious, unencumbered by integral ornament, an intrinsic feature of the southern Gothic architecture. The simple quadripartite vaults and transverse arches are emphatically outlined but spring from shafts which are pared down to the minimum while sharply profiled aisle arches spring directly from the smooth round piers without the hint of a capital. The blind triforium under low basket arches is more like a Renaissance balcony. Five pentagonal radiating chapels surround the apse while the rest of the 21 chapels are square. This very plain interior is the foil to two great treasures: the stained glass windows and the magnificent carved choir enclosure. Both were installed by the time the cathedral was consecrated in 1548 when the chapels and ambulatory were vaulted, although the choir had a temporary timber roof and the nave was still a skeleton.

The series of 18 Renaissance **stained glass windows**, 1507–13, were made by Arnaud de Moles for the ambulatory chapels. To produce the intense reds, blues, greens and golds, used here in large areas and to great effect, he took advantage of new advances in glass making and in the techniques of abrasion and annealing. The iconographic programme brings together monumental figures from the Old and the New Testament, a line up of prophets, patriarchs, sibyls, saints and apostles, with small scenes relevant to their prophesies or lives. The themes were probably furnished by the incumbent archbishop and donor of the stained glass, Clermont de Lodève (1507–38), a member of the great Amboise family. There are three key storiated windows. The Creation cycle in the **first chapel north** has figures of Adam and Eve and small scenes above and below of the Creation and the Fall. The three windows in the **main apse** dealing with the theme of the Crucifixion have magnificent fleur de lys in the upper register. In the central bay is Christ on the Cross with the Virgin, St John and Mary Magdalene. The window in the left bay contains Isaiah, the apostle Philip and Micah, and on the right King David, James the Great as a pilgrim, and a prophet. The Resurrection window, on the **south-west**, combines the apparition to Mary Magdalene, Noli me Tangere, in the central bay, and the Incredulity of Thomas with a small scene of the Supper at Emmaus. At the top Auch is represented by its coat of arms, and above the main figures are Claude de France, daughter of Louis XII, and her betrothed, the future François I, representing the two branches of the Crown, the Valois and the Orléans. At the base are more prophets and apostles and the arms of Clermont-Lodève (1507–38).

The visit to the **choir enclosure**, intended as it was to separate worshipping clerics from the hoi polloi, takes you into a world apart (pay to visit). A totally enclosed area, it is one of three in the Midi-Pyrénées, with Albi and St-Bertrand-de-Comminges, to survive church reforms in the 17C. The 113 **choir stalls** that line three sides are an extraordinary tour de force. Carved from heart of oak, richly patinated, the sanctuary contrasts in texture and abundance with the plain stone and the radiant stained glass. The enclosure was probably completed by c 1552–54 but there is no recorded date for the start of the work, calculated at c 1510–20. Gothic in essence, with late Flamboyant style baldaquins, the iconography of the age of humanism brings together biblical and mythological figures. The stalls are on two levels, the carved reliefs of the high backs of the upper 69 develop the theme of the Creation, starting with Adam and Eve in the north-west. The male-female alternance is maintained with figures representing the Old Law, including Moses, King David in several guises, sibyls and prophets and the Evangelists juxtaposed with allegories of virtue. The programme culminates with Saints Peter and Paul, the joint founders of the Christian Church and above the entrance to the choir are St Jerome, St Augustine and the Virgin. The lower stalls carry scenes from the life of Christ from the Annunciation to the Crucifixion in high relief panels on the end stalls. The misericords are decorated with lively and sometimes provocative anecdotes and the armrests with weird and fantastical beasts and demons. Hardly a surface is left undecorated.

Closing the choir to the east is a monumental retable (c 1609) by a local sculptor, Pierre Souffron II, with pilasters and columns in Pyrenean marble and two stone ambons. The four statues were salvaged in 1860 when the old *jubé*, sculpted in 1671 by Gervais Drouet, was dismantled. The mosaics in front of the altar were placed here in 1860.

The **crypt**, built to support the east end, has five undecorated radiating chapels corresponding to the main chapels. The 7C sarcophagus of St-Léotharde, from the former Benedictine Abbey of St-Orens d'Auch, is the most interesting piece. The cathedral **treasure** is in the former sacristy. The **St-Sépulchre chapel**, in the south east where the first stone was laid, is the only chapel of the apse without glass because it is against the canonial buildings. Its contains an important sculpted group re-enacting the **Entombment**, c 1500, with the usual line up of life-size participants in rigid postures: Joseph of Arimathea and Nicodemus at the head and feet of the body of Jesus as he is lowered into the tomb, the Virgin carrying the crown of thorns, St John, Mary Magdalene and Maries Salome and Cleophas. This particular group is flanked by four soldiers and covered by a gilded baldaquin with a Trinity and numerous angels. All ten chapels of the nave were dedicated to Notre-Dame when the sculptor, Jean Douillé was commissioned in 1662 to make 13 **retables**. Just two retables have survived complete, and part of another. The most noteworthy, in the Chapelle de l'Assumption on the right of the west door, was restored in 1964.

Among other furnishings are the early 16C ciborium above the 19C altar in the St-Sacrament chapel. A reconstruction (1803) of the mausoleum of Baron d'Etigny, originally at St-Orens d'Auch but demolished at the Revolution. The pulpit is 18C.

The *avant-choeur*, which replaced the *jubé* in 1860, underwent a transformation in 1970. The **choir organ** above the west end of the enclosure was given by Emperor Napoléon III and Empress Eugénie, an instrument designed for French Romantic music, it is signed Aristide Cavaillé-Coll. The **main organ** in the west end below the rose window, is one of the finest in the region and is used for concerts during the summer music festival. Built by Jean de Joyeuse, its installation was completed in 1694. The case is carved in chestnut and is decorated with caryatids, eagles and angel musicians, with Notre-Dame in the centre and reliefs of King David and St-Cecilia on the lower part.

South of the cathedral **Place Salinis**, created c 1863, is shaded by *mico-couliers*, trees of the Midi. Towering 40m above it is the 14C **Tour d'Armagnac** against the former canons' residence. It was originally built as a prison with a cell on each level.

East of Place Salinis the famous **Monumental Steps**, built c 1863 to the detriment of the old fortifications, descend to the banks of the Gers and the lower town via six flights of steps and three terraces. From the top, with luck, you can see as far as the Pyrenees. Covering the central section of the top terrace is a vast horizontal relief of words wrought in iron, called *L'Observatoire*. Conceived in 1991 by a Catalan artist, Jaume Plensa, and designed to be walked over—a very strange sensation in thin soled shoes, unwise in high heels—it is engraved with the biblical text of the Flood recalling the disaster of 1977 when the Gers burst its banks. Its other half, the *Faux Refuge*, is on the opposite bank (across the footbridge). Michelet's bronze statue of d'Artagnan, erected in 1931 on the level below, is far from *avant garde*.

The top terrace of the Monumental Steps leads to the **Pousterles**, ancient steep lanes with names such as Coulomates (*colombes*) and las Houmettos (*ormeaux*), linking the lower and upper towns, and to the old town gate, the **Porte d'Arton**.

At the end of Rue de la Convention on Place Garibaldi is the former pilgrim **Hôpital de St-Jacques**, rebuilt in 1765. Turn right into **Rue d'Espagne**. In the tiny courtyard is a splendid staircase. Rue de Valmy leads to **Place des Carmélites** with a wrought-iron cross and Place Salustre-du-Bartas, named after a Gascon poet (1544–90) born near Cologne (Gers) whose statue is in the square. The Municipal Library is installed in the former 17C **Carmelite Chapel** and can be visited.

The large **Place de la Libération** with a circular fountain was one of Intendant d'Etigny's creations, and overlooking it is the **Hôtel de Ville** (1777) which has a room with portraits of illustrious Gersois and a small theatre. At the end of the shady **Allées d'Etigny**, a statue of the great man, erected in 1817, surveys his work.

North of Place de la Libération on Rue Gambetta the **Maison de Gascogne**, the restored 19C grain market, is now used for *spectacles* and the post office opposite has taken over the former **Hôtel de l'Intendance** (1759). Cut through to **Rue Dessoles**, a lively, pedestrianised street, the old *Camin Dret*, with the 19C classical-style Church of St-Orens at the north end and some notable restorations of *hôtels particuliers* at Nos 40 and 45. Should you pass this way in Whit week, you will see on sale at R. Boiziot, the butcher on the corner of Rue Bazeilles, the much sought after quality beef from the *corrida* bulls at Vic Fezensac. The street leads back uphill to the Tourist Office. The former 18C **Episcopal Palace** is now occupied by the Préfecture.

To reach the **Museum of Auch** (tel: 62 05 74 79, closed Mon) in the old Jacobins Convent, take the road past the Préfecture and down Rue A. de Miles and Rue Gaudin (the museum is signposted). The 15C convent, radically modified in the 17C, was acquired and restored by the town in 1976. It has some fine Gallo-Roman exhibits, medieval carvings, examples of 18C decorative arts, ceramics, 18C and 19C paintings, and a regional ethnological collection of the 19C and 20C. The biggest surprise is the very rich **Latin American section** donated by Guillaume Pujos in 1921.

The **Gallo-Roman** and **medieval** exhibition on the lower ground floor is displayed in an attractive gallery looking out on the garden. It contains some brightly coloured Gallo-Roman frescoes (between 20 BC and 1C AD) found in 1962 at Villa la Sioutat, 9km from Auch. Among the funerary objects is a touching epitaph to a dog called Myia, and a beautiful perfume flask (after 2C AD) found intact in a sepulchre at la Hourre, Auch.

15

The Valleys of the Save and the Gimone

Total distance: 106km (66 miles).

This tour explores the two almost parallel valleys of the Save and Gimone, south-east of Auch, where the towns are predominantly brick, and includes the impressive fortified church of Simorre. This is *foie-gras* country par excellence.

L'Isle-Jourdain (pop. 5040, Tourist Information, tel: 62 07 25 57) was the capital of the lands belonging to the de l'Isle family, and it acquired its suffix at the time of the First Crusade (1096–99). Count Raymond de l'Isle and his countess accompanied Raymond IV Count of Toulouse, Raymond de l'Isle's cousin, on the march to the Holy Land. In Palestine the countess gave birth to a son whose baptism in the waters of the Jordan was from then on remembered in the name of the town. Raymond's brother, Bertrand de l'Isle (1044–1124), became Bishop of the ancient Lugdunum Convenarum, later known as St-Bertrand-de-Comminges. The dynasty died out in the 15C and the county was sold in 1421 to Jean IV, Count of Armagnac.

The town has two squares. The older, **Place Gambetta**—called the *marcadieu*—with arcades on two sides, is on the edge of the route built by the Intendant of Auch, d'Etigny. The other square contains the late-18C **Hôtel de Ville**, a sophisticated Italianate building in brick with a rusticated ground floor, the upper punctuated by wrought iron balconies. Adjacent is the Neo-Classical brick **halle** (1819), with a mass of elegant octagonal pillars, recently converted to house the European Museum of Campanology. L'Isle-Jourdain was the birthplace of Claude Augé (1854–1924), the creator of the *Dictionnaire complet illustré* (1889) which became the *Petit Larousse Illustré* in 1906, and the building opposite is named after him.

The town adhered to the Reform and, in common with most Protestant towns, the majority of its pre-17C monuments (castle, fortifications, church) were destroyed. The only bit of medieval architecture left, against the north-east of the church, is the brick **keep** of the château dismantled by Richelieu in 1621. The church was raised to collegiate status in 1318 by Pope Jean XXII. In the late 18C it was replaced by the severely Neo-Classical **Church of St-Martin**, designed in 1785 by Jean-Arnaud Raymond, which takes the form of two superimposed Greek crosses using the giant Doric order. The interior was entirely decorated in the 19C, the vaults (c 1879) by Engalières, and the murals (c 1889) by Terral. The reliquary chapel on the south contains the relics of St-Bertrand-de-L'Isle, Bishop of Comminges (1040–1123) and of St-Odon, second Abbot of Cluny (879–942), plus a relic of the True Cross.

Beside the N124 coming from Toulouse is one of the most impressive *pigeonniers* of a type found frequently in Gascony, and there are more along the D634.

Leave L'Isle-Jourdain by the D634, turn right on the D243, and left on the D39, 10km, to the **Château de Caumont** (tel: 62 07 94 20, July–Aug, at other times telephone), hidden away in woods up a long unmade track. The château was repurchased in 1979 by the de Castelbajac family, descendants of the original owners, who have undertaken the monumental task of restoration and who are likely to be your guides.

From the drive, the main body of the château is screened by outbuildings with false crenellations, neo-Gothic windows and turrets. When James MacMahon, an Irish mercenary with strong views on how his property should look, married Pauline de Montgaillard la Valette in the late 18C, he chose to transform it into the highly fashionable *style troubadour* subsequently ruining the buildings and himself. He also made an unsuccessful bid to breed merino sheep at Caumont.

The present residence, on high ground with a spectacular view of the Pyrenean range, was begun c 1535 on the site of the medieval fortress by Pierre de Nogaret la Valette, who had accompanied François I on his campaigns in Italy. He endowed his property with elements of Renaissance elegance and comfort without altering the basic medieval structure. However, the defences were dismantled after the Wars of Religion and the château was damaged by fire in the 17C.

The main building, built in alternate brick and poor quality stone from Auch, is arranged around three sides of a courtyard whose level was raised by MacMahon and lowered by the present owners who have restored most of the windows, including the oval ones at the base of the interior walls. At the exterior angles are square towers with steeply pitched roofs, and between these flanking the north entrance (16C) are two stairtowers with pepper-pot roofs. Along the east façade overlooking the courtyard is a gallery supported by huge stone corbels; the west wing (17C) has a rusticated loggia on the ground floor and the south is also 17C. Throughout the interior there are examples of MacMahon's Romantic intentions, including the vast hall or *Salon Troubadour* painted in neo-medieval *trompe l'oeil*. The second salon, of 1840, is in *style Pompéien* or Malmaison style. Also open to view are the library behind the door in the tower, the kitchen and the cellars, the first-floor corridor transformed by MacMahon and the bedroom known as La Chambre du Roi where, legend has it, Henri IV slept.

Most moving is the little chapel created by MacMahon and his son-in-law the Marquis de Castelbajac, one of Napoléon's generals and Ambassador to Napoléon III, for Caroline MacMahon, Marquise de Castelbajac who died at 18 in childbirth.

The small town of **Samatan** (pop. 1820, Tourist Office, tel: 62 62 55 40) 8km further south on the D39, is the location for the most famous of all the **marchés au gras** (foie gras markets) held on the edge of the town in three huge sheds beside the car park on Mondays from November to April. The duck and geese which serve as the basis of many traditional dishes in the Midi-Pyrénées are raised by Gascony's farmers and smallholders and sold at markets throughout the Gers during the winter.

On winter mornings at about 8am local producers rent a stall and start to unload from their vans trays of pale livers, each liver weighing anything from 400 to 900 grammes, setting them out on long trestles in one of the three vast sheds. The buying public awaits in eager anticipation for the moment when the whistle is blown, then the doors are opened and trading begins. Arrive well on time as the whole process of barter is rapid. The first market, for the *foie gras* itself, takes place at 9.45am; at 10.45 the poultry carcasses are sold; and at 11.30 is the *marché de volailles*, live poultry and other animals. Prices vary according to quality and season, at their highest around Christmas.

None of this is for the squeamish, yet it remains a reassuring indication of the importance that the French still put on the ritualistic exercise of producing, selecting and purchasing food. *Foie gras* has been produced since the 16C in Gascony, but the process was revolutionised in the 17C when maize was introduced into the region. The birds, after being reared normally for about six to eight weeks, are then subjected to *gavage*, force feeding, on cooked maize twice a day for about two weeks. Little of these large overfed birds goes to waste: the breasts become magrets, the legs confits, the rest of the flesh fritons, the blood a type of pâté, and the *gesiers* are often served warm in salads. Not surprisingly, Samatan has a museum of the history of *foie gras*.

Between Samatan and Lombez is a small artifical lake with a numerous facilities and an area for swimming.

2km away the community of **Lombez** (pop. 1238, Tourist Office, tel: 62 62 32 20) is gathered around the **Cathedral of Ste-Marie**. The diocese, founded in 1317, was one of several in the region created by Pope John XXII and lists 32 bishops until its suppression by Pius V in 1801. A plaque on the right of the west entrance records the visit of the poet Petrarch in 1330, arranged by Bishop Jacques Colonna (1328–41), of Italian extraction, who made Petrarch an honorary Canon in 1335.

The rather severe exterior of the brick church is characteristic of the Midi Toulousain with tall buttresses around the chevet, *mirandes* below the roof, and a five-tiered octagonal belfry with mitred bays. The foundations, belfry and first bay were constructed c 1346 and the west end has the typical blank face of meridional Gothic relieved only by a small roundel and the Flamboyant entrance in stone.

The interior is divided into two by an enfilade of pillars, similar to the Jacobins in Toulouse, but the north section is smaller than the south. Beside the first pillar on the left is a trap door which opens to reveal the floor level before it was raised as protection against flooding. The restored 12C baptistry in the north-west, part of an earlier church, below the tower, has an eight-rib vault and contains a remarkable collection of treasures.

Outstanding is the **lead baptismal font** referred to by Viollet-le-Duc in his *Dictionnaire Raisonné*: made of two separate pieces the lower is decorated with religious figures in medallions in the style of the 13C while the upper part has a frieze of profane scenes of antique design, possibly made up of two disparate pieces stored in the workshop, or just two styles; the stopper in the base suggests it was used for total immersion which was practised until the 9C. Other items worth noting are a late-15C sculpture of the dead Christ; 17C choir stalls in walnut, less grandly carved than those of Auch, but with some splendid atlantes on the episcopal throne; the altar, consecrated in 1753, in Carrara marble has a bas-relief carving by F. Lucas; the wooden balustrade from the chancel (1671–1710); some quality 18C ironwork by G. Bertin; and the 18C organ. The brilliantly coloured 15C–16C glass restored in the 19C, by the followers of Arnaud de Moles, illustrates Scenes from the Life of Christ and from the Passion.

The church shares the square with a fine **covered market** with brick pillars, and its walls with the houses to the south.

In the town is the hotel-restaurant *La Vallée*, tel: 62 62 35 10.

It is 14km on the D632/D17 to **l'Isle-en-Dodon** on the Save. This is a classic *bastide* with a central square surrounded by arcades and a Neo-Classical brick *hôtel de ville/halle* and several timber-framed houses in the adjacent streets. The 14C church has a fortified east end with battlemented towers and an octagonal belfry over the west porch. A Gallo-Roman stone altar is embedded in the east wall and the vivid 16C stained glass expresses a debt to the work of Arnaud de Moles.

Take the D6 for 9km in the direction of Gaujan.

Detour. The courage of the Resistance during World War II is commemorated by a Monument near Meilhan. At **Gaujan** take the D27a, and after 3km on the right a tall carved columnar monument marks the site where 84 *maquis* died on 7 July 1944. The D283, left just after the monument, follows the Lauze Valley through Aussos, to the vast 180ha **Lake of Astarac** which makes a refreshing interlude.

From Gaujan take the D12 north for 5km to the formidable brick church of **Simorre** (Tourist Information, tel: 62 65 36 34). Standing now in a large empty square, it was once part of a Benedictine community. The **abbey**, documented since the 9C, was originally established near here but, after it was destroyed by fire c 1140, the present site was chosen to start again. It was surrounded by 600m of walls and a ditch to protect the religious as well as the secular community, both under the control of the abbots. A cloister was built in 1240 and the new church, in brick, begun in 1292, was blessed in 1309 when a long drawn out feud between the abbots and the Counts of Astarac was coming to a end. The octagonal belfry and sacristy were added in 1350, and from 1442 the church was lengthened towards the west, using stone, while in the 15C the abbey buildings were embellished. With many changes during the 16C, fire damage in the 17C and repairs and demolition from 1756 until the Revolution, the monastic buildings were lost. In 1843 Simorre's historic and architectural importance was recognised and Viollet-le-Duc stepped in to restore and modify the church between 1844 and 1858. Further restoration was carried out in 1960.

A sturdy version of Toulousain Gothic with shallow articulation of the elevations, its military appearance is emphasised by the continuous crenellations added (or extended) in the 19C. The 14C stone façade was originally preceded by a porch with a Flamboyant doorway and you can see the gable embedded in the south-west wall. On each of the short transept arms is a small bell-tower. The striking exposed brick nave was entirely rib vaulted in the 14C. Over the crossing is an octagonal lantern on pendentives and ribs, with mitred openings. Although the west end is blank, the fenestration is surprisingly rich in the east part, with fine 14C tracery and a variety of stained glass, the oldest (1357) in the upper part of the square east end. Five windows of the choir and south transept have stained glass dated 1482, and one 1519. The stained-glass opposite the south door is 1525, and there is a 19C imitation of the original style in the north transept window. The very fine carved choir stalls, sadly mutilated in parts, were a gift in 1517 from Jean Marre, monk of Simorre who became Bishop of Condom. In the north transept there is an interesting 15C Pietà with several figures. The sacristy has murals of 1380; to visit tel: 62 65 36 34.

There are some pretty houses in the village and a simple hotel restaurant near the church, *Le Relais d'Arpèges*, tel: 62 65 32 05.

Continue north on the D12, for 12km to **Boulaur**, a serene and appropri- ately *Bon Locus* for the only active Cistercian community of nuns in the Gers who a few years ago took over a long-abandoned Fontrevist house founded in 1142. Visits are possible outside the hours of mass: ring the bell inside the door on the right of the courtyard marked *Entrée Monastère*. Note the barns to the left with wooden latticework typical of southern Gascony. The 13C and 14C abbey church with *mirandes* and a watch-tower was restored a few years ago. The spacious interior has a painted décor in the manner of the Jacobins in Toulouse. Most of the buildings and the fine wrought iron of the church are 18C.

Detour. The D626 heads west to **Castelnau-Barbarens** (6km) arranged in terraces around a castle which was razed in the 19C to make way for a parish church. It is worth stopping to investigate the 17C Notre-Dame de la Pitié, the arcaded streets and steep flight of steps, as well as for the views. In the direction of Auch is **Pessan** (about 6km) which once had a small abbey whose origins in the 8C place it among the oldest in the Gers. The Church of St-Michel is all that remains, with elements from the 11C to the 19C. The 11C church was damaged in 1250 although the transept survived and the east end, elegantly rebuilt c 1252, is dominated by a little square tower and slate spire. The crossing was raised and the nave has been heavily restored. There are some 15C choir stalls.

Further north (11km) on the D12 is all that remains of the **Abbey of Planselve**. Divided between two privately owned properties, it was opened to the public in 1992 and can be visited with a guide, Mme Denjean (tel: 62 67 77 87, 14.30 Sat & Sun, groups telephone). This was an important Cistercian Abbey whose origins in 1142 are well documented. It maintained a hospice and chapel for pilgrims on the edge of the property and prospered until 1557 when it was placed in the hands of commendatory abbots, which began the deterioration compounded by the Religious Wars, and it was finished off by the Revolution. In 1802 demolition began and much disappeared. The buildings are almost entirely in brick except for the structural elements. It is an unusual and interesting visit to the one or two buildings left, albeit in a haphazard state. The property was enclosed in a long brick wall, and the entrance is through the 14C gate-house which contains a model of the monastery in 1737. The lay workshops can be visited, with what may be a scriptorium, as well as the two beautiful *pigeonniers* near the Gimone.

Just east of Planselve on the N124 is **Gimont** (pop. 2950, Tourist Information, tel: 62 67 70 02), the only town in France where a *Route Nationale* runs not only straight through the middle of the town but through the **covered market** straddling it (thankfully there is a by-pass for the heavies). Originally surrounded by arcades, this massive construction has 28 octagonal piers supporting a timber roof, and was raised and rebuilt in the 19C—there are two dates, 1331 and 1825 on pillars east and west. This is an important *foie-gras* centre and there are *marchés au gras* on Wednesdays (except the summer), not in the old road-straddling *halle* but in the *marché aux grains* down the hill to the north. However, in the old market during May there are *courses landaises*—not the moment to choose to drive through.

Gimont, founded by the Cistercian Abbey of Planselve in 1266 in *paréage* with Alphonse de Poitiers, clings to a narrow promontory above the Gimone, hence the restricted layout. The **Church of Notre-Dame**, northeast of the *halle*, was planned in 1292 but the date above the porch is 1331. Mainly in brick, the later belfry is built over the vaulted stone sacristy with a Flamboyant window on the north, whereas the upper brick part is 16C or early 17C. The church contains some interesting items, including a 15C pulpit, an 18C altar in Caunes marble, and a small 15C Virgin. The most famous work (at time of writing removed for restoration) is a 16C **triptych of the Crucifixion** from Planselve which in Flemish tradition has a painted central panel and carved wings. There are relief sculptures of the Virgin, St Lazarus and an Angel of the Last Judgement, and Mary Magdalene and St Martha on the outside.

Gimont has a large lake with plenty of facilities.

Continue a further 13km north on the D12 for **Mauvezin** (pop. 1706, Tourist Information: 62 06 81 45), a village on a hill between the Arratz and the Gimone rivers. It was once an important stronghold, but in the 17C the castle was broken up into lots and the fortifications dismantled. It is laid out around a vast empty square surrounded by mainly 18C whitish limestone houses, with the 14C *halle* with stone piers to one side. The post office is in a 16C building, and the *hôtel de ville* is 17C. There is a Monday market.

Detour. 9km north on the D928 **Solomiac** (Tourist Information, tel: 62 65 02 57) is a late *bastide* (13C) on the Gimone with a 14C *halle* and 15C and 16C *couverts* (arcades) around it. The D165 (4.5km) goes through **Sarrant**, curious and picturesque, a circular village arranged around its church, a 14C tower over the old town gateway.

East of Mauvezin, on the D654, 6.5km, is arguably the prettiest *bastide* square and covered market at **Cologne** (Tourist Information, tel: 62 06 99 30). Wide open and spacious, it is surrounded by houses harmoniously combining well-restored brick, stone and timber, the oldest on the north and south. The *halle* itself is 14C. This is a simple structure, with a small square building in the centre (used for exhibitions) from which the roof radiates out supported by stone piers at the angles and wooden pillars elsewhere. The whole thing is topped by a small belfry and there are still 15C grain measures under the *halle*. Markets are held in the summer on Thursday and Sunday morning. Not far from here is the lake of Thoux-St-Cricq, organised for water activities.

It is 15km back to L'Isle-Jourdain on the D654.

16

Condom and the Ténarèze: Larressingle, Séviac

Total distance: 43km (28 miles).

This route includes three major but contrasting sites and an opportunity to visit Armagnac distilleries.

CONDOM (pop. 7836, Tourist Information, Place Bossuet, 32100-Condom, tel: 62 28 00 80) is the *sous-préfecture* of the *département* of the Gers, and capital of the Ténarèze, the central section of the Gers, which is named after a line of hills between the Adour and the Garonne which since time immemorial has been the north–south corridor linking the Garonne and the Pyrenees.

Condom is a pleasant town of mainly 17C and 18C handsome white stone *hôtels particuliers* more characteristic of Bordeaux and Aquitaine than Toulouse and the Languedoc. Variously described as the town of seven churches and the town of a hundred towers, the etymology of its unforgettable name is either a synthesis of *condate* and *dum*, meaning a hill at a confluent, or it is derived from *condominium*, a jointly controlled stronghold, as it was described when the ancient Vascon people from the Iberian peninsula, ancestors of the Gascons and the Basques, settled here c 721. A hundred noble families built a hundred fortified residences, hence the hundred towers. The number of churches has been whittled back, and the most important is the former Cathedral of St-Pierre.

Armagnac. The town is refreshed by the river Baïse, used in the 19C for transporting the precious Armagnac cargo to Bordeaux. It is still one of the main centres, with Auch and Eauze, for what is probably France's oldest distillate of wine, certainly older than cognac or calvados. When it was first produced in the 15C it was only used for medicinal purposes but during the 16C it started to acquire a different status and the production reached its peak in the 19C until the phylloxera epidemic in 1878. The area entitled to the Armagnac *appellation* was defined in 1909 and covers nearly 13,000 hectares (32,100 acres), the largest share in the Gers but running into neighbouring Lot-et-Garonne. The appellation is divided into three areas according to soil type: Bas-Armagnac, or Armagnac-Noir, to the west, is the largest area (7548 ha) with acidic, predominantly sandy soil which produces perfect grapes for distillation; the limestone of Haut-Armagnac to the east and south, representing (157ha), has grapes better suited to wines; the central region of Ténarèze (5127ha) has a mixture of clay and chalk with sand. White wine, low in alcohol and high in acidity, for distillation, is produced from three main grape varieties, Folle blanche, Ugni blanc and Colombard. Distillation has to take place by 31 March following the harvest and the alembic, or distilling vessel, is particular to the region. The wine is heated twice but distilled only once, whereas cognac is distilled twice, and maturation is in oak casks and not in the bottle.

Condom's facilities and position make it a good centre, as does the delight-ful 10-bedroom *Hôtel des Trois Lys* occupying a 17C building not far from the cathedral (tel: 62 28 33 33). The proprietor, Madame Manet, has a wealth of information on the region, and simply climbing the gracious staircase is an added bonus. The other attractive hotel, *Le Logis des Cordeliers* (tel: 62 28 03 68), is in a tranquil setting (Relais de Silence). The adjacent but independent restaurant, *La Table des Cordeliers* (tel: 62 68 28 36), occupies a converted Gothic chapel. Condom's market day is Wednesday, and two festivals are held in the spring, the *Bon Vivre*, to celebrate the quality of life (meaning food) in the Gers, and *Bandas y Peñas* (second Sunday in May), a colourful spectacle which brings a Spanish flavour to the town.

History. Condom is little mentioned until the 11C when a Benedictine Abbey was established and it became a stage on the Via Podiensis. It suffered the usual tribulations and political strife of the Middle Ages from both sides—the backlash of the Albigensian Crusades in Languedoc and the problems with the English in Aquitaine. It was elevated to episcopal see in the 14C but the Hundred Years War caused havoc until 1453. Just over a century later, having adhered to the Reformation, it was the theatre of more unrest during the Wars of Religion and the Cathedral was ran-sacked in 1569. Peace was restored with the Edict of Nantes in 1598, and the rebirth of the town dates from the 17C. Its most celebrated bishop was the great orator Jacques Bénigne Bossuet (1627–1704), named Bishop in 1670, but his contribution to the diocese was somewhat ephemeral as he was always too busy elsewhere.

On Foot. The town centre is **Place St-Pierre**, dominated to the north by the cathedral, opening to the east into Rue Gambetta and elegant houses on the south.

The **CATHEDRAL ST-PIERRE**. The Benedictine abbey, dedicated to St-Pierre, an important centre of learning, reached its apogee at the begin-ning 14C, and on the 13 August 1317, Pope John XXII, elevated Condom to bishopric with 130 parishes, a status it kept until the Revolution. The present cathedral was designed at the end of the 15C by Bishop Jean Marre (d. 1521), who rose through the ranks to become prior at Eauze and Nerac, as well as Confessor to the Queen, then to the King, before becoming Bishop of Condom. By 1511 work on the cathedral was already at an advanced stage and by 1521 the only parts still to be finished were the choir stalls and the roof. Bishop Hérard de Grossoles completed the work in 1524 and the cathedral was consecrated in October 1531.

Exterior. The rather gloomy south flank of the cathedral faces the square, the exterior generally in a rather sorry state and the south door very run-down despite some recent restoration. Built in a transitional style between Flamboyant and Renaissance, the best of the sculpture on the south is in the archivolts, the deep, ornate niches are empty and above the entrance are the arms of Jean Marre. Solidly buttressed all round, there is a 40m square tower over the west end.

Interior. The large aisleless 16C building without an extended transept is tacked on to the 14C Ste-Marie chapel at the east and the two parts are not exactly aligned. The wide nave with tiercerons has no triforium gallery, but is lit by the clerestory windows with grisaille glass. The nave piers have clustered shafts and carved capitals but the lierne vaulted choir is sur-rounded by undecorated cylindrical columns. The stone *jubé* is the third version, made in 1844 by the Virebent workshop in Toulouse, and forms a sort of pseudo ambulatory. The stained glass of the choir was made in a local workshop in 1861. A little light relief is added by an interesting group of **vault bosses** repainted in 1841, among them above the choir St-Sauveur, in reference to the dedication of the first church here, and St Peter the present patron, the builder, Jean Marre is represented by a sheep—*marrou* is Gascon for ram. Angel musicians evoke the celestial choir as well as the sumptuous liturgy of the 16C cathedral famed for its organ and counter-tenor chants; the Cross and Key of the town is in the south-east chapel and above the nave is the Royal coat of arms of Anne of Brittany, a portrait of Louis XII, and the fleur-de-lys.

The original, late Gothic-Renaissance pulpit, with an openwork baldaquin, is still in place. In the large chapels on the north are the tombs of Bishops Marre and Milon in the first, and in the third a carved walnut altar of 1704 salvaged at the Revolution from the pilgrim chapel, Notre-Dame de Piétat. A monument to Bishop de Grossoles stands in the sixth chapel. In the west tribune is the 17C **organ** built locally by Daumassens.

The west door opens into **Place Bossuet** where a worked metal cross with vines and corn motifs was erected in 1824. The Tourist Office is on the left. North of the cathedral is the **cloister**, built by Bishop Grossoles in the 16C with obvious stylistic similarities to the cathedral. There are double arcades on the east and west, and in the north-east corner is a doorway with Italianate decoration. Although commendable, it is over-heavy for the space. The buildings on the upper level have been occupied since 1861 by the Hôtel de Ville and the cloister serves as a public thoroughfare. On the north, between the old episcopal palace and the cloister, is the **episcopal chapel**, now part of the entrance to the Palais de Justice, also built in the first half of the 16C. An imposing Renaissance door links the chapel with the **Hôtel de la Sous-Préfecture**, the old episcopal palace begun in 1764 by Mgr d'Anterroches, the last Bishop.

The magnificent U-shaped stables with timbered ceilings have been converted to house the **Musée de l'Armagnac** (tel: 62 28 31 41 or 62 28 00 80, Mon–Sat, 10.00–12.00 and 14.00–18.00). Created in 1954, it retraces the history of the *eau-de-vie* and explains its production.

Round the corner at 21 Rue Jules-Ferry is the grandiose **Hôtel de Polignac**, 1780–85, now a school, with colonnades and wrought iron, built by the Abbot Marie Dorlan de Polignac, Prior of Layrac, on the ruins of the old citadel. The west façade overlooking the river is equally impressive. Further down the street is the former 18C Seminary of Mgr de Milon, now the Lycée Bossuet.

Rue des Eclosettes leads back via Rue des Jacobins to the covered market and from the south-east corner of the square the narrow Rue Voutée leads into **Rue Gambetta**, a lively, pedestrian street with the **Hôtel des Postes** (Post Office) in the old Neo-Classical Hôtel de Ville, and the pretty 17C Hôtel de Lagarde (Hôtel des Trois Lys).

In **Allée Général de Gaulle** (Rue Jean Jaurès) are stately 18C residences, such as the **Hôtel du Bouzet de Roquepine**, 1763, with *oeil de boeuf* windows in the façade, on the corner with Rue Roquepine. It was built on the line of the old fortifications as was the **Hôtel de Cugnac** next door. Laid out around three sides of a courtyard and closed to the street with formidable railings, the Hôtel de Cugnac is occupied by an Armagnac distillery, Maison Ryst-Dupeyron, and can be visited (tel: 62 28 08 08). Opposite, at the angle with Rue des Cordeliers, is **Hôtel de Cadignan**, 1775.

From Place de la Liberté turn right into Rue Cauzabon where on the left is the Louis XV-style Hôtel de Galard with a pilastered portico and mascaron motif. Place du Lion d'Or and Rue Charron which lead back to Place St-Pierre, also have some pretty houses. Rues Ichon and des Armuriers run down to the **banks of the Baïse** and **Pont des Carmes** south of which are gardens and a leisure area (there are river cruises during the summer, tel: 62 28 46 46).

Cross the Baïse and leave Condom by the D15.

From a distance, the bluff mass of walls and battlemented towers of **Larressingle** (5km) epitomise a medieval fortified village, albeit pocket sized. Called grandiosely by the locals the Carcassonne of the Gers, it is equally stunning once inside. The church was fortified in the 12C and later a 270m rampart was thrown around the church and castle, and the whole thing is still surrounded by a ditch. It was recognised by the popes in the 13C as the property of the abbeys of Agen and Condom and then became the official residence of the Bishops of Condom until the end of the 16C when they moved to Cassaigne, taking most of the transportable timber elements of the buildings with them.

The barrel-vaulted fortified **entrance** on the west, where there was once a drawbridge, is very narrow and the protection afforded by the walls and towers and the houses huddled up against them gives it a rather cosy feel inside. Opposite the entrance is the semi-ruined massive castle-keep on four floors with signs of later alterations and additions to make it more habitable. Nestling behind it is the little 12C Church of St-Sigismond; its west façade has a porch with Romanesque capitals and the Lamb of God in the tympanum. The half-dome of the 12C church was pierced when a two-bay extension was added to the east end in the 13C. The route to Santiago passed this way, and the other road from Larressingle (between the cemetery and the Marie) will take you down to the old pilgrim bridge, the **Pont d'Artigues**.

About a kilometre along the D15, turn right on the D278, left on the D114 (9km), across the vineyards to one of the most enchanting *bastides* in the Gers, the little circular village of **Fourcès** (pronounce the 's'). A bridge crosses the Auzoue, under the watchful eye of the 16C château. This tiny community has only about 350 inhabitants, but is decked out in blooms during the flower festival on the last weekend of April. The village probably developed around a primitive fortification, long disappeared, and was later enclosed in a protective wall, fragments of which remain, as does the pretty bell-tower astride the lane on the west. The old houses, some with arcades and others half-timbered, link to enclose the plane-shaded *place*.

Go south, 5.5km, on the D29 to **Montréal** (pop. 1182, Tourist Information, tel: 62 29 42 85). Built on an escarpment, it was one of the first bastides founded in Gascony, in 1256, and by the time it was finished in 1289 it was already under English domination. It has the typical *bastide* layout with a central square with arcades and a large church off centre, with aisles and primitive capitals and corbels in the east, bearing the scars of Protestant iconoclasm particularly around the south door. At the Tourist Information on the square, you can buy a combined ticket for the Gallo-Roman site at Séviac, and the two-room **Musée Gallo-Romain** *sur place* (Apr–May 15.00–18.00, Jun–Sept 10.00–12.00 and 14.00–19.00, Jul–Aug) crammed with items found at Séviac since 1868.

For eating, *Chez Simone* (tel: 62 29 44 40) in the village or, near Séviac, off the D29, the *hôtel-restaurant* (and museum) *de la Gare* (tel: 62 29 43 37), a converted railway station, perfect for children who can play outside in safety.

To reach **Séviac** (2km) head west from Montréal on the D15, turn left after the bridge and then right and follow the signs. The nonchalantly low-key setting belies the importance of the **archaeological site**, one of the largest in Gascony covering 2ha (tel: 62 09 90 35). Excavations in 1959 uncovered a classic Gallo-Roman **villa** with peristyle which dates from the 2C to the 5C. A large interior courtyard 35m square is itself bordered by a gallery 4m wide. The living quarters consist of mainly rectangular rooms and around them is another gallery. On the east is a large building with an apse heated by hypocaust and to the south, separated from the villa by an interior courtyard in which marble columns have been found, is a vast **thermae** with white and green marble slabs with the mosaics still in place in the piscina.

The most remarkable feature of Séviac is the beautiful and well made 4C and 5C **mosaics**. There are about 30 surviving pieces which vary in size, some are surprisingly complete and all astonishingly unprotected. The background colour is a creamy white and the designs are picked out in terracotta red, pink, olive green, dark blue and yellow ochre. Nearly all are repeat geometric patterns but a few have stylised fruit and vegetal designs. During the Merovingian era (6C and 7C) the villa was divided into smaller dwellings with transverse walls. On the south-east, traces of Merovingian Christian sanctuaries with a baptistry and necropolis can be identified.

Go back past Montréal on the D15, then turn right on the D113 to Gondrin, and left on the D931, to **Mouchan** (18km) where all that remains of the former Cluniac priory of St-Austrigile is the small but satisfying 12C church in the typical yellowish-orange stone of the region with a square tower (open May–Sept, afternoons). There are some simple carvings on the exterior and inside are 31 decorated capitals, mainly with a stiff leaf design similar to many at Flaran, although one has a a scallop-shell pattern, three have an overall design of interlacings, and five have storiated or animal themes. One of particular note, in the east end of the church, is carved on three faces with little scenes inscribed in arches.

From Mouchan take the D208 (3km) to **Château de Cassaigne** (tel: 62 28 04 02), set in 27ha of vines, which attracts 40,000 visitors a year, both to visit the building and to sample the Armagnac. The 13C castle became the summer palace of the Bishops of Condom at the beginning of the 16C when they abandoned Laressingle. It was remodelled in the stylish comfort of the Renaissance by Bishops Jehan de Monluc and Jean Duchemin both of whom were very attached to the château and died there. Their work forms the core of the building, but more restoration and rebuilding was carried out towards during the time of Louis de Milon (1693–1734) who was responsible for the restrained elegance of the present west entrance façade, and work continued on the gardens in the 18C. The Faget family, descendants of the Intendant of the last bishop, have owned the property since 1827 and have a long tradition of distilling Armagnac. A visit to the château includes a *diaporama* (audio-visual display) in English and French, and sampling the produce. The most spectacular feature of the interior is the beautiful brick vault of the kitchen, quite literally a *cul de four*, like the roof of a giant bread oven.

Detour. About 5km south (D208, D229) the Château of **Busca Maniban** (tel: 62 28 40 38, Easter–15 Nov, 14.00–19.00, closed Mon), built in 1649, in a marvellous setting above the vineyards, offers a visit to the house and the distillery. There is a typical Gascon *pigeonnier* nearby.

Flaran and La Romieu

Total distance: 52km (33 miles).

This excursion is within easy reach of Condom or Auch, and includes two former abbeys.

9km south of Condom on the D930 on the banks of the Baïse is the **ABBEY OF FLARAN** (tel: 62 28 50 19, all year, 09.30–12.00, 14.00–18.00, Jul–Aug all day, except Tues). The best preserved Cistercian edifice in the Gers, it is a beautiful group of 12C and 17C–18C buildings which were carefully restored after a fire in 1970. Apart from their architectural merit, they are used as a cultural centre, a centre for information on the pilgrim routes, concerts, exhibitions, and a *Son et Lumière* is held here in the summer.

Flaran was founded in 1151 and donations of land and property during the second half of the 12C enabled the construction of an important and very beautiful monastery. The upheavals of the 14C and 15C took their toll, and placed in the hands of secular abbots at the end of the 15C it continued to decline. In 1569 the abbey suffered devastating attacks by the Protestants, but in 1573 Abbot Jean de Boyer started restoration work on the church and repairs to other buildings were carried out through to 1603. In the 18C a general remodelling of the abbey was effected, particularly the guest quarters.

The entrance to the abbey is across the great courtyard with the church to the east and stables and outhouses to the west, and through the former *quartier d'hôte*. This building was conceived on the lines of a small gascon château as the prior's residence in 1759 with a grand staircase and stucco decoration. The **cloister** has been rebuilt twice since the 12C. All that remains of the 14C reconstruction is the west gallery, with rectangular piers subdivided by paired columns and capitals with vegetal motifs or hybrid animals and figures. The remaining galleries are very simple constructions with timber and tile roofs, and an upper floor on the north.

At the heart of the abbey is the extremely beautiful **Church of Notre-Dame**, begun c 1170, a rare example in the south-west of quintessential Cistercian architecture with the minimum of decoration and maximum light. It has a wide transept, square chancel and semi-circular main apse with two apsidal chapels on either side decorated on the exterior with a band of small arcades. These disappeared from the central apse when a brick and timber rising was added, possibly in the 17C. The crossing is vaulted with rectangular ribs and the three bay nave, raised c 1220, received a pointed barrel arch. A small rose window was inserted in the west. The south aisle is barrel vaulted but the north has ribs of a different style from the crossing. The numerous capitals all have stylised foliate, geometric or interlace motifs, and over the door from the cloister is a simple chrism. The west door has geometric friezes and reused marble columns.

Abutting the north transept are the 12C monastic buidings, the armarium (library), sacristy and the very gracious **chapter house**, which has nine ribbed bays supported by four marble columns in different colours and simple capitals. It opens on to the **cloister** with three richly moulded recessed bays supported by capitals on short marble shafts. The **monks' room** to the north is used for exhibitions. Above the chapter house was the **dormitory**, communicating directly with the church. The variety of fenestration indicates alterations in the 15C and the 17C, and in the 18C it was extended when individual and more comfortable rooms replaced the dormitory, an ironic decadence of the original Cistercian ethos.

A passageway in the north-east of the cloister leads to a traditional monastic garden with aromatic and medicinal plants and with an excellent view of the east end of the church. The garden façade was embellished by a monumental gateway in the 18C.

The **refectory** on the north of the cloister, was reduced in size at some point and adorned with elegant *gypseries* (c 1730–80). The kitchen and the warming house, either side of the refectory, were altered in the 18C. On the walls of the upper gallery, originally closed, are 18C mural paintings.

Also to visit is the **Madeleine farm**, restored in 1988, a section of which is used for exhibitions.

For eating (or staying) near Flaran, at Valence-sur-Baïse, *La Ferme de Flaran* (tel: 62 28 58 22), and at Castera-Verduzan, the *Auberge Le Florida* (tel: 62 68 13 22).

From **Valence-sur-Baïse**, a 13C *bastide* with a 14C church take the D142 and D42 (9.5km) to **St-Puy**, a charming village on the site of an ancient oppidum and the land of Blaise de Monluc (1500–77) Maréchal de France whose memoires were entitled *Commentaires*. At the many-times rebuilt **Château de Monluc** (tel: 62 28 55 02) you can discover more about wine, Armagnac and the Armagnac-based liqueur, *pousse-rapière*, a wickedly potent aperitif, in their beautiful vaulted cellars.

The D654 north-east brings you to **Pouy-Petit** and D232 to **St-Orens** (6km) which are two of the many fortified sites in the Gers.

From here you could visit **Terraube** (D42 north-east, 16km), a stunningly dramatic château, property of the Galard family since the 10C, and its little village.

From St-Orens take the D232/D204, cross the D7 and continue on the D204 to the D41 to **La Romieu** (16km). The two towers of the church high above the countryside announce the village of just over 540 inhabitants on the site of a Benedictine abbey founded, so it is said, by two monks returning from Rome c 1062. Its name, from the Latin Romaeus meaning pilgrims, was first mentioned in 1082. It was granted *bastide* status in the 14C at the wish of its great benefactor, Arnaud d'Aux born at La Romieu c 1260, cousin of Bernard de Got, first Pope at Avignon. The village was English from 1279 to 1453.

It is an out-of-the-way place with campsite and *gîtes*, an arcaded square, an old town gateway, an arboretum and a Gothic *lavoir*.

The **Collegiate Church of St-Pierre** (tel: 62 28 09 95, 14.00–18.00 every day) is an unexpected and interesting example of Gothic architecture. After an illustrious career, Arnaud d'Aux was made cardinal in 1312 and that year envisaged the construction of his funerary monument composed of collegiate church, cloister and residence. It was inaugurated on 30 July 1318. The church is approached through the 14C cloister which originally had two, possibly three levels. The Rayonnant bays, with two trefoil and a polyfoil opening in each, are divided by slender columns. Despite the degradations inflicted by the Protestant troops of Montgomery and at the Revolution, it still maintains an aura of peace and grace. The aisleless church, supported by massive buttresses, has a five-bay nave with the four tombs of the Cardinal and his nephews, also damaged. Below the octagonal tower on the east is the sacristy entirely decorated with some remarkable 14C frescoes. The eight walls are covered with octagonal medallions containing portraits of founders, biblical figures or geometric patterns and the vaults with a variety of angel musicians and censer angels. The other, square, tower is all that is left of the Cardinal's palace.

The D41/D931 bring you to Condom (11km).

17

Lectoure and the Lomagne

Total distance: 125km (78 miles).

This tour starts in Lectoure, and meanders through the Lomagne, the region between the Gers and the Garonne.

LECTOURE (pop. 4434, Tourist Information, tel: 62 68 76 98) is a town that seems to be *bien dans sa peau*, confident in its ancient if turbulent past, at ease behind its refined and genteel Neo-Classical façades, and solid as the rock it is built on despite the narrowness of the ridge. It merits a prolonged visit and is ideally placed for exploring the Lomagne. It is not as well equipped with hotels as Condom or Fleurance, but the *Hôtel le Bastard* (tel: 62 68 82 44), with an excellent restaurant but at times frosty reception, occupies an elegant late-18C town house. Market day is Friday, and not far away is the Lac des Trois Vallées.

The three main monuments in Lectoure, the former cathedral, the museum and the fountain of Diana, are at the east end of the town which has one main one-way street running east–west. The Tourist Information Office is next to the church.

History. Lectoure, capital of the Lomagne, has been occupied since the dawn of time. A Gallic tribe, the Lactorates, circumspectly surrendered to the Roman invaders c 120 BC and subsequently the Gallo-Roman city, capital of Novempopulania, flourished in the plain where several roads converged. The high ground was reserved for the temples dedicated to Jupiter and, more importantly, to Cybele, ancient Phrygian earth mother, a cult in which the sacrifice of the bull and ram, symbols of strength and fertility, was an important part of the ritual. An important find of *autels tauroboliques* was made in 1540 when the city wall was demolished east of the cathedral to make way for the new chevet and these are on display in the museum.

In the Middle Ages Lectoure was the main residence of the Viscounts of Lomagne and then became the headquarters of the powerful Counts of Armagnac until the siege of Lectoure, November 1472 to March 1473, when Louis XI's troops invaded and ransacked the town and murdered Count Jean V. Soon afterwards the town was reborn as a royal seneschalcy, only to suffer again during the Religious Wars.

In the 13C Bishop Giraud de Monlezun took a pledge of allegiance to Edward I of England, built an episcopal residence and repaired the cathedral. The **Cathedral of St-Gervais-et-St-Protais** is a fairly complex structure exposed over the centuries to the horrors of war and the caprices of individuals. The west façade, almost totally devoid of decoration, was erected in the 15C and has been subjected to many modifications and all too obvious restoration. Supported by two angle buttresses, the low arch of the entrance replaced the Gothic one in the 19C and the series of 10 niches above the door have almost melted away, such is the fragility of the limestone. The fenestration is very modest, with only a three-light window and a small oculus. The belfry on the north is impressive but not as impressive as it once was. The original version was demolished by Louis XI's army during the siege of Lectoure when the cathedral was part of the city defences. A tall spire was built in the 15C, but because emergency work was not carried out, had to be demolished along with the upper octagonal level in the late 18C. The five stepped levels, more ornate towards the top, are supported by angle buttresses which lost their statues in the Revolution. A tall isolated gabled buttress on the north flank of the cathedral indicates the incompleted rebuild of the choir in the 16C. The east and south sides of the cathedral can be seen from the adjacent Jardins des Marronniers and the courtyard of the Hôtel de Ville respectively.

Enter by the west door. A choir with apse and ambulatory in the style of the north of France was grafted to the single nave, typical of the Midi. The transition from nave to chancel is effected by an awkward triumphal arch partly obstructing the view of the high choir vaults. The two square bays of the nave are defined by six massive piers, the core of which are Romanesque and were designed to carry domes on pendentives in the manner of Cahors or Souillac. It is not clear whether the domes were ever completed because at the end of the 12C the nave was vaulted. Extensive repairs to the nave were carried out in 1480 and at the beginning of the 16C vaulted chapels separated by cylindrical piers with galleries were inserted. More damage and alterations to the nave followed in the 16C, 17C and 18C. The reconstruction of the chancel and apse began in the 16C at which time the five chapels to the east were completed. These square chapels are inscribed within the simple polygon of the east end with massive triangular sections of masonry between them. For financial reasons the work was abandoned until 1600 when the ten cylindrical piers were introduced to create the ambulatory. The choir vaults have three polychromed pendant bosses and the carved early-17C choir stalls were placed here in the 19C. The Chapel of the Assumption, to the left of the choir, has an 18C altar and elegant wrought iron, as well as a white marble statue of the Assumption of the Virgin, probably the work of an Italian sculptor. The Sacré-Coeur chapel of the nave has a series of 17C easel paintings of the Passion, and in two of the chapels are carved oak communion rails. The former baptistry contains a museum of sacred art.

The **Hôtel de Ville**, 1676–82, contiguous with the cathedral, was originally the episcopal palace. A majestically regular but unadorned building with numerous windows, the brick vaulted kitchen and cellars have been transformed into a fascinating **Archaeological Museum** (tel: 62 68 70 22, 09.00–12.00, 14.00–18.00, winter closing 17.00). Take note, the building does not always appear to be open when in fact it is, and the tickets are sold by the *concierge*, on the left as you enter. The entrance to the museum is to the right, below the magnificent cantilevered staircase set off by the scrolly outlines of the wrought iron balustrade.

The museum was opened in 1972, after a concerted campaign by the town. The unique collection of altars was always recognised as exceptional, yet in 1591 they were re-used at the base of the pillars of the *halle aux grains* where they stayed until 1842. By 1874 they were in the Mairie. The

Misericord in the choir enclosure, 1535, of the Cathedral of St-Mary, St-Bertrand-de-Comminges

Toulouse: the cloister, 1396, of the former Couvent des Grands Augustins, now a museum

Surrounded by cypress trees, the Romanesque basilica of St-Just-de-Valcabrère

The so-called Templar Church at Plan d'Aragnouet, in the Pyrenees close to the border with Spain

The white and gold painted east end of the church at Jézeau in the Pyrénées Centrales

The striking mosaic of the god Oceanus, now in the Archaeological Museum, Lectoure

(above, left) The remarkable 14th century frescoes in the collegiate church of St-Pierre, La Romieu

(above, right) Antoine Bourdelle's majestic bronze statue of Penelope, 1912, overlooking the Place Prax-Paris in Montauban

The beautiful stone openwork panel which is part of the screen, 1531, of the St-Raphael Chapel, Rodez Cathedral

Capital of Daniel in the Lions' Den, in the cloister, 1100, Moissac

*Sauveterre-de-Rouergue,
a bastide founded in 1281*

*The winter-time truffle market
at Lalbenque*

The remarkably well preserved 14th century Château du Bousquet

Albi: a view under the Pont du 22 août 1944

Figeac: La Place des Écritures, a courtyard enclosed by medieval façades with a giant version of the Rosetta Stone on the ground, 1990, by Joseph Kosuth

The attractive village of Brousse-le-Château on the banks of the Alrance river

The east end of the Church of Ste-Foy, Conques

seven rooms of the museum are arranged chronologically, the first part dedicated to local palaeontology. The Gallic era is represented by burial pits of the second half of the 1C BC, sculptures, pottery, including huge amphorae for wine, and coins. The showpiece, the **20 pagan altars**, from the 2C and 3C, are mainly in Pyrenean marble and decorated with the head of a bull (taurobole) or a ram (criobole). The engraved inscription on each stone records the date of the initiation ceremony involving the sacrifice of a bull or ram, and the name of the receiver of the rites. There are other pagan and Christian funerary monuments, and sarcophagi as well as mosaics exhibited in an attractive vaulted chamber dated 1680, one with an awesome portrayal of the god Oceanus.

On leaving the Hôtel de Ville turn left and left again and down to the bottom of Rue Fontelié to the **Fontaine de Diane**, a spring and pool covered by a 13C vaulted construction with a double arched opening and 15C iron grille. Water from this spring was used at the **Royal Tannery**, further down the street, now the Maison d'Ydrone, a retirement home. This important workshop, built in 1752–54, was one of the most advanced in its day and employed over 100 people. A double flight of steps leads down into the yard, and above the industrial building is a pretty ironwork gable which once contained the work's clock.

Turn up left along the Chemin de Saint Clair which follows the old city walls enclosing public gardens, cross the main road and continue on to the north-west side of town and the former home of the executioner, the 14C **Tour du Bourreau**, part of the old town walls. Wind your way back through the old streets past the **Hôtel de Castaing-Bastard**, Rue Lagrange, now converted to hotel-restaurant (see above), an elegant building with fine *gypseries* and fireplaces inside. Back on Rue Nationale, just after the corner with **Rue des Frères Danzas** is the 13C Tour d'Albinhac. To the west of the town is Cours d'Armagnac and, on the site of the castle of the Counts of Armagnac, is the hospital, begun in 1760 and completed in 1809–12. Behind the hospital on **Allées Montmorency** are the remains of the castle where the Duc de Montmorency was imprisoned after the battle of Castelnaudary (Aude) before being executed in Toulouse in 1632. Complete the amble along Boulevard Jean Jaurès built on the southern ramparts.

From Lectoure take the N21 in the direction of Agen and branch off on to the D7 and the D935 to St-Clar (15km). This is an important centre of garlic production and at certain seasons a slightly garlicky aroma will mingle with the scents of wild flowers. **St-Clar** is a *bastide* on a hill, founded jointly by Edward I of England and the Bishop of Lectoure, Géraud de Monlezun, in 1289, on the site of an earlier *sauveté*, resulting in two arcaded squares corresponding to the different periods of development. The older part, the Castelviel, is now picturesquely dilapidated in parts; its old church (12C and 14C) is in a very poor state and cannot be visited. The later *bastide* has retained its original orthogonal layout around the main square with a covered *halle* which consists of a simple roof supported by timber posts contiguous with the rebuilt (19C) *maison commune*. The church is a dull 19C neo-Gothic affair.

3km south of St-Clar is the **Château d'Avezan**, a severe 13C château on a bluff, with 15C and 17C additions, open Apr–Oct.

Return to the D7 and turn right on to the D40 (9km) to the **Château de Gramont** (tel: 63 94 05 26, 09.00–12.00, 14.00–19.00 Jul–Sep, rest of year 14.00–19.00). Part Gothic, part Renaissance, this is an excellently restored castle beside the river Arratz, the ancient frontier between Gascony and Languedoc.

It was first mentioned in 1215 when Simon de Montfort made it over to Eudes de Montaut and as a reminder of this the tower on the south is called Tour Simon de Montfort. The château was staunchly defended during the Hundred Years War by its châtelain, the Chevalier de Barbazan, who killed single handed six soldiers of the English army and for this act of heroism was permitted not only to use the coat of arms of France but was buried in 1432 with the royals at St-Denis. Gramont was inherited in 1491 by a member of the Voisins family, one of whom, Aymeric, was inspired to transform the medieval castle into a sumptuous Renaissance palace. From 1642 it passed through several hands and was more or less abandoned until it was purchased in the 1960s, restored, and bequeathed to the state. The visit is accompanied, and the visitors' entrance is through the Simon de Montfort Tower opposite the church where there is a small exhibition.

The château is composed essentially of two unequal wings. The smaller, known as the Châtelet, abutting the Simon de Montfort tower, is the older, dating from the time of the Montaut family, and incorporates elements of the 13C, 14C and 15C. The monumental main entrance, with the arms of the Montaut family above, was erected in the 17C. The upper part of the tower was removed and the arrow slits and cross windows are 19C fantasies. Inside is a large courtyard with the later and much larger wing, in bluish-grey limestone, on the north, c 1535–40. Steps lead up to the two doorways on the elevated ground floor level. This wing displays the idiom of the Renaissance—and uses the Corinthian and Ionic orders in an insouciant manner. Two small Gothic windows incorporated into the façade seem to indicate an existing building. The garden façade, flanked by pavilions in advance of the main façade, is slightly more ordered, and maintains the use of pediments for the smaller windows and entablatures for the larger ones. Inside the main entrance on the north, also reached by steps and a perron, is a staircase with late Gothic vaults with heavily moulded ribs.

The interior proportions and décor have been restored as far as possible, and the Grande Salle has a particularly fine monumental Renaissance fireplace. The upper floor of the Châtelet has been refurbished as for exhibitions and concerts are held regularly at the château.

Head now along the D40 (or the D88) and turn right onto the D86E for **Lachapelle** (11km). At the heart of this village resides a miniature rustic Baroque gem which offers a respite from medieval *bastides* and castles. The little **Church of St-Pierre** (13C) attached to the château and originally its private chapel, later became the parish church. But the main interest lies inside and first you need to obtain the key from the modernish house opposite (do not call between 12.00–14.00). Tiny though it is, the **interior** was entirely decked out in 1776 by a craftsman called Muraignon Champagne with an all encompassing scheme of gilded and painted woodwork, with panels, pilasters, mouldings, etc, and around the nave a superimposed series of arcades and loggias imitates the interior of a theatre. Apart from the dusty aspidistras, there are furnishings of a similar quality to the woodwork, including a pulpit and altars of the same date, a 16C statue of Ste-Quitterie, some late 16C–early 17C choir stalls with carved misericords, a 17C Virgin and Child, a relic of St Prosper, which came from Rome in 1777, and a two-eagle lectern presented by Napoléon III. There was some damage at the Revolution and the church was reworked to a certain extent in the 19C, but during more recent restoration a ceiling was removed to reveal the original gilded vault above the altar.

To the west of the D40 (D281 and D953, 6km) is the oldest *bastide* in the Gers, **Miradoux**, founded in 1253. It has an imposing but battered church, with a bare west end except for one rose and a pedimented Renaissance doorway. Across from the church is the Hôtel de Ville and built up against it is a 16C covered market.

Flamarens, 3km along the D953, is a tiny place with a château, 13C–15C, with one wing and a round machicolated tower looking out over the countryside. It was badly damaged by fire in 1943 and is under restoration but can be visited (10.00–20.00 Sat and Sun). The Grossolles family owned the château from 1466 to 1882 and the arms of Hérard de Grossoles, Bishop of Condom, 1521–43, with the date 1541, are above the door of the spectacularly ruined church. The belfry stands in isolated splendour with a two-bell gable. To the west of the village is the **Ecomusée de la Lomagne**, a museum of rural life centred around a typical 19C farm (tel: 62 68 76 98/62 28 62 95, Jun–Nov).

Take the D953 13km, to Auvillar.

Auvillar (pop. 1014, Tourist Information, tel: 63 39 57 33) is a small brick town of great charm built on an escarpment above the Garonne. The attractive Porte de l'Horlorge, the old city gate with a clock tower rebuilt in brick and stone in the 17C, is all that is left of the city defences demolished in 1572. At the centre of the town is a small triangular arcaded *place* surrounded by fairly grand 17C and 18C brick houses and one 16C building. The justly famous circular **halle**, its roof radiating out from a small central drum to rest on a sturdy Tuscan colonnade, was built in 1825 on the remains of a square market. Under its skirts are ancient grain measures. Auvillar reached its commercial high-point in the 18C, thanks to its port on the Garonne, now a *base de loisirs*, and to the manufacture of pottery. There is a collection of *faïence* in the Vieil-Auvillar museum.

The château, north of the marketplace, disappeared in the 16C but from the Place du Château is a tremendous vantage point over the vast Garonne valley and as far as the slopes of the Quercy. The **Church of St-Pierre** suffered badly during the Hundred Years War and the Wars of Religion resulting in a curiously disjointed exterior. An extraordinary ruined west tower, with two turrets and a belfry perched above the skeletal remains, was built in the 16C but almost entirely demolished in 1794, and then restored, along with the entire church, by Théodore Olivier in 1862. The church, rebuilt in the 15C after the Hundred Years War, is strikingly large, 43m long, and the older parts are in stone while the rest is in brick. The north apsidal chapel is all that is left of the earlier (late-11C/12C) church, with some carved capitals of that period. The apse is Flamboyant and the nave dates from the 15C and 17C. There is a Counter-Reformation retable behind the main altar.

For an example of pure 19C nostalgia, take the D12 and turn off after about 7km to Le Pin. The **Château St-Roch** (tel: 63 95 95 22, 14.30–19.00 Jul–Sep, weekends in winter) was the Flamboyant folly of a rich art collector, Georges de Monbrison, in 1860. This pastiche of a Loire château, all gables and turrets, was designed by Théodore Olivier, disciple of Viollet-le-Duc, and sits high in a 17ha park *à l'anglaise* benefiting from some fine views. The neo-Renaissance interior has high-quality woodwork and some beautiful tiled floors, plus painted décor in the Grand Salon by the Parisian Lechevalier-Chevignard. A hotel-restaurant uses part of the building, and the Disneyland appeal is completed by a tour of the park in a little train.

Take the D12/D15 (7.5km) to **St-Nicolas-de-la-Grave**, a small brick town whose most famous son was Antoine Laumet de Lamothe-Cadillac, coloniser and founder of Louisiana and of Detroit in 1701. His birthplace can be visited (tel: 63 95 92 55). St-Nicolas is close to the mighty meeting point of the Tarn and the Garonne, where medieval pilgrims crossed by ferry. It is now spanned by a monumental bridge and a 400ha lake has been created to provide a watering hole for tourists and locals with a *base de loisirs* and campsite.

The former **Abbey of Belleperche** is 12km away (D26) on the banks of the Garonne (14.00–17.00, Sat, Jul–Sept, or tel: 63 32 36 94). Founded c 1143–44, Protestants and Revolutionaries did for most of it, and all that is left is are the vast 17C/18C monastic buildings.

Follow the Garonne on the D26 and cross it again (D928, 11km) to **Montech**, which has an ancient forest to the south and the unique *Pente d'Eau* on the Canal Latéral de la Garonne to the north. Not exactly a water slope, but a system devised in 1984 to by-pass five locks by means of a mechanised structure straddling the by-pass canal which scoops up both boat and water. You can experience the technique first-hand by taking a boat trip on the *bateau mouche* from Montech (tel: 63 04 48 28).

To complete the tour of the Lomagne take the D928 to **Beaumont-de-Lomagne**, 22km, a pleasant *bourgade* with a mighty 14C covered market supported by a veritable forest of timbers. In the square is a statue to the mathematician Pierre Fermat (1601–65), who was born here. Beaumont, like St-Clar, has important markets to sell the high quality white garlic grown in the Lomagne. The markets are not, unfortunately, held under the beautful *halle* but at the *marché au forail* on Tuesdays and Saturdays from about June to September.

Lectoure is 40km by the D928 and D7.

18

Moissac

MOISSAC (pop. 12,200, Tourist Information, 6 place Durand de Bredons, tel: 63 04 01 85) is a modest town with a major and breathtakingly beautiful group of Romanesque sculpture in the former Abbey of St-Pierre de Moissac, once an important stage on the Via Podiensis to Santiago. Moissac draws crowds but never seems crowded and would make a convenient stopover for the present-day traveller. Near the motorway, convenient for Montauban, Toulouse, the Lomagne and Agen (see Blue Guide South West France) it has the advantage of rivers, the canal and the Tarn et Garonne Lake. The fertile valley is the market garden of the region, producing some 200,000 tons of peaches, melons, apples, pears, nectarines, cherries, plums, kiwis, strawberries and the unique Chasselas, a small sweet dessert grape with an *appellation contrôlée* label. Harvested early in the season, the *Fête des Chasselas* takes place on the third weekend in September when shop windows are draped with the luscious clusters. Market days are Saturday and Sunday. There are a number of hotels and a camp site on the banks of the Tarn. A pilgrimage documentation centre has recently opened. An all-season centre, the cloisters are open all year, and early November is the best time to photograph the sculpted tympanum.

On Foot. The approach to the abbey church is most dramatic along Rue de la République from Place des Récollets (the market/parking). Alternatively park in Avenue de Brienne, and take the steps down to the abbey. In the pretty Place Durand de Bredons, west of the church, is the Tourist Information Centre, exhibition hall and entrance to the cloisters.

The Church and Cloisters of the Abbey of St-Pierre de Moissac

History. The legendary founder of a religious community at Moissac is Clovis in 506, but it is more likely that the Benedictine monastery was founded by Bishop Didier of Cahors (630–655) at the time of Clovis II (639–657). The first documented evidence of its existence relates to gifts of land donated by Nizezius in 680 and to these were added gifts from 9C benefactors, the Carolingian monarchs and the bishops of Cahors. Moissac suffered incursions from all sides from the 8C to the 10C and, as the power of the Carolingians diminished in the south-west, the Abbey came under the protection of the increasingly powerful Counts of Toulouse who found it a valuable source of revenue. Its consequent decline was recorded in the chronicles of Abbot Aymeric de Peyrac (1377–1406). By 1030 part of the church had collapsed and in 1042 a fire put paid to the rest. There was no choice but to enlist the help of Cluny, then in full expansion, and St-Odilon was only too happy to add Moissac to the *'gîtes d'étape'* (Marcel Durliat, p 118) on the road to Santiago. A Cluniac monk, Durand de Bredons, was named Abbot of Moissac on 29 June 1048 and St-Pierre was permitted to maintain its abbey status despite its subordination to Cluny. Out of the ashes grew one of the richest, most influential abbeys in France with sculpture that transcends any other of the period. Durand de Bredons (1048–71) and Hunaud de Gavaret (1072–85) re-established the scriptorium and the illuminated manuscripts were undoubtedly a source of iconographic and stylistic inspiration to the sculptors. Durand de Bredons became Bishop of Toulouse from 1060 and through him Moissac played a leading role in Gregorian reforms in the 11C. The abbey was also one of Cluny's springboards into Spain, and part of a spiritual network woven across northern Spain and south-west France carrying artistic influences in both directions.

The consecration of a Romanesque church on 6 November 1063, constructed on the apse of the earlier Carolingian church, is recorded on an inscription in the choir. The monastic buildings were blessed by Urban II in 1096. The cloister, completed in 1100, was created during the time of Abbot Ansquitil (1085–1115) who also added the massive porch and belfry at the west end of the church. Ansquitil's successor, Abbot Roger de Sorèze (1115–31) fortified the west end and was responsible for the famous monumental doorway. In the 12C the church was transformed into an austere aisleless building intended to receive cupolas similar to Cahors (it is not known if these were built.) Consecrated in 1180, it was damaged by fire in 1188 and by Simon de Montfort in 1212, when the cloisters also suffered. A long period of stagnation was interrupted by the abbacy of Bertrand de Montaigut (1260–95) who restored the cloisters. Aymeric de Roquemaurel (1431–49) and Pierre and Antoine de Carmaing (1449–1501) repaired the monastery after the Hundred Years War when the church was reconstructed in Gothic style and the brick part of the belfry was added. The church as we now see it dates from this period.

Pierre de Carmaing placed the abbey under the indirect control of Commendatory Abbots in 1466. In 1626 secular canons replaced the monks, plunging it into decline, and the library of some 120 manuscripts, already neglected, was sold to Colbert. In 1767 some of the monastic buildings were demolished and at the Revolution other buildings were sold and the cloister sculptures were damaged. At the beginning of the 19C the northern part was returned to the parish and a small seminary installed, but c 1845 the refectory was demolished to make way for a section of the Bordeaux-Sète railway although the church and cloister had been classified historic monuments in 1840. Yet, the first restoration work on the cloister, supervised by Questel, began in 1838–42 and in the 1850s Viollet-le-Duc and Théodore Olivier worked on the porch and belfry.

Exterior. The famous **tympanum** over the south entrance of the abbey church is simultaneously enthralling and profoundly moving and the impact never diminishes. The church, however, is a hotch potch of Romanesque and Gothic, a testament to successive building campaigns which transformed the late 12C stone church into a 15C Gothic church of brick. The Romanesque bays, with the windows and mouldings still in place, were arbitrarily divided and submerged by the buttresses to support the higher levels. The belfry was altered and amended in the 15C and 17C. In 1985 the paving immediately in front of the portal was dug out to counteract damp problems, and beneath it a paving of brick and pebbles dated 1611 was revealed. When this was removed the two 12C steps up to the narthex were uncovered and the portal restored to its original proportions.

On the engaged column on the east of the porch is the effigy of Roger de Sorèze, Abbot from 1115–31, but his opposite number is unidentified, and there is a horn player on one of the merlons.

The remarkable **south portal** was executed between 1120 and 1125, twenty years after the cloisters, and shows the influence of Cluny in the vaulting and the cusped or scalloped trumeau and door jambs. Hints of colour suggest that the sculptures were once polychromed. All the surfaces of the doorway are enlisted to carry images which present a coherent and developing theme from the Incarnation to the Last Judgement climaxing with the Christ of the Parousia. The tympanum sculpture is a seminal and transcendental work by an individual of unique creative genius to convey a supernatural and inspirational vision; the narrative and anecdotal scenes on the outer wings of the portal carry a didactic and moralising message.

The whole programme cannot be assimilated at one glance. Unseen when facing the portal straight on is **Prophet Jeremiah**, the single most moving figure, attenuated to blend with the narrow east face of the trumeau. His head inclined, hair and beard flowing, he exudes gentleness and sorrow rather than doom and gloom, but there is also a suppressed dynamism and tension in the crossed legs and floating drapery. The figure of **Isaiah** on the right-hand jamb is smaller, less impressive, but like Jeremiah he carries his prophesy on a scroll. To his left (our right) his prophesy is confirmed: an Annunciation (some of the panels suffered badly from damp and the Angel was poorly remade in the 19C) and Visitation (also a copy) are followed by a combined **Epiphany and Nativity**, the Virgin seated on her bed holds Jesus while Joseph is behind and an ox munches benignly. The frieze above contains a series of animated scenes which read from right to left: the **Presentation at the Temple**, Jesus is held by Simeon while the Virgin offers two doves; the **Flight into Egypt** with the Virgin tenderly embracing her child as the false idols fall from the Temple at the arrival of the true God. On the left (west) side of the portal, the badly damaged images in the lower register represent lust. Avarice is the death of a rich man, mourned by his widow, whose soul is departing with demons (the angel arrived too late). Above this, **Lazarus** lies dying at the rich man's door while dogs lick his sores, but an angel gathers up Lazarus's soul, symbolised by a little nude body of which now only the feet remain, and delivers it into the bosom of Abraham. St Luke, seated on the left, unrolls the text of his gospel.

A rather strangely contorted **St Peter**, a diabolic animal at his feet, old but vigorous, with the key of the Holy Kingdom prances on the left door jamb, and on the west face of the central trumeau is **St Paul**. With the same plastic virtues as Jeremiah, he shows a different character, tense and alert but acquiescent and receptive, his open hand contrasting with Jeremiah's closed around a scroll. Between Paul and Jeremiah three pairs of lions and lionesses on a floral background move restlessly up the trumeau to the lintel of reused marble with an earlier frieze on the under edge. On the outer face are eight carlines or large thistles encircled by foliage spewed out of the mouths of beasts at each end.

The famous **tympanum** rests on this lintel. It is composed of 31 figures on separate blocks. The theme is an Apocalyptic Vision based on the text of Revelations IV, 2–11. Two sources of stylistic and schematic inspiration have been proposed: the first is a Spanish illumination of the Commentary on the Apocalypse in the *Beatus* of St-Sever, c 1070; or it was linked to the painted décor and mosaics of the interior of the church. The **Christ in Majesty enthroned**, one hand raised in blessing, the other on a book, dominates and focuses the composition. On his head is a crown and around it a large, richly decorated cruciform halo. His gaze is immobile and his beard and hair highly stylised similar to that of Jeremiah and St Paul. The rest of the composition fluctuates and flows around him in infinitely restless movement. Closest to him, swooping in and out, are the four apocalpytic beasts, also identified with the symbols of the four Evangelists (Rev. IV, 7) and flanking them two seraphim. Around the throne are the four and twenty elders (Rev. IV, 4) crowned and carrying a musical instrument (rebec or viol), goblet or perfume flask, symbolic of the prayers of saints, who represent the twelve prophets of the Old Testament and the twelve apostles of the New Testament. There is repetition but no monotony, each figure meticulously detailed and in varied poses, craning their necks as they listen attentively. The horizontal lines which structure the composition lose their rigidity behind the undulations which evoke the 'sea of glass like unto crystal ' (Rev. IV, 6) and around the outer edge a beautifully carved ribbon ornament, running from the mouth of a beast on the left to a Cernunnos head on the right, adds to the mobility of the scene. The details of the entire sculptural programme merit a great deal of attention. The conceptual originality of this creation is matched only by the skill and subtlety of its execution.

Interior. Cross the threshold into the square narthex (c 1110–15), where everything is on a massive scale to support the belfry tower. Solid pillars with engaged columns support heavy square ribs. Two of the huge capitals have foliate motifs and the others show Samson slaying the lion and lambs in the jaws of wolves.

The interior of the church is rather less remarkable than the rest. The church is a typically aisleless southern Gothic design painted in a rather shocking yellow, a modern (1963) rendition of the original 15C décor which is conserved in the first chapel on the right. The transformation began in 1431 with the construction of a polygonal choir following which the walls were raised and the vaults built. There are shallow chapels between the buttresses.

Among the **furnishings** are three Gothic polychromed groups: a 15C Flight into Egypt in wood (the figure of Joseph is 17C), a stone Pietà flanked by Mary Magdalene and St John, 1476, with donor figures, and a 15C Entombment (restored in 1985) in walnut of eight figures arranged around the body of Christ: Joseph of Arimathaea, Nicodemus, St John and the Virgin, Mary Magdalene, Mary Cleophas and Mary Salome. The wooden Christ on the Cross (1130–40) is contemporary with the portal sculptures and very close stylistically, but the cross itself is probably 13C. An ancient marble sarcophagus, possibly 4C, was used as the tomb of Raymond de Montpezat, d. 1245. The organ case, mid-17C, carries the arms of Cardinal de Mazarin, Commendatory Abbot (1644–61), who paid for it with a fine for neglecting his duties, and the instrument was remade by Cavaillé-Col c 1865. The early-16C choir enclosure was once gilded and polychromed and has lost its original statuary. Through the screen on the left can be seen the plaque recording the dedication of the church of 1063 on the north wall (lighting). The carved wooden altar rail and stalls are 17C as are the two panels representing the martyrdom of St-Ferréol.

The entrance to the cloister is in the north-east corner of Place Durand de Bredons through the exhibition centre or via the Tourist Office.

CLOISTER (open every day except 25 Dec and 1 Jan. Closed 12.00–14.00 except July and Aug). The almost square cloister on the north side of the church is a on a grand scale (40m by 37.5m), and only one dark shady cedar planted about 150 years ago encroaches on the regularity. 116 slender columns, alternately paired and single, on a continuous low wall support capitals of a dramatic form which widen out from a narrow base like an inverted pyramid or a flower, emphasised by a deep cut away abacus above. All the faces of the capitals and the impost blocks are carved. This is the oldest and largest collection of **Romanesque carved capitals** anywhere still in their original place and the date of the original cloister, 1100, is recorded on the central pillar of the west gallery. Although the capitals are all original their initial order was upset when the arcades were remodelled in moulded brick in the 13C.

A light timber framework supports the roof of the galleries. In the southwest corner is the stairway to the gallery above the narthex, with a domed vault supported by twelve heavy ribs, overlooking the church and the forecourt. More steps lead up to the *chemin de ronde*. There are displays of sculpted elements from earlier buildings and some original elements from the south portal in the chapter house and chapels on the east side of the cloisters.

The **angle pillars** have carved reliefs on reused Pyrenean marble sarcophagi representing eight of the apostles, each identified by an inscription. Durand de Bredons, Abbot of Moissac and Bishop of Toulouse, is on the central east pier. The forms are stylised, static and diagrammatic, similar to the ambulatory reliefs at St-Sernin, Toulouse, although details vary to convey the individuality of each apostle, and while the figures are full frontal the heads are in near profile. All are dressed in tunics and cloak except James who wears a chasuble.

The **capitals** were damaged during the Revolution when many of the figures lost their heads, but there is a remarkable amount still intact and the ratio of storiated to decorated capitals is 45 out of 76. Some have brief notations and, at eye level, they acted as contemplative visual aids designed to affirm the Faith. The iconography is based on both the Old and the New Testament. Particularly important are episodes from the Life of Christ, from the Incarnation to the Last Supper, and to these are added apocalpytic scenes concerning the Second Coming, selected martyrdoms, parables and miracles, but no scenes of the Passion. The capital, No. 47, at the south-east angle, at a prominent position between the church and the chapter house, portrays the Martyrdoms of Peter, patron of the abbey, and Paul, and below a tiny cavity in the column contained a miniscule shrine with the relics of the two saints until 1793.

Because the order of the capitals has been jumbled there is no way of knowing how they were originally organised—for example, the iconographic programme begins with the Fall, No. 42, followed by No. 17, Cain and Abel, the Sacrifice of Abraham, No. 1. No. 29 brings it all to an end with the vision of Holy Jerusalem. The angel, the holy messenger, is the most frequent motif appearing in both the Old and New Testaments. Pure and immaterial beauty is represented by the exquisite foliate and decorative capitals.

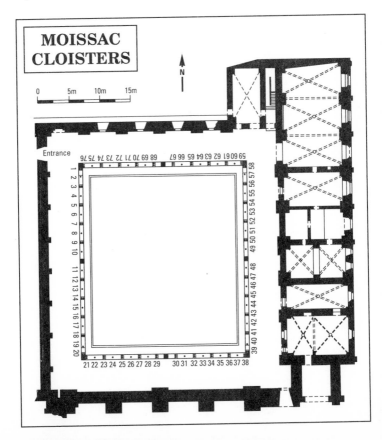

This list of the pillar reliefs and capitals starts opposite the entrance to the cloister in the north-west corner and proceeds anti-clockwise.

Western Gallery

North-west pillar, St Philip (west face)

1. The sacrifice of Abraham
2. The glorification of the Cross
3. Acanthus leaves
4. Birds
5. Daniel in the lions' den/Announcement of the birth of Christ to the shepherds
6. Acanthus leaves
7. The devil unleashed
8. The raising of Lazarus
9. Palm leaves
10. Fantastic figures and animals

Central pillar with inscription: 'In the year 1100 of the Incarnation of the Lord Eternal, this cloister was constructed, at the time of Dom Ansquitil, Abbot. Amen.'

St-Simon on the east face

11. David anointed by the Prophet Samuel
12. Vegetal design
13. Birds and animals
14. Acanthus leaves
15. The eight beatitudes or the eight conditions of blessedness from the Sermon on the Mount
16. Lions rampant
17. Cain and Abel
18. Vegetal design
19. The ascension of Alexander
20. David's victory over Goliath

South-west pillar, St Bartholomew (west face)

Southern Gallery

South-west pillar, St Matthew (south face)

21. Herod's feast
22. Birds among plants
23. The city of Babylon
24. Birds
25. The dream of Nebuchadnezzar, King of Babylon
26. The martyrdom of St Stephen
27. Acanthus leaves
28. David and his musicians
29. The Holy City of Jerusalem

Central pillar, red marble panel

30. The final defeat of Satan by St Michael
31. The symbols of the four Evangelists
32. The Canaanite woman and the Centurion
33. The parable of the good Samaritan
34. The three temptations of Christ in the Desert

35. The revelation of St John at Patmos
36. The Transfiguration
37. Imprisonment of St Peter
38. The Baptism of Christ
South-east pillar, St Paul (south face)

Eastern Gallery
South-east pillar, St Peter (east face)
39. Samson wrestling with the lion
40. Two martyrdoms: St Peter and St Paul
41. Vegetal design
42. Adam and Eve and the Fall
43. Acanthus leaves
44. The martyrdom of St Laurence
45. Christ washing the disciples' feet
46. Palm leaves
47. Lazarus and Dives
48. Eight eagles or dragons and human heads
Central pillar, Durand de Bredons: Abbot of Moissac 1047–71, Bishop of Toulouse 1059–71
49. Four figures seizing eagles by the neck
50. Wedding at Cana
51. Vegetal design
52. The Epiphany/Massacre of the innocents/Herod at the gates of Jerusalem
53. Palmettes and animals' muzzles
54. Acanthus leaves
55. The martyrdom of St Saturnin
56. Acanthus leaves
57. The martyrdoms of St Fructuosus, St Augurious and St Euologius
58. Annunciation and Visitation
North-east pillar, St James (east face)

Northern Gallery
North-east pillar, St John (east)
59. Angels wrestling with dragons
60. Eagles
61. Vegetal design
62. Two miracles of St Benedict
63. Birds
64. The miracle of St Peter healing the paralytic
65. Vegetal design
66. The Celestial Kingdom
67. The miraculous draught of fishes
Central pillar with grey marble slab
68. Daniel in prayer in the lions' den/Prophet Habakkuk bringing food to Daniel
69. A procession, possibly the crusade to Jerusalem
70. Vegetal design of Mozarabic influence
71. The symbols of the four Evangelists

72. Birds
73. Meshach, Shadrach and Abednego in the fiery furnace
74. Scenes from the life of St Martin
75. Scrolly design of Mazarabic influence
76. Jesus and the Good Samaritan
North-west pillar, St Andrew (north face)

The **town** has no medieval buildings left and very few of the 16C or 17C. The attractive **Abbot's Residence**, east of the church, houses the **Musée Moissagais**, a museum of folk and popular art (combined ticket with the cloister). Frequently rebuilt, the oldest part of the building is an 11C chapel in the south tower with 12C paintings on the vault and the rest is 17C and 18C.

At the end of Rue de la République is the market place, built on the site of an old convent, with the *halle* of 1895 and Halle de Paris, 1930. Cross the canal by the Pont St-Jacques, the only swivel bridge left, to the banks of the Tarn (by car from the end of Pont Napoléon, 1882), and the *Grand Moulin de Moissac* (hotel-restaurant, tel: 63 04 03 55), rebuilt after a fire in 1916, the only reminder of the very important 18C mills and navigation on the Tarn. This part of town was rebuilt after the floods of 1930.

A section of the Lateral Canal to the Garonne, cut between 1843 and 1847, is carried over the Tarn by a magnificent **aqueduct**. To reach it, cross the Tarn in the direction of Castelsarrasin, turn left towards the camp site and follow the road for about 1km. The usefulness of the canal was shortlived as the railway was inaugurated in 1856.

On the N113 west, just after the railway station, is a church dedicated to **St-Martin**. This is the oldest sanctuary in Moissac, built on the site of a Gallo-Roman hypocaust. Incorporated into the chancel is the old church with a flat east end, dating from the end-6C or early-7C. It was extended to the west in the 10C using an already existing wall with large rounded buttresses. More repairs and alterations were carried out from the 13C–15C. The church was saved from destruction in 1922 and is now under restoration.

19

Montauban

MONTAUBAN (pop. 53,278, Tourist Information, Ancien Collège, tel: 63 63 60 60), a pink brick town on the banks of the Tarn, is an attractive, lively, and slightly dusty place within easy reach of Cahors, Albi, Moissac, and the Garonne and the Aveyron valleys. It has good rail links, is near the A62, and has the largest number of hotels in the Tarn-et-Garonne. There are a number of museums and gardens and big markets on Wednesdays and Saturdays at Place Prax-Paris plus stalls every day on Place Nationale. There is jazz in July and ballet in August.

History. Always a major town in the south-west, Montauban lost its status as *chef-lieu* of a huge *généralité* in 1790 and became part of the Lot, but some negotiating during a visit by Napoléon in 1808 resulted in the creation

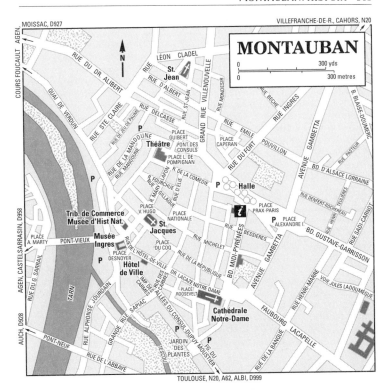

MOISSAC, D927

VILLEFRANCHE-DE-R., CAHORS, N20

AGEN, CASTELSARRASIN, D958

AGEN, D928

AUCH, D928

TOULOUSE, N20, A62, ALBI, D999

of the *département* of Tarn-et-Garonne, which acquired choice parts of Quercy, Gascony, Rouergue and Languedoc, and Montauban was reinstated. Famous as the second Protestant stronghold in France after La Rochelle, in common with Protestant towns in the south-west, it has few pre-Reformation buildings. Less obvious in the hurly-burly of today's activities is that Montauban was one of the first *bastides* in the region, founded in 1144 by the Count of Toulouse, Alphonse Jourdain. The town enjoyed tremendous prosperity after the Albigensian crisis as a commercial centre, benefiting from its position between two navigable rivers, the Tarn and the Aveyron. Access and defence were improved by the Pont-Vieux across the Tarn, erected c 1303, and during the Hundred Years War (1337–1453) the town, taken by Captain John Chandos in the name of the Black Prince, became the last frontier town between Guyenne and the Languedoc until 1368.

The recovery of the town's commercial status at the end of the 15C engendered a brilliant cultural life in the early 16C and resulted in the establishment of numerous schools which were a breeding ground for humanist ideas and the support of Calvinism. The first Religious War had a profound effect on the town: Protestant zealots set fire to the cathedral on 20 December 1561 and all the other churches were destroyed except St-Jacques which became their own church or *temple*. After the Edict of Nantes in 1598 Montauban became a Protestant place of safety, with a college financed by Marguerite de Valois (1552–1615) and a Calvinist academy. This situation lasted until La Rochelle fell in 1629 and with the Revocation of the Edict of Nantes in 1685, the Protestant community took flight. Montauban, already a powerful administrative centre, grew prosperous again through trade in wool, silk, leather, pottery and brick, stimulated by the opening of Royal Routes across the south-west. This wealth was converted into elegant Neo-Classical brick town houses. The most obvious symbol of the Counter-Reformation is, however, the Neo-Classical Cathedral built partly in stone. Just before the Revolution the town's economy slowed down and the essence of the 18C town was conserved and the few new buildings followed the pattern of the old, resulting in a town centre with an extraordinarily unified architecture. Montauban was the birthplace of two eminent artists, painter, Dominique Ingres (1780–1867) and sculptor, Antoine Bourdelle (1861–1929).

Montauban is on a plateau overlooking the Tarn, and the two levels can be confusing. Park in Place Desnoyer alongside the Tarn south of the Pont-Vieux and steps or a lift take you up to the Musée Ingres.

The **MUSÉE INGRES** (tel: 63 22 12 00, generally 10.00–12.00, 14.00–18.00, closed Mon, times vary according to season), one of the major museums in the Midi-Pyrénées, is installed in the former Episcopal Palace, a brick building of 1664, which occupies the site chosen by Alphonse Jourdain to build his castle. In the same place in 1360 the English started to build their garrison, Château Renaut, later incorporated in the defences during the Religious Wars. The English guardroom is the lower basement of the museum. The wide-ranging collection, with items from the 4C to the 20C, occupies most of the five floors.

In 1851 Ingres donated 54 paintings and antique vases, and at his death in 1867 more than 4000 drawings, his personal collection of paintings, and memorabilia with the proverbial violin (*violon d'Ingres* = hobby). His friend and pupil Armand Cambon (1819–85) was the first curator of the museum, and there are a number of works by him and other epigones. Works by Bourdelle were donated by his daughter and have been amplified from national collections.

The work of **Dominique Ingres** (Montauban 1780–Paris 1867) is exhibited in six elegant rooms on the first floor, with ceilings *à la française* painted in 1868, looking out over the Tarn, and over Bourdelle's epic **Monument to the Dead of 1870**, (1893–1902).

Ingres studied in Toulouse under Roques, then in Paris in 1797 he entered the studio of David. After several attempts he won the Grand Prix de Rome in 1801 but he did not go to the Villa Medici until 1806. The works at Montauban, if not his greatest or best known, demonstrate his range. Two small landscapes, rare in Ingres' repertoire, were probably painted in Rome shortly before the summer of 1807. Among the best of the portraits here are of his friend the Italian sculptor **Lorenzo Bartolini**, 1806, who persuaded him to move to Florence between 1820 and 1824, and the **Portrait of Madame Gonse**, 1840s, the sort of accomplished work for which the painter is best known. It is a flattering likeness of a mature fashionable woman in a serene pose, with scrupulous attention to the quality of textures of flesh and fabric. **The Dream of Ossian**, 1812–13 and 1835, the ultimate Romantic painting from an artist whose work is a constant balancing act between Classicism and Romanticism, was commissioned by Napoléon for the ceiling of his bedroom at the Quirinale Palace, which he never got around to sleeping in. This curious work, based on the greatest literary hoax of the

18C, was originally oval, but Ingres repurchased it and squared it up with the help of assistants. The Gobelins' tapestry version of the most classical of subjects, the **Apotheosis of Homer**, woven in 1867, is based on a commission for the ceiling decoration in Charles X's museum at the Louvre in 1826. There are three other versions of **Roger Freeing Angelica** (Louvre, London and Detroit) but the Montauban painting of chivalry and sensuality, of hard metal and yielding flesh, was painted in 1841. There are a number of works and studies which demonstrate Ingres' great debt to Raphael.

Among the possessions given by Ingres are a delightful little painting of Ingres' Studio in Rome (1818) by Alaux and the Portrait of a Spanish Girl by Coello. The huge collection of drawings is rotated thematically.

Paintings by the followers of Ingres, Hippolyte Flandrin (1809–64), Théodore Chassériau (1819–56), are scattered through the gallery. On the top floor are French and European paintings from the 15C to the 18C, including a number of fine Italian works donated by Ingres.

The work of **Antoine Bourdelle** (Montauban 1861–Le Vésinet 1929) is in the main room on the ground floor. Bourdelle, from a poor background, like Ingres studied first at Toulouse. At the age of 18 he discovered a close identification with Beethoven and felt that he heard sculptures and the museum owns one of the many versions of the composer. In Paris Bourdelle studied with Falguière and Dalou, then from 1893 to 1906 he was an adjuster in Rodin's studio. Bourdelle's work breaks down into two phases. The first, described as Dionysian, with works of explosive, unrestrained nature, produced the **Monument to the Dead of 1870–71**, which was not unveiled until 1902 because its design was considered too conversial for a public monument. The dynamic **Hercules the Archer** (1909), is a pivotal work between the two styles, before he moved from an analytic to a synthetic approach. The Head of Apollo, c 1900, typifies his classical, Apollonian phase, which brought him into line with the early 20C. In 1911 he worked with August Perret to design **Reliefs for the Théâtre des Champs-Elysées**, 1911. Bourdelle's constant concern was the relationship of sculpture to architecture, and Montauban is graced with several fine examples of his work.

In the lower basement are local Gallo-Roman, Merovingian, Carolingian and Medieval exhibits. The main room of the first basement with particularly beautiful brick vaults, is used for temporary exhibitions, and has a collection of 18C and 19C regional ceramics. Other local painters represented are François Desnoyer (1894–1972), a local Fauve, Marcel Lenoir (1872–1931), and Lucien Andrieu (1875–1955).

From the museum, turn right up **Rue de l'Hôtel de Ville**. In a courtyard in **Rue des Carmes** is an elegant brick loggia. The grandiose bleached face of the Neo-Classical **Notre-Dame Cathedral** makes precisely the contrast with the rest of the town that was intended. Shortly after the Revocation of the Edict of Nantes Louis XIV's architects conceived a church which would symbolise the Counter-Reformation and celebrate the power of the monarchy. Its design and the type of materials used played an important psychological role. The first stone was laid on 10 April 1692 and the cathedral was consecrated on 1 November 1739. The original plans were drawn up by François d'Orbay (1634–97), son-in-law and associate of Le Vau, and modified by Robert de Cotte (1656–1735). The façade has a Doric peristyle of four columns and the Ionic order above. The interior is imposing and austere, with the Doric order used throughout. It takes the form of a Greek cross with 16 arcades, 87m long in total, the nave barely longer than the choir. The pitted originals of statues of the four Evangelists by Marc Arcis commissioned for the façade in 1719 have been brought inside and replaced by reproductions. The pendentives of the dome are decorated with the Four Virtues.

The most important work is **Ingres'** painting of **The Vow of Louis XIII** (1824) (timer light switch on the wall left of the altar), commissioned for the cathedral by the Ministry of the Interior in 1820 and carried out in Florence. It shows Louis XIII placing France under the protection of the Virgin of the Assumption. The result is an eclectic work which bears out the duality of the theme. Ingres modelled his Virgin of the Assumption on Raphaelesque Madonnas, but she is a wordly creature, imperious and sensuous, bathed in a diffused light and framed by drapes held back by voluptuous angels. The king is painted in harsher tones with a direct light falling on his face and upstretched arms to emphasise the contrasts of the metallic sceptre and crown and ermine robe.

Also worthy of note is some fine late-18C–19C wrought iron, a monumental candlestick with dolphins and a vast lectern and 18C choir stalls. A 15C console with Bruniquel marble is used as an altar with a 16C statue on it. The organ, built in 1675, came from St-Jacques and has kept its original case. In one of the chapels on the left of the choir are gilded stucco sacred ornaments by Ingres père.

North-west of the cathedral between Rue de l'Hôtel de Ville and Boulevard Midi-Pyrénées is the old town. At the end of Bd. Midi-Pyrénées is the **Information Centre** in the former Jesuit College, a large 17C brick building, with *mirandes*. Outside Bourdelle's majestically graceful bronze statue of **Penelope** (1912) overlooks Place Prax-Paris where the markets are held. **Rue de la Comédie**, behind the Information Centre, leads to Place L. de Pompignan in front of the theatre, and another Bourdelle sculpture, **Sapho** (1925).

From the square the Pont des Consuls goes over the Vallon de la Mandoune. Take Rue d'Elie to **Place Nationale**. In keeping with the rest of the town but unique in the realms of urban décor or *bastides*, the buildings around the square are entirely in brick, incorporating with great subtlety different types and qualities of brick, some sections possibly designed to be rendered, some purely decorative, harmonious yet varied. At ground level is a double arcade, also unusual, with arches at each angle, following the layout of the original *place*. Two sides were destroyed by fire in 1614. Plans were drawn up by Pierre Levesville and were carried out; then, in 1649, the two remaining sides were consumed by flames and a new campaign of building was led by Charles Pacot following Levesville's plans. Some houses were not completed until 1708. The last restoration was at the beginning of the 1980s and the brickwork is showing signs of deterioration.

West of Place Nationale is **Eglise St-Jacques**, the only church spared by the Calvinists. Built as a parish church dedicated to St James of Compostela, the fortified west end dates from the 13C, but after the Hundred Years War major repairs were carried out and the chevet dates from 1481. The octagonal Toulousain style belfry has three levels of openings and was restored in the 18C. It still carries scars inflicted by royalist bullets during the siege of 1621—it is a pity no one has taken a pot-shot at the amazingly repellent ceramic reproduction of Raphael's Vision of Ezekiel above the west door. The characteristic regional aisleless nave with chapels was extended in the 15C and revaulted in the 18C. Sad and sombre with peeling paint, the Chapelle St-Jacques (south) has gilded stucco work by Ingres père.

South of St-Jacques is the the municipal library in a grand building overlooking Rue du Général Piquart with **Bourdelle**'s **Dying Centaur** (1914). Lower down on the right is the **Musée d'Histoire Naturelle** on Place A. Bourdelle, open Tues–Sat, 10.00–12.00, 14.00–18.00.

The **Pont-Vieux**, a very strong construction in brick and stone and originally fortified, was begun in 1311. Straight rather than hump-backed, because of the difference in the levels of the two banks, it has seven high arches. The extremity of each triangular cutwater is in stone as are the bases of the piers, which has helped it withstand the exceptional floods of 1441, 1766 and 1930.

Return to the banks of the Tarn via the steps or lift next to the Ingres Museum. There is a memorial to Ingres of 1868, by Etex, in the square on the left, and further along the Impasse des Carmes and Rue Sapiac is the refreshing **Jardin des Plantes**, created in 1860 as an arboretum where the Tescou meets the Tarn. There is a bust of A. Quercy by Bourdelle.

To the north, on the banks of the Tarn in **Cours Foucault**, laid out in the late 17C by Intendant Foucault, is Bourdelle's great monument to the dead of the First World War, **La France veillant sur ses morts**, a contrast in style to the 1870 monument.

20

Two tours: Bas Quercy and the Quercy Blanc

Causse de Limogne, east of the N20: Truffles and Abbeys

Total distance: 83km (51 miles).

The southern part of the Quercy has a rugged and desolate charm, with endless vistas and excellent walks. Rainfall and rivers disappear rapidly through the porous limestone plateaux which at their highest are only about 360m and the land provides quantities of stone. Stone was used by primitive man to build *dolmens* between 2500 and 1500 BC, of which there are over 500 in the Lot. Stone walls, stone *croix de chemins* outside villages, houses built in stone with *bolets* (covered terraces) and *souillardes voûtées* (kitchen annex), stone for rural buildings such as the practical *pigeonnier* and *moulin à vent*, the country is brindled with old dry-stone shelters called *cabanes*, *cazelles* or *gariottes* and there are communal facilities, *lavoirs*, *fours à pain* and *fours banaux* in many a modest village. The vegetation is low key: juniper, or the abundant spiky blossoms of the *Mimosa des causses* (Cornus) that scumble the February landscape with yellow, and most typical is the seemingly insignificant small oak. At the roots of some of these trees nestles the greatest treasure of the *causses*, the magnificent truffle, and in winter, when the *causses* are at their most severely beautiful, is the time for the epicurian, the season of *truffes* and *foie gras*.

If you are keen to snuffle a truffle, come to **Lalbenque** in the winter. This small town (pop. 868; south-east of Cahors, 16km on the D6) has the most important **truffle market** in Midi-Pyrénées on a Tuesday at 14.00, from the end of November to the end of March, the optimum time being January.

Truffles. The distinctive, slightly bitter aroma wafts down the street from the outdoor market where truffles enveloped in a napkin in a small basket are laid out on trestles. The price is totally dependent on supply, a kilo can fetch anything between 1500 and 2500 Fr., and the contents of a basket are sold as one lot. Trading does not begin until the whistle is blown. The prospective purchaser writes a price on a slip of paper and if the vendor keeps it, the price is acceptable. A type of underground mushroom, the only variety sold is the *Tuber melanosporum*. The most surprising discovery for the uninitiated is that a truffle is rock hard and resembles a lump of coal. The spores begin to grow in July and do best in a warm, humid season and nowadays the *trufficulteur* is more likely to use dogs than pigs to find them. Since the beginning of the century there has been a huge decline in the production of truffles. Around 1900 the Lot produced more than 200 tonnes of truffles a year, today it is between 5 and 20 tonnes. Truffles can be eaten raw or cooked, grated on a salad of endives, cooked with leeks and potatoes or on their own in in a delicate puff-pastry case, in omelettes and other egg dishes, with pasta, and with all meat dishes.

Near the Mercadial (between the D19 and the D6 north) is a superb carved stone cross.

Leave Lalbenque towards the north-east on the D10 for **Aujols** (11km) which has a *lac-lavoir*, like a village pond, surrounded by washstones and houses with *bolets*. There are more typical houses at **Concots** (D10/D911, 10.5km) which has an old tower called the tour de l'Horloge. **Limogne-en-Quercy**, 11.5 km along the D911, capital of the Causse, has a Sunday market and truffles on Fridays in the winter. There are several dolmens nearby and about 5km further along the D911 is a windmill, just past the turning to **Promilhanès**.

Go through that village, D84/D53/D55, to **Laramière**, whose windmill has no sails and whose priory has seen better times. Yet, a visit to the privately-owned **priory** (next to the church with three bells) is worthwhile (tel: 61 85 51 48). An Augustinian priory was founded in 1148 on a rocky site above stream and the buildings formed a square. The Religious Wars destroyed a great deal and the Jesuits who took it over in the mid-17C made many alterations. Despite all the abuse there are still some interesting elements, including the 13C chapel, albeit drastically altered by the Jesuits who divided it into two horizontally, the Romanesque pilgrim hostel, and above all the chapter house painted with geometric designs and carved capitals representing Blanche of Castille and Louis IX (St-Louis).

About 6km away, D55/D115, on the border of the Quercy and the Rouergue, in the *département* of the Aveyron, is the **Abbey of Loc Dieu** (tel: 65 29 51 17, July–Sept), a former Cistercian monastery. It is confusing at first sight as the abbey is camouflaged by a 19C pastiche of a Loire château, and its landscaped park is in total contrast to the *causse* wilderness. The abbey suffered the fate of most religious foundations, decline, destruction and dismemberment, but at its lowest ebb, in 1812, it was purchased by the Cibiel family of Villefranche-en-Rouergue who have restored and renewed the buildings. Monks from the Limousin founded it in 1123. A stone in the church to the right of the door records two dates, 1124, the beginning of the abbey, and 1159, the start of the definitive church, completed 30 years later. The church, chapter house and cloister of the abbey can be visited.

The pure and simple lines of the exterior have been maintained and straightforwardly restored. A large part of the nave is 12C, laid out as a Latin cross. It has a shallow transept with four square chapels and a pentagonal apse. The walls were heightened in the second half of the 13C and the apse c 1300, explaining the tall narrow two-light plate tracery windows and one in the west end. Above the crossing is a square tower with three bays of two-light openings and a steep roof. Generally free of decoration or ornament, according to the rules of St-Bernard, the drama of the interior depends greatly on the play of light and shade with an occasional decorated capital, impost and carved boss. The pointed barrel vaulting of the aisles gives way to rib vaults over the the later parts. The third important stage of building, or rebuilding, began in 1470 and is represented in the three galleries of the late Gothic cloisters where the low wide arches and vaults spring from decorated imposts attached to massive cylindrical columns. The chapter house, rebuilt at the same time, has three openings on to the east gallery and is divided into three equal naves, the vaults supported by two slender clustered columns. The rest of the abbey was turned into a comfortable home in the Romantic manner of the 19C. In 1940 when the French art treasures were at risk, this small château in the Rouergue became the repository, for a short time, for none other than the Mona Lisa and La Belle Ferronière. Summer concerts are held here.

Take the D926 west for 10.5km and turn left on to the D33 at Parisot and in 9km you come to the lovely **Abbey of Beaulieu en Rouergue**, (tel: 63 67 06 84, Palm Sun–Sept, 10.00–12.00, 14.00–18.00, closed Tues), like all Cistercian abbeys, established near water and woodland. Since 1974 the lay brothers' dormitory is used as a centre for contemporary art. Visits to the abbey are with a guide. The church is a rigorous structure, begun c 1275 and completed in the 14C, rhythmically articulated by tall buttresses, narrow lancets and seven plate tracery rose windows. It has been heavily restored. The chapter house, with three open bays and traces of coloured wall paintings, is a superb piece of 13C architecture. Most of the monastic buildings were repaired and amended in the 17C and 18C. This is a stunning place and the temporary exhibitions are an added bonus.

Just past the abbey turn right on the D20 and then the D19, 10km to **Caylus** (pop. 1425, Tourist Information: tel: 63 67 00 28), in the valley of the Bonnette, its old centre hidden in a hollow beside the main road and the tall spire of the church indicating its presence. Rue Droite, which runs the length of the village from the church to the Place de la Mairie and the quaint alleyways which intersect it, have examples of Gothic or Renaissance houses, most notably the **Maison des Loups** (14C) with Gothic windows and high-relief carvings. In the market place is a 14C *halle* with 18 octagonal pillars protecting the old grain measures.

Further west, above the market on a terrace overlooking the valley is a 13C *donjon* of the ruined castle. The **Church of St-Jean-Baptiste** (14C/15C) has a stone steeple (15C) and steep slate-covered roof with tiny dormers. The entrance on the north-west is decorated with a continuous frieze, a Virgin and Child on the right of the door and animals on the left. The elegant seven-sided apse dates from 1470 and the tall lancets contain stained-glass of the same date mixed with glass added during restoration in 1868. Hidden away, despite its monumental size, arms upstretched, is an anguished **Christ** (1954), pinned to the wall by one hand. This was carved from the trunk of an elm by **Ossip Zadkine** (1890–1967) who made Caylus his home in the 1950s. There are several inscribed tombstones in the floor of the church, the most beautiful, near the Christ, is that of Coligny, Chevalier de Malte, killed at the siege of St-Antonin, 21 June 1622.

Detour. 6km south of Caylus on the D19, the **Château de Cas** at Espinas (tel: 63 67 07 40, 10.00–12.00, 14.00–18.00, July–Aug, closed Mon), a medieval castle transformed in the 16C into a Renaissance château, was entirely restored this century to repair damage wrought by the Revolution and the Second World War.

About 4km north of Caylus, on the D19, **Lacapelle-Livron** has the remains of a Templar-Hospitallers commandery (13C–18C) with a fortified Romanesque church adjoining it (private) and just outside Lacapelle (1km south) is a tiny isolated Gothic Chapel of **Notre-Dame des Graces** in a marvellous position on the cliff above the Bonnette (key with Abbot Jourdes).

Take the D85 and the D20, 13km to **Puylaroque** (pop. 600), in the Tarn et Garonne. A village of great character, it was probably an important agricultural centre in the 13C and 14C. The old narrow streets fan out from Place E. Capin to climb the ridge which drops sheer at the south-west. At the start of Rue de la République is the most complete of several Gothic houses, with large arcades and geometric tracery in the three upper windows, reminiscent of Cordes or Lauzerte. The church, with evidence of many periods of alteration and restoration, has fragments of Romanesque sculpture, and the streets all converge on Place de la Citadelle with the remains of the château.

The D17 will bring you in 13km to **Caussade** (pop. 6224) a funny old place that feels lived in, famous for its straw hats and markets (Mondays and *foie gras* November to March). At the junction of the N20 from Cahors and the D926 from Villefranche-de-Rouergue, it is a good springboard to the Quercy Blanc, Montauban and Moissac, or the Aveyron Valley.

The Quercy Blanc, west of the N20

Total distance: 46km (28 miles).

The Quercy Blanc—a white limestone plateaux—like the Bas Quercy, includes several delightful places in a landscape scattered with windmills, fountains and pigeonniers.

From Caussade, take the N20 and D20, 14.5km, to **Montpezat-de-Quercy** (Tourist Information, tel: 63 02 07 04), a lovely medieval stone and timber village with Gothic and Renaissance houses, a small arcaded square closed at one end by the Hôtel-de-Ville, a 14C town gateway, and 16C tapestries in the **Church of St-Martin**. The town's great benefactors were the family des Près, who numbered several prelates among them. The church, completed by 1339 and consecrated in 1343, was designed by an architect from the Popes' Court at Avignon. Harmonious, sober, clean and white, the church is built into a hollow in the slope of the hill to the east of the town centre. The west end is simple, with one rose window and behind the church is a marvellous group of timber-framed houses, the old Cannons' College or living quarters built in the mid-14C. Go armed with some 1Fr pieces for lighting.

The main interest of the church is its furnishings and fittings. In the choir are the famous made-to-measure **tapestries**, of Flemish origin, which have been here since 1520 when Jean IV des Près presented them to the church on the occasion of his elevation to Bishop of Montauban. They are stitched, not woven, and are made up of five panels with 15 scenes of the legend of St Martin of Tours. Above each scene is an explanatory octosyllabic quatrain in old French verse. Note the animated compositions, the architectural detail and the shimmering colours. They read from left to right. The first panel shows St Martin, in the town of Amiens, about to share his cloak with a beggar. Then follow other, less well-known, episodes in Martin's life—his dream, his journey across the Alps when he is stopped by robbers, his ordination as Bishop of Tours and chasing away pagan beliefs. It shows him effecting conversions and cures in Germany. The last tapestries change emphasis and are concerned with the battle between good and evil. Finally there is a reminder to attend mass.

There are two funerary effigies of the benefactors, left and right of entrance to the choir: Cardinal Pierre des Près (1288–1361) in Carrara marble, and his nephew Jean, Bishop of Coïmbra in Portugal then of Castres from 1338–53, in Quercy stone, formerly polychromed. The painting (16C) above the dean's stall represents Jacques des Près, d. 1589, the last bishop in the family. The 26 stalls are 15C and have carved misericords. Other worthy objects include in the first chapel south, Notre-Dame de Pitié de Montpezat, 1475, sculpted in sandstone in Villefranche-de-Rouergue, and polychromed in the 19C. An object of veneration in the 16C, there is still a pilgrimage the third Sunday in September. In the next chapel is an alabaster diptych, 15C/16C, made in Nottingham, with scenes of the Nativity, the Resurrection and the Ascension, and in the third chapel is a headless St Anne and the Virgin, 13C. In the second chapel on the north is an English 14C alabaster Virgin with Doves. There are two 14C reliquary caskets in the last chapel.

Detour to the little Chapel of **Notre-Dame-de-Saux** (ask for the key at the presbytery or at the Hôtel-de-Ville, Montpezat). Take the D20, in the direction of Cahors, 500m after the sign 'Montpezat', turn left to Saux and at the crossroad straight on, then follow the signs (about 5km). The charming little rural church with a belfry is in the middle of woods and is the frame for some precious 14C murals.

The D38/D4 brings you to after 12km to **Castelnau-Montratier** (pop. 1782, Tourist Information, Mairie, tel. 65 21 94 21), a pretty village perched above the Barguelone and the Lutte and overlooked by three windmills (Cahors road), one still working, at the centre of a fruit-growing region. The village is arranged around a triangular *place* with chestnut and linden trees and some old houses.

Wriggle your way west (D74/D19/D31/D34, about 20km) to **Lauzerte** (pop. 1566, Tourist Information, tel: 63 94 61 94), which justly deserves its qualification as one of the most beautiful villages in France. Saturday market. It clings to a rock dominating the Cahors-Moissac road and the land from which it derived its wealth. It has a profusion of fine old houses that have been lovingly restored, an arcaded square, the Place du Marché, and an interesting Gothic church enlarged in the 17C containing some outstanding Baroque retables. Another church at the bottom of the hill also contains a fine 17C retable. It is the sort of place that attracts artists and craftsmen and has a modest hotel, the *Hôtel du Quercy* (tel: 63 94 66 36).

21

Cahors

CAHORS (pop. 19,665, Tourist Information, Place A. Briand, tel: 65 35 09 56) is easy to reach on the N20 from Paris or from Toulouse, or by train. It is the sort of outstanding smallish town that the French do so well, at ease with its historic past and equally comfortable in the 20C. It occupies a peninsula surrounded by rocky cliffs formed by the Lot River. Allow enough time to do justice to the major monuments, the cathedral and the Pont Valentré, as well as to the medieval town, which has been the focus of much care and restoration. Throughout the summer there are exhibitions, concerts and river trips. The local wine is excellent, with a cuisine to match. There are a number of good hotels in and around the town, and all the other usual facilities. The very best place to eat in Cahors is the restaurant *Le Balandre* (tel: 65 30 01 97) in the *Hôtel Le Terminus*, newly renovated (tel: 65 35 24 50), Avenue Freycinet, just north of the railway station (packed out on weekdays at noon, so reserve). Next to the Hôtel de Ville is one of the better restaurants of Cahors, *La Taverne*, in Place Pierre Escorbiac, tel: 65 35 28 66.

The town is divided unequally in two by **Boulevard Gambetta**, a shaded avenue running north–south lined by 19C institutions. There are three bridges crossing the Lot, Pont Louis-Philippe, Pont Cabessut, and the old Pont Valentré, which will be closed to traffic when the replacement is finished. There are car parks behind Place Briand (via Quai Cavaignac and Rue d'Hautesserre), near the Pont Valentré, and further north on Bd. Gambetta.

History. The antique city of Cahors, known by the 1C BC as Divona and from the 3C as Civitas Caducorum, was capital of the Cadurque people, the site of an ancient shrine linked with the cult of water. Gallo-Roman Divona occupied most of the peninsula for some centuries but Frankish invasions in the 6C brought this culture to an end and barely a stone of the antique city remains. Already Christianised by the 5C, the rebirth of the town is attributed to Didier, Bishop from 630–655. In the 12C a new cathedral and cloister replaced an earlier building and when the troubles of the Cathar heresies had passed, the town expanded and in the 13C became a banking centre. Their reputation was enhanced when Dante expelled the Cadurcien bankers or moneylenders, *Caorsins*, to *Inferno*. In 1316 a Cadurcien, Jacques Duèze, from a Caorsin family originally from Castelnau-Montratier, became Bishop of Fréjus, then of Porto, and was elected second Pope at Avignon from 1316–34 as John XXII. He bestowed many favours on his town including, in 1332, a university which enjoyed a good reputation until the 17C, and a vast programme of urban renewal was undertaken. In 1360 the Treaty of Brétigny placed Cahors, as part of Aquitaine, under English control but, as the first town to break with the Treaty, it remained so for only 10 years. By the 17C Cahors' zenith had passed and it was mainly a town of lawyers and magistrates. In 1680 the ramparts, by then redundant, were demolished.

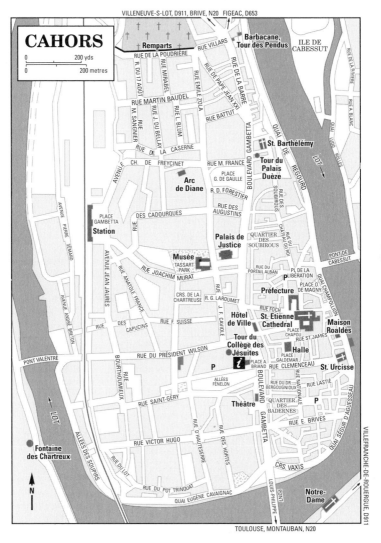

VILLENEUVE-S-LOT, D911, BRIVE, N20 FIGEAC, D653

CAHORS

0 _____ 200 yds

0 _____ 200 metres

On Foot. The walks are arranged around the two parts of the town, east and west. The medieval town is on a slight slope.

The Cathedral and the Old Town

The visit is a figure of eight turning on the cathedral, and is by no means exhaustive. Look out for details, and look inside courtyards.

Start on **Place Chapou** in front of the cathedral. The *place* itself is named after a hero of the Resistance, Jean-Jacques Chapou (1909–44), whose bust is outside the south door of the cathedral, but was created at the beginning of the 14C as was the former **Episcopal Palace** on the north side. Almost totally rebuilt in the 17C and considerably altered again in the 19C, it is now used by the Préfecture of the *département* of the Lot.

West of the *place* the sign *'Gambetta Jeune et Cie, bazar génois'* was discovered when the Crédit Agricole took over their premises. **Léon Gambetta**, born in Cahors 1838, the son of an Italian grocer, went into the legal profession before embarking on a career in politics. A vociferous defender of the French Republic, during the siege of Paris by Prussia in 1870 he fled in a balloon and organised resistance from the provinces. He became President of the Chamber in 1879 and of the Council in 1881 and died in an accident in 1882.

On Wednesday and Saturday mornings one of the best **open-air markets** in the Lot fills Place Chapou, a positively sensual experience of sight, taste and smell, bringing together regional-seasonal produce such as strawberries, *Cabecou* and *cèpes*. There is a flower market on Sunday mornings and a market every day in the *halle*, built in 1869. Two of the many heavenly delicacies found in Cahors are *pruneaux fourrés* (stuffed prunes) and chocolate covered walnuts.

THE CATHEDRAL OF ST-ETIENNE (ST STEPHEN). A veritable text book of architecture from the 12C to the 18C, the cathedral was begun c 1109–12 to replace an earlier building and work went on almost continuously until the 13C. Major modifications were carried out in the 13C and 14C, and in the cloister in the 15C. More changes were made in the 18C and restoration began in the 19C.

Exterior. There are three entrances to the cathedral around the west, two of them open. Taking them in chronological order, the oldest is the recently restored small **south door**, c 1130, a pretty trilobed opening under a double round-headed arch where the points of lobes are divided and rolled. The brick arcades above are a later addition. The Romanesque **north portal**, one of the masterpieces of Romanesque sculpture in the Midi-Pyrénées, disappeared from view in the 18C. It was rediscovered in 1840 and for some time mistakenly thought to have been moved from the west. In fact during the 12C, the orientation of the streets had a different emphasis, the main north–south route through the medieval town corresponding to the present Rue Clément Marot. Recently the street in front of the portal has been lowered restoring the porch, as far as possible, to its original proportions. A deep, slightly pointed arch protects the sculpted **tympanum** generally thought to date c 1140–50.

The main theme of the relief is the Ascension of Christ, but unusual emphasis is given to the patron saint of the cathedral, the protomartyr, St Stephen. The work has stylistic links with Moissac, but the composition is more rigidly compartmentalised, less free flowing, although there is a serious attempt to introduce variety to the individual figures and a certain animation to the composition. Christ, isolated in an oval mandorla, is flanked by two dancing or gesturing angels which emphasise the upright figure of Christ and form a link with the other parts of the composition. Either side of the Virgin below, her hand raised towards Christ, are the eleven apostles present before Pentecost (when Judas is replaced by Matthias) framed in trilobed arches. It is not easy to make out the eleventh apostle who is squeezed into the left-hand corner beside the provocative back view of the tenth. There is a striking uniformity, unlike Moissac, in the size of the main protagonists.

The anecdotal scenes in the **spandrels** of St Stephen's martyrdom are in a different mood and tempo. On the left, Stephen professes his faith to the Sanhedrin, some of whom wear bonnets. On the opposite side, present at the stoning of Stephen is Saul, at whose feet the false witnesses place their mantles. One of Stephen's persecutors is sheltering in the foliage of the extrados. The hand of God linking the upper register to the lower, is part of Stephen's vision of the Trinity. Banal scenes of hunting and aggression fill the outer archivolt and the cornice above the portal is peopled by a series of witty little figures whose torsos extend into the billet moulding and whose legs appear in the medallions on the underside. The rosette decoration extended into the upper part of the portal in the early 20C.

A grand scheme of renovation and Gothicisation was undertaken from 1280 to 1324 at a propitious moment both politically and spiritually and at a time of great prosperity. It coincided with the urban reorganisation, the reaffirmation of the Orthodox Church after the Cathar heresies, and the need to renovate part of the cathedral. In a desire to harmonise the building, the cupolas were covered by a single roof and the east end was raised. The **west end** was added 1308–16, its sparse decorative features emphasised by a barely articulated surface. The elevation is divided horizontally by two moulded string courses supporting high relief sculptures and, apart from these and the hood mouldings carrying sculptures, all the decoration, made up of blind arcades organised into a square, is concentrated around the Rayonnant rose window, innovative for the period. The upper parts of the belfry-porch were completed in the 17C.

Interior. The porch or narthex is linked to the nave by a descending flight of steps. Around the upper section are murals, 1316–24, with twelve scenes from the Creation to the Expulsion, restored in 1988 and the organ (1702–06), placed in the porch in 1722, was moved forward to its present position to expose the murals. The surprisingly vast aisleless **nave**, 20m wide, probably begun c 1120, was one of a group of 77 Romanesque domed churches in Aquitaine. The **cupolas** at Cahors, on pendentives and carried by massive arches and six strong piers, are the most audacious, 18m in diameter and 32m above ground. In the western cupola is a rare monumental Gothic **mural**, the Prophets in the corolla and the martyrdom of St Stephen in the apex. The walls of the east end were raised in 1280—just two Romanesque capitals survive on the north—bringing it to a height commensurate with the nave and making feasible the insertion of tall windows. The St-Anthony chapel was added in 1491, and the more original **Notre-Dame chapel** (also called the *Chapelle Profonde*) was consecrated in 1484 by Bishop Antoine d'Alamand. The decoration introduces the Cadurcien rose motif together with *bâtons écotés* and suns with undulating rays. These motifs became very popular on secular buildings in and around Cahors until the beginning of the 16C. The Immaculate Conception panel was almost totally destroyed after the Religious wars, but the vaults still have their original decoration. The retable, 1679–81, dedicated to the Virgin, was designed by Gervais Drouet of Toulouse and made in Cahors.

Survivors from a revamp of the interior during the 18C are the main altar (1702–06), in red marble from Caunes (Languedoc), and the red marble north gallery (1734) which resulted in the disappearance of the north portal and the pulpit (1738). The walls were plastered in white to set off the marble. Fragments of 14C paintings discovered in the apse during restoration work in the 19C led to the repainting, or reinterpreting, of all the painted decoration. This was completed in 1874 and coincided with the installation of the new **stained glass**, commissioned in 1872 by Bishop

Grimardias from Joseph Villiet of Bordeaux in 1872. The iconography is based on cycles of the life of Christ, the life of the Virgin and local saints as well as the life of St Stephen. It is very high quality, among the best in the Lot.

The Flamboyant **cloister**, reached by the door in the south of the choir, with complicated lierne vaults, replaced the 12C cloister. Work began in the east gallery and continued through two building campaigns of 1497–1509, and 1514–53, demonstrated by the variation in the doorways which carry the coats of arms of successive bishops, and discrepancies in height and decoration of the arcades. A few mouth-watering samples of late Gothic sculpture survived the Reformation, notably the glorious Virgin of the Annunciation on the angle pillar in the north-west, with long wavy hair falling on her shoulders. The pendant boss above is decorated with Christ and angel musicians and there is more carving on the door opposite.

The **St-Gausbert Chapel** (open July–Sept, except Mon) off the east gallery, the former chapter house, has a small collection of religious artefacts, and has late-15C/early-16C murals.

The south-east door leads to an enclosed courtyard with the engaging **Archdeacon's House** on the south and west. Two Gothic houses around a stairwell were given a Renaissance face-lift c 1520–40 with mullioned windows, rinceaux, busts in medallions, pilasters and candelabras.

Leave the cathedral complex by a vaulted passageway leading into Rue de la Chantrerie. A complex building opposite dating from the 14C, called **La Chantrerie**, was used from the 17C by the cathedral chapter to store their wine presses or vats. Its name comes from its proximity to the old residential quarters of the cathedral cantors and it is thought to have been built as a type of warehouse or commercial centre. An exemplary restoration, the façade has two two-light windows with columns flanking a vast overhanging chimney breast above four Gothic arcades and it is now used by the Musée du Vin (tel: 65 23 99 70, 10.00–12.00, 15.00–19.00, Jul–Sept).

Turn right and right again into **Rue St-James**—a re-used 13C carved head on the angle with Rue du Petit-Mot, and a vegetarian restaurant at No. 41, *l'Orangerie* (tel: 65 22 59 06). In the courtyard at **No. 27**, part of the old cathedral choir school, a 12C–13C construction with 14C doors and windows, is now used for temporary exhibitions. Maison Manhol, **No. 18**, is a characteristically symmetric 17C façade with *mirandes* at the top. Just before the corner with Place Chapou is a 15C façade. Turn left at the end of Rue St-James and walk alongside the *halle*. On the left, **No. 53** is worth noting.

The area south of the cathedral is known as the **Quartier des Badernes**, the lower quarter where the titled bourgeoisie or *nobles de robe* built their houses. The grander houses are concentrated around the **Rue Nationale**, the old Rue Droite which led to the Pont-Vieux. **No. 116** has Cahors' most voluptuous Baroque entrance with volutes, an oculus and a heavy panelled door carved with luscious fruit and flowers. **No. 128** is early 13C, with squat arcades and the outlines of a gallery with three three-light round-headed bays. In the next block is a medieval façade with two 15C windows.

On **Rue du Dr. Bergougnioux** is a 17C doorway belonging to the same house while the tower on the right has mullioned windows with *bâtons écotés*. No. 77 has a Renaissance window with fluted columns similar to the style of Nicolas Bachelier. The 16C *hôtel* at **No. 40** is a charming if delapidated example of the arbitrary juxtaposition of successive decorative modes without regard to overall harmony: next to Cadurcien Gothic windows (1480–1500), with *bâtons écotés*, is a triple bay of more Italianate design (c 1530) exploiting the idiom of the early Renaissance. The interior mid-16C façade is altogether more disciplined and shows a better understanding of the use of the classical orders.

Back in **Rue Nationale**, **No. 186** has a whole gamut of openings, from the 15C to the 17C. Where Rue Nationale runs out of Place Rousseau are a variety of details, and in the street elevation of the Résidence du Lavoir are restored 13C windows and gargoyles of a dog and a bear. If you continue to the end of the street, you arrive opposite the emplacement of the Pont Vieux.

Return to **Rue Lastié** which has a number of beautiful buildings. On the left, **No. 35** has a fine 14C window with bar tracery and round the corner on Place St-Priest is a restored 17C open Toulousain style staircase. On the right is a medieval house with the outline of a crocketed gable above 14C windows. **No. 117** is a particularly fine 14C jettied house with three Gothic windows above and a low 16C arch to the shop below.

Behind several of the attractively restored 15C and 16C half-timbered façades in **Place St-Urcisse** are restaurants. The early 13C **Church of St-Urcisse** was altered in the 14C but has retained its late Romanesque door and Gothic capitals around the south door (in the garden of the neighbouring building), whereas the west porch is contemporary with the west façade of the cathedral (c 1320) and similarly has a large rose window above the portal. On the central pillar is a standing Virgin and Child protected by a carved baldaquin. Inside (if you can get in) are storiated capitals of Original Sin and the Life of Christ. In Rue Clémenceau is another vegetarian restaurant, *Marie Colline* (tel: 65 35 59 96).

Continue north along **Rue St-Urcisse**. The Romanesque house at **No. 62** has a restored early-13C brick façade, and the adjacent one a timber *soleilho*. Back at Place St-James, turn right and on the right in **Place Henri IV** is **Hôtel de Roaldès**, one of the best known houses in Cahors, but heavily restored. It changed hands many times, but in 1636 passed to a family of magistrates, the Roaldès. At its core is a 13C tower in brick, and facing the river is a beautiful *soleilho*. The façade on Place Henri IV is richly decorated with the Quercynois idiom of the end-15C–16C: roses, *bâtons écotés* and flaming suns. Continue along the riverbank to **Place Champollion** where there is a colourful 19C monument to **Clément Marot** (1495–1544), poet, statesman and sympathiser with the Reformation, by Turcan, Denys Puech and Olivier Merson.

It is worth making a detour across **Pont Cabessut** for views of the old town and the restaurant on a barge, *Le Fil des Douceurs* (tel: 65 22 13 04).

Leading out of Place Champollion is the pretty, shady **Place Olivier-de-Magny**, built on the old cemetery of the church of la Daurade. The only reminders of the old church and the 17C Benedictine convent attached to it are a piece of 12C nave and 15C chapels. The restored house with a tower in **Rue de la Daurade** dates from two campaigns of construction, c 1250 and late 13C–early 14C. On the corner with Rue C. Marot stone arcades support a timber-framed upper floor with brick nogging, a 13–14C building. One of these houses is a popular restaurant, *Le Rendez-vous* (tel: 65 22 65 10). Turn right into **Rue C.Marot**. The 17C house at **No. 12** is on the site of the birthplace of Olivier de Magny (1530–c 1561), lyric poet and secretary to Henri II. **Place de la Libération** has a variety of buildings—note **No. 44** with three symmetrical bays rebuilt in 1633 and a spiral staircase inside the doorway of 1642. The small streets north-west of the square are worth exploring: No. 3 Rue St-Pierre has a group of 16C/17C sculpted heads. No. 40 **Rue du Portail Alban** has a stair-tower with a 16C door decorated with *bâtons écotés* and 19C Neo-Classical portal.

North of Place de la Libération is the **Quartier des Soubirous** (meaning upper or superior), served by **Rue du Château du Roi** and its continuation **Rue des Soubirous** where the principal urban palaces were built. Note the mixture of Baroque and medieval at No. 58 Rue du Château du Roi, and one of the few remaining exterior timber staircases in the courtyard of the 13C/14C mansion at No. 43. Turn into **Rue du Four Ste-Catherine**, a narrow and picturesque street leading down to the riverside. At the end on the left is **Collège Pélegry**, the only remaining building of the university, somewhat disfigured by recent additions but still bearing the coat of arms of the college. At the end of the impasse is the late 15C battlemented stairtower and around the doorway is a splendid profusion of *bâtons écotés*, one of the best examples of Cadurcien sculpture at the end of the 15C. The college, founded in 1368 by Raimond and Hugues de Pélegry for 13 poor students, survived until 1751.

The **Château du Roi**, in the next block on the right, acquired the title when it became the temporary residence of the King's representative in the Quercy in the 15C. In the 14C it had belonged to relatives of Pope John XXII, the De Via family, who probably built it, and in the 19C it was turned into a prison. At No. 102 **Rue des Soubirous** is a 14C house, No. 88 is a late-15C–16C town house decorated with *bâtons écotés* and a fine Gothic door.

The most remarkable medieval building in Cahors is the 14C **Palais Duèze**, attributed to Pierre Duèze, brother of Pope John XXII. The vast urban palace was arranged around a square courtyard. What is left can best be seen from Rue Albe and Place Thiers. The **tower**, on Boulevard Gambetta, 34m high, was the highest in the town, a certain mark of prestige, and favoured the style of the preceding century with two-light Romanesque windows. The palace was subsequently taken over by the Prince of Wales in 1364, but the main wing was demolished in 1405.

The renovated **Hôtel de l'Escargot** (tel: 65 35 07 66) incorporates part of the old palace. The **Church of St-Barthélémy**, enclosed within the same walls as the Duèze palace, was partly rebuilt in the 14C. A rigorous building, orientated north–south, the monumental entrance at the base of the belfry is similar in style to that of the cathedral and to St-Urcisse The upper part of the imposing belfry-tower has blind arcades in brick. Inside is a plaque commemorating the baptism of the Pope in 1245, and some 15C murals.

Return to the centre down Boulevard Gambetta or the parallel streets.

The Pont Valentré and the western part of the town

On foot or by car, follow the tree-lined Quai Cavaignac round the south perimeter of the town to the **PONT VALENTRÉ**, the emblem of Cahors and the most famous medieval fortified bridge in France. When the construction of the Pont Valentré began in 1308 the town already had two bridges, the Pont Vieux to the south, and the Pont-Neuf to the east, realised between 1254 and 1291. The slow progress of the Pont Valentré was traditionally blamed on satanic forces, but the problems were as much financial as technical despite a grant from the king in 1312. The bridge was in use by 1335 but not completed. As hostilities with the English increased and the defences of the town were being improved and extended, there was an added impetus in 1345 to complete the bridge, although work continued until 1378. Restoration began in 1879 under the supervision of Paul Gout who, in tribute to the legendary diabolic intervention, sculpted a little devil clinging to the angle at the top of the central tower.

Its six wide arches and the three high towers 40m above the river, are a magnificent sight. The arches each end had a portcullis and there was a barbican on the eastern bank. Quite narrow, there are passing bays on the bridge. A dam below the bridge, which has existed since the 14C, links the lock (1808) to the 16C Périé Mill downstream. Just upstream is the old pumping station of 1853 and a reconstruction of a pre-16C wooden *bâteau-moulin*. Above that is the site of the ancient **Fontaine des Chartreux**, supposedly the source of the sacred fountain, Divona, around which the Gallo-Roman town developed. The fountain springs from a natural reservoir under the Causse de Limogne about 20km east. Quai Valentré has been pedestrianised and prettified with flowerbeds and is the departure point for a variety of river cruises on the Lot, made navigable again in the last few years, in both directions (tel: 65 22 67 80). There is also the inevitable Petit Train.

The remaining **fortifications** are at the north of the town, extended in the mid-14C to protect the entire peninsula and to incorporate religious communities outside the *cité* walls. It had two fortified gates and eleven square towers. Four survive—**Tour St-Jean** dominating the east bank, **Tour Morlas** and **St-Mary** in the centre, and **Tour du Pal** on the west. Of the gates, only the Porte St-Michel opening on to the cemetery is left and the barbican, which protected the eastern Porte de la Barre, still stands high above the river. There is a scrap of the antique thermae, the **Arc de Diane**, in an incongruous setting on Avenue de Freycinet behind Place de Gaulle. North of the *place* in Espace Bessières is the Musée de la Résistance (tel: 65 22 14 25).

Moving south from the Arc de Diane, on Rue Emile Zola, is the municipal museum, **Musée Henri-Martin** (tel: 65 23 14 00, July–Sept), installed in the former Bishops' Palace since 1906. It contains Gallic and Roman archaeology, pre-Romanesque, Romanesque and Gothic elements from lost buildings, and 14C, 15C and 16C religious art (closed for repairs at the time of writing). The Henri-Martin Gallery has a collection of works given to the town by the Toulousain painter and his son, Martin Ferrères. Henri Martin (1860–1943) studied in Toulouse and Paris under J.P. Laurens and started out as a Salon painter. In 1889 he adopted Neo-Impressionism and in the 1890s became known for his decorative work. The 18 works exhibited in Cahors are from this period when the subject matter of his work was increasingly concerned with idealised scenes of contemporary life and idyllic pastorals. He was influenced by the work of the Italian divisionist painter, Giovanni Segantini, and owes a debt to Puvis de Chavannes.

Behind the Tourist Information Centre on Allées Fénelon is the pretty tower of the **Jesuit College**, 1674, and around **Place A. Briand**, recently endowed with a new fountain, at the centre of town, are the public buildings of the 19C. The **Hôtel de Ville**, on Boulevard Gambetta, was rebuilt in 1840, but in the passageway which cuts the building (Rue Fondude) are the remains of the 17C door and 13C windows of the old residence of the seneschal. Next to the Hôtel de Ville is the restaurant *La Taverne* (tel: 65 35 28 66).

On Foot or By Car. There are two vantage points on the cliffs to the south for views over Cahors. The **Mont St-Cyr** to the south-east is reached by crossing Pont Louis-Philippe to the faubourg St-Georges, and, after the fountain, a footpath on the left takes you up past the ruins of the Hermitage of St-Cirq with its cypresses, to the summit and a spectacular view of the whole town. It is possible to return by a path descending to the faubourg of Cabessut to the east of the town. By car, from St-Georges take the D6 (direction Lalbenque).

For a superb view of the Pont Valentré and the river, cross the bridge, turn right and then left to the **Croix Magne** on the Pech d'Angély.

22

The Lot Valley

This is an extraordinarily beautiful river although slightly less well-known than the Dordogne Valley or Tarn Gorges. A stay in the Midi-Pyrénées could be organised around the Lot, which enters the region in the east of the Rouergue at St-Laurent-d'Olt and leaves the west Quercy approximately 240km later. It flows past or near to major sites such as Cahors, Conques, Figeac, St-Cirq-Lapopie, Entraygues and Espalion, through wide valleys and narrow gorges. These excursions follow the Lot as far as Entraygues.

West of Cahors, the vineyards

Total distance: 110km (69 miles).

This itinerary follows the Lot's meandering route west of Cahors where the vineyards reach down to the water's edge, and is an opportunity to do a little wine tasting.

The potential of river transport was exploited as early as the 13C and it became the major route for exporting overseas via the Garonne and the port of Bordeaux. By the 17C navigation had improved with numerous locks and by the 19C up to 300,000 tonnes of freight was carried a year until the railway put paid to it. For 60–70 years there was no traffic on the Lot but recently 70km was made navigable and pleasure boats offer a variety of excursions of between Luzech, Cahors and St-Cirq Lapopie. The cargo most closely associated with the river was wine. The strong dark wine of Cahors was carried to Northern Europe and became the communion wine in Russia. The Romans cultivated wines here by the 3C and Pope John XXII took Quercynois wine-growers to Avignon to cultivate Châteauneuf du Pape. The Bordelais resented the competition and did what they could to block exports but the final death-knell to river transport and the wine trade was phylloxera which destroyed the vineyards in the 1880s. In 1961 new vinestock of traditional types, Auxerrois and the Merlot, was planted in the valley and production and quality has gradually built up until 45 communes qualified for *Appellation d'Origine Contrôlée* in 1971. Like many of the smaller wine growing areas, there is an emphasis on improving the quality of the wine and it is possible to buy excellent Cahors at a reasonable price. Many of the vineyards offer a *dégustation*.

Leave Cahors on the D911 north (direction Fumel), to **Mercuès**, 5km. The ancient *bastide* is entirely dominated by the **Château de Mercuès**, a favourite residence of the Bishops of Cahors since 1212, now a luxury hotel and one of the leading restaurants in the region (tel: 65 20 00 01). The owner, G. Vigouroux, is a wine dealer and the cellars can be visited.

Turn left on to the D12 and cross the river to **Douelle** (4km), a once important river port now used only by pleasure boats. The 15C church, heavily restored last century, has a model of a boat suspended from the nave vaults. Return to the right bank and the D12 where the vineyards start in earnest. At **Caillac**, 2km on the D10, the Church of St-Pierre and St-Paul was built in the 11C/12C but the only Romanesque elements to survive are on the south entrance. The church was rebuilt from the beginning of the 16C and a delicately sculpted Renaissance doorway was inserted, with the profiles of Adam and Eve on the lower right.

Take the D145/D9 up the **Col de Crayssac** for a great view down to the loop in the river encompassing the vineyards of **Parnac**, known as the capital of Cahors wine since the cooperative of the Côtes d'Olt was installed there. **Caïx**, a boating centre (tel: 65 20 18 19) on the Lot, has an immaculately tended domaine belonging to the Danish Royal Family, a small part-12C church and a sculpted cross (1772). Stay on the D9 to Luzech (about 10km from Caillac).

Guarding a particularly tight meander in the Lot is the great 13C keep of **Luzech** (pop. 1580, Tourist Information, tel: 65 20 17 27). After the Albigensian Crusades the bishops and Barons of Cardaillac each had a castle, the episcopal fort on the higher ground and the seigneurial one lower down. The medieval town clustered around the castle is still enclosed in part of its protective walls and there is an old gateway just below the château. In the Grande Rue, the old main street, the restored 13C Maison des Consuls houses the Tourist Information and a small museum of local archaeology. Place du Canal, now the main street, was originally a canal or moat dividing the medieval town from the *barri* (suburb) which itself has existed since the 13C. An important market is held here on Wednesdays.

Two short expeditions can be made from Luzech. The first (on foot) takes a path from the château up to the plateau above the isthmus, called the **Impernal**, a prehistoric and Gallo-Roman site, the source of most of the exhibits in the museum. The other is to follow the Lot (possible by car) to the opposite extremity of the peninsula where the Flamboyant chapel, **Notre-Dame-de-l'Isle**, is submerged in vineyards on the very banks of the Lot. Built by Bishop Antoine de Luzech c 1505 in a style reminiscent of the cloisters at Cahors, it was a pilgrimage chapel for sailors and still has a pilgrimage in September.

Return to Luzech by the west of the headland past the 14C/15C Church of St-Pierre, restored in the 19C. Take the left bank, D8, 5km, to **Albas** perched on top of a cliff. This was a wine port and another favourite watering hole of the Bishops of Cahors, especially in the 16C. The episcopal residence was restored by Antoine d'Alamand c1485, and is decorated with Cadurcien roses. There is just one medieval gateway standing. Cross back after 3.5km to the *bastide* of **Castelfranc**. Surrounded by hills, the 14C church with a splendid belfry-tower helped defend the town against the English in 1355. About 3km north on the D45, **La Masse** is a group of houses forming a square around a Romanesque church and slightly further on

(2km) is **Les Junies Priory**, founded for women between 1343 and 1355. The austere Church of the Madeleine (key at house opposite the Cross), on the banks of the River Masse, has some 14C stained glass with the figures of the founder, Gaucelme de Jean, his nephews and the family coat of arms. There are traces of the adjacent cloister and of the vaulted chapter house.

Cross the river again on the D45 (6km) to **Anglars-Juillac** in the middle of vineyards. The restored Romanesque church in the centre of the town has a belfry-gable, and around the upper part of the abside is a motif special to the valley, consisting of pierced metopes. The church was remodelled in the 16C but the Renaissance door with a sculpture of the Crucifixion is sadly damaged. Follow the left bank 5km to **Bélaye**, a picturesque *castrum* or village around a castle on a narrow spur above the river which was acquired by the Bishops of Cahors c 1236 with parts of the old city walls and lovely views towards Prayssac.

(Prayssac, on the right bank, is one of the starting points for the **Dolmen Circuit**—others are Castelfranc or Les Junies—a walk indicated by arrows.)

On the left bank the D8 continues 6km to Lagardelle and to the Church of St-Pierre-ès-Liens at **Pescadoires**, a priory founded in 1037 and attached to Moissac. It has lost its apse, but is still interesting for its squat square belfry supported by a cupola and the exterior decoration. **Château Lacoste** at **Grézels** (2.5km) has a museum of the wines of Cahors (tel: 65 21 34 18, July–Sept). Built in the 13C, rebuilt in the 16C, and restored in 1960, it is still an impressive structure built around a quadrangle with two square and two round towers.

Stay on the D8 for 4km and cross the river to **Puy-l'Évêque** (pop. 2302), an interesting and ancient little town built on an escarpment on the right bank, descending in concentric terraces to the banks of the Lot where there used to be a major port. A stronghold of the bishops, it was occupied by the English during the Hundred Years War who reinforced the defences so well that the town withstood attack during the Religious Wars. At the highest point the Bishops' tower, c 1230, is the only part of the episcopal fort still standing and the Esplanade de la Truffière at its base is a good vantage point. On the same level are the 14C Château de l'Ychayrie and a small 16C castle. One level down, enclosed in a second enceinte, the Château de Bovila has a late-Gothic door with *bâtons écotés*. The 14C fortified Church of St-Sauveur, slightly distanced from the town, on the D911, was remodelled in the late-15C by Bishop Antoine d'Alamand who added the superb porch belfry with a Flamboyant portal and above it a Crucifixion with the Virgin and St John. There is a market on Tuesdays.

Worth a **detour** is the Romanesque church at **Martignac** (4km north), both for the building itself and for the 15C/16C murals of Christ in Majesty, an Entombment, the Deadly Sins and the Virtues, symbolised by angels, and the Saved received into Paradise by St Michael.

The D119 brings you (6km) to one of the major Romanesque churches in the Quercy at **Duravel**. The key is kept at the *boulangerie*. The **church** has kept many of its Romanesque elements, despite radical restoration in the 19C, and has a 15C west entrance. The lateral door is 12C and around the east end are decorated corbels and a frieze of palmettes; the pierced metope motif appears here as at Anglars-Juillac. The square belfry over the crossing is 14C. The church was part of an important priory, founded in 1055 and affiliated to Moissac, which acquired the relics of three oriental hermits, Agathon, Poemon and Hilarion, guaranteed to attract pilgrims. There are storiated capitals inside with the Martyrdom of St Peter, and scenes of Hell, punishments, and the Archangel Michael. Behind the altar a red sand-stone sarcophagus contains the relics of the three saints, and in the nave are a Gothic holy-water stoup and a Gallo-Roman relief decorated with vines. The small, square Merovingian crypt, built to contain the relics, has four pillars and ten engaged columns supporting the groin vaults. Two of decorated capitals are exceptional: one with a peacock, its tail spread, standing above a serpent; the other with an inscription recording the consecration of the sanctuary.

Veer off on the V8 behind the church to **St-Martin-le-Redon**, in the Thèze Valley, leaving the vineyards for more wooded scenery and different rural architecture. Follow the road for about 10km, cross the D673 and turn right. Just inside the Lot-et-Garonne is the magnificent **Château de Bonaguil** (tel: 53 71 05 22/ 39 75). It is everything that a castle should be, standing erect on a rocky promontory, with 13 towers and turrets, 350m of perimeter walls, and military architecture ranging from the 13C to the 18C. There is plenty to see, including fascinating 16C and 17C graffiti.

From the D673 take a sharp right turn to **Montcabrier** (6km), a 13C *bastide* with a 19C covered market and Church of St-Louis with a 14C Rayonnant rose window in the west and a stunning belfry-gable with six arcades. Inside is a statue of St-Louis with a beard to the left of a dusty 17C retable. Take the D673/D660 and go through **Goujounac** (13.5km), an immaculate village in golden stone with flowers and shrubs and a small Romanesque tympanum with a Christ in Majesty in the south wall.

After 3.5km turn left on the D45 to **Les Arques** which has a virtually unsullied 11C Romanesque **church** with unique mozarabic-inspired capitals and a crypt. The tiny village, with about 170 inhabitants, made a huge impact on the Russian born sculptor, **Ossip Zadkine** (1890–1967), who had an on-going love affair with the Midi-Pyrénées from the 1920s and bought a house in Les Arques in 1934. Intellectual, musician and poet as well as sculptor, his arrival in this bucolic village must have been something of a revolution. The **Zadkine Museum** (tel: 65 22 83 37, 11.00–19.00, 15 Jun–Sept, 14.00–18.00, weekends rest of year) opened in 1988 in his former studio converted into a small attractive gallery which has recently been extended. The exhibits are on loan from the Zadkine Museum in Paris, but several of the large wooden sculptures were conceived in Les Arques: **Daphne** (1939), hewn from a massive trunk, and **Diane** (1941) in poplar and polychromed, a work he always kept in his home; and the stark, highly emotional **Pietà** (1939–40) in the church. Stylistically his work owes a particularly heavy debt to Cubism and primitive sculpture but emotionally it is expressionist. The work here shows his range including sculpture, prints, phtotographs and tapestries. Les Arques has the project for his first major monument, for Rotterdam in 1947, The Destroyed City, and bronzes of his most successful work, **Orpheus** (1948), the dynamic **Arlequin Hurlant** (1956), **Arbre des Grâces** (1962) and the compact and polished **Pomone** (1960).

Zadkine participated in the restoration of the Romanesque **Church of St-André-des-Arques** (across the D45, 1km from the road), and discovered in 1954 some remarkable 15C murals which have, unfortunately, deteriorated.

The Lot Valley, east of Cahors

Total distance: 136km (85 miles).

Follow the Lot from Cahors on the D653 to the east. In places this is a wide, fertile valley, lined with walnut trees and poplars, cultivating tobacco, sunflowers and strawberries; in other parts it is confined within high cliffs. There are a number of picturesque villages, numerous castles, and always beautiful scenery.

Laroque-des-Arcs has four churches, the most eyecatching is the tiny Chapelle St-Roch (1842) above the English Castle, and at **Lamagdelaine** is the little 12C Church of Notre-Dame-de-Velles on the banks of the Lot. After 15km you arrive at **Vers**, named after the river that cascades through the village and from whose source, at St-Martin-de-Vers, came the water carried about 30km to Cahors by the Roman aqueduct, sometimes over sometimes underground. The best preserved portion of the aqueduct is visible at the foot of the cliffs above the lock.

Take the D622 for 14km to **Bouziès**, divided into two communities by the river. Cross to the port of **Bouziès-Haut** for river cruises (tel: 65 30 22 84/65 31 26 83). A spectacular **walk** along the old towpath of Ganil built in 1877 starts from the railway bridge, part carved out of the overhanging cliff, to St-Cirq-Lapopie.

From Bouziès-Haut to St-Cirq-Lapopie by car: either stay on the same bank and take the narrow and winding D40 or return to the D622 and cross again further up-river which has the advantage of the view of St-Cirq across the Lot (7km).

The curious name **St-Cirq-Lapopie** from the patronymic Pompeius, which became La Popia, is a memorably stunning village stretched out on a ridge overlooking the Lot. This is the best known attraction on the Lot and has developed into a well-manicured village with lots of artists, boutiques, cafés and tourists. Dominating the scene is the 16C church, but it has little of interest. At the highest point, next to the church, are the remains of a feudal castle. At the extreme east is the Porte de la Pélissaria leading to the river where there were once tanneries. The attractions of St-Cirq did not go unnoticed even by the most sceptical of men, André Breton, leader of the Surrealist Movement, who purchased an old auberge here in the 1930s, and was joined by Foujita and Man Ray. Exhibitions of modernism are held at the **Château of St-Cirq Lapopie** (tel: 65 31 27 48, July–Sept). River cruises can be made from St-Cirq.

Staying on the south bank of the river, take the D8, (7km) to the **Château de Cénevières** (tel: 65 31 27 33, Easter–Nov) high on a cliff. This is a charming privately-owned château (the owners will show you round) part of which is 13C, but in the 16C the fortress was transformed into a Renaissance residence. There are painted decorations on the walls of the so-called Alchemist's room.

Cross the river to the D622 and continue 8km to **Cajarc** (pop. 1059, Tourist Information, tel. 65 40 72 89), which, like St-Cirq, has an exhibition centre, the **Centre Georges Pompidou** (tel: 65 40 63 97, spring–autumn) for contemporary or modern work. Georges Pompidou frequently visited the Quercy, and Cajarc was the birthplace of the writer Françoise Sagan. A pleasant old town with a market on Fridays, it is enclosed within a circular boulevard; it has good facilities, including a lake, and river cruises (tel: 65 40 72 89).

Stay on the D622 to **Larroque-Toirac** with its impressive and visitable château (tel: 65 34 78 12, July–Sept) built into the rock and **St-Pierre-Toirac** (13.5km), a tumble-down place with old houses with *bolets*. At the centre is an austere 12C church with carved corbels, raised and fortified in the 14C, which contains numerous decorated capitals, many of them storiated. There is a light at the back of the church. Merovingian sarcophagi are laid out to the south of the church. The D662 takes you to Figeac via the historic and picturesque village of **Faycelles** (13.5km).

To continue along the Lot, cross the bridge at St-Pierre-Toirac which takes you into the *département* of the Aveyron and the D86, a pretty route along the Lot ending at Capdenac Gare (15km), the 19C conurbation whose raison d'être was the railway (1856). Quickly leave Capdenac Gare for **Capdenac-le-Haut** (3km), a beautiful village commanding a key defensive position high on the north bank above a kink in the river, promoted as the site of ancient Uxellodunum. Often beseiged in the past, it has ramparts, two Gothic gateways with a barbican, a 14C square keep which houses the Tourist Information (tel: 65 34 17 23) and a small museum (June–Sept).

The N140 follows the Lot for about 15km through Bouillac and La Roque-Bouillac and crosses the river at Boisse-Penchot. Turn left after the bridge on to the D42 and after 5km left again on to the D963. After 6km cross the Pont d'Agrès and turn right on the D42, another 6km to **St-Parthem**. This is a stunning village, as is **La Vinzelle**, standing sentinel over the Lot valley. This is the region to taste *estofinado*. **Almon-les-Junies** is the *centre mondial* for this dish at its three restaurants: *Chez Jean Ferrières* (tel: 65 64 04 65), *Chez Georgette Trayssac-Romiguières* (tel: 65 64 04 69) and *Chez André Cavaignac* (tel: 65 64 04 90).

Just 1.5km from the **Pont de Coursavy**, where the Dourdou runs into the Lot, on the D901, is **Grand-Vabre**, the reputed resting place of Dadon, founder of Conques, marked by the chapel Notre-Dame-de-la-Nativité, restored in 1978. The 15C parish church has a relief with a Pietà with Ste-Foy and Ste-Catherine. Restaurant *Chez-Marie* (tel: 65 69 84 55). (See Route 25, Conques.)

The Lot Valley (D141/D107) from here is a pleasant drive through a sparsely inhabited countryside, wooded with oaks, silver birch and box to **Entraygues** (24km). The terraced slopes either side of the valley before Entraygues are frequent reminders of the many abandoned vineyards of the Pays d'Olt, but a few have been revived between Le Fel and Espalion. (See Route 26, Olt Rouergat.)

23

Souillac, the Causse de Martel, the Dordogne and Célé Valleys and Rocamadour

Total distance: 110km (69 miles).

This itinerary covers the northern part of the *département* of the Lot, often described by its old name, the Haut Quercy, in an almost round trip, starting at Souillac.

SOUILLLAC (pop. 3570, Tourist Information, Bd. L-J. Malvy, tel: 65 37 81 56) is the first town of any importance on the N20 after entering the region from the north. A pleasant town in pale stone, on the Borrèze, a tributary of the Dordogne, it is well equipped with hotels and other accommodation which makes it a good base.

The main monument is the Romanesque **Abbey Church of Saint-Mary**, 1075–c mid-12C, part of a Benedictine abbey. The church has survived although the monastic buildings of that period were destroyed in the 16C by the Protestants. The abbey was restored and repaired in the 17C and 18C. The appearance of the church is rather sterile, despite the arrangement of polygonal radiating chapels opening off the apse, perhaps because of the heavy restoration in the 17C and 19C and the crisp white stone and the large empty area around it. To the west are the remains of the 10C belfry.

The most interesting feature of the church is remarkable **Romanesque reliefs** on the reverse of the west door, possibly moved here in the 17C. The **tympanum** is a complicated illustration, framed by three arches, of the dream of the monk Theophilus, apocryphal hero of the Miracles of Our Lady who, having sold his soul to the devil, had to ask for the Virgin's intercession for its recovery. Heavenly forces, represented by the Virgin descending from the clouds and angels, oppose the forces of evil made up of dragons and other beasts. This animated scene is framed by the figures of St Peter and St Benedict. The **trumeau** is a masterpiece of tumbling and intertwined figures of humans, and monsters, biting and snarling, representing Sin, Chaos and Pardon. The Prophet Isaiah on the right door jamb, a graceful figure with crossed legs, flowing beard and hair and swirling drapes which cling to his limbs, is a more vigorous version of Moissac's Jeremiah and extended to fill a larger space. The rather less wonderful figure on the opposite jamb is the patriarch Joseph or Josea.

The cavernous two-bay **nave** is covered by two cupolas on pendentives and supported by massive interior buttresses, in the tradition of a number of churches in the west of France, and above the crossing is a third cupola. It is devoid of decoration except for some interesting carved capitals in the capacious east end. The furnishings include a 16C retable of the Mystery of the Rosary, a painting of Christ's Agony on the Mount by Chasseriau (1819–56), and 18C choir stalls. From the narthex is the entrance to the crypt, discovered in 1948, which incorporates the foundations of an earlier church and elements of the Carolingian chancel as well as 11C–13C sarcophagi.

Adjacent to the church, installed in the 17C monastic buildings in 1988 and in total contrast is the **Musée de l'Automate** (tel: 65 37 07 07, June & Sept every day 10.00–12.00, 15.00–18.00; July & Aug every day 10.00–19.00). This is a magical place, a wonderland of mechanised dolls and models arranged thematically and activated in rotation to perform all sorts of acrobatics and contortions, the most comprehensive collection of its kind in Europe with more than 1000 pieces, from 1862 to 1960. An absolute must for children of all ages, especially on a rainy day.

From Souillac follow the Dordogne river on the D43 to Belcastel. The Grottes de Lacave (tel: 65 37 87 03, Apr–Nov) includes a visit by electric train and lift to underground lakes and spectacular concretions. Stay on the D25, between the roches de Monges and the Rochers Sainte-Marie to Meyronne, then cross the river to St-Sozy (D15) and turn right (D114) to Creysse, a pretty village at the foot of a rocky outcrop with a Romanesque chapel.

Take the D23, 29km, to **Martel** (pop. 1402, Tourist Information, tel: 65 37 30 03), the principal town on the Causse de Martel. Famed for its **seven towers**, its legendary founder is Charles Martel (c 685–741).

As the ancient capital of the Viscounty of Turenne it became a free town in 1219 and has retained much of its medieval character. The **Palais de Ramondie** at the centre of the old town, built in 13C–14C but altered later, has interesting late Gothic windows. It contains the Tourist Information and the Musée d'Uxellodunum (tel: 65 37 30 03, Jul–Aug), a small archaeological museum. Nearby are the 13C Hôtel de la Monnaie, the Tower of Henri Court Mantel, and the sturdy 17C covered market. South of the market is Maison Fabri, a 15C house with a round tower built on the site of the house where Henry the Younger, son of Henry II, died in 1183. In Rue Droite, south of Place des Consuls, are more old *hôtels* and at the eastern end of town is the 14C **Church of St-Maur**. The Romanesque tympanum in the porch, from an earlier church, has a Last Judgement with Christ surrounded by angels presenting the instruments of the Passion and sounding the trumpets of the resurrection. Inside there is a 15C Christ on the Cross, some 16C glass in the east end, and 18C panelling and pulpit. In the 16C Grenier d'Abondance, on the Fossés des Cordeliers, is a walnut press, the Moulin de l'Huilerie Castagné (tel: 65 37 38 39, summer).

Return to the Dordogne valley at **Gluges** by the N140, cross the river and continue on the D43 through the rocky formation of the Cirque de Montvalent to Carennac (18km).

Carennac is an attractive village on a backwater of the Dordogne with an ancient **priory** which, despite periods of abuse, has retained a certain charm, with its Romanesque tympanum and group of Gothic sculptures. The Cluniac priory dedicated to St Peter was probably begun towards the end of the 11C. In the 15C the cloister and chapter house were rebuilt. Even before the Revolution the monastery was in a lamentable state and this was not helped by the sale and distribution of most of its possessions soon after.

The priory buildings surrounding the church were remodelled in the 16C and 17C and incorporate the façade facing the river known as the *château*, probably begun in the 15C on the old defences. The Romanesque sculpted **tympanum** above the church porch is the most impressive element of the architecture. Protected by a deep porch and supported by a cluster of four pillars in the centre and two at each side, with simple capitals, it is a finely chiselled but rigorous composition of great clarity. The centre rectangular panel, the full height of the tympanum, is dominated by the hieratic figure of Christ, his hand raised in blessing, framed by an oval mandorla. In the spandrels are the symbols of the four Evangelists. The space on either side is divided horizontally into two registers containing the Apostles with small crouching figures in the extreme corners. A delicately carved vegetal *rinceau* outlines the composition and the narrow lintel has a regular pattern of alternating pearls and little animals.

It is reminiscent of the reliefs of the north porch at Cahors. To the east an 11C door with a double arch and four decorated capitals is signed by the mason, *Girbertus*. The modest 12C church has a barrel vaulted nave and some interesting capitals. There is a shallow transept and a cupola on pendentives above the crossing and a few touches of polychrome in the vaults. The sadly mutilated cloister has one Romanesque gallery on the south whereas the rest was rebuilt in Flamboyant style in the 15C, also reminiscent of Cahors. In the restored **chapter house** is the 16C **Entombment**, a moving ensemble of sculptures with a hint of the original polychrome. Gathered around the Christ are the life-size figures of Nicodemus and Joseph of Arimathaea, with Mary, in the centre, on her right St John, and Mary Magdalene holding the ointment jar, plus two Maries.

Take the D30 (8km) to the hamlet of Prudhomat-Castelnau in the shadow of the **Château de Castelnau-Bretenoux** (tel: 65 38 52 04, all year). This is a truly impressive example of feudal architecture, emphasised by the blood-red colour of the ferruginous limestone it is built in and its position on a plateau with a commanding view over the borders of the old provinces of Périgord, Limousin, Auvergne and Quercy. The castle follows the triangular form of the plateau and has a massive tower at each angle, a semi-circular one in each side and a square keep on the south-west. The Barons of Castelnau appeared in the 11C, and the castle remained in the hands of the descendants or a branch for 38 generations until 1830, but only after the last member, Albert de Luynes, was forced at the Revolution to demolish the upper part of the towers and fill in the ditches. In 1851 a fire caused extensive damage. Jean Monliérat, the last private owner from 1896 to 1932 and a well-known member of the Opéra Cominique, restored it in part before donating it to the State.

The earliest section of the building is late-12C or early-13C with two-light round-arched windows. Major programmes of enlargement and fortification were carried out in the 14C and 15C and assured its defence during the Hundred Years War. In the 16C and 17C it was transformed into a more hospitable residence. It has a collection of medieval sculpture and Jean Mouliérat's collection of religious art, among other things.

In the village the collegiate church built in the 15C by Jean de Castelnau still has its carved wooden stalls, Renaissance windows and a 14C Virgin.

From Bretenoux take the D940, 10km, to **St-Céré** (pop. 4025, Tourist Information, tel: 65 38 11 85), a lively town with a market every Saturday and a fair the first and third Wednesday of each month. It also holds an important summer music festival (tel: 65 38 29 08). This is a very popular holiday centre, particularly for campers, in green and pleasant surroundings.

In the centre of town, around Rue de la République, the main street, and Rue du Mazel, are some 15C, 16C and 17C houses, with medieval and Renaissance features. The quai des Récollets, on the bank of La Bave, has pretty views on to the river, the old houses and bridges. The *Hôtel de France* has a highly recommended restaurant (tel: 65 38 02 15).

The artist **Jean Lurçat** (1892–1966) lived here for over twenty years and his work can be seen in two places. In town, off Place de Marcardial, the **Casino** (tel: 65 3819 60) combines an art gallery for temporary exhibitions, shop and café, and a permanent collection of Lurçat's tapestries and ceramics. The two towers high above St-Céré mark the 14C château purchased in 1945 by Jean Lurçat. **St-Laurent-les-Tours**, **Atelier-Musée Jean Lurçat** (tel: 65 38 28 21, Easter, and 14 Jul–Sept), reached via the D904, is a fascinating insight into Lurçat's later work. He started his career as a painter and came under the influence of the important movements of the early 20C, but he is best known as a tapestry designer, the most prolific of his generation, a medium he began experimenting with in 1917. The large rooms of St-Laurent-les Tours, which Lurçat decorated in his own inimitable style, create a perfect setting for his highly idiosyncratic and vividly coloured tapestries. There are also tapestry cartoons, a large number of paintings, sketches, ceramics, fabrics and furniture, demonstrating the full range of Lurçat's work. Madame Simone Lurçat, the painter's widow, donated the collection to the *département*.

West of St-Céré, in the direction of Rocamadour, is a pretty route with a series of interesting sites.

Head west from St-Céré on the D673 and turn left after 2km to the **Château de Montal** (tel: 65 38 13 72, open Palm Sun–end Oct), a gem of a Renaissance château with a sad story. It was built by Jeanne de Balsac who inherited a fortune in 1503 from her father, Robert de Balsac d'Entragues, Governor of Pisa during the French occupation of northern Italy. Widowed in 1511, she began the construction of Montal for her son Robert but he was killed six months after his departure for Italy in 1523.

This small château is characteristic of the new innovations introduced into France from Italy in the early 16C and indicative of the culture of its chatelaine. Only two wings were ever completed. Despite its present apparent composure, Montal suffered the worst degradation at the end of the 19C when it was stripped of all its decoration and sold off in job lots. It was purchased just before the First World War by a wealthy industrialist and enlightened patron, Maurice Fenaille, who, after years of patient searching, recovered many of the original pieces and/or commissioned copies and Montal was made whole again. The façades facing the country-side have the characteristics of a feudal fortress but the interior courtyard elevations are luxuriously decorated with an Italianate vocabulary of friezes, pilasters, candelabra, allegorical subjects and statues in niches, and high-relief busts which are memorials to Jeanne de Balzac's family. There is a very grand staircase, sculpted on the underside. In the rugged Quercy, Montal is a haven of 16C refinement.

3km west of Montal, on the D673, is the **Grotte de Presque** (tel: 65 38 07 44, Easter–Oct) one of many caves that can be visited in the region. About 4km after the caves, the D38 will take you through the **Cirque d'Autoire**, where a 30m waterfall cascades into the gorge and opposite, in the sheer cliff face, are the ruins of the château des anglais, the description given to most rock-fortresses of this kind in the region. A little further (3km), nestling on both banks of the the valley is **Autoire**, a model Quercynois village. Gathered around a simple church (12C, 14C and 15C) and a 16C manor house, the buildings are in pale gold stone or half-timbered with hipped roofs of russet-coloured tiles. Take the D135 (2km) to the equally alluring **Loubressac**, a fortified village overlooking the valleys of the Bave and the Céré.

Return to the D673 via the D118 to La Poujade and the D14 (6km).

The porous limestone of the *causses* allows water to penetrate and is the reason for the abundance of underground rivers and caverns in the region. The most remarkable, for its size and complexity, and probably the most famous of the underground rivers is the **Gouffre de Padirac** (tel: 65 33 64 56, Apr–Oct). This magical visit, lasting about 1½ hours, is made by lifts, on foot and by boat through a series of galleries and lakes (2.5km on the D90).

Continue straight on along the D673 for 13km Rocadmadour.

ROCAMADOUR (Tourist Information, tel: 65 33 62 59) is the principal attraction in this part of the Midi-Pyrénées, but its magnetism is hard to define. In the Middle Ages the challenging aspect of this inhospitable ravine and the difficulties of access probably contributed to the penance of a pilgrimage, but today the site has been fully exploited to welcome the visitor with numerous hotels, restaurants, souvenir shops, car parks, and the ubiquitous little train, not to mention the installation of lifts to carry people up and down the cliff. The drama of the *cité* clinging to the rock above the Alzou valley is best viewed from **l'Hospitalet** on the plateau above.

There is parking at l'Hospitalet, near the lifts to the south, and at the bottom of the valley.

History. The first mention of a church at Roc-Amadour was in the 11C when the two Benedictine abbeys of Marcilhac and Tulle disputed the site. The monks of Tulle won the day and this was when a Marian cult associated with Rocamadour was first recorded. Its reputation was enhanced by a Book of Miracles of Our Lady of Rocamadour written in 1172. The pilgrimages of St-Bernard, c 1147, and Henry II Plantagenet in 1170, put the site securely on the map, and other pious notables followed in their wake. At its apogee, in the 14C, Rocamadour may have catered for as many visitors as it does today. The troubles of the Reformation started a decline until in the 19C Rocamadour was in a ruinous state. In 1829 a group of ecclesiastics instigated the physical and spiritual revival of the site and reinstated an annual pilgrimage in 1835. This is in the week beginning 8 September, and on the evening of the 14 August there is a candlelight procession.

On Foot. Start from **Porte de l'Hospitalet**. Of the old pilgrim hospital of St-John only fragments of its chapel remain, incorporated into the 19C chapel. The *Voie Sainte* brings you down into the village on Rue Roland le Preux through the first of five fortified medieval gateways, Porte du Figuier. There is a lift to the sanctuaries before the second and most picturesque gate, **Porte Salmon**. Either branch left here, passing behind the houses to arrive at **Porte Basse** at the far end of the village, or go straight down the main street, **Rue de la Couronnerie**, which has a few genuinely old buildings. Near the 15C Hôtel de Ville is the **Tourist Information Centre** and the 216 steps of the **Grand Escalier** leading to the Religious City. Beside **Porte Hugon** is a house called La Louve.

The **Cité Religieuse**, sadly lacking in spiritual warmth on non-pilgrimage days, is made up of a number of sanctuaries which were massively restored and rebuilt in the 19C, the best features being fragments of 12C and 15C frescoes. The sanctuaries are on different levels but all lead off a common *parvis* or forecourt centred on the first rocky resting-place of St-Amadour where, so the story goes, in 1166 his body was exhumed intact centuries after his death. (All the sanctuaries can be visited July–September, the parish **Church of Notre-Dame** is open all year, and the Basilica St-Sauveur from Easter to All Saints.) The main sanctuary, the Church of Notre-Dame, was rebuilt after a rock fall in 1479 and damaged in the 16C. It was restored and enlarged in the 19C. To the right of the 15C portal is a fragment of a wall-painting (also 15C) of ghoulish skeletons, The Three Dead and the Three Living. Inside, above the altar (1889) stands the famous 12C Black

Virgin, one of a series of enigmatic black Madonnas which remain largely unexplained. Originally a reliquary statue, it has suffered over the centuries and Madonna and Child acquired crowns in the 19C. Rocamadour has connections with the sea, represented by ex voto models of boats. The most phoney of all the accoutrements associated with the place has to be the replica of Roland's faithful sword Durandel, embedded in the rock above the Notre-Dame Chapel, a reference to the legend that Charlemagne's companion offered his sword to Our Lady of Rocamadour.

On the exterior wall of the 12C **Chapel St-Michael** are some remarkable but damaged late-12C/13C **frescoes** of the Annunciation and Visitation, and there are more in the apse. Below the chapel was the canons' calefactory (warming room), leading to the gatehouse which has been opened at each end to offer some good views over the village. The so-called Abbey Palace, mainly 19C, houses the Museum of Sacred Art dedicated to Francis Poulenc (1899–1963) who composed the Litanies to the Black Virgin. On the north-east side of the terrace is the largest sanctuary, the **Basilica of St-Sauveur**, originally 12C, its west end built into the cliff face and supporting a wooden gallery. A rectangular space divided into equal naves by two piers with eight columns from which spring diagonal ribs, it is lit by diffused light from the five windows in the east but is confusing as it has been reorientated, with the altar in the north. Steps from St-Sauveur lead down to the **Church of St-Amadour** underneath, the least altered of the medieval buildings with heavy squared ribs similar to the narthex at Moissac. The sacristy was created later from the cistern of the keep. The three further sanctuaries of St-Blaise, St-John and St-Anne, containing the 17C altar from the Notre-Dame Chapel, close the terrace to the east.

To get to the **château** (ramparts only) (14C and 19C) built at the top of the cliff to protect the shrines (and to the south car park) you can either follow the Stations of the Cross (1887) or take the second stage of the lift. Rocamadour has on offer a whole variety of tourist attractions—La grotte des Merveilles (tel: 65 33 67 92, Apr–Oct), a Monkey Park, an Eagle Rock, a Butterfly Garden, or a walk in the Alzou Gorges. There is abundant accommodation in and around the site, but for convenience combined with tranquillity, try *Le Troubadour* (tel: 65 33 70 27) a small new hotel on the Padirac road.

On the D673, 9km west is the **Moulin de Cougnaguet** (tel: 65 38 73 56, 09.00–12.00, 14.00–17.00, Apr–Oct) a 14C fortified mill with four pairs of millstones which still grind into action.

Gourdon and the Bouriane, the Henri Giron Museum

Total distance: 37km (25 miles).

This is a short itinerary, a continuation of the previous one, in a region between the Dordogne the Lot Valley and the Causse of Gramat around the N20, known as the Bouriane.

From Payrac on the N20, head 3.5km south then turn right on the D673 and go 4.5km to **Le Vigan**. This small town has a curious church, part 14C—the three bay nave—and part 15C—the complicated east end. During restoration work in 1960 Romanesque capitals from an earlier building were uncovered in the foundations.

The **Henri Giron Museum** (tel: 65 41 33 78, May–Oct) 3.5km from the centre, was created in 1991 around a private collection. Henri Giron (1914–) was born near Lyon and now lives in Brussels. Self-taught, his paintings are almost always of women and he has developed a very distinctive figurative style. In a delightful rural setting, another feature of the museum is its excellent restaurant (telephone in advance).

The main town of the Bouriane, **Gourdon** (pop. 4880, Tourist Information, tel: 65 41 06 40), situated on a limestone mound typical of the Bouriane landscape, is a busy little town with an eclectic summer festival, *Rencontres Estivales*, a medieval carnival, and a butter market on Thursdays in July and August. The old town has a 13C gateway, and Rue Majou (Mayor), the old main street which climbs up to the arcaded main square, has some good 13C to 16C buildings. The surprisingly large but simple Church of St-Pierre which was built in the 14C, has 14C, 15C and 16C stained glass and some gilded 17C carvings. Steps behind the church lead up to the summit and an orientation table.

The **Grottes de Cougnac**, 5km north on the D704 (tel: 65 41 22 03, Apr–Oct), discovered in 1949, have both fantastic concretions and paintings in black and red of animals and human figures.

From Gourdon go back through Le Vigan, take the D1, and cross the N20 to Séniergues, with its cruciform Romanesque church, then right on the D10, 24km, to **Labastide-Murat** which, as the name suggests, was a *bastide*. Originally called Fortanière, in 1852 Napoléon III allowed it to be re-named after the brother-in-law of Napoléon I, Joachim Murat (1767–1815), King of Naples. He was born in the little house which is now the **Murat Museum** (tel: 65 31 11 50, July–Sept) created with gifts from the family.

24

Figeac and excursions: Assier, Gramat, the Célé Valley

FIGEAC (pop. 9665, Tourist Information, Hôtel de la Monnaie, Place Vival, tel: 65 34 06 25), *sous-préfecture* and the second largest town in the Lot, shares the top of the list of medieval towns in the Lot with its neighbour Cahors. The smaller of the two, Figeac has an almost intact medieval centre with a variety of beautiful houses from the 12C onwards, built in a combination of stone, brick and timber. What is so exciting is that new architectural gems are still being discovered. Figeac also has a superb little museum dedicated to the Egyptologist, Champollion, who was born here. It is a quite perfect centre for exploring the Lot and the Aveyron, easy to reach on the N140 between Gramat and Rodez, and Cahors (D653) and trains via Capdenac Gare. It has all the facilities you would expect from a medium-sized town. The most loving restoration is the *Hôtel du Château du Viguier du Roy*, a luxury hotel with a welcoming atmosphere in the centre of town (tel: 65 50 05 05).

History. The town developed on the banks of the Célé around an abbey founded in the 9C, enriched by pilgrims on their way to Rocamadour and Santiago. On the major north–south route between Marseilles and the great fairs in Champagne, it grew into a huge mercantile centre with a wealthy merchant class. The merchants had trade links from the Levant to northern Europe, they amassed great wealth, and enough power to challenge the abbots and eventually form a secular oligarchy. These factors combined to create a brilliant period in Figeac's architectural history from the late-12C to the end-14C. Such was the prestige of the town that at the beginning of the 14C it was placed under the direct guardianship of the king through his representative, the *Viguier*. The Hundred Years War and plague epidemics slowed the economy, the Wars of Religion destroyed buildings. By the 17C and 18C there was no more international commerce and the Figeacois turned to other trades and its buildings adapted to different requirements. However, the medieval layout barely altered. It was not totally untouched by zealous restorers in the 19C and modernisers in the 20C—Place Vival was opened out, the canal was filled in—but from 1970 Figeac has looked forward to its past with enthusiasm.

On Foot. Figeac is worth many hours' exploration; and do investigate the courtyards. Start the visit in Place Vival in the south-west of the town where there is parking. On the south of the place is the 13C **Hôtel de la Monnaie**, for a long time considered representative of Figeac although only the back elevation is authentic, and it had nothing to do with minting money. The front was reconstructed in the 1900 with windows from another building, and the square was opened up in 1920. It has large arcades on the ground floor and more ornate openings on the first with 12C two-light windows with a variety of tracery. Under the eaves is a *soleilho*. The Hôtel de la Monnaie contains the Tourist Information and the **Musée du Vieux Figeac**, a small museum of traditional life in the Quercy with stone carvings of all periods including a monumental Renaissance doorway from the Hôtel de Sully, destroyed in 1900, prehistoric objects, furniture, and the 13C matrix of the town seal.

Take the Rue Ortabadial behind the Hôtel de la Monnaie, and turn right on Rue Balène. Much of the west of this little street is given over to the **Château de Balène**, now used for exhibitions, a large urban palace built in the 14C. Its tower was dismantled in 1900, but it has original windows with late Gothic tracery and mouldings. The Hôtel d'Auglanat, at No. 1, on the corner, is also 14C, with a low-arched doorway and a deep hood moulding.

You come now to **Rue Gambetta**, the main street running north–south, continuing over the Célé to the south, with smartish boutiques and a lot of interesting façades. Characteristic of the medieval houses in Figeac are the large arches at street level, intended for storage and workshops. The basic shape remains the same over the centuries, but the mouldings of the arcades become more highly profiled in the later buildings. The older, more modest houses, have tall, narrow doorways at the side with a staircase immediately behind, necessitating an outward opening door. Look out for No. 13, **Hôtel de Livernon**—built in 1367, it had the first rectangular windows and one is still in place on the tower—and also the 16C timber and brick façades at Nos 28 and 27. The Crédit Lyonnais building, reconstructed after a fire in 1900, has series of Romanesque three-light windows. **No. 34–43**, a beautiful 14C *hôtel particulier* with an inner courtyard and a diversity of windows on the street façade, can be visited (tel: 65 34 28 00, June–Sept, and weekends out of season).

Rue Clermont, half-way down Rue Gambetta, also has a series of 13C trefoil windows, a huge arch and a 17C balustrade. The most outstanding is 14C/16C Hôtel Dumont de Sournac (Hôtel de Bonnes Mains) with a corbelled out chimney-breast.

Turn right into Place E. Michelet to the **Church of St-Sauveur**. The Abbey of Figeac, rival to Conques, was affiliated to Cluny in 1047 and its entry into the Cluniac domain precipitated the building of a new church towards the end of the 11C. The partly completed building was consecrated in 1093 and work continued through the 12C to 14C. After the Protestants left in 1623 repair and consolidation work began, but during the 18C and 19C the cloisters and monastic buildings were lost and saddest of all was the demolition of the abundantly carved west end, known as *La Grotte*, in 1823. The only remains are the upturned capitals used as bases for holy-water stoups. The rectangular tower is 17C, whereas the unspectacular west entrance dates from 1823. There are traces of the Romanesque building on the north, juxtaposed with Gothic extensions and 17C alterations. To the south the façade is more regular and the chapter house was built in the 13C. The east end is blocked off, but there is a view of it from Rue du Monastère.

Steps lead down from the narthex into the **nave**, which took its present form in the 17C but has retained the general layout of a pilgrimage church, with aisles and ambulatory. The 12C engaged columns on square piers support the 17C groin vaults of the seven-bay nave. The south elevation has a blind triforium and 14C clerestory whereas the north was rebuilt in the 17C when the vaults were replaced and has no triforium. The crossing vaults date from 1920, built after the 18C dome collapsed in 1917, whereas the transepts have their original 13C decorated vaulting, some of the oldest in France, and a deep cornice supported by a carved corbel table. There is a rose window in each transept. The mock-Gothic choir and most of the ambulatory were built in the late-17C/early-18C although the radiating chapels are late 12C, as are the carved capitals including a Christ in Majesty and Martyrdom of St Stephen. The stained glass, which is all 19C, has recently been restored and some of the best is in the clerestory. In the last bay of the south aisle is a wooden relief of the Dream of St Martin.

Opening on the south side is the 13C **chapter house** (light switch on the left by the curtains) with a 17C carved and painted wooden décor. The glass dates from 1883 and the central window is dedicated to Prince Louis Napoléon. To the south, where the cloister once stood, is Place de la Raison, shaded by chestnut and linden trees, the *pétanque* arena.

Go back aross Place Michelet to **Rue Roquefort** where the overhanging angle tower with an elegant base and crenellated *soleilho* identifies the 16C town house built by Galiot de Genouillac, builder of the Château d'Assier. Much of it has disappeared, but you can enter the courtyard through the pedimented doorway, and in the stairtower is a spiral with a coiled central core.

Walk through to Rue Plancat, Place Sully and **Rue Emile Zola**, also known by its former name, Rue Droite or Rue Drecha, the oldest street in Figeac with a number of wonderful restored and unrestored medieval houses. The whole street is worth exploring. The 14C **Hôtel du Viguier du Roi**, Nos 48–50, is a group of houses dating from the 12C, 14C and 18C around a series of courtyards and was the *viguier's* residence from 1302 to the Revolution. (If you have time for nothing else, stop for tea here.) The oldest part on the corner with Rue Delzhens has characteristic arcades and a magnificent Romanesque window on the *piano nobile* of two-light bays divided by carved piers and subdivided by columns. Although partly reconstructed and restored, there is some original carved detail. Note also the sculpted head of a man in the 14C façade.

At the heart of the old town the triangular **Place Champollion**, formerly the Place Haute, is surrounded by picturesque buildings. The Romanesque (12C) house at No. 4, the **Maison du Griffon**, is considered to be the oldest house in Figeac. It has arcades at ground level (obscured) and three-light windows with sculpted elements on the first floor. South of the *place* is a restored 14C house with a series of superb traceried windows on a deep moulded course, and a battlemented *soleilho*.

The little Rue des Frères Champollion, north-west of the *place*, leads to the **Musée Champollion** (tel: 65 34 66 18, 10.00–12.00, 14.30–18.30, Jul–Aug; out of season, closed Mon, check times), a small museum of Egyptology installed in 1986 in the restored 14C and 16C house where **Jean-François Champollion** (1790–1832) was born. The museum has three rooms devoted to Champollion, arranged thematically. The first contains a documented account of his life and career. He began studying Egyptian hieroglyphics when he was at the Lycée in Grenoble, returned to Figeac in 1816–17, and visited for the last time in 1831. He did not visit Egypt until 1928 when he was already Curator of the Egyptology Department at the Louvre.

The Salle des Ecritures Egyptiennes contains a cast of the Rosetta Stone given by the British Museum in the 1950s. This room is devoted to Champollion's research and his major work in deciphering the inscriptions on the stone which was discovered during Napoleonic expeditions in Egypt in 1799 but held in England since its capture in 1801 when the British took Alexandria. In 1822 Champollion announced in a letter to M. Dacier, dated 27 September, that he had pierced the mystery of hieroglyphics, by comparing the picture images with known scripts. The stone records a decree drawn up by Egyptian priests at Memphis on 27 March 196 BC and bears three versions of the same inscription, in Egyptian hieroglyphics, in Greek and in demotic script. The gallery contains few, but good, pieces including examples of scripts on different types of materials such as papyrus parchment, and on different supports—stellae, fragments of architecture—and also has instruments used by scribes. The third room is concerned with the illustrations of the after life—pantheons, divinities, mummies and sarcophagi. There are frequent temporary exhibitions on the top floor.

The Egyptian-medieval experience does not end when you come out of the door of the museum because at the end of the impasse is a courtyard, **La Place des Ecritures**, opened in 1990 to mark the bicentenary of the birth of Jean-François Champollion. The courtyard is enclosed by beautiful medieval façades and on the ground is a giant version of the **Rosetta Stone**, the creation of an American artist, Joseph Kosuth. The text, enlarged nearly 100 times, is engraved on black Zimbabwe granite arranged on several levels to follow the contours of the site and to symbolise the passage from one language to another. The courtyard is used for summer concerts. A French version of the hieroglyphics is engraved on the glass door of a vaulted cellar and because of the transparent surface is as difficult to decipher as the original.

There is an exit from the courtyard to Rue Seguier, but go through the terraced gardens which contain papyrus from Egypt and Mediterranean plants and through the 17C **Hôtel de Colomb** where there is an exhibition on the local heritage.

Return to Rue Emile Zola to climb either Rue Boutaric or Rue Delzhens up to le Puy (Mount Viguier), a commanding position over the red-tiled rooftops and beyond.

The **Eglise Notre-Dame du Puy** is on the site of an ancient cemetery and the first Christian sanctuary dedicated to Notre Dame la Fleurie. In 1372 the Romanesque church was destroyed by *routiers* and rebuilt and enlarged. Most of the exterior decoration, now damaged, is concentrated around the projecting west front, c 1345. Between the Protestants, who turned it into their temple in 1576 and the area into a citadelle, and the Catholics, who took their revenge on the building when the Protestants left in 1622, there was not a great deal left. Between 1666 and 1693 it was repaired in its original style reusing original stone where possible, the major change being the transformation of the three central naves into one wide one, only the first bay retaining the earlier five-nave layout. In the east end four Romanesque storiated capitals have survived. The monumental retable, carved in walnut, was made locally in 1696, and has a profusion of columns, vines, putti, reliefs and statues and a painting of the Assumption. There is a 18C wooden sculpture of St James, and an early-19C altar with a clothed Virgin and Child dedicated to Notre-Dame-la-Fleurie who, according to a legend, caused roses to open in the snow one Christmas Day.

Leave le Puy by **Rue St-Jacques**, a narrow, twisting alleyway, turn left on Rue Colomb, and right on to Rue Maleville, spanned by a vaulted passageway belonging to the 15C Hôtel de Laporte, with an oriel window. Follow Rue St-Thomas to Rue de Crussol which runs downhill and on the right is the 16C/17C **Hôtel du Crussol**, now a bar, with an elegant galleried courtyard, external staircase and colonnaded *soleilho*. In Rue d'Aujou turn left and at the junction with Rue Séguier and Place Carnot is a notable house, the **Maison Cisteron**, which also has a colonnaded *soleilho*. The lower floor with arcades is medieval, the angle turrets are 16C, and the wrought-iron 18C. The covered market of 1900 in **Place Carnot** replaced the 13C *halle* knocked down in 1888. Market day is Saturday. Around the square are *soleilhos* built from the 16C to the 19C in a variety of forms.

Rue Gambetta leads out of the south-east corner of Place Carnot, and on the narrow north façade on the building at the corner with Rue de la République is a Romanesque relief sculpture of a Green Man. At No. 30 **Rue Caviale** is the **Hôtel de Marroncles**, a fine and rare example in Figeac of an early 16C house with mullioned and transomed windows, and further along on the left is the 18C Hôtel de Salgues, the *sous-préfecture*, with an angled entrance and courtyard. There are many fine **doorways** in the town, from the 12C to the 20C, and the oldest door is 16C. At Place Barthal turn left and you are back in Place Vival.

Excursions from Figeac: Assier and Gramat

Total distance: 47km (29 miles).

Between Figeac and Gramat. Leave Figeac on the N140 to the north-west, and turn right on the D18 to **Cardaillac** (10km) a village with a glorious past and a great deal of charm, with old stone buildings lining narrow alleys. The feudal Barons of Cardaillac were one of the most powerful dynasties, and by 1300, with 20 parishes under their control, they dominated the Haut Quercy. The original community was divided between the fort—the ruins can be visited—which existed by 1064, to the south-west, and the village. To the east was the priory and Church of St-Julien, established by 1146, rebuilt in the 17C. Le Musée Eclaté (tel: 65 40 10 63, July–Aug) is a musem of local history. Cardaillac is also known for its restaurant, *Chez Marcel* (tel: 65 40 11 16), imperative to book.

Return to the D140 and turn left on the D653. About 13km from Cardaillac is a village in a totally different vein, **Assier**, with a church and the remains of a vast and luxurious château, more reminiscent of the Loire Valley than the Quercy, both built by Galiot de Genouillac, Seigneur d'Assier, (1465–1546). Proud, ambitious and flamboyant, a soldier and administrator under three kings, Charles VIII, Louis XII and François I, he became Seneschal of Quercy in 1526 and Grand Ecuyer de France.

The **Château d'Assier** (tel: 65 40 40 99, every day July–Aug, closed Tues rest of year) was begun in 1525, after Galiot's return from the Italian campaigns. Built around four sides of a vast rectangular courtyard, the château was sold off piecemeal by its owners, descendants of Galiot, in 1768. The little that remains conveys the grandeur of the project and the exhuberant but empirical use of knowledge acquired in Italy or in the Loire Valley. The **church**, Gothic in essence but Renaissance in detail, was built by Galiot in 1540, his coat of arms in the pediment. A continuous frieze around the church is concerned with military exploits and techniques, constituting a catalogue of artillery and fortifications. Inside the church is the funerary chapel Galiot built for himself, with an accomplished stellar vault, and two effigies of the First Master of the Artillery: standing in armour and recumbent in court dress.

On the other side of the N140/D940, 7km, is the well-kept village of **Lacapelle-Marival**, built in local stone whose colour ranges from pinkish gold to grey, with a small rectangular halle (15C) its tile roof supported by stone pillars. The tall keep of the castle (tel: 65 40 80 24, July–Aug) 13C, 15C and 18C, dominates the the village and shelters a grand staircase and frescoes.

On the N140, 2.5km after the junction with the D940, is the tiny *bastide* of **Rudelle** with an ancient ford and bridge, founded in 1250 on the Figeac–Rocamadour road. It is worth a visit for its unique and impressive fortified church complete with crenellations and machicolations (the upper part owes much to 20C restoration). Other villages characteristic of the region, built in pale stone with wide arches and hipped or steep pointed slate roofs are **Rueyres** and **Aynac**, each with a small (private) château.

The *Lion d'Or* (tel: 65 38 73 18) at **Gramat** (14.5km on the N140) (pop. 3643, Tourist Information, tel: 65 38 73 60) has an excellent restaurant specialising in local produce.

(See Rocamadour, Route 23.)

The Valley of the Célé

Total distance: 54km (34 miles).

This beautiful drive west of Figeac could be part of a round trip combined with the Lot Valley (see Route 22).

Leave Figeac on the D13 and after 6km take the left fork on the D41. The Célé winds first through a lush, tamed landscape now planted with maize, sunflowers, and occasional vines and tobacco, whereas from the 14C to the 18C saffron was a major crop. Its cliffs then close in to form a narrow defile with tiny villages cramped to the rocks or sheltering at the base.

At the T-junction just after **Ceint d'Eau** take the D41. The little community of **Corn** (8km) has the traces of a castle and some lovely farms nearby. **Ste-Eulalie** (4.5km) is a hamlet with prehistoric painted caves, a Romanesque chapel built into the side of the *causse* and a fountain dedicated to Ste-Eulalie. A further 2km and you see across the river the steep roofs of the tiny community (68 residents) of **Espagnac-Ste-Eulalie**, in a picturesque huddle at the foot of the cliffs. A nunnery was established here in the 13C, and despite the English invasions survived until the Revolution. The remains of the convent buildings surround the garden and what is left of the cloister. The Church of Notre-Dame de Val-Paradis has partly disappeared, but still standing is the unusual and picturesque 13C jettied half-timbered belfry, as is a section of the nave. To visit the **church** (10.30–12.00, 15.30–19.00) ask Mme Bonzani in the house with a wooden gallery past the archway on the right of the Chemin des Dames. The north door of the church opens into the 13C nave and grafted to it is the much higher 14C apse. It contains three tombs with recumbent statues of the 13C and 14C and an 18C gilded retable.

Brengues (2.5km) shelters a pre-Romanesque church with rounded corners, heavily restored in 1835. It has a market on Thursday evenings.

At 9km is **Marcilhac-sur-Célé**, the outstanding site of the valley. Surrounded by cliffs in shades of white, grey, ochre and pink, the village runs down to the river's edge (excellent picnic area) sheltering at its heart the ruins of a once very important **abbey** dedicated to St-Pierre, and attached to Moissac. Formerly prosperous, it was pillaged during the Hundred Years War, and from 1461 the abbots attempted to revive and rebuild the church and the protective walls around the village. Damaged again by the Protestants in 1659, it received its final blow in the 19C, but the ruins of the **church** still give an idea of its initial importance. The west portal, flanked by the bases of towers and the ruined first bays of the nave, with massive cruciform pillars, is reminiscent of Conques. Above the entrance are five primitive Romanesque reliefs, possibly re-used, of a Christ in Majesty flanked by the sun and the moon, and two angels, with St Peter and St Paul below. The present church, now used by the parish, incorporated the remains of the earlier one in the 15C. The chancel is protected by a narrow ambulatory, and it has conserved its 17C stalls and pulpit. The best preserved Romanesque building is the late-12C **chapter house** which contains some beautiful capitals framing the door and early rectangular rib vaults. North of the chapter house are more sculpted capitals. The monastic buildings have almost entirely disappeared although two of the five defensive towers are still in place.

Just after **Sauliac-sur-Célé** perched above the valley, or from Liauzu (12.5km) turn right on the D40 to leave the lush valley for the evergreen oaks and junipers of the arid Causse de Livernon and the **Musée de Plein Air du Quercy-Cuzals** (tel: 65 22 58 63, Apr–Nov), 4km. This is an open-air museum of rural life in the Quercy of about 50ha and provides enough material for a visit lasting a couple of hours or a whole day. Two complete farms have been reconstructed as well as a *pigeonnier* and a *cazelle*. There are 25 small museums of rural crafts, crops and animals and a section devoted to water, a rare commodity in the Quercy, and seasonal activities are demonstrated. It is an ideal place to take children.

Return to the D41, and **Cabrerets**, at the confluence of the Sagne and the Célé, which has a semi-troglodite castle, the **Château du Diable**, clinging to the cliff face opposite the bridge. An ancient stronghold of the local barons, the castle was destroyed in 1390 to prevent it falling into the hands of the English. At the other end of the village is an imposing 15C château.

Turn right in the village for **Pech-Merle Centre of Prehistory**, combining a visit to the Museum of Prehistory and to the Caves (tel: 65 31 23 33, Palm Sun–1 Nov). The **caves**, discovered in 1922, are some of the most interesting in the region, both for their natural formations and for the scope and beauty of the images they contain. For conservation reasons groups to the caves are strictly limited to 20 people so it is advisable to arrive early in high season. The museum gives an introduction to the region from Paleolithic time to the Iron Age, and there is an audio-visual presentation. The underground visit covers some 1.2km and numerous galleries, not difficult but sometimes damp. The natural formations include the usual stalagmites and stalagtites, but also upright calicite discs and white cave pearls; yet far and away the most awe inspiring are the marks left by man. The images are mainly executed in black (carbon), and red (iron oxide) and date from 20,000 to 15,000 BC, the Solutrean to the Magdalenian periods. The majority of the nearly 80 representations are of **animals**, the most beautiful frieze being the famous dappled **horses**, c 18,000 BC, one of several using or inspired by the natural contours of the rock.

The Célé flows into the Lot at Bouziès (see Route 22, Lot Valley).

25

Conques and the Dourdou Valley

CONQUES (pop. 362, Tourist Information, tel: 65 72 85 00) is truly a heavenly place in a magnificent but isolated site clinging to the side of a natural amphitheatre or *concha* at the confluence of the narrow Ouche gorge and the Dourdou valley. The village, built entirely in silvery-yellow schist, the steep roofs clad in gradated fish-scale tiles, forms a protective terraced semi-circle above the Romanesque abbey church of Ste-Foy (St-Faith). The church has a huge well-preserved sculpted tympanum over the west door, and the community has managed to hang on to a unique and priceless collection of religious objects. There is a Cultural Centre and a recently-opened centre for Romanesque Studies. Among others, there are also two good hotel/restaurants, the *Hôtel Ste-Foy* (tel: 65 69 84 03), and the *Hostellerie de l'Abbaye* (tel: 65 72 80 30) (guarded by a female dragon).

It is advisable to park in the car park (follow signs) at the east of the village and walk down past the Cultural Centre to the **ABBEY CHURCH OF STE-FOY**. It is said that in the 8C a hermit called Dadon settled in this place and the pious community that developed adopted the Benedictine Rule. The Abbey's reputation was firmly secured in 866 when the relics of a young Christian, Ste-Foy, martyred in the 3C, were furtively translated from Agen to Conques. To house the relics a church existed by the end of the 10C (c 980) and Ste-Foy's first miracle was in 983. Books of miracles in the 11C enhanced her reputation for curing eye problems and liberating prisoners.

The cult became very popular throughout Europe and Conques became a major stage on the *Via Podiensis* to Santiago. A larger church dedicated to Ste-Foy was begun by Abbot Odolric (1030–65), and continued by his successors, Etienne II (1065–87), Bégon III (1087–1107) and Boniface (1107–25). The result was one of the finest, albeit small, examples of a pilgrimage church, but the abbey was so powerful that, unlike many on the pilgrim route, it remained independent of Cluny. Ste-Foy suffered over the centuries, and at the Revolution the Chapter was dissolved, the property sold and most of the 12C cloister disappeared. Help was desperately sought in the 19C as the church threatened collapse. Salvation came in 1837, in the shape of Prosper Merimée, the newly appointed Inspector of Historic Monuments who, accompanied by Stendhal, visited Conques. Repairs began in 1839, and have gone on ever since.

Exterior. A terrace above the east end of the church provides a rare view onto the chevet of this gloriously satisfying building, made up of abutting sections rising in a pyramid to the octagonal lantern-tower, rebuilt in the 15C and 19C. The clerestory of the choir has six blind arches supported by carved capitals and alternate windows to light the altar. The church was begun in red sandstone in the first half of the 11C and continued in yellowish limestone with schist infill. Steps go down to the level of the church and from here its considerable height comes into perspective. The oldest door, in the north transept, has smallish, finely carved capitals with interlacing and palmettes. Take the route round the east end where vaulted cavities for tombs are inserted between the chapels and superimposed engaged columns flank the windows and support the cornice. The second oldest doorway on the south transept also has decorated capitals. You come then to the most important monument on the exterior, the **Tomb of Bégon III**, probably moved here in 1834, in a deep recess with an inscription celebrating the accomplishments of the abbot, in particular as benefactor of the cloister. The relief panel represents Christ enthroned between the abbot on Christ's right and Ste-Foy, acting as intercessor, on the other side. The figures have characteristics—little ears, pierced eyes, centrally parted hair—typical of the work of the Master of the Abbot Bégon. As you climb the incline you pass on your right the Fountaine de Plô, Dadon's source of water.

The fairly severe **façade** was probably built during the abbacy of Boniface (1107–25). It is buttressed by two tall square towers culminating in the 19C belfries, and between them is an oculus, two round-headed windows and polychrome stone rose motifs. A deep arched hood protects the celebrated **tympanum**. Endearingly anecdotal, the 120 figures, in a style closer to the Auvergne than Languedoc, are arranged rather like a strip cartoon in tidy compartments. The message is clear and numerous inscriptions reinforce it. The subject is a **Last Judgement**, based on Matthew 25, a didactic warning of reward and punishment. On the left is an orderly composition appropriate to Heaven in contrast to the confusion of Hell on the right. Christ enthroned at the centre, raises his right hand to show the way to the chosen and with his left hand he indicates the path of the damned. Extending beyond the mandorla, his hands orchestrate the composition and establish a symbolic link between him and mankind. Angels above support a cross, others sound the horn and carry the instruments of the Passion, and on Christ's left four more carry the book of life and a censer and ward off evil. On Christ's right the blessed line up, the Virgin first, the blue of her cloak still visible, followed by St-Peter and Dadon. Next is an abbot, leading Charlemagne by the hand with members of the Carolingian royal family.

Then the three martyrs St-Caprais, Bishop of Agen, St-Prime and St-Felicien who died with Ste-Foy, and crouched in the corner the monk Ariviscus, perpetrator of the holy theft. The three arcades below represent the abbey church and the manacles represent ex voto offerings by Christian prisoners saved from the Moors by the intervention of Ste-Foy who is presented prostrate before the hand of God. Next to her the dead rise from their earthly tombs. Framed in a series of arches in the lowest register is Abraham flanked by the Wise Virgins, martyrs and prophets, all about to be received into Paradise by way of an open door, whose hinges and lock are carved with infinite care. The weighing of souls is going on in the centre, a sly demon attempting, unsuccessfully, to bring the scales down on his side, watched by Archangel Michael. Juxtaposed with the Gates of Paradise are the Jaws of Leviathan into which the damned are being stuffed by a hairy demon. All the deadly sins and a few more are represented with their appropriate punishments: Sloth, Pride, Lust, Greed, Gluttony, Envy, and Anger is particularly gruesome, a man cuts his own throat while a demon sucks out his brain, the inverted world of a man roasted by a hare, and so it goes on—Gossip, Power, Fornication, Heresy—and in the upper corner a money forger, forced to swallow molten metal, is surrounded by his money-forging equipment. The inscription on the lintel is: Sinners, if you do not reform your morals, know that you face a terrible judgement.

Interior. The interior is magnificent. In the tradition of churches along the pilgrim route, it was designed with an enclosed choir where the clergy could worship undisturbed while crowds of pilgrims filed past the relics. The height of the narrow **nave** (22.10m) is impressive but it is modest in length, just six bays, and the total length of the church is 56m. The vaults are sustained on alternate round and square piers with attached shafts and the groin vaulted aisles have transverse arches. The half-barrel vaulted gallery takes the thrust of the high vault, and enriches the overall design of the interior with elegant double openings divided by pairs of slender columns. Indirect light falls on the nave from the aisles and the galleries and directly from the windows in the west façade. There is one deep and one very small chapel on each arm of the ample transept. At the crossing four piers rise to arches supporting the octagonal Gothic lantern which gives light to the crossing but which has also given rise to endless problems finally dealt with by underpinning the structure in 1982 and rebuilding the lantern. An enfilade of columns, rebuilt in the 19C, marks off the choir, presumably built on the foundations of the earlier church, from the ambulatory. Around the choir are 12C and 13C wrought-iron screens.

The church has a total of **250 carved capitals**, 212 of them inside, most with decorative motifs such as interlacings, palmettes and acanthus. Animals and decorative motifs combined with figures start to appear around the apse but storiated capitals are infrequent. The fourth pier north has a Last Supper on the south face, and the martyrdom of Ste-Foy on the east. On the north-east pier of the crossing is a child in a loincloth between two eagles. On the south of the choir is the Sacrifice of Abraham, a symbol of the Eucharist. The earliest storiated capitals in the **south transept** have scenes from the life of St Peter. A group of sculptures of the Annunciation, high in the **north transept**, are of the same period as the tympanum (c 1107–25) and may have been belonged to the west portal ensemble. The Virgin, who is spinning, and the Angel Gabriel are framed in separate arches. In the angles of the transept left and right are St John the Baptist and Isaiah. The south transept chapel dedicated to Ste-Foy contains typically, but incongruously, a 17C gilded reredos and panelling. On the south wall is a rather damaged 15C fresco of scenes from the martyrdom of Ste-Foy. In 1993 new glass was installed, designed by the artist Pierre Soulages, after lengthy research for a glass with varying qualities of luminosity.

Virturally nothing remains of the Abbot Bégon's **cloister** except in spirit. On a lower level than the church, its tragic destruction began at the Revolution, and Mérimée arrived just too late. The low wall of the small, square cloister has been rebuilt to delineate the space and the two small arches on the east were part of the entrance to the chapter house. From the south-east corner of the cloister is the entrance to a little cemetery suspended above the Ouche gorges.

On the west are six bays of the façade of the **refectory**. About **30 capitals** of the cloister, in pale coloured limestone from the Causse, have been conserved and reused or exhibited in the museum. The entrance to the refectory gallery has the **most famous capital of Conques**, an original and charming composi- tion depicting the construction of the cloister. Eight masons, seven holding the tools of their trade and one with a horn, look out over the cloister wall which fills two thirds of the capital. The capital opposite has four identical armed warriors on the angles. The beautiful **pool** in the centre, made at the same time as the cloister, but reassembled and restored, is carved in serpentine stone and decorated with 18 small columns and capitals alternating with masks and atlantes, all in miniature but no less skilfully carved.

In the refectory gallery is the entrance to **Trésor I**. This is an absolutely unique and glittering collection which escaped the iconoclasts and treasure seekers of the late 18C through the timely action of the locals. The centre- piece is the **reliquary statue** known as **Ste-Foy en Majesté** (St-Faith in Majesty) a curious and disturbing work belonging to a type of cult image traditional in central France in the Middle Ages. Its chilling gaze and strange proportions instilled pilgrims with sufficient awe to persuade them to part with money or jewels. Made up of disparate pieces, some 4C or 5C, put together in the 10C, it has a basic wooden frame covered wih embossed sheets of precious metals, filigree, precious and semi-precious stones and enamels and contained part of the skull of Ste-Foy. Over the centuries the offerings of pilgrims, ranging from ancient cameos and intaglios to a Gothic monstrance, were added. A second reliquary of Ste-Foy found under a flagstone in the choir during restoration work in 1875 consists of a small casket covered in embossed leather decorated with enamels, with bones wrapped in fine fabric and a delicate belt. Other reliquaries, many of them reworked, include the lantern-shaped Pepin's shrine, 9C–10C, a triangular reliquary with a large rock crystal in the apex called the A of Charlemagne, the portable altar of Ste-Foy, early 12C, and Bégon's altar, dated 26 June 1100, in porphyry with niello and silver gilt ornament. From the goldsmiths of Villefranche-de-Rouergue are a charming small silver statue of Ste-Foy, presented on 2 August 1497, and a magnificent processional cross (1503) which also bears an image of the child-saint. A series of four 16C Aubusson tapestries describe the events leading to the execution of Ste-Foy.

The Musée Joseph Fau or **Trésor II** is next to the Information Office. In the basement are Romanesque capitals mainly from the cloister, and on the other floors a collection of religious carvings, furniture and tapestries.

The **village** is very small. The main street, **Rue du Abbé Floran**, runs the length of the village, east–west. **Rue Charlemagne**, on the lowest level, takes you under the Porte du Barry, one of the 11C gateways and past the Romanesque Fontaine du Barry, and eventually to the Pont Romain over the Dourdou in the lower village. However, just as it leaves the upper village a left fork goes to the tiny 16C Chapelle St-Roch and a **beautiful view** of the village. **Rue Haute** (Rue Emile-Roudié), as its name suggests, runs along the top of the village above rooftops and alongside some picturesque houses. To the west of Rue Haute is Rue du Château, named after the 15C/16C **Château d'Humières**, the grandest house in the village. Round the corner **Porte de la Vinzelle**, with a 17C polychrome statue of the Virgin, straddles the route the pilgrims usually took on the next stage of their journey, passing the 17C Oratoire de la Capelette.

The Pilgrimage of Ste-Foy is the second Sunday in October.

From Conques to Rodez

Total distance: 35km (22 miles).

There are some remarkable viewing sites for Conques, the most photogenic of villages. The nearest is just off the D901 in the direction of Rodez, turn left immediately opposite the Pont Romain to the Site de Bencarel across the Ouche from Conques. Alternatively cross the Pont Romain (not Roman but derived from the Islamic name for Christians or pilgrims, *roumis*) very, very narrow (not suitable for camper vans) and climb.

It is a pretty drive along the **Gorges du Dourdou** on the D901. At the end of the Gorges is the Moulin de Sagnes, a 17C mill built in the red sandstone of the valley. After storms, the river itself runs red. (From St-Cyprien, see detour below.)

The **route south** runs through the *vallon* or *rougier* of Marcillac, a valley washed in the purplish-red of the local sandstone where the cultivation of vines on the south-facing slopes was introduced by the monks of Conques in the 11C, and flourished until phylloxera killed the vines in the 19C. It never completely recovered and wine production is greatly reduced. In Valady, D962 or D204, from Marcillac, you can taste the local wine at the Caves des Vignerons du Vallon.

The village of **Marcillac**, almost entirely in red sandstone, is a testimony to better times, with several fine old houses grouped around the 14C–15C church to the south of the D901. A seemingly disproportionate number of them are attractively refurbished as *Maisons de Retraite* (retirement homes). A market spreads out under the trees alongside the D901 on Sundays, and a procession at Whitsun to mark the ancient festival of La St-Bourrou (*bourgeon* = bud) starts from the Chapel of Notre-Dame-de-Foncourieur 1km north of the village.

Salles-la-Source, in truth three villages on three levels niched in a south-facing hollow, has a 20m cascade on the higher level, various châteaux and churches on the lower level, and, between the two, installed in 19C buildings, a **museum of local crafts**, part of the Musée de Rouergue (tel: 66 67 28 96), which traces the history of agriculture and wine making, using an old spinning mill with a keel-shaped timber roof.

From Salles take the D85 south. **Souyri** has a Romanesque church fortified in the 15C. Take the D568 to **Onet-le-Château**, a 14C and 15C castle with 16C modifications, formerly the residence of the Chapter of Canons of Rodez (visit exterior only) but from the terrace is a marvellous view of Rodez. Return to the D901 and after *l'Hostellerie de Fontange* (tel: 65 42 20 28), a 16C château-hôtel with a superb dining room, turn right to Rodez.

The Dourdou Valley and the Causse du Comtal to Bozouls

Total distance: 45km (28 miles).

South of Conques on the D901, at **St-Cyprien-sur-Dourdou** (15C church and belfry), turn left on the D46 to **Lunel** (15C church and Pietà) and the **Pic du Kaymard** (707m), the highest point in the canton of Conques. At this point the various geological strata come together: granite of the plateau, red sandstone of the valley, and the yellow limestone (used in the Church of Ste-Foy) of the Causse du Comtal.

At **Polissal** turn right on the D904 passing on the right the restored 14C tower of a former Commandery of the Templars. (18.5km) **Villecomtal** is a spread out fairly dilapidated 13C *bastide* in sandstone and slate, with the remains of the old fortifications including the gateway, the tour de l'Horloge. The church (14C–15C) has a small polychrome 15C Pietà and a finely carved altar rail and pulpit (?18C).

A pretty route winds along the Dourdou Valley to **Muret-le-Château** with its ancient castle (11C and 15C). Above the village is a waterfall. Return to the D68 and 2km before Rodelle is the **Grotto of Ste-Tarcisse** (15C) and a modern chapel with a monument to the local sculptor, Denys Puech (1854–1942), born in Bozouls.

Rodelle (little Rodez) is perched above the left bank of the Dourdou and crowned by the ruins of a castle of the Counts of Rodez. A Carolingian site, the church is part Romanesque, part 15C and has a very touching and unusual late Gothic polychrome Pietà, Christ's head supported by St John, Mary Magdalene at his feet.

Descend to the D20 to **Bozouls** (pop. 2060, Tourist Information, tel. 65 44 92 20), between the Causse du Comtal and the Lot Valley. Here the Dourdou has created a remarkable natural site carving its route deep into the tender rock for about 700m. The newer part of town on the right bank has a small square with a **Monument to the Dead** designed by **Denys Puech** for his native town. Across the bottom of the ravine is a bridge reached by Rue de l'Hospitalet passing near two old towers, and the route climbs again on the opposite bank to the medieval village through a fragment of the old outer walls. The recently restored Romanesque **Church of Ste-Fauste**, with Gothic chapels on the south, has some interesting storiated capitals and 15C sculptures of the Virgin, St Peter and St Anthony in the porch, and is sometimes used for concerts.

The D988 takes you to Rodez or Espalion (see Route 26).

26

Rodez, the Olt Rouergat and the Aubrac

RODEZ (pop. 24,700, Tourist Information, tel: 65 68 02 27), the *préfecture* of the Aveyron, is a bustling town on a hill above the Aveyron river. The *département* of the Aveyron, the largest of the Midi-Pyrénées, embraces the high open spaces of the limestone *causses* and the Monts d'Aubrac, serene and green valleys, and the dramatic gorges of the Aveyron, Lot and Dourbie. It is often referred to by its old name, the Rouergue, and its people as the Rouergats.

The old part of the town, around the great roseate pile of the cathedral, has been spruced up over the last few years. Arterial roads from Rodez radiate out to all parts of the Aveyron, the N140 links it with the N20, and it also has a small airport and rail links with Toulouse and Paris. There is plenty of accommodation.

History. Ancient Segodunum was called Ruteni by the Romans and became an important Gallo-Roman oppidum stretching almost as far as the modern town until the 3C. The counts and bishops maintained a fierce rivalry lasting several centuries, and from the 13C the Comté of Rodez passed to the d'Armagnac family who made a great impact on the town. The Cathedral of Notre-Dame was the last great cathedral begun in the Midi during the 13C and took 300 years to built under the supervision of twenty bishops.

On Foot. From the N88 head for the centre of town. There is a convenient car park near the **Tourist Information Office** on Place Maréchal Foch. **Place Foch** is a large open square, with a white marble statue, **Naïade de Vors**, 1859, by Denys Puech, symbolising the Gallo-Roman supply of water from the Vors to the town. The former **Jesuit College Chapel** (Chapelle de l'Ancien Lycée Foch) is a sober 17C Baroque building, now used for concerts. The attractive galleried interior has conserved the original Louis XIII painted woodwork, pink and grey stone architectural elements and rendered walls decorated with portraits of Ignatius de Loyola and other leading Jesuits. To the west of the Place Foch is the **Tour Maje**, now incorporated into a hotel (tel: 65 68 34 68), the most important of the 30 fortified towers which once protected the town. Turn right into **Rue Penavayre**. Just before the end of the street there is the pretty Gothic courtyard with a well, in a former canonical residence.

The **CATHEDRAL NOTRE-DAME DE RODEZ** is the major monument of the town. On 25 May 1277 the first stone of a new cathedral was laid following the collapse of the belfry of the old church in 1276 which took with it the choir and part of the 10C nave. The new building, modelled on the great Gothic cathedrals of northern France, continued in fits and starts until 1562, but despite the span of some 300 years, there is little architectural hiatus. The cathedral was brought to the state we see it today at the time of Bishop Georges d'Armagnac, 1530–62.

Exterior. The chevet was completed between 1277 and 1300. Five pentagonal radiating chapels are separated by large sparsely decorated rectangular buttresses, and flying buttresses, rare in the Midi, help to take the thrust of the ambulatory vaults.

The pride of the Rouergats is the free-standing **belfry tower** on the north flank of the cathedral, 87m high. Begun in 1513 under the supervision of the master-mason Antoine Salvanh, it was completed by 1529. It is made up of three progressively more elaborate stratified octagonals and around the top are angels with censers, saints and apostles, culminating in the figure of the Virgin of the Assumption. In 1793–94, when irreparable damage was done to the cathedral, the belfry was saved by replacing the statue of the Virgin with an allegory of Liberty, and the four Evangelists with martyrs of the Revolution, including Marat.

The Flamboyant **portals** on the transepts, c 1440–c end of 15C, are executed in fragile limestone and lost most of their figures during the Revolution. But the iconographic programmes seem to have been complementary: the Incarnation on the north portal and the Redemption on the south. The great **west elevation**, dominating the Place d'Armes, was completed c 1562. This part is more typical of the region—sheer and massive with little decoration, and no west door. Incorporated into the city walls, it was built towards the end of the 15C. The austerity is relieved by the elegant Rayonnant rose window, in place by 1529. Work continued on the southern tower during the episcopate of the humanist, Georges d'Armagnac (1500–85), and his secretary, Guillaume Philandrier, editor of Vitruvius, who introduced new concepts of architecture into the Rouergue. The upper part of the south-west tower is constructed in the style of a classical temple, and above the central bay, incongruously placed between the two crocketed Gothic spirelets, is a Renaissance gable, c 1562.

Interior. This is a large, essentially Rayonnant cathedral, with aisles and ambulatory but with very little integral ornament, typical of meridional Gothic. Whether this was dictated by financial or aesthetic considerations is debatable. The shallow undulations on the piers of the main arcades, as opposed to sharply profiled shafts typical of most Rayonnant cathedrals, are also found in Narbonne, as is the elimination of capitals in favour of a smooth elision from the surface of the piers to the finely moulded ribs and arcade arches. Another tradition in the Midi, possibly to reduce the amount of bright light entering, or due to lack of funds, is to reduce the glazed section of the clerestory to only part of each bay. The 11 pentagonal chapels in the east were completed between 1277 and 1300 but the Romanesque nave was still in existence until the 15C. The last bays of the nave and the façade towers brought the building to near completion at the beginning of the 16C.

The plain interior is a setting for some interesting elements which survived the late 18C. The 15C Flamboyant **jubé** avoided destruction at the end of the 17C but was damaged after the Revolution and lost all 38 statues. It was finally removed in the 19C but not altogether destroyed and re-sited in 1872 inside the south door. Some **choir stalls**, 1478–88, were damaged when the *jubé* was removed, but the elaborate episcopal throne plus 62 higher and 14 lower stalls are original. The remainder are 17C, as is the balustrade above. On the exterior of the choir enclosure a 15C mural was discovered in 1978 with scenes from the the the life of St-Eloi (588–659). The charming late-14C statue of **Notre-Dame de Grace** has lost most of its colour and all of its precious stones. The **27 chapels** contain a variety of **furnishings**. The oldest piece is the 10C marble **altar table** on the north wall of the axial chapel (there is a light). The main altar until 1525, it has an inscription recording that Deusdedit, the Bishop (961–1004), ordered it to be made. In 1662 it was painted with an Annunciation and used as a retable. In the chapel vault are 14C **frescoes**, probably part of a cycle originally covering the whole chapel, were discovered under plaster in 1986. There are more frescoes (1340–50) in the north-east chapel of the choir which resemble stained glass, with 18 of the 24 original figures, identified by their symbols or by an inscription, and others discovered in 1994 in the south-east choir chapel.

The most important late Gothic carved **retables** are found in the two central chapels on the south of the nave. The Mount of Olives from the last quarter of the 15C(?) has delicately sculpted and polychromed limestone figures in a richly decorated surround. The adjacent St-Sepulchre chapel is closed by an elaborate openwork Gothic screen, but of the 12 statues only five on the interior, four sybils and an Ecce Homo, are original. The vast **altarpiece** in three registers inside the chapel, 1523, introduces elements of Renaissance decoration into a late Gothic context. The lower register contains a polychromed Entombment characteristic of many in the region, but in addition are three small reliefs, and crowning the ensemble is Christ stepping out of his sarcophagus. The most important painting in the cathedral is on the wall opposite—**Tobias and the Angel**, 1715, by Antoine Coypel (1661–1722).

The **entrance to the sacristy**, c 1525, is finely sculpted, as is the screen of the **St-Raphael chapel** opposite, part of the stone choir enclosure of c 1526–27. It contains one superb openwork panel carved with a vase, garlands and cherubs. The 16C **canons' tribune** is above the St-Sacrament chapel in the north west. Relics were displayed in the chapel which has remarkable coffered vaults. There is a very fine carved walnut **organ case**, 1628, in the north transept.

The **Evêché** (Bishops' Palace), north of the cathedral, built in 1694 but partly reconstructed in the 19C, derives much inspiration from Fontainebleau. From inside the courtyard is a good view of the belfry and of the 15C Tour Corbières in the city walls.

In the south-east corner of **Place d'Estaing**, east of the cathedral, a vaulted passageway leads to the best courtyard in Rodez in the 15C **Maison de Benoît**. Typical of the transitional late Gothic style, it has a Flamboyant gallery and a tower decorated in the idiom of the early Renaissance. The old streets around the cathedral have small shops and boutiques. Rue de Bonald (north-east) leads to **Place des Embergues**, an imaginatively reinvented area, and Rue Cusset, south of Place d'Estaing, leads to something similar called **Place des Maçons**.

From Place d'Estaing, take Rue Touat, left into Rue Monteil, right into Rue Neuve and left into Rue Camille Douls, past **Place Raynaldy** which has been given a new look, keeping parts of the old buildings.

On Place Clemenceau is the **Musée des Beaux Arts Denys Puech** (tel: 65 42 70 64). The Aveyronnais sculptor, Denys Puech (1854–1942), conceived the idea of a museum for Aveyronnais artists which was inaugurated in 1910. A campaign of renovation, 1984–89, has created a very attractive installation in the building designed by André Boyer for the contents of Puech's studio and work by his contemporaries including Maurice Bompard, Tristan Richard, Raymond Gayrard and Eugène Viala. The upper floor and basement have temporary exhibitions from the museum's collections.

Puech's work, displayed on the ground floor, is a technical *tour de force* with a tendency to convey sleek, sentimentalised, and mildly erotic female or hermaphrodite nudes in mythological or allegorical guises. Lighthearted

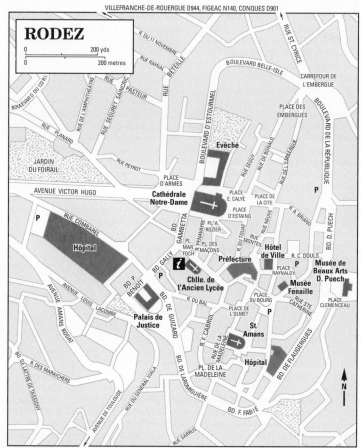

VILLEFRANCHE-DE-ROUERGUE D944, FIGEAC N140, CONQUES D901

RODEZ

0   200 yds
0   200 metres

VILLEFRANCHE-DE-ROUERGUE, ALBI, MILLAU, N88

it makes no apologies for ignoring completely any attempt at psychological insight. Works include a portrait bust of his wife, Princesse Gargarine Stourdza, 1908, and Mézence blessé, which won him the Prix de Rome for sculpture in 1884. The head of the muse in Muse d'André Chenier is a portrait of the singer Emma Calvé, born in Decazeville, but we are not told who was used as model for the deliciously rounded bottom and soles of the feet.

Take Rue Ste-Catherine and where it meets Rue St-Just is **Musée Fenaille**, in two buildings, their façades updated in the 14C and 16C (reopening 1995). **Place du Bourg**, the medieval commercial centre, has a market on Wednesdays and Saturdays and is framed by some interesting jettied and half-timbered houses. In the middle of the square is a bust of A. Blazy Bon, 1778–1846, by Puech. The elegant 16C **Maison de l'Annonciation**, is named after the Annunciation relief sculpted on the angle and the Préfecture occupies the **Hôtel d'Ayssènes**, 1716, on Place

Charles de Gaulle, more reminiscent of the châteaux of the Loire Valley than the Rouergue. A bronze plaque near the entrance was erected to the memory of Jean Moulin (1899–1944) sous-préfect of the Aveyron and hero of the Resistance.

Maison Trouillet is a late 15C house with some fine decoration as is the late-Gothic **Maison d'Armagnac** (1525–31), Place de l'Olmet. A rib-vaulted passage leads to a tiny Italianate courtyard with three miniature galleries and a stairtower with Renaissance windows. Further south is the **Church of St-Amans** on the Place des Toiles, a little square with a fountain, the site of a Gallo-Roman necropolis. Reputed to be the oldest church in the Rouergue, most likely 11C or 12C, it contained the relics of St-Amans, St-Quintien and St-Dalmas. In 1752 the decision was taken to rebuild the Romanesque church before it fell down. Much of the old building material was salvaged and reused, including the Romanesque capitals, and rebuilding lasted from 1758 to 1764. The result is a Baroque exterior in dark pinkish-red sandstone with an impressive west façade reminiscent of Venice, in contrast with the pure Romanesque style interior. The cupola was painted by a local artist, Salinier, with scenes from the life of St-Amans, and 16C tapestries have the same iconography. There is a 15C Pietà, a curious 16C statue of the Trinity and a reliquary casket in Limoges enamel.

The Olt Rouergat and the Aubrac

Total distance: 135km (84 miles).

In Occitan the Lot was known as the Olt, and Olt frequently appears in the toponymy. This section of it, across the northern Aveyron, marks the southern boundary of the Aubrac. Of strategic importance in the Middle Ages, a line of castles protected each crossing point. The last part of this itinerary is an excursion into the Aubrac.

At the confluence of the Lot and Truyère, 21km north of Rodez, **Entraygues-sur-Truyère** (pop. 1400, Tourist Information, tel: 65 44 56 10) has plenty of facilities in the town and surroundings (campsites, shops) and four two-star hotels including the *Hôtel de la Truyère* (tel: 65 44 51 10) and the *Ferme-Auberge de Mejanassère* (tel: 65 44 54 76).

The best part of the town is close to the 13C–14C bridge over the Truyère, claiming to be the oldest bridge in the Rouergue, but restored in the 17C. Spanning the Lot is the Pont Notre-Dame. Between the two is the old town with jettied houses and covered passageways called *cantous*. Two towers of the château built by Henri II, Count of Rodez, when he founded the *cité* in the 13C are still standing and the remainder is part of a 17C modification. It is a centre for exploring the rugged and off-the-beaten-track country around the Gorges de Truyère, which is good for hiking and fishing.

Take the D920 for 17km along the Gorges du Lot to **Estaing**, a very picturesque small town between the Lot and the Coussane, with a tall castle. The elegant 16C bridge at Estaing is protected by a chapel and decorated with a wrought-iron cross and a statue of Bishop François d'Estaing (1460–1529) whose family built the castle. It now houses a religious community but you can visit the 17C terrace overlooking the valley (bell in the courtyard). The 15C church behind the château has a belfry and a pretty clock tower with a bell, and outside the Flamboyant porch are two very weathered carved crosses. Inside are sculpted bosses, some modern glass, and the usual Baroque retables and reliquaries. The narrow streets around the church are worth exploring for the fine schist houses and for the tanneries on the Coussane east of the church.

A further 10km is another small town on the Lot, **Espalion** (pop. 4614, Tourist Information, tel: 65 44 10 63), on the old Languedoc–Auvergne route, midway between Rodez and Laguiole. It is an obvious touring centre and attractive place with typical Aveyronnais slate-roofed red sandstone houses, an ancient triple-arched bridge, and markets on Tuesday and Friday. The *Hôtel Moderne* (tel: 65 44 05 11), is a good place to stay and an excellent place to eat. The local **museum** in the 15C Church of St-Jean (10.00–12.00, 14.00–18.45 Jun–Sept, except Sun) has a famous collection of holy-water stoups and one room, amazingly, devoted to the history of the diving suit because two Espalionais pioneered underwater apparatus. A section of the **Musée de Rouergue** is housed in the former prison (1838–44).

1km south-east of Espalion on the D556 is the **church** of **Perse**, all that is left of the priory of St-Hilarion. The small church in the reddish regional stone is part 11C, part 12C. It has a stunning belfry gable and a south portal of note with a sculpted tympanum representing Pentecost. On the lintel is an animated scene of the Apocalypse and the Last Judgement and in the west spandrel four little figures represent the three Magi and the Virgin and Child.

3km further along the valley is **St-Côme d'Olt** (pop. 1198, Tourist Information, tel: 65 48 24 46). The bridge, decorated with a cross, existed in the 14C but has been frequently rebuilt and the town fortifications have all but disappeared. The medieval château (Mairie) opposite the church was built in the 12C inside the walled *cité*, the towers added in the 14C and restored in the 15C. There are several attractive medieval houses, and rich farmers of the Aubrac built the 17C and 18C houses, some with pavilion roofs. The most original roof, however, is the **church** steeple, a tall witch's hat with a twist, intentional or otherwise, the ultimate flame on the Flamboyant church, 1522–32, attributed to Antoine Salvanh, master mason of the belfry of Rodez. The carved portal has a pair of particularly splendid Renaissance doors (1523) in oak with panels containing busts, animals and linenfold; each door is studded with 365 star-shaped nails. The wooden Christ (16C) is carved in walnut, the Pietà is 18C, and the remainder of the furnishings 19C. To the north the Chapelle des Pénitents, the first church in St-Côme, has kept its Romanesque features although the porch was added in the 18C.

Cross back over the river to St-Côme-d'Olt, via the D6, 10km, where the 15C church at **Lassouts** incorporates sculptured elements of an 11C church damaged by *routiers*, including a simply carved Romanesque tympanum with a Christ in Majesty and on either side six apostles. High relief carvings of an owl and two bulls surround the tympanum. The church has conserved some Romanesque altars and in the south chapel a very fine Romanesque piscina is embedded in the wall.

The scenery becomes very pretty on the descent D6–D988 (14km) to the beautiful village of **Ste-Eulalie d'Olt** whose 16C and 17C houses were built by wealthy weavers. The 15C Château des Curières de Castelnau is well preserved, and an old mill has been transformed into a hotel-restaurant, *Le Moulin d'Alexandre* (tel: 65 47 45 85). The church is interesting, with an 11C east end, and a pre-Romanesque altar recording the consecration of an earlier church c 1000. In the 12C the church doubled up as a citadel and c 1530 it was enlarged by two bays to the west. Successive alterations are fairly obvious from the exterior.

Another 3km or so on the D88 brings you to **St-Geniez d'Olt** (pop. 2200, Tourist Information, tel: 65 70 43 42), a charming town spanning the river with definite possibilities as a touring centre: Hôtel de France (tel: 65 70 42 20).

An important town in the 19C, it has some fine 18C and 19C *hôtels particuliers*, albeit in need of attention. Whereas its former wealth was due to cloth and leather, today it is renowned for its strawberries. In Rue de l'Hôtel de Ville is the cloister of an Augustinian convent founded in the 14C and rebuilt in the 17C now occupied by the Mairie. The adjacent **Church of the Pénitents Blancs** shelters a precious small late-15C triptych, with the Epiphany represented by ten gilded wooden statues, and painted panels of a Circumcision and a Nativity. Through the cloister and across Place de la Mairie is the **Tourist Information Office** installed in the Baroque **Chapel of the ·Pénitents Noirs**. The chapel, completed in 1705, has a painted wooden ceiling and a magnificent altarpiece (due for restoration).

On the riverbanks are the old tanners' houses; on the other side the parish **Church of St-Geniez**, built in the 12C but extensively renovated in the early 18C, has a stately double staircase. It contains the tomb of Mgr Frassyinous (1765–1841) Grand-Maître of the University at the Restauration, sculpted by M. Gayrard. The steps south of the church climb to the **Monument Talabot** by Denys Puech to the wife of the first Directeur Général of the Railway PLM from where there is an excellent view.

Take the D19 out of St-Geniez, a narrow winding road with views of the Lot to start with. The D19 then turns north across the Pays de Boraldes, the most mountainous part of the Aubrac.

The Aubrac is a beautiful high plateau at the opposite end of the Midi-Pyrénées to the Pyrenees, and far less well known. Part of the southern Massif Central, it is shared between the Aveyron, the Cantal and the Lozère. Although its highest point is 1400m, there are no abrupt peaks but soft reliefs scattered with strange rock formations, smoothed and rounded in the Ice Age and eroded by time. It is particularly suited to those seeking outdoor pursuits, fishing, walking, riding, skiing in the winter, and for the plant lover in everyone. 1300 species of flowers have been identified, growing according to altitude, soil conditions and human interference, and the Aubracophile will claim that it has more flower power in early summer than the Pyrenees. Fields of narcissi and daffodils, tall spiky yellow gentian, wild geraniums, calament or tea of the Aubrac, with a tiny pink flower, digitalis, euphorbia, anenomes, campanulas, German and English types of broom, wild orchids of all varieties, some resembling bees and spiders, some that smell of goat and little sprial ones, and so on. The most fascinating of all must be the carnivorous plant of the peat bogs, *Drosera Rotundifolia*. There are also prehistoric plants called *Ligulaire* of Siberia and an orchid called *Malaxis Paudoas*. And wild raspberries, juniper and bilberries for those who enjoy gathering. (For more floral information and organised walks, tel: 66 32 56 02.)

The pastures are occasionally interrupted with patches of woodland: beech in the north-east, at their best in autumn, chestnut to the west, and pubescent oaks in the valley. The landscape is broken up by dry stone walls and stone shelters called *burons*, once used by the shepherds or cheese makers, now mainly abandoned. Cattle and sheep reign supreme, but the gentle Aubrac breed of cattle is the champion. The race was revived in the 1980s and has proved its worth both for beef and milk production. When the traditional transhumance is celebrated on the Sunday nearest 25 May

(St-Urbain's Day) the cattle are beribboned and garlanded and make their stately way towards the higher ground. The villages and sturdy churches are in dark granite or basalt, the roofs of the same material, sombre in winter against the snow, and there are frequent carved *croix de chemin* in the same dark stone, marking the old pilgrim route or standing outside a church.

The small community of **Prades d'Aubrac** (925m) (18km) is built in dark basaltic stone with the silhouette of the octagonal belfry and spire of the church built in 1540 and a 15C polychrome stone Pietà. Unusually for the Rouergue the vaults have pendant bosses.

Stay on the D19 through Bonnefon to the granite village of **St-Chély-d'Aubrac**, 16km, a stage on the route to Santiago remembered by the sculpted pilgrims' cross on the ancient bridge over the Boralde. About 4km along the D533 north, turn left to the Neck of Belvezet, a high volcanic peak created from a solidified lava lake which due to erosion resembles organ pipes. Another 4km brings you to the village of **Aubrac** (1250m), a fearsomely exposed place on a winter's day at the crossroads for the ski centres. The Dômerie d'Aubrac, a pilgrim hospice founded c 1120, had a battalion of knights, monks, nuns and *donats* (lay brothers) under the control of the Dom, who protected travellers; and such was its reputation that it attracted hundreds, even thousands of pilgrims. Disbanded at the Revolution, many of the buildings demolished, still standing are the hospital, rebuilt in the 15C and now private property, part of the enceinte called the *tour des Anglais*, and the Church of Notre-Dame built early in the 13C, unadorned inside and out, with a belfry dating from 1457.

From Aubrac it is 19km to **Laguiole** (pop. 1264, Tourist Information, tel: 65 44 35 94), the small dynamic capital of the Monts d'Aubrac, held up as a shining example of the exploitation of local resources. There are several hotels, and the local restaurateur-hotelier, Michel Bras, one of the most famous in the region, uses local ingredients, especially plants and vegetables in his restaurant *Lou Mazuc* at the *Hôtel Michel Bras*, tel: 65 44 32 24, just outside Laguiole on the Aubrac road. More down-to-earth is the *Hôtel Regis*, tel: 65 44 30 05.

The town's economy is built on its cattle, the Aubrac, celebrated in the marketplace/car park by a bronze sculpture of a bull by Georges Guyot, 1947; on its cheese, called Laguiole, produced since the 12C but now vigorously marketed and made into a dish called *aligot*, mixed with potatoes and cream; and on its famous knives, *couteaux de Laguiole*, with bone handles, invented by Pierre-Jean Calmels in 1829.

On the corner of Place du Forail is the local Musée du Haut-Rouergue. Rue du Faubourg and Rue du Couvent, with a cross marking the old pilgrim route, take you up to the church, mainly rebuilt in the 17C after the Religious Wars, with scallop shells sculpted on the porch.

The **Château du Bousquet** (tel: 65 48 41 13, open from 14.30 during school holidays) is just 6km away on the D42. It is privately owned and the owner, Pierre Dijols, will probably take you round. This medium-sized château is everybody's dream of a medieval castle and stands on a small hill with little to interrupt the view of it. Constructed mainly in basalt, it is a remarkably well preserved example of 14C military architecture. Solid and compact, it has four round angle towers and two square ones, the east orientated one enclosing a small chapel facing the rising sun, all six with high roofs. There are almost continuous machicolations and a two-level parapeted walk around the upper part.

The origins of the château are uncertain, but it may have been built by the Hospitallers on the Montpeyroux family's fief to protect the oldest and most direct pilgrimage route from Le Puy-en-Velay to Conques, the Route de Godescalc. In the late 1680s this fortress became the residence of the Roquefeuil family, who owned it until 1900, and made several alterations, notably to the windows. Their coat of arms appears on the painted ceiling of the Gothic chapel which also contains statues and a life-size Crucifixion which miraculously survived the Revolution. The present staircase is 100 years old, the Grande Salle is richly furnished and the kitchen, with smoke blackened ceiling, musicians' gallery, vast fireplace and bread oven, is a delightful part of the visit.

Return to the D921 via St-Rémy-de-Montpeyroux. After 11.5km is a turning left to what little remains of the 12C **Abbey of Bonneval** (closed Sun) now occupied by nuns who sell the chocolate they make. (See Routes 22 and 26, Lot Valley, Rodez.)

27

Villefranche-de-Rouergue and the Gorges de l'Aveyron

Total distance: 85km (50 miles).

This is a route of views and valleys with some exceptional sites of scenic and architectural interest, and a good choice of hotels and restaurants.

VILLEFRANCHE-DE-ROUERGUE (pop. 13,000, Tourist Information, B.P. 239, 12202 Villefranche-de-Rouergue, tel: 65 45 13 18) is a perfectly delightful market town beside the Aveyron at the centre of an important agricultural region. At its heart is the *bastide*, founded in 1252 by Alphonse de Poitiers and fortified in 1342–43. The importance of the town was measured by its markets and fairs and these are still active. The weekly markets (Thursday), held on the central square, animate the town with colourful stalls and fragrant goods. Fairs were always monthly outside the city walls and still are, except the walls have gone and leafy avenues replace them.

There are three important religious monuments to visit: the Gothic collegiate Church of Notre-Dame, the 17C Chapel of the Pénitents Noirs, and the 15C Chartreuse St-Sauveur on the other side of the river (Pénitents Noirs and the Chartreuse, open 1 Jul–15 Sept except Tues, guided visits, enquire at the Tourist Office). Villefranche is an ideal centre for exploring the Aveyron, and within easy reach of Rodez, Figeac, Albi and Cahors. The *Relais de Farrou* at St-Remy, north of Villefranche, (tel: 65 45 18 11) is one of a number of hotels of all categories in the area, and the restaurant *Bellevue* (tel: 65 45 23 17), near the Chartreuse, is recommended.

On Foot. The **Tourist Information Office** is on Promenade du Guiraudet, near the main bridge. Follow the river bank past **Rue de la République** at the end of the pedestrian bridge, Pont des Consuls, the old main street leading to the centre, and take **Rue Polier**, lined with interesting old buildings. Turn left at Rue Etroite and cross Rue de la République from where you have a view of the mighty belfry of Notre-Dame. Continue straight on down Rue du Paradis and Rue de la Monnaie, turn right on Rue du Segeant Bories. This brings you to a small square with the only **fountain** in the town, le Griffoul, dated 1336, and the **Musée Urbain Cabrol**, of archaeology and local history (10.00–12.00, 14.00–18.00, June–Sep, except Sun). Turn left on Rue Marcellin Fabre and almost immediately on the right is a very splendid late Gothic **doorway** at the foot of a stairtower. Further up Rue Bories is a stairtower, c 1490, with a finely carved doorway on your left, and in Rue Marcellin Fabre something similar.

Rue R. Flassadiers and Rue Campmas bring you to the **Chapelle des Pénitents Noirs**, begun in 1641 is one of the best Baroque churches in the Midi-Pyrénées. Soberly classical from the exterior but with a curious octagonal lantern, the interior under restoration is another dimension. In the shape of a quadrangle with mitred corners, eight main ribs support the wooden lantern which originally had more openings. In the 17C the walls and timber ceiling received painted décor. The ceiling, completed in 1701, includes scenes from the Legend of the True Cross. The overall effect was altered in the 18C when the pilasters were marbled (1784) and stucco reliefs added but some of the marbling has been removed and the paintings underneath restored. In 1709 the gilded retable was installed with scenes of the Passion on four panels. In the gallery are 15C stalls from Loc-Dieu Abbey, in dire need of attention, bought at the time of the Revolution by the Pénitents and deposited here.

On Place St-Jacques the door marked Hôtel de la Charité is on the site of the old pilgrim *hôpital*, and in Rue St-Jacques is the façade of the 15C Chapelle St-Jacques. Turn left into Rue Cabrol and right into Rue Halle, the site of the old grain market, which arrives above **Place Notre-Dame**. Among the tall arcaded houses surrounding the square, is the **Hôtel de Raynal** on the south, a pretty early Renaissance façade with *bâton écoté* mouldings around the door and first-floor windows and carved label-stops including an Annunciation. The door opens into a coffered passageway and a very small Renaissance courtyard with the remains of a sophisticated décor.

The overpoweringly huge belfry-porch of the **Church of Notre-Dame** straddles the north-east corner of the square. The first stone of the church was laid in 1260, shortly after the foundation of the *bastide*, the vaults were completed in 1480, and it was consecrated in 1519. The Flamboyant belfry was completed c 1560, although the spire was never built and it is topped off with a rather inadequate structure. It takes the traditional form of Gothic churches in the Midi, of a nave without aisles and chapels, with tall windows, between the buttresses. The east end of the church is Rayonnant, the west Flamboyant. The choir has heavily restored 15C glass, a gift of Charles VII. The stalls with misericords (c 1480) by André Sulpice, a very active workshop, were badly damaged at some point. The pulpit is also 15C. The medallion of the altar in the north transept is attributed to Pierre Puget. The church contains paintings recovered from convents or other religious houses in Villefranche.

The streets south of the church are worth exploring, notably Rue Guillaume de Garrigues, which leads back to the river.

By Road. The **Chartreuse de St-Sauveur** on the D922 about 1km from the town centre is one of the few charterhouses to have been preserved and is a relatively unknown treasure of the Rouergue. To visit, see above.

When the charterhouse was begun in the 15C, Villefranche-de-Rouergue was a flourishing commercial town with some 8000 inhabitants. It was built with the fortune bequeathed by a rich draper, Vézian Valette, who, having decided to endow the construction, departed in 1450 for Nicolas V's Jubilee in Rome and died there shortly afterwards. His widow, Catherine Garnier, took over the task and work began in 1451. Such was the size of the donation that the church, the large cloister and the chapter house were completed in seven years, the small cloister between 1458 and 1460, and a chapel was added in 1528. Apart from a few outbuildings and the development of the agricultural annexes in the 17C, it was not altered until the community was dispersed in 1790 when it was bought by the town and used by the hospital until a few years ago. The architecture and decoration is uniformly Flamboyant and has been subjected to very few restorations.

The Carthusian order, founded by St-Bruno in 1086, was strict but not as strict as the Cistercian rule. The monks lived according to the rules of solitude, silence and devotion while fulfilling the needs of a communal life. To accomplish this they lived in twelve hermitages, small self-contained maisonettes on two floors with gardens, opening on to the large cloister.

The large **west porch** of the church protects a portal and carved door panels with two monks holding the coats of arms of Vézian Valette and Catherine Garnier. Inside is a simple space, the nave and polygonal choir divided by a screen. The **choir** contains 30 stalls, c 1461, with decorated armrests and misericords and beautiful carved panels, from the workshop of André Sulpice. North of the altar is a memorial to the founders and their tomb with engraved effigies and an inscription. There is some original glass and richly carved bosses and brackets. On the north is a 16C chapel.

The **vestibule**, between the church and the chapter house, has 15C glass, and the **chapter house** itself resembles a chapel with a polygonal apse and three admirable windows with a Nativity and choir of angels, St-George and Ste-Catherine, and carved capitals and bosses. The **refectory**, which has a beautiful pulpit, is usually closed. The magnificent but soberly uniform great Gothic **cloister**, 60m by 40m, has remained intact. Around it are twelves hermitages, two of them original. The small cloister is more ornate and quite outstanding with twenty bays decorated with pendant bosses sculpted with the arms of the founders, sixteen different adaptations of the reticulated tracery, and crocketted pinnacles and gargoyles on the piers. In the south-west, near the refectory, the lavabo has a carved relief of the Washing of the disciples' feet.

From Villefranche-de-Rouergue, pick up the D47 on the right bank of the Aveyron to Monteils, then branch off on the D149 to Najac (22km), stretched out precariously along the ridge of a cliff above a loop in the Aveyron Gorges.

Najac (Tourist Information, tel: 65 29 72 05) draws visitors because it is such an attractive site, and in their wake follow the arty-crafty shops and little train, but also all types of facilities and activities. Two popular hotel-restaurants are the *Oustal del Barry* (tel: 65 29 74 32) in the village, and in the valley, the *Hôtel Belle-Rive* (tel: 65 29 73 90), convenient for the railway station with an occasional train from Toulouse or the north.

At the west of the village is the castle, rebuilt by Alphonse de Poitiers in 1253. The *cité* and the *bourg* developed below it, separated by a wall and gateway from the faubourg (or *barry*) to the east until the 18C. The **Place du Faubourg** is the only part that can be described as a *bastide* and is known to have existed in 1258. More of a wide street than a square it has a fountain and *couverts* on the south. The houses close in as the street descends into the *bourg*, framing a view of the castle. There is an ancient fountain (1344) carved from a single block of granite on the left.

Rue du Château marks the entrance to the *cité* and climbs up to the **château** (tel: 65 29 70 92, guided visit, Apr–Sept). Alphonse de Poitiers incorporated a 12C castle, including the Tour Carrée, into his fort adding four linked towers and a tall keep with three floors. The castle is surrounded by a wall with a square tower and a justice tower. Despite many periods of disruption by Seigneurs, Cathars, English, Protestants and *Croquants* (peasants) the château was finally ruined in the 19C when it was used as a quarry.

Further east still is the 13C **Church of St-Jean l'Evangéliste**, built after the Albigensian heresies by the Cathar community, forced by the Inquisition to replace the 12C Church of St-Martin. Erected 1258–75, it is one of the first Gothic churches in the Rouergue. Severe but well built, without aisles and a flat east end, the plate-tracery windows of 1320 have mid-19C glass. Among the furnishings are the original altar, used as a step for 150 years and returned to its rightful place in 1966, a 15C Crucifixion with a 16C Virgin and St John and a curious iron cage in which a candle burned continuously in front of the statue of the Virgin (14C). The roads are narrow and winding.

From Najac take the D564 then the D594 (direction Laguépie) and turn right on to the D958 to Varen (11.5km).

It would be easy to drive past **Varen** without noticing its treasures. On the main road itself is a Romanesque **church**, second-half 11C, originally part of a Benedictine monastery dedicated to Notre-Dame and St-Pierre, which became a collegiate then the parish church of St-Serge. The simple west entrance opens into an eleven-bay austere vessel with a continuous tunnel vault and a flat apse. There is no transept and the nave is buttressed by narrow aisles ending in semi-circular apses over crypts. There are windows only on the south. The interesting group of carved **capitals** is concentrated around the choir and apses, inside and out. The interlace motif in the south chapel is the oldest c 1070–80. Others have vegetal and animal elements and even storiated including Daniel in the Lions' Den, archangels Raphael and Gabriel. The most accomplished capitals in the choir may be as late as the early 12C, and some carry traces of polychrome. Over the choir is a domical vault supporting the belfry.

The flat apse is a mystery. Altered in the 14C, there are Romanesque capitals on the exterior (St Michael and the dragon, Samson and the lion), it was possibly transformed from semi-circular at some point to make an access, then closed when the situation changed.

It is worth taking some time to explore the village. On the south side of the church the 15C château has been transformed into the Mairie, and further on is a pretty fountain. Between the two, the 15C town gateway leads to the old streets, the market place and eventually a restored mill on the banks of the Aveyron.

Detour. The D33 takes you through the pretty village of **Verfeil**, with a small covered market and Baroque altar, and on to the Abbey of Beaulieu-en-Rouergue, 12km, (see Route 20).

Stay on the D958 (which becomes the D115) following the Aveyron for 15.5km then cross the river into St-Antonin-Noble-Val. Turn left over the bridge then keep following the road round to the right until you are north of the town at a large tree-lined junction with the D19.

St-Antonin-Noble-Val (pop. 1882, Tourist Information, tel: 63 30 67 01) is a superb and not over-prettified town, crammed with vestiges of medieval houses. It dips its feet in the Aveyron and is overlooked by the craggy Roc d'Anglars to the south.

A Benedictine monastery, established in Nobilis Vallis in 763, protected the relics of St-Antonin, martyr of Pamiers in the Ariège. The town grew around the abbey, now replaced by the presbytery and the *école maternelle*, at the south-west of the town where the little Bonnette runs into the Aveyron. The availability of water maintained a thriving leather industry in the Middle Ages and the streets bear witness to a very prosperous past, although St-Antonin too had its share of upheavals. There was a small spa at the beginning of the century and now there is a water bottling plant. The watery aspect is also an advantage for tourism, and just outside the town are facilities on the river for canoeing and swimming. Its Sunday morning market is animated, and there are hotels and restaurants. The **Roc d'Anglars** is a scenic expedition, as are the **Grottes de Bosc**.

Walk down **Rue de la Pelisserie** and take note of the narrow side streets and details of medieval windows and decoration. St-Antonin contains one of France's oldest civic buildings, the **Hôtel de Ville** or **Maison Romane**, on Place de la Halle. It is used by the Musée du Vieux St-Antonin (tel: 63 30 63 47, Jul–Sep).

This is a magnificent example of Romanesque architecture realised 1150–55. The main building of three bays abuts a tower on the south and on street level are four large archways. The main elevation has an open gallery, its full length divided by piers into three four-light bays. The piers carry some remarkable sculpture. On the right are Adam and Eve, and on the other, a figure holding a book and a sceptre with an eagle is the Emperor Justinian. This suggests that the large room on this floor originally had a judicial function. Each bay is divided by paired columns with carved capitals, seven figurative representing the vices, and eleven vegetal. On the top floor are three two-light bays with round arches under a continuous moulding. Indentations in the façade once contained coloured enamelled ceramic discs (the museum has some fragments). The tower has two superimposed two-light windows, the upper trilobed opening was remade in the 19C, and the Tuscan-style campanile was added by Viollet-le-Duc in the 19C.

Opposite, the **halle** of 1840 shelters a 15C discoidal stele with a Crucifixion on one side, and on the other the Virgin and Child between two bishops, one of them St-Eloi or Eligius. South-west is the elegant **Mairie**, of 1751, formerly the convent of the Génovéfains (Tourist Information). Next door is the neo-Gothic church of 1862 and behind the Mairie are some beautifully restored houses with galleries and *mirandes*. A buffer town during the Hundred Years' War, for a time the English had their garrison in Rue Guilhem Peyre, behind the Maison Romane, a street with many other small and interesting details. Most definitely a town to linger in.

Go back across the Aveyron to pick up the D115, passing below **Penne** perched precariously on the cliff above the road (see Route 34 Cordes), and stay on it for 22km, then turn left on the D1 and almost immediately right to **Bruniquel** (Tourist Information, tel: 63 67 24 91). This is another picturesque ensemble on a rock between the Aveyron and the Vère. On the threshhold of the Quercy, the Albigeois and the Rouergue it grew wealthy from important medieval fairs dealing in flax, hemp and saffron. The main street leading up the hill from the church, 17C and 19C, passes under one of the three remaining gateways of the old ramparts past 14C, 15C and 16C houses. To the left is the recently restored **Maison Payrol** (tel: 63 67 26 42, open Apr–Sept w.e., and 15 June–15 Sept) named after an important local family. The restorations have revealed a fascinating sample of civil architecture from the 14C to the 17C, built above an ancient vaulted cellar. Samples of different periods include a room for receiving pilgrims or travellers, medieval wall paintings, fireplaces, a variety of windows, and a remarkable 15C sculpted ceiling over what was once a granary. There is also a collection of stone carving and documentation recording the history of the village and the château.

At the summit are the two **Châteaux de Bruniquel** (tel: 63 67 27 67, Apr–Nov), the property of the Counts of Toulouse in the 12C and divided between two branches of the family in the 14C. The Château Vieux still has its 12C keep, called the Tower of Queen Brunehaut after the legendary Merovingian queen who reigned over the Quercy c 600, as well as the 13C–14C ramparts. The main part of the building was extensively altered in the 18C and 19C with the addition of an arcaded terrace looking out towards the Aveyron Valley. Changes were made in the 17C and 18C to the Château Jeune, built between 1485 and 1510.

There is a hotel and some restaurants and, across the river, the Grotte de la Magdaleine.

From Bruniquel either cross the Aveyron immediately and follow the right bank (5km), or keep on the D115 and turn left and under the road to cross the Aveyron to **Montricoux**, a small unspoilt town remarkable for the number of 15C and 16C timber-framed houses using mud brick or wattle and daub infill. To the west of the village the 13C–16C **Church of St-Pierre** was once the chapel of a Templar Commandery; one of the vault bosses is carved with a tau-cross. The tall octagonal brick belfry was added in c 1549 to a massive stone base. The church has a narrow nave and pentagonal apse decorated with a mural of the Annunciation by Marcel Lenoir (1872–1931), and modern glass in the windows. The Counts of Montricoux had a funerary chapel here. Among the fittings are an ancient stoup and font, a 12C statue of St Peter, and diverse retables, including one with a model of St-Eutrope in a glass coffin (17C).

Opposite the church is a large square tower with shallow buttresses. The former keep of the Templar Commandery has been integrated into an 18C château which houses the **Musée Marcel-Lenoir** (tel: 63 67 26 48, 10.00–12.00, 14.30–19.00, May–Sept). Enter through the west door of the château. This is a private collection of the work of Lenoir who was born in Montauban and died in Montricoux, displayed in an elegantly colourful setting. The 121 exhibits, among them many portraits, demonstrate the influence of the Nabis and Maurice Denis as well as Lenoir's interest in fresco technique and his mystic tendencies. The visit also includes the 12C Templar *salle de garde*.

Take the D78 to **Bioule** (9km), a tiny community at whose heart is the modest stone and brick Château de Cardaillac (tel: 63 30 95 62, 15.00–18.30, Jul–Aug, weekends June & Sep) on the banks of the Aveyron river. Owned for five centuries by the powerful family of Cardaillac, the château was built at the beginning of the 12C, almost entirely rebuilt in 1329, and modified in the 16C. The St-Sauveur chapel has 14C murals, and in the late 15C the Salle des Preux received its painted décor.

Montauban is about 20km on the D115.

Between Figeac and Villefranche-de-Rouergue

Total distance: 100km (62 miles).

This itinerary could as easily be done from Rodez or Figeac, and ties in with the Lot Valley to the north, or Conques.

D1/D922 **Villeneuve-d'Aveyron** (**en-Rouergue**), an attractive little town at the edge of the D922, 10km north of Villefranche-de-Rouergue, acquired the status and privileges of *bastide* in 1271 after the *sauveté* that had grown around an 11C monastery was acquired by Raymond VII, Count of Toulouse in 1231 and became a royal *bastide* in 1272. In 1359 the *bastide* was fortified and there are four main gateways, the **Tour Savignac** or **Cardaillac**, built in 1359, **Porte Manhanenque** and **Porte Isaurenque** which lost their towers in the 18C, and **Porte Haute**, integrated into the fortifications in 1486.

Villeneuve has preserved much of interest from its past, including a number of 15C and 16C houses, with traceried or mullioned windows, notably around Place des Conques and Rue Pavie, lined with arcades. The **church** is made up of two parts. The centrally planned 11C Chapel of St-Sépulchre has a ribbed dome centred upon an oculus and supported by four columns. It was extended by the Church of St-Pierre et St-Paul (nave and polygonal apse) in the 13C. In the north apsidiole are medieval frescoes of a Christ in Majesty with the symbol of the Evangelists and scenes from a pilgrimage.

Leave Villeneuve on the D40, and just before Naussac turn right on the D87 to **Peyrusse-le-Roc** (18km). This was an important fort belonging to the Counts of Toulouse, but the village was abandoned in the 17C in favour of Villefranche-de-Rouergue. The access to what is left—12C and 13C towers and the remains of the *cité* clinging to a steep rock—is possible but not easy, but it is all very picturesque. The village **church** has works by Hervé Vernhes, a local artist, which light up automatically as you enter and include the altar which is in solid elm, a Crucifixion in walnut behind it, and a series of paintings on canvas. The village puts on a medieval fair in August.

Now continue on the D87 to **Montbazens** (8.5km), turn right on to the D5 and left after 2km taking the D994 and D658 to Bournazel. The **Château de Bournazel** is a high point in the development of Renaissance architecture in the Rouergue. Two massive round towers of the medieval château mark the entrance, but on the other side is a complete change of style. Built presumably in 1545, the date found on the north wing, it is now a retirement home but can be visited. It shows a highly individual interpretation of the influences of antiquity and of Italy, with a disciplined use of the classical orders but demonstrating certain differences to the classicism of the north of France. It was damaged by fire in 1790 and restored in 1964 and is being restored again.

From Bournazel take the D595 and D253 to Rignac and then the D997/D285 (15km) to **Belcastel**, on a cliff at the edge of the Aveyron, a bit of a sham, but a very good one. Twenty years ago the village had almost completely disappeared, but the enthusiasm of the architect Fernand Pouillon for the castle was contagious and a concerted effort has created something rather magical.

The village climbs the slope up to the ruins of the château, and a superb **bridge** completes the scene. At the end of the bridge is the 15C **Church of**

St-Mary Magdalene, extended in 1891. It contains an old altar found under the flagstones, and on the left the mausoleum and tomb of Alzias de Saunhac, Seigneur de Belcastel, builder of the church. Nearby are three 15C statues, the Virgin and Child, St Anthony Hermit and Mary Magdalene and a 15C St Christopher with the infant Christ on his shoulders in the north transept. The little village has much to offer, including a camp site and two restaurants, both good, the more up-market *Restaurant du Vieux Pont*, tel: 65 64 52 29 (with accommodation), and *Restaurant Couderc*, tel: 65 64 52 26.

From Rignac follow either the D1 or the more devious D47 back to Villefranche-de-Rouergue (28km). See Route 34 Cordes.

28

Millau, Montjaux and the Lévezou

MILLAU (pop. 22,500, Tourist Information, Avenue Alfred Merle, BP 331, 12103 Millau, tel: 65 60 02 42) is a *sous-préfecture* of the Aveyron, at the most eastern extremity of the Midi-Pyrénées on the corridor (the N9 which will become an autoroute in the next few years) between the ClermontFerrand and Montpellier. The town is on the right bank of the Tarn near the confluent with the Dourbie, and it is surrounded by the omnipresent Grands Causses, limestone plateaux on the edge of the Cevennes.

The town, although not as obviously eye catching as Rodez or Albi, is vibrant, active and constantly being improved. It is a good centre for exploring south-east Rouergue, the neighbouring *départements* of Lozère and Hérault. Accessible by train, it has a large number of hotels of all categories. The modern *International Hotel* has a view of the *causse* and a good restaurant (tel: 65 60 20 66), and in a different setting, 2km south-west of Millau on the D992, the *Hôtel-Château de Creissels* (tel: 65 60 16 59), has a restaurant in a vaulted cellar (tel: 65 60 31 79).

History. Ancient civilisations, c 2500–1500 BC, inhabited the caves in the region and erected dolmens and menhirs, but it was not until about the 2C BC that people came down from the hills. The Celtic tribe, the Rutenes, called their settlement Condatomagos, market-town on the confluent. The Romans established an important pottery manufacture from 10 BC to AD 150, and throughout the Middle Ages it was a major commercial centre, trading leather, cloth and copper with goods from the Languedoc seaports. By the 8C the town was known as Amiliavum, eventually to become Millau. After a series of feudal alliances, it achieved autonomous rule in the 12C by an oligarchy of consuls, but lost its independence in 1361 and came under English domination. It picked itself up again during the period of peace following the Hundred Years War, then, unlike most of the Rouergue, embraced the Reformation in the 16C. The leather trade, and especially glove making using the pelts of lambs sacrificed to assure sufficient milk for cheese production, was already well established and expanded with the town through the 18C to flourish until the 1930s—everyone wore gloves in Millau. There are still a few individual *gantiers* (glovers) at work in Millau and the two great industries, pottery and glovemaking, are represented at the museum. Most of the medieval buildings were destroyed at the time of the Reformation, but the town has retained its medieval layout.

On Foot. At the centre of Millau is **Place du Mandarous**, a half circle, where four large boulevards meet. The **Tourist Information Office** is to the north-west, off Boulevard de la République and the old town is south of the *place* enclosed in a mandorla of boulevards which replaced the city walls. Take Rue du Mandarous and turn left on to **Rue Droite**, the former main street, parallel with the river, a pleasant, pedestrianised street of small shops. There are still one or two glove makers (L'Atelier du Gantier at No. 21), family businesses with ancient machines in their shop windows, where you can have gloves made to measure, surely the ultimate leather luxury. This brings you to **le Beffroi**, the belfry which is the leitmotif of Millau, towering 42m over the old town. The lower square section of the tower is all that remains of the 12C tower which was part of the city defences and represented seigneurial power. It was bought by the town in 1613 and subsequently became a symbol of municipal authority. The upper octagonal section was built in 1614 to contain a bell and the town clock.

The vast **Place Emma Calvé** (underground car park) is named after an Aveyronnaise opera singer, heralded locally as *Notre Carmen* (1858–1942), a role she sang 1389 times. After the Beffroi turn left to the large **covered market** (markets on Wednesday and Friday), a huge metal and brick construction with cellars, which was erected in 1899 and renovated in 1984–85, part of a project of *Haussmanism*, when Bd Sadi Carnot and Rue Coussergues were created.

Return to Rue Droite and continue on to **Place Grégoire**, which has some interesting 17C façades, doorways and a corbelled out angle tower. This in turn leads to **Place du Maréchal Foch**, the prettiest, and the oldest, square in Millau. It was the only public space in the old town and is arcaded along one side with a colonnade of cylindrical piers which, according to popular tradition, come from cloisters destroyed during the Religious Wars. However, the capital, possibly part of the old pillory, above the stone table in the north-west has an inscription in Occitan: '*gara que faras enant que comences*', the salutary message that you should think about what you are going to do before you begin. The oldest houses on the north are 15C–16C, in the centre is a cool fountain of 1835, and on the east the Ecole Paul Bert occupies the old Grain Market built in 1836. There are a couple of café/ restaurants.

North of the square is the **Church of Notre-Dame de l'Espinasse**. This is a mainly 17C church, rebuilt after the Reformation with money raised from tolls on the Tarn for nine years. When it reopened in 1646 it was the only parish church in Millau until 1828. Little remains of the Romanesque church consecrated in 1095 except perhaps the lower walls of the heavily buttressed east end and the base of the belfry, which was rebuilt in the 17C in Toulousain style. The west façade is pure Baroque. The interior space is straightforward, without aisles but with the addition of a gallery on three sides, and a seven-sided apse. The apse has modern murals by Jean Bernard (1940) and the glass, blues to the north and pinks to the south, was made by Claude Baillon in 1984.

On the south-east side of Place Foch is the **Musée de Millau** installed in the 18C Hôtel de Pégayrolles (tel: 65 59 01 08, 10.00–12.00, 14.00–18.00 every day Apr–Sept, rest of year closed Sun and BH). Sober but genteel, the building is arranged around a U-shaped courtyard and has a fine staircase inside. The museum is divided between archaeology on the left and gloves to the right. The **archaeological section** has an area devoted to local palaeontology with the fossilised footprint of a dinosaur. The Bronze Age is also represented. The Gallo-Roman period, from 1C–4C, takes most of the space with artefacts from the site of Graufesenque just south of Millau. It includes pins, lamps, fibules, money, figurines in white and in terracotta pottery, bronze statuettes, goblets and mosaics and some glass, and pots as far as the eye can see. The potters of Graufesenque were expert in sigillated pottery, clay pots with stamped-on moulded motifs and decorated with a red slip fired to a high temperature. The techniques, stages and periods of production from 10 BC to AD 250 are explained. Ceramics from Graufesenque were exported as far as Scotland, North Africa, even India. There is a room devoted to Millau from the 10C to the 18C and another to a week in the life of an everyday Rutene.

Up the stairs on the right of the entrance is a pretty octagonal room with a coffered vault and **gloves of all kinds**—long, short, coloured, flashy, sporting, old, new, and some from Buffalo Bill's last show in Paris. There is all you every wanted to know about glove making from tanning the skins (*megisserie*) to glove design and, if you time it right, you may hit on an exhibition of modern sculpture based on leather. There is also an exhibition of dolls, which may or may not appeal to children (the dinosaur footprints will probably fare better) with ... mini gloves.

Turn left out of the museum, through the covered passageway, right on Rue Guilhem Estève and left on to Rue Haute to the **Quartier du Voultre**. The Dominican convent was destroyed by the Calvinists who took over the 16C church, and, after much toing and froing, a new Protestant Temple was built in 1869. The Porte du Voultre was probably part of the old fortifications and gave its name to the leather workers' quarter. Rue du Voultre comes out into Boulevard de l'Ayrolle, built on the old city ditches. To the left is the Tarn and the Rue de la Tannerie will bring you to **Pont Lerouge** (1821) next to which are two arches of the 12C bridge and a 15C mill.

If you turn right at the end of Rue du Voultre you will find a little way along on the left a small elegant colonnaded building, the grandest **lavoir** ever, in which citizens could wash their linen in public, built 1749 as part of the urbanisation and modernisation scheme. It takes the form of a Neo-Classical semi-circular pavilion with arcades.

Return to the old quarter down Rue St-Martin. **Rue Peyroliers** which crosses it has interesting façades and will bring you back to Rue Droite. The **Church of St-Martin**, on the south side of Place E. Calvé, is a small simple church with a large Baroque painting of the Descent from the Cross attributed to the Flemish 17C painter Gaspard de Crayer (1584–1669).

The site of Graufesenque is, except for the very energetic, a five-minute car ride away on the other side of the Tarn. Cross the river by the Pont du Larzac towards the D992, go 350 degrees around the roundabout and take the small road (signposted) to **Graufesenque** (09.00–12.00, 14.00–18.30, every day except BH). On the plain where the Tarn and the Dourbie converge, the settlement covered some ten hectares of which 4000 square metres have been excavated. The site is well maintained and the visits are accompanied.

Excavations from 1973 to 1981 uncovered traces of three successive periods of habitation. The Celtic and early Gallo-Roman period, 2C–1C BC, when there was intense commercial activity with the Mediterranean. From the 1C to the first half of the 2C, the workshops of Gallo-Roman potters attest to a massive production of pots for export. Later, from 150 to 300, there was a marked deterioration in the quality of the dwellings. The variety of buildings exposed demonstrate the organisation of the community, and include the modest dwellings of the potters and others, as well as two sanctuaries. There are also roads, gutters, drains, thermae and hypocausts, to support the domestic side of life. The most fascinating are all the buildings related to the enormous **production of pottery**: workshops, wells, clay storage areas, and of course kilns. Three kilns have been uncovered, the largest, 6.80m by 11.30m, could have held between 10,000 and 40,000 vessels at one firing. The industry was run on the lines of a cooperative, with a multitude of support activities, and at the height of its production there were about 500 potters working at Graufesenque.

Between Millau and Rodez, the Lévezou

Total distance, 110km (68 miles).

This is not the fastest route between Millau and Rodez, but crosses the high Plateau de Lévezou separating the two main towns of the Aveyron, and divides the two parts of Rouergue, the wetter, wooded west and the dryer east benefiting from Mediterranean influences. High (1000m) and exposed, its numerous artificial lakes are a big attraction to visitors looking for outdoor pursuits.

From Millau, take the D911 and turn left after 10km to **St-Beauzély**, on the D30, a high fortified village with a 16C castle (exhibitions). The 12C Gramontin priory of **Combéroumal**, on the D171 west of the village, was an austere Grandmontain monastery (Limousin), solid and practical, and can be visited.

Take the D30 for about 5km and turn left, to wind through chestnuts and oaks, magnificent in the autumn, to **Castelnau-Pégayrols** (4km), a sensational red sandstone place, picturesquely dilapidated—a satellite dish here, a bit of sculpted cornice there, interesting windows, rabbits in the yard—in a cluster of 15C and 16C houses grouped around the château. The village is fortress-like, above the Muze, with two churches, both dating from the 11C. The larger, the parish Church of St-Michel, was begun in the 11C but was subsequently modified in the 13C and 15C. The older Church of Notre-Dame (11C–12C) in the cemetery has some wall paintings.

Follow the D515 then the D993 8km to **Montjaux**, the most stunning of this series of villages clinging, as the best always do, to the side of a high escarpment and looking out over the Grands Causses and the Muze valley towards Roquefort. Washed in red, the houses are arranged in tiers stretching out along the hillside, with a stocky Romanesque church at the far end. The ruins of an old château, supposedly on the site of a temple dedicated to Jupiter, look down on it, and there is a 'newer' château (16C–17C) below. The delightful **church**, in pink sandstone with blue-grey slate roofs, originally part of a priory attached to Chaise Dieu (Auvergne), shows the stylistic influence of that region. It is mainly 12C, with some parts 15C and the façade and belfry rebuilt in 1856. Over the crossing is a domed lantern on pendentives, and the roof of the apse has just been restored. It has a number of capitals with large simple carvings of animals and birds, monsters in combat and fantastic beasts.

D993 to Bouloc, then turn on to the D44 to **Les Canabières** (12.5km), a severe schist hilltop village which seems to be made up entirely of farms, if the aromas are anything to go by. The first Templar Commandery in the Rouergue was established here and the church made over to them in 1120. Unlike the village, the church porch is in pinkish sandstone, and the tympanum has carved reliefs. The low narrow church has a few carvings inside and an upturned capital used as a holy water stoup.

Now take the D73/D993 north-west for about 5km to **Salles-Curan** (Tourist Information, tel: 65 46 31 73), 17.5km, which has become an important centre for tourism next to the vast **Lac de Pareloup**, 1300ha, into which a thousand streams pour their contents to supply the hydro-electric stations on the Tarn.

Salles-Curan is a strange mixture. There are narrow streets with dilapidated houses, a bit of 19C kitsch in the form of a polychromed statue of the Virgin with a rakish starry halo of which the Bishops of Rodez, who had resided there in the 15C, may or may not have approved, and a bit of modern. The bishops' residence is now a hotel, *Hostellerie du Lévezou* (tel: 65 46 34 16). The **church** is also 15C and has some fine carved choir stalls adorned with a whole range of beasts and vegetal motifs. The human figures have fared less well. There is some restored 15C glass. The Renaissance house below the church with an angle window is where the *dimes* (tithes) were collected.

The D577 circumscribes the lake, about 26km, an interesting irregular outline with many fjords, large enough for swimming, sailing and water skiing. North on the D993 and D922, 15km from Salles-Curan, is another lakeside resort, **Pont-de-Salars** (Tourist Information, tel: 65 46 82 46). Its lake is small but has the same facilities. Both centres have top quality campsites and there are enough activities in the region to make it ideal for family holidays.

From Pont-de-Salars take the D911 and turn right after about 8km on to the D112 to **Inières**, a charming village with a fortified **church**. It protects a superb Annunication group c 1470, which probably came from the Cathedral of Rodez. About 8km north-west on the D112/D666 is another impressive little fortified church at **Ste-Radegonde**, with similarities to Inières, but on top of the machicolated tower is an arcaded belfry with a pointed roof. From here to Rodez is 4km (see Route 26).

To return to Millau, take the D88 and turn off at Sévérac-l'Eglise and follow the D28 through Vaysse-Rodié, for the view, to **Vezins** (17C château, Jul–Sept, pm) on to Bois-du-Four and **St-Léons** (25km), the village where the eminent entomologist Jean-Henri Fabre was born (museum, Jul–Aug, pm). Then pick up the D911 again (48km).

Or simply **stay on the D88** to **Sévérac-le-Château** (pop. 2500, Tourist Information, tel: 65 47 67 31), also a good base at the point of entry to the Rouergue, with train connections, midway between Rodez and Millau, handy for the Causses and the Aubrac, and with a number of hotels. The medieval town is entered through a fortified gate and dominated by the ruins of a large feudal castle. The château, which can be visited, shows the signs of wear and tear resulting from frequent conflicts and subsequent restorations. Then take the N9 to Millau (81km).

29

The Causse Noir, Gorges de la Dourbie, Nant, and the Templar towns of the Larzac

Total distance: 124km (77 miles).

This is a tour which begins at Millau where the Doubie meets the Tarn, having carved a route through the Causse Noir and the Causse du Larzac. The route plunges straight into the valley, brindled with Romanesque churches, and justly described as the *Jardin du Rouergue*. There are steep, narrow, winding roads to be negotiated to reach some of the out-of-the-way sites, although the valley itself is not difficult. The route then crosses the barren and spectacular Causse du Larzac through the Templar villages of La Couveratoirade and Ste-Eulalie-de-Cernon, to return to Millau via the N9.

Leaving Millau, cross the Tarn by the Pont de Cureplats and take the D991 which almost immediately penetrates a deep rift between the limestone cliffs, quite magnificent at all seasons, but especially in autumn. At **Massebiau** there is a tight loop, past two castles, le Pépissou, just a tower, and le Monna, which protected the access to the Causse Noir. The scenery becomes more rugged, and the villages scattered along the valley are the inheritors of medieval forts defending the territory. **La Roque-Ste-Marguerite** is a small community with a château (rebuilt in the 17C) and church (11C and 18C) picturesquely clamped to the cliff.

  Detour. There are roads from here across the Causse Noir, to the **Grottes de Dargilan**, to the extraordinary natural phenomena of **Montpellier le Vieux** and **Roquesaltes**, groups of rocks resembling ruined and deserted villages, and to remote villages and views of the valley.

  2km after Ste-Marguerite the road crosses the Dourbie, and you may catch a glimpse above of the abandoned village and château of **St-Véran** and the Church of Notre-Dame des Treilles. These can only be reached with difficulty along a winding and vertiginous track. Walking would be the safest way up.

  Similarly **Cantobre**, on the other side of the valley, is another vertiginously spectacular spot where the dolomitic rock and buildings merge into one craggy mass. There is a good view of the village from the D991 for those who opt out of the winding D145 which leads up to it along the valley of the Trévezel. The entry to the town is through the old gateway and at the summit is a part Romanesque (11C) church, rebuilt after the Wars of Religion.

The valley now widens out, becomes gentler, and fulfils its description as the Garden of the Rouergue. On the edge of the route is the **Church of Notre-Dame des Cuns**, the most complete Romanesque church in the valley, built in golden limestone, compact and sturdy, with a polygonal apse, the only addition being a chapel in the 15C. Like many Romanesque churches in this vicinity, which have similar characteristics, it was affiliated to St-Victor de Marseille.

Nant (Tourist Information, tel: 65 62 25 12), 32km from Millau, is a charming village, all the more attractive because it entails no climbing. On the banks of the Dourbie, it has a graceful 14C bridge, an arcaded 16C market with huge stone pillars and vaults (no longer used as a market), and the town hall occupies an elegant 18C building with staircase and stucco. There is also a notable church with a massive, fortified west end. Once an important Benedictine abbey, the **Church of St-Pierre** is all that remains. The 12C rectangular fortified narthex with high relieving arches was amended two centuries later with the addition of a Gothic door and also the tower. Chapels were added to the nave in the 14C and 19C, and the windows were enlarged in the 19C but the pentagonal east end has conserved many of its 12C elements. The interior is impressive and subtly lighted. The nave, not on exactly the same axis as the chevet, has pointed barrel vaults supported by pairs of engaged columns on high bases. There are **121 sculpted capitals** altogether, mainly cubic in form, with stylised vegetal or geometric designs, they seem to be the work of several sculptors and some probably from an earlier church. There is a short transept with apsidal chapels, and the crossing is covered by a cupola on simple pendentives. The apse is semi-circular from the interior with three windows and simple decorations.

The D55 from Nant leaves the valley to cross the high and sometimes desolate **Plateau du Larzac** (14.5km) to La Couvertoirade. (Alternatively follow the D999 along the Dourbie to St-Jean-du-Bruel then the D999/D7, to join the D55, 26.5km). The Larzac is a large territory of some 1000 square km, grazed by huge flocks of sheep, cultivated with cereal crops in some parts, small bushy vegetation in others. It was once covered in forest but was cleared for agricultural purposes over many centuries, reaching its present condition in the 18C. Donations of land in the Rouergue were made to the **Templars** from the mid 12C, but the acquisition of the Church of Ste-Eulalie in 1151 was the watershed. Convenient for the Mediterranean, with important links to the Massif Central, land for crops and horses—these factors all contributed to the installation here of the Knights.

La Couvertoirade is probably the best known of the Templar establishments. Given to the Templars in 1159 by the Viscount of Millau, the town was a dependence of the Commandery of Ste-Eulalie until it was made over to the Hospitallers after the Templars were disbanded. The sight of it is very impressive, enclosed in the walls the Hospitallers built around the town in the 15C, in a hollow in the rugged *causse*. The only entrance is through the Porte du Haut (the Porte du Bas collapsed in 1917) because the remarkably well preserved walls prevent any other access. A community was mentioned here in the mid 11C. It is not known exactly when the Templars took over, but some time after acquiring Ste-Eulalie and La Cavalerie. They were given land in the area in 1181, and by 1249 had built the castle, so probably around 1200.

Once inside, on the right is the 17C/18C **Hôtel de la Scipione**, with a permanent exhibition about the Templars. Just before it is a flight of steps which leads up to the **ramparts** for an overall view of the village and a closer look at the defences made up of a series of fortified towers and curtain walls in an irregular shape determined by the rock on which it is built. The castle, incorporated into the enceinte in 1439, is now just a ruin. The **church** opposite, a simple vaulted building with a tall tower that looks little different from the military buildings, was probably built by the Hospitallers in the 14C after the St-Christol chapel, outside the walls, was abandoned.

There are three rustic corbels on the façade and inside two discoid stelae and a carved boss above the choir. Near the church is the communal oven, and below the flight of steps is a public reservoir, Les Conques, supplied by rainwater from the church roof. There are a number of delightful houses particularly along **Rue Droite** on the south, which formerly linked the two entrances, lined with 16C and 17C buildings with exterior steps up to the door and vaulted cellars beneath.

Take the D185 from La Couvertoirade and turn right on to the N9 at **La Pezade**, to leave it again almost immediately left on the D7. Just before Cornus turn right on the D65 and then fork left on the D77. The arid *causse* landscape gives way to green pastures, with sheep as far as the eye can see.

After 23km you arrive at **Ste-Eulalie-de-Cernon**, its five defensive towers and the church tower standing proud above the red roofs in an altogether softer, prettier setting as you come off the plateau. Park outside the walled village, and pass under the tower to the **Grande Rue** which leads up to a large open square with a 17C fountain. This was the cemetery until 1641, and marks the divide between the fortified town enclosed in walls by the Hospitallers in the 15C, and the earlier Templar castle. An earlier church here, on the site of the present one next to the château, was made over to the Templars in 1151 and gradually, by fair means or foul, they became the principal landowners of the Larzac coming at times into conflict with their neighbours. The new **church** was well built but sober, with an unaisled four-bay nave, the transverse arches springing from simple foliate capitals on engaged columns, ending in a semi-circular apse. In 1648 the decision was taken by Commander Jean de Bernouy de Villeneuve to reorientate the church creating a new main entrance, with a fine 17C door with broken pediment and statue of the Virgin in the former apse. Either side are the only old chapels (13C), and the belfry was rebuilt in 1842. The remainder of the chapels were opened out in the 19C.

The **château** was built around four sides of a courtyard, but the oldest part, the façade on the square, can hardly be said to look much like it was at its inception, sometime between 1187 and 1249, given the many vicissitudes and owners it has suffered. Of the four original square towers flanking it, only one remains. The courtyard can be reached via a vaulted passageway (near the toilets, and the door may be closed). To the 12C and 13C building a wing was added in 1648 to provide an upper floor with a grand staircase, murals, and mullioned windows.

For a stunning **view** over Ste-Eulalie, take the D561 to the south, and continue up across open land again and turn right on the D23 to **Viala-du-Pas-de-Jaux**, about 10km, which has a massive fortified barn built in the 15C.

The D23 will take you 10.5 km over the edge of the Causse du Larzac into **Roquefort-sur-Soulzon**, famous for its **cheese** and probably the best known place in the Aveyron.

Two producers offer visits to the cellars or caves where the cheese matures: *Société des Caves et des producteurs réunis de Roquefort* (all year), and the smaller *Caves A. Alric* (Le Papillon) (summer only). The société's tour, including an audio-visual, an animated demonstration of the creation of the caves, and guided visit, helps to explain the existence of all those sheep on the *causse* and the price of Roquefort cheese. Five dairies with milk from 800,000 sheep owned by 2,500 farmers produce the cheese to which the *Penicillium Roqueforti* is introduced. It is then wrapped and left to mature in these cold, damp and draughty caves on long trestles—row upon row of silver discs—to acquire its blue veining and distinctive flavour. There is a tasting (and buying) at the end. Only around the end of March is there a great deal of activity in the cellars, otherwise the cheeses, except for being turned regularly, are mainly left to their own devices. It is a variation on the theme of visits to caves and caverns (plenty around the *causses*) which are always good value when it gets too hot outside.

Detour. Another small fortified village, **St-Jean-d'Alcas**, in good restorative order and enclosed in walls in the 15C but not by the Hospitallers, can be reached from Roquefort, on the D93/D293, about 9km , or perhaps more easily by the D999/D923 (10.5km).

The last real Templar *cité* is at **La Cavalerie**, unfortunately submerged in a small town on the edge of a busy route so that it has nothing like the appeal of the other two. From Roquefort take the D992 and turn right after 4km on to the D999 and either wiggle along the Cernon Valley (D77) or continue 17km straight on to La Cavalerie on the east of the N9. More than half of the 15C protective walls are still in place, punctuated by three huge towers at the angles and over the main gateway. Along the old streets inside are houses from the 15C–17C. The church, begun in the 12C, was almost entirely rebuilt in 1760–61, but inside some fragments of the old building can still be seen.

Millau, a further 20km, has to be approached from the south-east because the **view** from the N9 (to be absorbed into the new autoroute) is quite spectacular.

30

Castles on the Tarn: the Tarn Valley, from Millau to Albi

Total distance: 138km (86 miles).

The Tarn Valley, as well as the Gorges de la Dourbie, are quieter alternatives to the Gorges du Tarn. (Millau is nevertheless well placed for a visit to the gorges which are part of Languedoc-Roussillon.) This is a gentle amble along the Tarn from Millau to Albi, giving time to enjoy the river scenery, and the pictureque villages and castles.

This perambulation could begin where the valley, as opposed to the gorges, starts (or ends) which is at **Le Rozier**, 21km upstream from Millau, a pretty village where the Gorges du Tarn and the Gorges de la Jonte converge. From there to Millau is a scenic drive between strange rocky outcrops and canoe hire, boat trips and endless camp sites on the river banks. In the field beside the river near **Mostuéjouls** is the little Church of Notre-Dame des Champs, with a *clocher-peigne*, a comb-like belfry. From Le Rozier you will arrive at Millau on the N9 (Avenue Jean Jaurès).

From Place du Mandarous in the centre of **Millau**, take Boulevard de l'Ayrolle, and at Place des Martyrs de la Résistance go straight on, staying on the right bank (do not cross the river) along Avenue de Calès (D41) which looks singularly unpromising for a while, the scenery at first very different from up river, much wilder and dryer and the villages formidable, untamed and untouched by the urge to prettify.

Peyrac and **Comprégnac**, in stone with *lauze* roofs, were once wine villages, but the terraced slopes surrounding them show little sign of cultivation. However, around **Candas** there are a few vines among the woods, and Montjaux looks down from its rocky nest (via the D41, see Route 28). Stay in the valley, where you may see herons, on the D96 towards St-Rome-de-Tarn and continue to the junction with the D993 (23km from Millau). If you want views, climb up to **Viala**; but if you prefer a boat trip on an idyllic section where the Tarn flows through steep wooded cliffs called the Rasps, go to the boat station at **Mas de la Nauc** (D73) (tel: 65 62 59 12, open Apr–Nov, check departures; Jun–Sept, every day).

St-Rome-de-Tarn, on the other side of the river (D993 south), is an attractive village surrounded by old vineyards. (Basic hotel-restaurants at Viala and St-Rome.) The D31 climbs via St-Victor and drops down again to cross the river. (A branch right takes you to the Chapel of Notre-Dame du Désert.) This is hydro-electric country and the plant of Le Pouget at Le Truel (6.5km) can be visited (tel: 65 46 50 89).

Cross on to the right bank (D200) until it meets the D25, then turn left back across the Tarn, past some beautiful *pigeonniers*, and over the Dourdou into **St-Izaire** (9.5km). This impressive site was chosen by the Bishops of Vabres for their episcopal château towering above the reddish-stone houses arranged in terraces above the valley. The **château** can be visited (15.00–18.00 Sun & BH May–Sept, all day 14 Jul–Aug). A large square building, built between the 14C and 17C, it has a little look-out tower on the angle towards the village and a variety of fenestration. Inside is a chapel with 14C frescoes and a marquetry ceiling.

Return on the D25 to **Broquiès** (9.5km), with its old houses and views, and take the pretty D54, 8.5km to Brousse-le-Château. **Brousse-le-Château** is first and foremost a formidable castle with ramparts and towers clinging to a high rocky spur between the Tarn and the Alrance, with a sheer drop towards the Tarn. It is also a pretty village on a hill with tall houses lining the bank of the Alrance, linked to the road by an ancient humpbacked stone bridge reputedly dating from 1366. Facing all this is a recommended hotel/restaurant, *Relays du Chasteau*, tel: 65 99 40 15.

Cross the bridge (on foot only) and take the winding path up to the **castle** (open 14.00–18.00 May–Sept, 10.00–12.00 Jul–Sept). Brousse was first mentioned in the 10C and the considerable buildings have been consolidated and restored. Through the 13C gateway is a grassy area with the main building to the left. It is enclosed in a 15C enceinte incorporating earlier constructions. Almost totally intact, the ramparts follow the contours of the rock to make an irregular polygon, narrower at the south-east than the north-west, with a multitude of openings for a variety of weapons. A ditch was dug at the north-west early in its history and above it stood the highest tower in the region, la Picardie, dismantled in the 17C with only the base remaining. The oldest of a variety of towers, built towards the village, is 14C. The château stayed in the hands of the d'Arpajon family from the 13C until 1700. After the 15C they turned the main lodgings into something more habitable. These buildings contain the well, a bread oven (restored in the 19C), stables, large rooms with fireplaces and a 17C staircase. Some of the towers were also used as lodgings or as places of captivity. There is a little museum of tools and pieces of masonry, part of a menhir, stucco and furniture. A wonderful place for children.

The early Gothic church in the village and its cemetery replaced the chapel inside the fortified enclosure. A little rustic edifice, it has a small belfry and a very simple plate tracery rose window. A tiny house adjoins the east end.

From Brousse stay on the D902 for 5.5km, until it crosses the river and departs for Rodez. The road on the left bank becomes the D33 and follows the Tarn for about 5km when it leaves the river to climb up to **Coupiac**. Here is another imposing **castle** being slowly restored, but of a different character from Brousse-le-Château (open Easter–Oct, Jul–Sept, guided visits 10.00–19.00, tel: 65 99 79 45). Built in the 15C on a rock in the middle of the village, three high round towers bear down on it. There were probably four to start with, but the châtelain, Louis de Panat, was forced to dismantle a quarter of his castle by Louis XI after partipating in a local revolt in 1465, and the section between the north towers was rebuilt in the 16C and amendments continued until the 18C. Part fortification, part luxury residence, it has arrow slits, cannon holes, *chemin de ronde* and machico-lations for defence, ogee and mullioned windows, Renaissance dooways, fireplaces, two spiral staircases, a vaulted kitchen and latrines for comfort. It is also a *gîte*, with dormitory accommodation. For something like five centuries Coupiac has owned an authentic relic of the *saint-voile* (holy veil), hidden during the Wars of Religion and forgotten until a bull happened to uncover it. In 1968 an **oratory** was built behind the castle to display the relic and, still venerated, there is a pilgrimage at Assumption. The neo-Byzantine décor of the oratory was painted by Nicolas Greschny, born in 1912 in Estonia, who made his home in the Tarn.

Another relic is the beautiful 11C **tympanum** from the first church, Notre-Dame de Massiliergues, now under the archway west of the 19C **parish church**. Semi-circular, it has a monogram of Christ, or chrism, very unusual in the Rouergue, with a cabled outline inscribed in a tilted square. On either side are angels and small flowers or stars.

Some 8.5km (D60/D33) from Coupiac is the charming village of **Plaisance** with a gem of a little hotel-restaurant, *Les Magnolias*, for a real culinary treat, in a 14C house where Paul Valéry once lived (tel: 65 99 77 34). At the top of the hill in the village is a small **church**, part 12C, part 15C/16C. Steps lead up to the porch to a door with deep roll mouldings and bulbous capitals and bases. The apse is also decorated, and above the south transept door is an ancient re-used typmpanum with a chrism similar to Coupiac, flanked by two lions and daisies. Inside are storiated capitals, including Daniel in the lions' den at the crossing and leaping lions in the north-west transept. The crossing is covered by a lantern on pendentives supporting the chunky belfry.

Another good place to eat, just 11km up the road at **St-Sernin-sur-Rance**, is the *Hôtel-Restaurant Carayon* (tel: 65 99 60 26). The town is also the world centre for *gimblettes*, a small hard cake with caraway seed. Its third claim to fame is the statue, on Place du Fort, of the wild-boy of the Aveyron who is thought to have been raised by wolves. He first came to light in the district of Lacaune in 1798, and in 1800 he spent a few days at a house in St-Sernin-sur-Rance. François Truffaut made a film about him.

St-Sernin, on a spur high above the confluence of the Rance and the Merdanson, has a fine 16C/17C bridge and was an important medieval stronghold. In the older part of town to the south is the 15C Hôtel de Ville and the church of the same period with a square rustic belfry and a small bell. In the south wall above a sundial is a pretty stone rose window. Inside the church is a lierne-vaulted chapel with Christ and the four Evangelists on the bosses, carved brackets and a varied window tracery.

The start of the D999 to Alban has some dramatic hairpin bends. **Alban** is not a terribly inspiring place but in its modern **Church of Notre-Dame** is an interesting mixture of decoration and fittings. The west façade has modern abstract coloured glass by Bruno Schmeltz and an old balustrade. The portal is in late 18C style and the interior is decorated with murals (1957/58 and 1967) by Nicolas Greshny. A crowned Madonna and Child, possibly 16C, is on the main altar, and against the north wall is the most outstanding piece, a 16C **wayside cross** sculpted on three sides with scenes of the Passion. It was found in the old cemetery in 1927, and is considered the best of its kind in the Tarn.

Wind back down to the banks of the Tarn on the D53 and turn left on to the D77. On the approach to Ambialet (22.5km) there is an excellent view of the dramatic site where the Tarn forces its way through high cliffs to form a tight loop and a narrow isthmus. **Ambialet** (Tourist Information, tel: 63 55 32 07) is on the isthmus, and on the cliff above is a priory. Park on the river bank in the village. There is a small hydro-electric plant and the weir is the other side of an archway next to the 19C EDF building. When not in flood this is a pleasant walk. Over the bridge is the tried and trusted *Hôtel du Pont* (tel: 63 55 32 07).

The priory on the cliff can be reached on foot by following the stations of the cross up a path which starts near the car park, or you can go by road. At the summit is a wide terrace with spectacular views and a long flight of steps leading up to the west end of the little 11C **Church of Notre-Dame de l'Oder**. There is still a religious community in the priory but the much-restored church can be visited. The deep porch has four carved capitals supporting a square belfry and the interior is very plain and simple with huge square pillars and exposed stone. The three-bay nave is barrel vaulted and the aisles have half barrel vaults. There are shallow transepts and a trilobed east end.

From Ambialet it is 15.5km to **St-Juery** along the D172. As you arrive in St-Juery turn right (direction Arthes), crossing the Tarn at the Saut du Sabo, then turn immediately left and left again on the D70 to **Lescure**. The 12C Church of **St-Michel-de-Lescure** is signposted left (V4) just before Lescure centre (open afternoons July–Aug or when there are exhibitions) and, once part of a Benedictine abbey, it has the best **Romanesque sculptures** in the Albigeois. The **west door** has a wealth of sculpted decoration including four elaborately carved archivolts, mouldings, carved corbels and cornice, and capitals reminiscent of the Porte des Comtes at St-Sernin, Toulouse. The inner capitals have eagles and lions, and the outer ones the Sacrifice of Abraham, the Temptation of Adam and Eve, Lazarus and the Dives, and the sinful receiving punishment. The **east end** is also richly decorated. The nave has three bays with cruciform pillars and aisles but is covered by a wooden roof, as are the aisles and the crossing. The belfry collapsed at some point bringing down the cupola and and was rebuilt, as was the apse. There are a number of carved capitals of varying degrees of sophistication: at the entrance to the choir two storiated capitals, Jacob and Esau and Daniel in the lions' den; at the crossing, a rare floral motif, eagles, and lions rampant, all influenced by Moissac; several of the nave capitals are of a more traditional design, and include dragons with crossed tails and the Sacrifice of Abraham. There are several foliate capitals with the vein of the main leaf emphasised.

Go through Lescure passing the 16C brick gateway on your left and join the N88 which will bring you, in 3km, to the centre of Albi (see Route 33).

31

The Rougier and the Monts de Lacaune, the Abbey of Sylvanès

These excursions from Lacaune, between the *causses* of the southern Aveyron and the Monts de Lacaune at the eastern end of the Tarn, offer more scenery than monuments, although there are numerous dolmens and menhirs in the region and the Cistercian Abbey of Sylvanès.

LACAUNE (Tourist Information, tel: 63 37 04 98) is a small unpretentious spa nestling under slate roofs on the edge of the Monts de Lacaune in the Haut Languedoc Regional Park, midway between Albi, Millau and Béziers, excellently placed for the *causses* to the north and forests and lakes to the south. At an altitude of 800m, it is dominated by the peak of Montalet at 1260m. The town's main monument is the **fountain des Pisseurs** in Place du Griffoul, erected in 1559 by four consuls, a reminder, according to the publicity blurb, of the diuretic properties of the waters; symbolic of the four consuls say others. In the same square is a small folk museum, Le Musée du Vieux Lacaune. The church, built in 1668, has modern windows and a new organ which is used for recitals in the summer.

In the region of the Monts de Lacaune are a number of **menhirs**—monolithic blocks of flat stone usually carved on one face with rudimentary male or female features—created at the end of the Stone Age, c 3500–2500 BC, by peoples who lived in the Lacaune mountains. However, their symbolism and significance is still wreathed in mystery. They take some seeking out although one menhir stands outside the Tourist Information Office. Ask inside for more information and maps on how to find them.

Market day is Sunday. The Lacaune is famous for *charcuterie* and *salaisons* (sausage, cured and dried meats) and for the bottled water of Mont Roucous. The town and surrounding area caters well for visitors, and the *Hôtel Fusiès* (tel: 63 37 02 03) at the centre of town is a traditional French hotel owned by the same family for 300 years, with a highly recommended restaurant. The family also owns the Casino, 500m away, with numerous facilities.

The Rougier and the Abbey of Sylvanès

Total distance: 86km (54 miles).

Leave Lacaune by the D607 north-west, on the boundary of the *départements* of the Tarn and the Aveyron, through woods and views—the most spectacular panorama is at Roquecézière, 900m, dominated by a monumental statue of the Virgin. After 18km make a detour right on to the D645 to the small folk museum at **St-Crépin**, containing examples of menhir statues from the St-Sernin region (tel: 65 99 68 66, 10.00–12.00, 14.00–19.00, Jul–Aug). Return to the D607, turn right on to the D33, and go 7km before turning right again on to the D91. After 1km there is a turning left (C6) to **Notre-Dame d'Orient**, a beautiful hidden hamlet around a large redsandstone church. The austere and unadorned exterior has the date 1666 on the south-west gable above a huge sundial and a disproportionately small belfry on the east.

At the beginning of the 17C Franciscan friars re-established a community here after the Religious Wars and built a model Counter-Reformation church. The uncomplicated interior space is crammed with Baroque busyness on a predominantly blue background. The walls are covered with *trompe l'oeil* pilasters, candelabra, rinceaux and, behind the retable, draperies. The curved ceiling is the most original part, covered in wood panels in a sort of herringbone design. The altar is decorated with paintings in medallions and the retable is quite splendidly over-the-top with, in the centre, the Virgin and Child, crowned in gold. The central section is set off by pairs of Corinthian columns, and flanking it are statues of St Francis and Ste-Clair while the whole thing is liberally sprinkled with angels. The polychromed relief medallions contain saints important to the Franciscan order. There are more Baroque altarpieces in the chapels of the nave and the Ste-Marguerite chapel has a very fine worked leather antependium.

Return to the D91, a pretty up-and-down winding route following the Rance, past gentle pastures, tiny villages and deserted farmsteads. Continue for 7km to **Combret-sur-Rance**, a typical once-fortified medieval village of the southern Aveyron in an impressive site. It has an old *halle de justice* and a restored church with a fine porch.

An old bridge brings you after 9.5km to **Belmont-sur-Rance** (pop. 1000) on a hill above the Rance dominating the countryside with its celebrated 75m-tall crocketed spire, contemporary with the spire of Rodez Cathedral and in similar red sandstone. It stands over the west end of the Gothic collegiate **church** (1515–24) at the top of the village which has a fussy Flamboyant tympanum and Renaissance and Gothic fenestration in the tower. The houses near the church have some nice Renaissance details and the steep streets serve as gutters.

Leave on the D113/D51 to Camarès (19.5km) along the sinuous route following Rance Gorges. The *ville haute* and the lower town of **Camarès** are divided by the Rance which is spanned by a picturesque bridge with one very high and two smaller arches. This is a popular tourism centre with plenty of facilities and in the old town on the left bank is small hotel with a reasonable restaurant, *Hôtel du Vieux Point* (tel: 65 99 59 50). The area around Camarès is called the Rougier and derives its name from the red soil, a mixture of sandstone and marl.

Take the D12 out of Camarès for about 8km, turn right, go through **Montlaur** taking the D101 towards the north-west and then turn left after crossing the Grazou (about 4km). After 1.5km you will see on your right the **Château de Montaigut** (tel: 65 99 81 50, 10.00–12.00, 14.30–18.30, Easter to 1 Nov) atop a conical hill. The views over the Rougier de Camarès and the Grauzou valley are marvellous and sometimes stretch as far as the Monts de Lacaune.

The château, which has retained its early medieval, possibly 11C, layout, originally controlled the route from St-Affrique to Camarès and has been saved by a long programme of restoration. The huge château-keep, a massive but simple construction, is protected to the south by an enceinte around a courtyard with stables and outhouses. In the lower vaulted rooms are a deep cistern carved out of the rock and a cellar—safeguards against siege. The transformation from severe fortress to comfortable and decorative residence began in the 15C with the addition of a large fireplace and ogee doorway, and was carried further in the 17C, with the insertion of large windows, more fireplaces and sophisticated decoration in stucco known as *gypseries*. There is an exhibition on stucco and the plaster used was quarried and milled to the north-west of Montaigut. (These sites can be visited on foot, ask for the pamphlet *Sentier du Plâtre*.) There are other small exhibitions of archaeological finds and military architecture on the way up to the attic of the castle.

At the bottom of the track to the château is a small farmhouse which has been turned into a museum with geological exhibitions and a reconstructed farm interior of 1914 with commentary (press the button) on the upper floor. There is also a tiny church.

Return to the D101 and turn left towards **Gissac**, an amazingly empty, furrowed valley, typical of the Rougier with dark red soil and bright green vegetation. After Gissac take the D92/ D10 and turn left on the D540 to Sylvanès (15km).

The **Abbey of Sylvanès** (tel: 65 99 51 83, open 16 Mar–31 Dec, guided visits Jul–Aug) is in the green and wooded valley of the Cabot. It is one of several old abbeys in the Midi-Pyrénées which have experienced a renaissance in one form or another in the last twenty years or so. Sylvanès' new role is as an important cultural centre where courses are held nearly all year round and concerts in the summer.

It was founded in 1132 by a repentant brigand of noble birth, Pons de Léras, and four years later the community adopted the Cistercian rule. The **church**, a very fine example of Cistercian architecture, was begun c 1151 and its construction lasted nearly a century, resulting in an interesting juxtaposition of Romanesque and Gothic building techniques. The church was left almost untouched by the Calvinists and the Revolution although the monastic buildings fared less well. At first glance the abbey is a bit disappointing, the church crunched in a hollow against the side of the road. The west end is plain with just two small doors (for the dead to the north and the lay brothers to the south), and a Rayonnnant window with end-13C–early 14C glass and a small arcaded belfry over the crossing. The east is far more inspiring, the flat chevet pierced with four rose and three lancet windows, and a cornice of small arcades running around the exterior. Some of the wrought iron is 12C. Even more uplifting is the interior, with the play of light from the many windows on the uncluttered, beautifully porportioned elevations. The five-bay aisleless nave is a forerunner to the aisleless Gothic churches in the Midi. The nave, transepts and choir have pointed barrel vaults, whereas primitive rib vaults are introduced at the crossing and in the first bay of the nave. There is a door in the first bay of the nave which opened into the cloister and two doors in the south transept gave access to the monastic buildings.

Only the east wing of the **monastic buildings** has survived, plus an incomplete gallery of the **cloister**, probably built later than the rest, towards the end of the 13C. The rectangular sacristy with a low vault has a decorated tympanum over the door to the cloister and the chapter house has one single bay of vaulting with rectangular ribs springing from carved imposts in the angles. The walls were stuccoed in the 18C. Finest of all is the **monks' room** or scriptorium, saved from near ruin by an important programme of restoration, and used as a refectory or for concerts. Four central columns divide it into ten vaulted bays with rounded ribs similar to the chapter houses at Escaladieu and Flaran, although, built c 1160–80, it probably pre-dates either of these.

Return through **Bains-de-Sylvanès**, where the mineral waters were exploited in the 17C and 18C, and take the D92 to Fayet and the D12 to **Brusque** where, it is said, Thomas à Becket stayed. From here there is a choice of scenic routes to Murat-sur-Vèbre on the D922: the D92 along the Dourdou (19.5km), or the slightly longer D12 (26.5km).

Murat-sur-Vèbre (Saturday market) is a typical town of the Lacaune, where the houses huddled together shoulder to shoulder are not only roofed in slate but have overlapping slate shingles on exposed walls. There is an 11C church and all around are magnificent beech forests, glorious until late autumn. Between here and Lacaune, either side of the D622, are the **menhirs**, some signposted. There are two off the D169 north, more around **Moulin-Mage**, one at Rieuviel, one in the middle of a farmyard at **Haute-Vergne**, and a huge one in a field on the left of the D622 not far before the junction with the D607.

The Lakes

Total distance: 71km (44 miles).

The second itinerary from Lacaune is a scenic drive around the large lakes to the south, and another chance to go menhir hunting, a sort of monumental treasure hunt for children, with the bonus of a beach at the end for swimming.

Leave Lacaune to the east on the D622 and branch off to the right after 8.5km on the D62 to the **Lake of Laouzas** (7km). By turning left on to the D162 you come to the beach but the road continues on around the lake, through the village of Villelongue to the dam at the south. A further 7.5km brings you to **Salvetat-sur-Agout**, in the Hérault, an important tourist centre on the cliffs beside the Agout. Although it is categorised as one of the *plus beaux villages de France*, with its tall, austere slate clad houses catching the sunlight, it is not a run-of-the-mill picturesque village. Nearby are plenty of water-based activities on the Lake La Raviège with a beach at the west.

32

Castres

CASTRES (pop. 50,000, Tourist Information Théâtre Municipal, tel: 63 71 56 58 and 63 35 26 26) is a pleasant, leafy, prosperous town in the southern Tarn built mainly in stone on the banks of the Agout. It is comparable in size although less well-known than Albi and without the same visual excitement but with a charm and character of its own. At the centre of an important agricultural region, there is an excellent and very friendly market four times a week (Tues, Thur, Fri, Sat). The town owns an important collection of Spanish art exhibited in the Goya Museum, and holds the Goya music festival in July. Castres is convenient for Albi and, over the Montagne Noire, Carcassonne. There is plenty of accommodation of all categories and other facilities available and, on the edge of the Regional Park of the Haut Languedoc—encompassing the Sidobre, the Montagne Noire and the Monts de Lacaune—it is an ideal base for the pursuit of outdoor activities.

History. An important stage on the Via Tolosane to Santiago, Castres had a major Cathar community at the end of the 12C, and was elevated to a bishopric by Pope John XXII in 1317, a status it maintained until 1801. The town enthusiastically embraced Calvinsim to become a Protestant place of safety second only in the Region to Montauban. In 1576 Henri IV helped the peaceful return of the Catholics with the institution of the Chambre de l'Edit to legislate over disputes between Protestants and Catholics. Between the Edict of Alès in 1629, and the Revocation of the Edict of Nantes, 1685, Castres enjoyed its most brilliant period: the population increased, monasteries were reinstated and most of the town was rebuilt. Architects were introduced from the Ile de France to build a new episcopal palace and design a garden typical of the Grand Siècle. Despite the Neo-Classical emphasis, the most emblematic buildings, in an area whose economy has been based on leather and textiles since the Middle Ages, are the medieval houses of the textile and leather workers on the banks of the Agout. Castres was the birthplace in the 19C of the politician and pacifist, Jean Jaurès, and there is a small museum devoted to his life.

On Foot. There is some parking in front of the **Tourist Information Office** installed on the ground floor of the theatre. The **Municipal Theatre**, opened in 1904, was designed by Joseph Galinier of Toulouse, a pupil of Garnier, architect of the Paris Opera House, and restored in 1982. It is an imposing *Belle-Epoque* building, and is used for all types of shows, concerts and exhibitions, and can be visited. Opposite is the former **Episcopal Palace**, used by the Hôtel de Ville and the Goya Museum. Jules Hardouin-Mansart drew up the plans for this soberly classical building, inaugurated in 1675. Around three sides of a courtyard with a monumental staircase, the unadorned façade serves as a backdrop to the dark greens of the yew trees and box hedges of the **formal garden** designed by Louis XIV's gardener, André Le Nôtre (1613–1700). Planted on the site of the southern ramparts and ditch, the garden began to take shape in 1696. The knot-gardens nearest the palace have box hedges trimmed into a fleur-de-lys pattern and the yews have a variety of designs. Along the river is an avenue of limes as old as the garden and new trees are being prepared for a takeover. The chestnuts are a mere 80 years or so old.

The **Goya Museum** (tel: 63 71 59 30, closed Mon except July, Aug), on the first floor of the Bishops' Palace, is a very pleasant, usually quiet, museum with an excellent collection of Spanish works. Inspired by the donation in 1893, by the son of the local painter Marcel Briguiboul (1837–92) of three paintings and complete sets of etchings by Goya, the museum has concentrated on Spanish works since 1947, and regional funding since 1972 has helped to make this one of the most important Spanish collections in France. The museum often holds temporary exhibitions with a Spanish bias.

The **Spanish primitives** (14C–15C) are among some of the most beautiful works in the museum. A large part of the collection is of works from the golden age of Spanish painting in the 17C. These include a replica of the Prado Portrait of Philip IV (1634–36) attributed to Velazquez (1595–1660), a sweetly gentle *Virgin Mary with a Rosary* (c 1650) by Murillo, and Zurbaran's *Carthusian Martyr* (c 1636). There are works by Francisco Pacheco, by Coello, a Juan de Valdés (1622–90) room and an Alonso Cano (1601–67) room.

The room dedicated to **Goya** (1746–1828) has three of his works, and paintings inspired by him. The masterpiece is the calm, self-assured **Self-Portrait with Glasses** (c 1797–1800) painted some years after his illness. The second portrait is of **Don Francisco del Mazo** (c 1815). Filling the whole of the end wall of the gallery is the huge **Session of the Royal Company of the Philippines** (1815), an atmospheric work with a veiled criticism of bureaucracy. The museum also owns original prints of Goya's Los Capricos, the Disasters of War, and Los Proverbios, as well as Tauromachy. Among the modern works is a token Picasso.

Leave by the courtyard. On the north-west side is the Tour St-Benoit, c 1100, the last remaining fragment of the Abbey of St-Benoit, with a 17C roof, and opposite is the large and ordered south flank of the Baroque **Cathedral St-Benoit**. Begun in 1678 and consecrated in 1718, the project was never completed to the specifications originally envisaged by the architect Guillaume Caillau. The interior is rather dreary in spite of the *trompe l'oeil*, but there is some nice woodwork and a number of large paintings by Cammas, de Rivals and Despax. The coloured marble altar of 1763 is covered by a grandiose baldaquin made in 1768 by the Cailhive workshop.

Back in the daylight, go round the east end of the cathedral where the space is enhanced by an elegant 19C colonnade made from columns salvaged from the old abbey and a small square, **Place du 8 Mai 1945**, the only sizeable square in the town centre before the Revolution. The Passage St-Vincent opens into one of the main commercial streets, **Rue Alquier-Bouffand**, which was almost entirely rebuilt after a fire in 1724. Turn right to the Pont Neuf.

The most original features of the town are the colourful timber **craftsmen's houses** on the banks of the Agout whose bases are large arcaded stone cellars, perhaps 14C, opening directly into the river. These houses were once the homes and workshops of tanners, weavers and dyers. They were restored in 1979 and, for better or for worse, restoration is still continuing. From the **Quai des Jacobins** is another good view of them, and the pleasure boat *le Miredames* (tel: 63 71 56 58, Apr–Nov) leaves from across the Pont Vieux to make a half-hour trip to Gourjade Park, an open air leisure centre.

The **market** (Tues, Thurs, Fri, Sat) is held on **Place Jean-Jaurès**, a tree-lined square created in the medieval heart of Castres in 1872, adorned with a pretty fountain with angels at one end and a statue of Jean Jaurès at the other. In Rue Malpas, *La Mandragone* restaurant (tel: 63 59 51 27) is recommended.

Take Rue Emile Zola from the west of Place Jean-Jaurès, and turn right into Rue Frédérick Thomas. **Hôtel de Nayrac** on the left (occupied by Société Générale) was built in 1620 by a wealthy draper, Jean Oulès, using brick and stone, in the manner of the Renaissance mansions of Toulouse or Albi. The three linked façades have elegantly decorated dormers, and the main entrance, flanked by paired Doric pilasters with a huge coat of arms, is on the right. A screen wall closes the courtyard and under the arcades on the street were, originally, boutiques. The plaster has been removed from the 17C façades of Nos 14 and 16 uncovering the timber frame, known in Castres as *corondat*.

Place Pélisson, a small smart junction decorated with a fountain, has a Renaissance style building at No. 8, a nice-looking restaurant (*La Feuillantine*, tel: 63 59 26 33), and a tea shop as well as the **Centre National et Musée Jean-Jaurès** (tel: 63 72 01 01, closed Mon, except Jul and Aug). Attractively installed in an old printing works since 1988 it records the life and work of Jean Jaurès, socialist leader, parliamentary orator, journalist and historian born in Castres on 3 September 1859 and assassinated on 31 July 1914. Deputy for the Tarn in 1885, in 1889–93 he turned to socialism and championed causes such as the miners' strikes in Carmaux, independence of the glassworkers in Albi, and Dreyfus. He was described as the apostle of peace but his pacifist ideals led to his assassination on the eve of the First World War. The museum has a permanent exhibition, documentation centre, and holds temporary exhibitions.

Turn left on Rue Sabaterie, and left again. From No. 4 to No. 14 **Rue des Boursiers** there is a string of 16C and 17C façades, and No. 1 has a late Gothic doorway. Turn left into **Rue Emile Zola** and right into Rue Tuboeuf. **Rue de l'Hôtel de Ville** runs parallel with Rue E. Zola. Linking them is another old street, **Rue Victor Hugo**, with Castres' second religious monument, **Eglise de la Platé**, rebuilt in 1743 by the Jesuits, and sought after for its organ. The accomplished Italianate façade on Rue Victor-Hugo superimposes Doric and Ionic orders. Squashed between the buildings around it, the Florentine style campanile can best be seen from Rue de la Platé.

The Baroque interior has a grandiose main altar flanked by six red marble columns supporting a canopy and the retable in Carrara marble of an Assumption of the Virgin by Italian artists, 1754. There are paintings by the ubiquitous Despax, of a Visitation and an Annunciation. The superb organ with a sumptuous gilded organ case supported by atlantes and adorned with angel musicians, was installed in 1764 and decorated by a local artist called Chabbert. It was restored by Alfred Kern from Strasbourg in 1980 and is used for concerts.

Opposite Rue de la Platé, in **Rue de la Chambre de l'Edit**, is the **Hôtel de Viviès**, built in 1585. Considered one of the best pieces of late Renaissance architecture in the town, it was corrupted with Baroque additions and the whole building is rather tired looking. Nevertheless it has been brought into the context of the 20C by the **Centre d'Art Contemporain** (tel: 63 59 30 20, open every day) for resolutely modern exhibitions.

Rue Tolosane, at the west end of Rue de la Chambre de l'Edit, is flanked by two piers of the old **Porte Tolosane**. **Hôtel de Poncet**, Rue Gabriel Guy, is an elegant building with a balustraded terrace supported by caryatids and a loggia with Ionic columns reached by a monumental cantilevered staircase.

Rue de la Chambre de l'Edit brings you back to the Théâtre Municipal.

The Sidobre

Total distance: 76km (48 miles).

Immediately north-east of Castres is the granite plateau of **the Sidobre**, 600–700m, on the edge of the Massif Central. Wooded in places, scrubby moorland or marshes elsewhere, the attractions of the Sidobre are scenic and its main curiosities are the strange biomorphic rock formations. Giant granite boulders, smoothed and rounded by time, isolated or in a tumbled confusion called a *chaos*, have acquired descriptive names: *Roc de l'Oie* (goose rock), *Trois Fromages*, *Chapeau du Curé*, etc. This is an area for walks and picnics, beside the Lac du Merle or the valleys and gorges of the Agout.

The most significant architectural site in the Sidobre is just 9km from Castres on the D89/D58, the small village of **Burlats** in woods beside the Agout. The **Church of St-Peter** was part of a large Benedictine Priory founded c 1160. It was wrecked during the Religious Wars. The sacristy on the north is occupied by the Mairie and the remains of the Romanesque cloisters are now the schoolyard. The east end of the Romanesque church is mainly intact, so is the north transept door in the form of a triumphal arch with the remains of two carved capitals, one with birds the other storiated. The west door has a similar but more elaborate arrangement of a triple portal and seven vigorously sculpted capitals once supported by slender columns. The skeletal ruin of the nave is separated from the chancel by a double transverse arch and some of the capitals, decorated with heads and volutes, have survived.

Standing isolated near the river is the ravishing **Pavilion of Adelaïde**, a rare masterpiece of Romanesque secular architecture, named after a legendary lady remembered in the songs of troubadours. A simple rectangular stone building, it has recently undergone a careful restoration and its outstanding features are the beautiful two-light windows on the upper floor—four on the south façade and one on the west—carved with a variety of motifs. The floors are divided by stringcourses on which the upper windows rest. The first floor has large and small openings, and at ground level are three arched openings (as found at Figeac or Cordes).

The **Bistoure Tower** to the east was part of the Gothic ramparts, and near the bridge is the 12C **Maison d'Adam** with the outlines of one Romanesque window. Its carved elements found their way to the USA.

Turn left over the bridge, and left again on to the D4, 7km to **Roquecourbe**, an old textile town on the Agout with overhanging houses around the square. From here the D55 follows the winding route of the Agout through wooded gorges for 21km to the little schist town of **Vabre** (Tourist Information, tel: 63 50 40 12) overlooking the Gijou, once an important textile centre, its medieval bridge revised in the 19C. It now hosts several fairs, festivals and sporting events throughout the summer.

8km along the D53 is the **château** at **Ferrières**, the grandiose home of the Calvinist leader, Guillaume Guilhot, governor of Castres in 1562. A medieval castle that was revamped over several centuries it has been sadly neglected and its magnificence is crumbling. There are still, however, many traces of the wholesale application of early-Renaissance idiom to bring it into line with the desire for luxury and comfort in the 16C. On the other side of the road there is a Protestant Museum (tel: Mairie, 63 74 03 58, open Jul–Aug) in the Maison du Luthier which follows the history of the Huguenots in the Haut Languedoc. The road continues around the Sidobre to **Brassac** (7km), another schist and slate town on the Agout with a Gothic cobbled bridge and a 17C château at each end. It is close to the Forest of Castelnau and on the route to the lakes (Route 31). The D622 west brings you 24km back to Castres.

At **Lafontasse** is a Renaissance church with a tabernacle.

The natural phenomena of the Sidobre can be explored further on the D30 and D58.

Mazamet, the Montagne Noire and Sorèze

Total distance: 52km (33 miles).

This is the gateway to the **Haut-Languedoc Regional Park**, 145,000ha of natural beauty, wild flowers, beech, conifers, and of wildlife, a walking centre par excellence with 1800km of signposted paths. The **Pic de Nore**, 1210m, is the highest peak of the Black Mountains, from where you can see Monts de Lacaune and the Pyrenees. Guided walks in the park from Arfons, near Dourgne, every Tuesday in July and August (tel: 63 70 31 10).

17km south-east of Castres on the N112 is **Mazamet** (pop. 11,500, Tourist Information, tel: 63 61 27 07) enclosed in the Montagne Noire. An essentially modern town and gastronomic centre at an important junction, it revolves around the Place de l'Hôtel de Ville, and still has a Protestant community. The Temple Protestant is indicated by the medieval tower of St-Jacques, and the Catholic Church of St-Sauveur was built in 1740. In Maison Fuzier (tel: 63 98 99 76) is the local history museum, Musée Mémoire de la Terre, of burial rites in the Albigeois over the centuries.

The D118/D54 climb steeply out of Mazamet into the forest 5km, to **Hautpoul**, a village vertiginously perched above the Arnette valley, a Cathar stronghold fortified by Pierre Raymond d'Hautpoul in the 12C, beseiged by Simon de Montfort in 1212, then ravaged during the Religious wars, with parts since salvaged.

Come back down to the D118 (Carcassonne to the south) and at Mazamet either take the very small winding D53 on the edge of the mountain, or return to the D621 through **Labruguière** (16km) an industrial centre with an ancient town at its heart built in concentric circles. It also has the Musée Arthur Batut (tel: 63 50 22 18, Apr–Sept). Inventor of aerial photography in 1888, Batut was born in Castres in 1846.

Massaguel (D85/D50, 9km) is a charming village with a non-visitable château and a church with modern glass. 2km from Massaguel is **Dourgne**, a small town with a large fountain, arcades and a winding route, on the D12, up into the forested slopes around the little mountain village of **Arfons** (660m) on the ancient pilgrimage route, and 3km from the Lac du Lampy. On the Castres side of Dourgne are the abbeys of Ste-Scholastique, built between 1895 and 1927, and **St-Benoît-d'En Calcat**, 1890–1936, two Benedictine houses. The brotherhood publishes religious books, and has a shop selling books and other crafts they produce. Stay on the D85 for 7.5km.

Sorèze (Tourist Information, tel: 63 74 10 22, and the Maison du Parc Regional, tel: 63 74 11 58/63 74 16 28), enclosed within avenues of plane trees, is a most attractive and well-to-do small town with jettied houses. The **Collège de Sorèze** has been a private school since 1682. On the site of a Benedictine abbey, founded early in the 9C and affiliated to Moissac in 1119, but totally destroyed during the Religious Wars, the Benedictines of the Congregation of St-Maur rebuilt the abbey in 1637 and later opened the school for the sons of impecunious gentlefolk. In 1776 it was elevated to Royal Military Establishment. One of its most famous pupils was the future South American statesman Simon Bolivar (1783–1830).

The crenellated tower and octagonal belfry of **St-Martin**, towering above the college and the village, are all that remains of the 15C parish church. The remains of the apse below the tower are open and unprotected since the church disappeared exposing the Flamboyant decoration in the interior.

2km away is the miniscule but remarkably active copper village of **Durfort**, with several shops and a small Copper Museum (tel: 63 74 22 77, June–Sept). There are lakes at **Cammazes** and **St-Ferréol** which supply water to the Canal du Midi, and they provide a refreshing summer interlude.

33

Albi

ALBI (pop. 46,579, Tourist Information Place Ste-Cécile, tel: 63 54 22 30) is the best known and most decorative of the brick towns of the Tarn and Garonne valleys, eliciting many comparisons with Tuscany and much pink prose. Yet the ochres, roses, reds and purples do not disappoint. The cathedral, on a spur above the Tarn, dominates and protects the town beneath it. Albi's most famous son, Henri Marie Raymond de ToulouseLautrec Monfa (1864–1901), was born in a house in the old town and the Albi museum contains the largest single collection of his works. Albi is well served by roads, with a new autoroute linking it to Toulouse and by rail and air connections (flights to Paris and Lyon). It makes a perfect centre from which to explore the whole of the *département* of the Tarn, Toulouse, and the southern Aveyron. It is very well equipped with hotels and restaurants. In the town centre are the *Hostellerie St-Antoine* (tel: 63 54 04 04) and the *Hôtel Chiffre* (tel: 63 54 04 60) and nearer the station the *Hôtel d'Orléans*, (tel: 63 54 16 56), all family run hotels. On the outskirts of Albi beside the river is the luxury *Hôtel la Réserve* (tel: 63 47 60 22).

History. Settled by the 4C BC, Civitas Albigensium was mentioned for the first time c 400 and was head of a diocese in the 5C. By the 7C the *cité* was taking shape under the shared power of the Church and the Counts. At the break-up of the Carolingian Empire the Counts of Albi became vassals of the Counts of Toulouse but the infamous Trencavels, Counts of Béziers, Carcassonne and Albi, protectors of Cathars and self-styled counts, rivalled them in the 13C until the Albigensian Crusade (1209–29). Contrary to popular misconception, the town was not beseiged during the Crusade and the nominal connection possibly refers to the region. Some half century after the Crusade, the Orthodox Bishops undertook the rebuilding of the cathedral as a symbol of their sovereignty. Despite the usual problems of the Middle Ages, the town's prosperity increased during the late 15C and 16C thanks largely to *pastel*. At about the same time two Bishops of Albi, Louis I and Louis II of Amboise, great patrons of the arts, decorated the interior of the cathedral. The metallurgical, mining and glass industries, which developed in the 19C, have mainly disappeared.

On Foot. Place du Vigan, created in the 18C, marks the divide between the medieval quarter and the modern town. It extends south with a pleasantly tree-covered area where a clothing and hardware market are held on Saturdays. The description give below concentrates on the old town, signalled by the medieval tower above the offices of La Dépêche. Note that the town makes a feature of signposting the streets with their old Occitan names as well the modern ones.

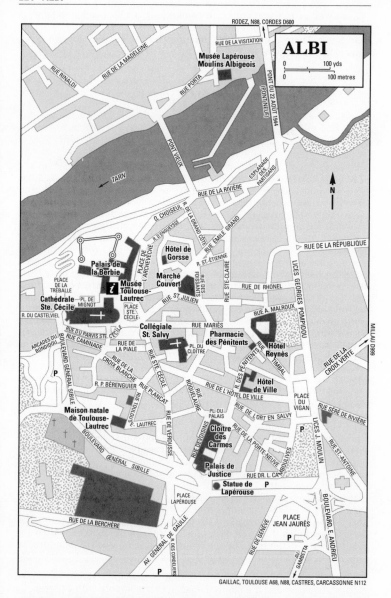

At No. 14 **Rue Timbal**, north-west of the *place*, is the **Hôtel de Reynès**, built by a rich *pastel* merchant c 1520. The small Italianate courtyard is the most sophisticated of the period in Albi, combining a stairtower in the tradition of Gothic buildings with the elegance of a Renaissance loggia. On the south façade are two busts in medallions, reputedly of François I and

Claude de France. Almost opposite, on the corner of Rue des Pénitents, is the 16C **Maison Enjalbert** or **Pharmacie des Pénitents**, an outstanding timber-framed house using the vocabulary of the Renaissance, triangular pediments, Ionic and Corinthian pilasters. Turn left into **Rue Mariès**. The massive south flank of the cathedral suddenly looms into focus. On the left is the slightly run-down **Place du Cloître** at the east end of the **collegiate Church of St-Salvy** with one 12C stone chapel and a thrusting 15C brick structure. The sign to the *cloître* takes you through a passageway to the modest and secret cloistral remains with just one gallery left, Romanesque-going-on-Gothic, begun in 1270. The tomb of Vidal de Malvési, creator of the cloister, and his brother, is against the church. Salvy was made Bishop in the late 6C and in 943 his relics were translated to this site. The cult of St-Salvy was widely venerated in this region during the early Middle Ages.

Interior. Despite successive modifications from the 12C to the 18C, the interior is quite harmonious, if gloomy. The lower parts of the four east bays, completed c 1100, are heavily restored. Lateral chapels were added during the 14C and 15C and the chancel and two preceding bays, rebuilt in the 15C, are Flamboyant. Louis d'Amboise consecrated a new altar in 1490. The clerestory was added in the 18C, as was the rose window. The early 16C organ was transferred from the cathedral in 1737 by Moucherel, and is used for concerts. Behind a wrought-iron screen is a group of c 15C polychrome figures (light switch on the right), an Ecce Homo and members of the Sanhedrin. A replica of the 12C wooden image of St-Salvy stands behind the ornate Baroque altar with a baldaquin of 1721. The original Romanesque north entrance has been almost obliterated by a pedimented version but the sculpted capitals are still in place. The three-tiered belfry, the **Tour de la Gâche**, on the right is a text-book example of changing styles and proves that Albi was once more white than red. The Romanesque base, c 1080, with Lombard style blind arches and the second stage, c 1220–40, both in white stone, are topped off with a late-14C brick crown and watchtower.

Turn left into **Place Ste-Cécile**. On the far right is the Bishops' Palace and the **Tourist Information Office**. The austere and inscrutable fortress of faith, the **CATHEDRAL OF SAINT CECILIA**, totally dominates the square. A great undulating heap of brick that looks as if it were tipped all of a piece from a celestial mould, it epitomises southern or meridional Gothic with none of the fractured restlessness of the High Gothic of northern France. It took about 100 years to build, at a time of sprirtual renewal and pecuniary rigour, between 1282 and 1383. Basically a skeletal structure supported by buttressing with non load-bearing walls, its originality is due both to the brick, a cheaper and faster means of building, and to the massive rounded buttresses which echo, and were probably inspired by, the fortifications of the adjacent Bishops' Palace. Its seriousness reflects the cause of its main champion, Chief Inquisitor Bernard de Castanet, Bishop of Albi (1277–1307), in reaffirming the authority of the Roman Catholic Church following the subversive effects of the Cathar heresies in the 12C with a church that resembles a fort. There are no walls of glass, possibly a question of economy, or as protection against southern sun, and the lower lancet windows were added in the 15C. The silhouette of the cathedral was altered in the 19C during work to solve the problem of water infiltration when the roof, which originally had wide overhanging eaves and rested directly on the vaults, was raised by the architect César Daly, a disciple of Viollet-le-Duc. The 19C work is demarcated by the gargoyles and the lighter brick. Daly began prettifying the roofline with small belfries to match one already existing, but local disapproval led to their demolition. The cathedral stands isolated like a beached ship since the houses that surrounded it were cleared away in the 18C–19C.

Savour it. Follow the south flank along Rue du Parvis Ste-Cécile. The Bondidou River, now underground, precluded a west entrance. Cross the road to the car park and go down the **Arcades du Bondidou** for a sensational view of the cathedral then turn right at the end to join **Place du Château** and the very ancient quarter of Castelviel with its miniscule *places*. **Rue du Castelviel** is overwhelmed by the 78m tiered belfry of the cathedral. The tower, built between 1355 and 1366, is articulated by quarter-circle relieving arches between great rounded buttresses but the rhythm changes in the octagonal upper level, 1485–92. From **Place de la Tréballe** there are steps down to the *Berges du Tarn* (riverbank).

Follow the north flank of the cathedral past the small door which was reserved for the clergy and down Rue de la Temporalité, into the light of **Place Ste-Cécile**. Head for the sole public entrance to the **Cathedral** on the south, going through the archway built by Bishop Dominique de Florence (1397–1410) using a rounded tower that was part of the fortifications of the episcopal city, and climbing up to the entrance under the early 16C crocketed Flamboyant baldaquin and filigree tympanum. The sculptures of the entrance were remade by César Daly between 1865 and 1870 when the baldaquin was closed in.

Interior. Nothing quite prepares you for the contrast. After crossing the threshold of the Flamboyant vestibule c 1510–20, often from bright sunlight to initial gloom, there is a moment of shock, even recoil, faced with the excesses of the interior. The interior was transformed in the calm years of nascent humanism before the Reformation. A basically simple, unified space, without aisles, the interior buttresses form the lateral chapels and support a rib vault rising to a height of 30m. The coherence of this space was disrupted before the end of the 15C by the elaborate choir enclosure. The two great bishops, uncle and nephew, Louis I (1474–1503) and Louis II (1504–10) of Amboise, were responsible for the metamorphosis—two powerful men from a great family of prelates and ambassadors with access to the latest artistic trends in the Loire, in Burgundy and in Italy. There is no written documentation extant relating to the work as all the archives of the cathedral were destroyed during the Revolution. The all-over *trompe-l'oeil* pattern of the chapels and walls conceived c 1509–20 has been subjected to numerous restorations, especially in the 19C.

The **Last Judgement** on the west wall is thought to date from the time of Louis I, whose striped colours fill the lower space. This is the largest surviving wall painting of the period in France and was probably executed by Franco-Flemish artists, contemporaneous with Hieronymous Bosch. Applied directly to the brick, it covers some 200 square metres. The composition is organised according to tradition but there is one disturbing omission: the key figure of Christ in Judgement. In the 17C different priorities permitted the piercing of an opening through the wall to the chapel where the relics of the first Bishop of Albi, St-Clair, lie and consequently this work is arranged around a void.

The composition is divided vertically, the blessed on the right of the void, lined up in orderly fashion on a calm blue ground, and opposite, with a murky ground, is hell in all its confusion. It is also divided horizontally into three main registers and Heaven is subdivided into three hierarchies: angels, the 12 apostles, and a line-up of the saved with St-Louis and Charlemagne, and others now unidentifiable. Below is the theatre of the

Resurrection where those mortals already judged hold the Book of Life open on their chests. Opposite them sinners are thrown back to the underworld. The bottom register is Hell, depicted in as much horror as the artists could muster and compartmentalised into scenes representing each of the seven deadly sins which are annotated in old French, from left to right: Pride, Engy, Anger or Wrath, Sloth is missing, Avarice or Greed, Gluttony and Lust, each with the appropriately grisly punishments.

In quite a different artistic timbre, high above this didactic message, is the splendidly Baroque Moucherel **organ** (1734–36) supported by two muscular atlantes. The carved case is mainly in oak, and the figures, including the joyful angel musicians, are in lime. Restored to its original sounds in 1981, it is one of the best instruments in France and is frequently used for recitals. When the need to accommodate large congregations arose after the destruction of several parish churches at the Revolution, the main altar was placed at the west in the 19C to avoid opening out the east end which would have necessitated dismantling the precious Gothic choir enclosure. The black marble altar with enamels was made by two Parisian artists, Jean-Paul Froidevaux and his wife, in 1980.

The magnificent Flamboyant **jubé**, c 1474–84, which divides the nave from the chancel, a profusion of ogees and lacework, pinnacles and broccoli leaves, was carved in tender limestone which has hardened over the centuries. The cutting and under-cutting of this scintillating work is a tribute to the technical virtuosity of French stonecarvers. The original 75 statues in the niches have disappeared; those that are there are replacements.

The visit to the **choir** is a few francs well spent. Around the ambulatory, on the outside of the choir enclosure, is a procession of magnificent late-15C (c 1480) **polychromed statues**. They represent Old Testament prophets, priests and kings, those who have not yet seen the light but predict or prefigure the Coming of Christ. Inside the entrance, turn to face the door, for the ultimate **Virgin of the Annunciation**, her sweet face framed by long hair and her hand on the Bible, as she receives the message of the Angel Gabriel on her left (on the exterior of the enclosure). Of the 48 large format sculptures over 30 are around the ambulatory. They are in excellent condition but would benefit from a thorough restorative clean. The figures stand in ornate niches, most carry a banderole and several are identified by name. The image makers, who counted some Flemish among them, had a penchant for the anecdotal and descriptive use of costume and fashion, but also the expressive quality of each individual. Note **Isaiah**, looking a bit like a prosperous bourgeois merchant, and **Jeremiah**, appropriately grave. **Simeon**, the High Priest of the Temple, at the axis, is the linchpin between the Ancient and the New Law. His importance places him on the opposite side of the screen from the Virgin and Child. (Below Simeon is a plaque commemorating the quick action of a local official to save many of the 254 original carvings from destruction at the Revolution.) The only other women are **Esther** and **Judith**, the latter wearing a rich red brocade dress hanging in heavy folds and a bejewelled headdress. The two great Christian Emperors, **Charlemagne** and **Constantine**, stand sentinel opposite each other over the north and south entrances to the choir. Inside the choir (enter on the north) are the **Apostles**, those who have seen the light, but the carvings are not as accomplished as the ones of those that went before. Seek out at the west end, on the reverse of the *jubé*, the small but voluptuous **St Cecilia** with her attributions, a crown of roses and lilies, a portative organ and a martyr's palm. All around the western part of the chancel, above the 120 oak stalls, are 70 delicately sculptured **child angels**, each holding a musical instrument or scroll, and above them are the Arms of Louis d'Amboise. The canopy of the **Episcopal throne** is a tour de force of undercutting. The modern altar table of white marble is a refreshingly simple piece.

What little medieval glass, c 1320–25, there is, is in the high windows at the east. Works in the chapels include a fresco of the Resurrection and The Legend of the True Cross (c 1460–70), both heavily restored. In the east chapel are four paintings sent from Rome by Cardinal de Bernis in the 18C.

The **vaults** were **painted** between 1509 and 1512 by Bolognese artists who worked suspended in baskets. The iconographic programme, like the chancel statues, unites the Old and New Testaments. The New Testament figures are painted in gold, the others in silver, on a deep blue ground, and have hardly been touched since they were painted. The scenes are arranged in the form of a triumphal procession from west to east with St Cecilia in the centre, and tell of the return of man to God under the guidance of the Church culminating in the Christ of the Second Coming surrounded by the symbols of the four Evangelists. On the boss nearest to the organ are the 11 fleurs-de-lys, the arms of France in the 14C. Among the scenes most easily recognisable reading from west to east are the Last Supper, the Transfiguration, the Coronation of the Virgin, St Cecilia and Valerian, the Annunciation, then Cecilia and Valerian again at each extremity of the next bay, the parable of the Wise and Foolish Virgins, the Coronation of the Virgin again, and the Tree of Life. Adam and Eve are easy to recognise in the east bay. This significant work was the first major example of Italian Renaissance art in the Midi, and compares very closely to the decoration of churches near Pavia in Northern Italy.

In the north-west chapel, the Chapel of the Rosary, is a 14C **Sienese polyptych**. In the north-east chapel of the nave is a disagreeable modern reproduction of a statue in St Cecilia in the Trastevere, Rome, as she was found in her tomb in 1599.

Before tackling Toulouse-Lautrec you might take the opportunity for a breather in one of the loveliest places in Albi, the **Gardens of the Bishops' Palace**. Make as if going to the museum, but at the foot of the steps turn left and take the short cobbled incline which brings you to a terrace high above the Tarn. As you move forward to the edge of the terrace the river, spanned by the old and newer bridges to the right and the rail bridge to the left, comes into view framed by the brick façades of the old suburb of La Madeleine opposite. On the horizon is what appears to be a replica of the cathedral. (This is the 19C Church of **Notre-Dame de la Drèche**, 5km away (N88 north, D90), with an important painted interior. On the site of a 13C church, it is an ancient place of pilgrimage and shelters the 12C statue of the Madonna of La Drèche.) On the right is the great mass of the **Palais de la Berbie**, the name derived the from old Occitan word *Bisbia* meaning Bishops' Palace. Archbishop Hyacinthe Serroni (1678–87) installed the formal garden and the vine-shaded walk on the old ramparts, reached via the steps in the south-west corner. The statues in the alcoves are 18C.

The Berbie, both palace and fortress, is a powerful building of disparate parts, begun in the second half of the 13C by Bishop Durand de Beaucaire and completed by Bishop Bernard de Castanet c 1277, to protect their authority vis à vis the town and as part of the town's defences. Built entirely in brick, tamed and modified over the centuries, its architecture complements the cathedral. The oldest part is the **Tour Notre-Dame** on the east overlooking Place de l'Archevêché. The mighty **Tour St-Michel** on the west was completed in 1277 while the bastions along the Tarn were probably constructed during the Hundred Years War. The Bishops of Amboise amended the east wing and Bishop Gaspard Daillon de Lude added the *salon doré* and the monumental staircase. By 1790 the building was taken over by the State although the episcopal see was reinstated in 1823.

Used for temporary exhibitions and, during the Albi Summer Festival, open air concerts, the main function of the Berbie since 1922 has been to house the **TOULOUSE-LAUTREC MUSEUM** (tel: 63 54 14 09, daily Easter–1 Oct, rest of year closed Tues). The museum owns 210 paintings and more than 600 drawings, lithographs and posters by Toulouse-Lautrec, the majority of which were donated by his mother, Countesse Adèle, encouraged by Lautrec's oldest friend and supporter, the art dealer Maurice Joyant. It also has an eclectic collection ranging from local archaeology, two superb authenticated paintings by Georges de la Tour (1593–1652), and one by Guardi (1712–93) as well as a vast group of 19C and 20C works by local artists and by such notables as Corot, the Pont-Aven Group, Vuillard, Bonnard, Matisse and Dufy and sculptures by Rodin, Bourdelle and Maillol.

Henri de Toulouse-Lautrec is a legendary figure, a direct descendant of one of the oldest and most prestigious dynasties in south-west France, the Counts of Toulouse. But through a tragic quirk of fate he was also mis-shapen and ugly. Most importantly he was a dedicated painter caught up in the social debates of his time and revered and protected by his family. He was born within sight of the cathedral, to Adèle Tapié de Celeyran and her first cousin Alphonse de Toulouse-Lautrec. The main occupation of the eccentric count and his family was hunting, but they could all draw. In 1878, at the age of 14, Henri slipped on the polished parquet in Albi and fractured a leg and, the following year, broke the other leg. The bones did not knit and he remained just over five feet tall, so he drew instead of riding. Until 1881, when he went to Paris to become a professional artist, his time was divided between the different family estates. By 1884 he was established in Montmartre and he pursued his profession among the Parisian avant-garde and sub-culture of Montmartre which he evokes in all its gaiety and squalor. He travelled prodigiously but not far; he knew Van Gogh, the Pont-Aven Group, and Degas, whose work he admired most; he also knew Wilde, Whistler and Beardsley and was heavily influenced by Japanese prints; he made use of the effects of theatrical lighting; he assimilated Art Nouveau tendencies; and the popular illustrations of the 1880s were possibly the single most tangible influence on his art. Lautrec's *annus mirabilis* was 1892, when he produced his first colour posters which brought fame to him and to the people he portrayed. His posters were his main contribution to 20C art, but in fact he only made 32 lithographs for posters in the last ten years of his life. He died in 1901 at the Château de Malromé, near Bordeaux.

The **permanent exhibitions** take up the first, second and third floors. (There is a lift.) Fourteen galleries are dedicated to Toulouse-Lautrec, with paint-ings by his family, paintings of him by his friends, including Vuillard in 1898, and self-portraits. Lautrec's earlier paintings reflect the influence of his first teacher, René Princetau (1839–1914), and the aristocractic milieu. There is a tiny, rather inept, portrait of 1881 of his father on horseback, dressed as a Caucasian, his falcon on his wrist. The paintings are arranged themati-cally rather than chronologically, although at the beginning these coincide. A form of diluted Impressionist landscapes gives way to linear studies of figures and interiors. In 1882 he moved to Leon Bonnat's studio and then to

Cormon in Montmartre. By 1885 his work was becoming far more experimental and his social conscience was stirred. **La Buveuse** or **Gueule de bois** (1889) for which Suzanne Valladon, Lautrec's mistress, posed shortly before they separated, is a comment on isolation and self-destruction. Compare this dejection with the quiet dignity of the two portraits of another woman seated and alone, his mother, **Comtesse Adèle de Toulouse-Lautrec**, painted c 1881 and 1887. The large painting of **Maurice Joyant en baie de Somme** (1900), dressed in yellow oilskins and sou'wester that Lautrec had acquired from the States and wanted to paint, took 75 sittings. There are dandies and women with complicated coiffures, in a style he developed after 1889 in thin oils on board with a breathtaking fluidity and economy of line.

The galleries with the hard-core Montmartre works are to the north. Sensual, erotic, funny, tender or wickedly satirical, with a straightforward realism that was considered outrageous at the time, Lautrec's critical observation and technical prowess come together. Representative of his work are the two famous versions of **Au Salon de la Rue des Moulins** (1894), one a pastel study in preparation for the oil painting. A studied and carefully orchestrated piece in large format (1.115 x 1.325m), it is the culmination of his studies and sketches of *maisons closes* (brothels) and their occupants, made from 1891 to 1895. In these galleries are all the music-hall stars found in the posters: Yvette Guilbert, Jane Avril, La Goulue, Loïe Fuller, 1893, a swirl of veils and graceful arabesques.

The **second floor** contains original **lithograph stones**, which Lautrec prepared himself, and the **posters**. Lautrec's earlier work and experiments are synthesised in this flattened decorative formula which projected the art of the poster into the 20C. He was a man with a foot in two camps, the Establishment and Parisian sub-culture and this dichotomy is brought into perspective in this museum.

The 19C and 20C collection is on the third floor.

The **quartier de la rivière** on the slopes of the Tarn has many beautiful old buildings, some in a sorry state but the majority most thoughtfully renewed. Set out from Place de l'Archeveché (note the 16C slate roofs and dormers) on the south-east of the Berbie. Rue d'Engueysse has some jettied houses with open galleries or a *soleilho* (sometimes called a *galetas*) originally used for drying crops, including *pastel*.

There is a choice of restaurants in this area, down Que Choiseul and on the river bank. The pointed arches indicate the oldest part, c 1220, of the much-modified **Pont Vieux**, and the brick sections indicate the enlargements made after 1820 to allow the carts carrying coal and glass to pass.

Across the river is the **Faubourg du Bout-du-Pont** which developed in the 11C, and on the right in Rue Porta is a terrace overlooking the river. Just after the fork with Rue Porta enter Square Botany Bay (beside the Altea Hotel), and the **Musée Lapérouse** devoted to the life and times of Jean-François Galaup de Lapérouse, sailor and explorer, born near Albi in 1741, who was active at Hudson Bay against the English during the American Wars of Independence. The old mills of Albi were below here.

Return by Rue de la Visitation and the Pont Neuf, 1866, renamed **Pont du 22 août 1944**, to commemorate a combat between members of the Resistance and a German column. On the west side of Lices Georges Pompidou is the 19C Lycée Lapérouse, where Jean Jaurès, the local socialist hero, taught philosophy, 1881–83. He played a key role in encouraging local glassmakers to form the Verrerie Ouvrière d'Albi in 1896, one of the first worker-managed enterprises in France.

Between **Esplanade des Partisans**, the river and Rue Emile Grand is a tangle of narrow streets. Rue de la Grand'Côte was one of the most important before the 18C. At the end of Rue Emile Grand, with the angle of Rue St-Etienne and Rue des Foissants, is the crumbling stone **Maison Pierre-Raimond de Rabastens**, the oldest house in Albi (12C). Quite a contrast is the spruce, turn-of-the-century brick and steel **marché couvert** (covered market) 1901–02. There are some stalls in the market every day but it positively bustles with activity on market day (Saturday). The best house nearby is the 16C **Hôtel de Gorsse**, in a courtyard at the top of the steps north of the market. Return to Place Ste-Cécile along Rue St-Julien, where No. 16 has a *soleilho*.

South of the cathedral is a mainly pedestrianised and up-market quarter, with restaurants and chic boutiques among the carefully restored medieval, Renaissance, 18C and 19C houses. From the south-east corner of Place Ste-Cécile, take **Rue Ste-Cécile**. Where Rue Puech-Bérenguier and Rue de la Croix-Blanche meet is the pretty **Maison du Vieil Alby** for regional exhibitions, and in **Rue Toulouse-Lautrec**, No. 10 is an attractively restored late-Renaissance courtyard. Further along on the right are the home of Lapérouse at No. 14, and the Hôtel du Bosc, where Toulouse-Lautrec was born and where, in 1878, he broke his leg.

Continue to Rue de Verdusse and turn right to **Place Lapérouse** with a large monument to Lapérouse by Nicolas Bernard Raggi (1791–1862) erected in 1853. Rue Devoisins opens into Place du Palais where the **Palais de Justice** occupies the former Carmelite Convent, an early 17C brick building around a small cloister. Take the street opposite to join **Rue de l'Hôtel de Ville**. This once most prestigious street is lined with some of the best noble houses, the most outstanding at Nos 13, 14 and 17, and No. 16, the **Hôtel de Ville** since the 18C. Above the doorway of the restored 17C façade is the coat of arms of Albi and inside is a very attractive brick courtyard. Rue de l'Hôtel de Ville leads back to Place du Vigan.

34

Cordes, Monestiés, the Ségala, Sauveterre-de-Rouergue

Total distance: 70km (44 miles).

CORDES-SUR-CIEL (pop. 900, Tourist Information, Maison Fontpeyrouse, tel: 63 56 00 52), described locally as the *Perle des bastides*, is the showpiece of the northern Tarn, one of the oldest and most picturesque *bastides* in the region, its charter granted by Raymond VII of Toulouse in 1222. The suffix *sur-Ciel* was officially recognised in 1990 to distinguish it from Gordes in the Vaucluse, and is not such a fantasy as it seems. If you are lucky enough to be near the village just after dawn on a clear autumn day you are likely to see the mists gather in the Cérou valley and swirl around the base of the hill. Many postcards by the local photographer Pierre Blanc prove it (found in the newsagents in the lower town). Apart from the spectacular site, the detail that qualifies it as a two-star entry is its unique group of Gothic houses.

There is a choice of hotels, restaurants and cafés in and around Cordes including the *Grand Ecuyer* (tel: 63 56 01 03) installed in a Gothic *hôtel-particulier*, the delightful hotel-restaurant *Hostellerie du Vieux-Cordes* (tel: 63 56 00 12), and nearby is the *Hostellerie du Parc* at Les Cabannes (tel: 63 56 02 59). By Midi-Pyrénées standards, Cordes can get busy in the summer, and on a Saturday morning the market, held at the bottom of the hill, does cause some confusion. Since the beginning of the century Cordes has attracted a number of artists and artisans and there are some classy shops as well as a few trashy ones.

The best way to get to the top of the hill is to walk, not as daunting as it looks. There is some parking at the top, but better to park in the lower town (car park to the west off the D600). Alternatively there is a little train from Easter to autumn (not lunchtime).

Cordes is made up of four concentric enclosures, the first two dating from the *bastide* built in 1222, the others later. The suburb of La Boutellerie on the eastern side remained outside the protected perimeter. Start from **Place de la Boutellerie** and take the no-entry to cars road, which takes you past the Chapel of the old Hôpital St-Jacques on the right to the junction with the **Pater-Noster steps** on your left—as many steps as there are words in the Lord's Prayer—and the **Porte de l'Horlorge** on the right, with a clock and a round tower. This was the eastern entrance to the fourth enceinte, built in the 16C to enclose the four *faubourgs* surrounding the medieval fort since the 14C. It gets steeper here.

There was never a feudal castle at Cordes, but around the next bend the mighty **barbican** comes into view on a clifflike base with a tiny spring of water welling from the corner. It was part of the third enclosure built at a time of great prosperity and population explosion at the end of the 13C or early in the 14C when the earlier enclosures were consumed by new buildings. The road turns the next corner to arrive at the **Porte du Planol**, 1222–29, built parallel with the wall, preceded by a semi-circular tower facing outwards. As the defences became redundant and the community grew, the four 13C gateways of the two original enclosures were engulfed by the buildings around them. Opposite is the late 15C Maison Gorsse, with early Renaissance windows regrettably now shuttered.

The road then turns left to pass through the **Portail Peint**, barely altered since the 13C when it would have had two portcullises and a wooden door, to the heart of the *bastide*. Immediately on the right is the entrance to the **Musée Charles Portal** (tel: 63 56 00 52, 14.00–18.00 Jul, Aug, otherwise Sun and BH), a private museum of local archaeology and history with a remarkable and eclectic collection.

On the **Grand Rue** are the best of the famous **Gothic houses**, a remarkable group with traceried windows and sculpted decoration, that appear to date from nearly a century after the foundation of the *bastide* when the bourgeoisie made fortunes from linen and leather and the population of Cordes could have been around 5000. The best are to the south, built into the side of the hill with an average of three floors on the town side but up to five or six facing the countryside. On the ground floor are large arches of varying size giving access to the courtyard, stables or boutiques. The first floor is the most ornate, corresponding to a large room the width of the building lit by a series of windows, the decoration usually concentrated around the windows and on the stringcourses linking the bays. The rhythm of the bays and the carvings are slightly different for each house. As the population decreased the occupants moved to the lower floors, partitioned the interior, blocked doors and windows, especially when windows were taxed in the 17C, sliced off the relief carvings to hang shutters, but left the upper floors unmolested. When the time came to restore the houses, the second floor often served as a model for the lower one. The names are an invention of the 19C inspired by nothing more than the decoration on the façade.

The first on the left is the **Maison Carrié-Boyer**, considered to be among the earliest built between 1295 and 1320. On three floors, the façade aggressively altered, it remains an example of how most of the houses were left in the 19C. Next to Maison Carrié-Boyer is **Maison Prunet**, of about the same date, with three arcades on the gound floor and three of two-light Gothic windows outlined by a deep moulding with a carving in the apex and a circular oculus above each pair. It houses the Sugar Museum. The next house, **Maison du Grand Fauconnier**, is one of the three masterpieces. Two of the original birds of prey from the façade are in the Charles Portal Museum. This house, thought to date from the first half of the 14C, is one of the most carefully executed façades, with five arcades at ground level. The first and second floors have series of traceried windows, arranged in different rhythms, and high relief carving on the mouldings, capitals, label stops and at the apex of the hood moulds.

The **Yves Brayer Museum** (tel: 63 56 00 40, Apr–Oct), with 17 paintings donated by the artist, is on the first floor of the Grand Fauconnier, through the small courtyard and up the stone spiral staircase. Opposite are a flight of steps leading to **Place de la Bride**, an open square where shady chestnut trees, café tables and a terrace overlooking the countryside have replaced the public buildings of the *bastide* such as the *maison commune* and the prison. Immediately below to the north you see steep steps connecting the different levels.

Descend the steps next to the Hôtel de la Bride to the **halle** where the two major streets converge. There was probably a market here in 1276, but it was rebuilt in 1358 and the 24 octagonal pillars have been repaired so often it is unlikely that any are entirely 14C; the chestnut roof timbers were replaced in the 19C. The depth of the well (85m) indicates that it was only used for emergencies, in any case there were other wells and cisterns. There is no regular market held here, but there are occasional fairs: medieval festivities on the 14 July—*Les Fêtes du Grand Fauconnier*—and a Gargantuan Feast in September. There is a summer Music Festival.

Continue past the market to the **Church of St-Michel** (open in the summer), a rather disappointing edifice with a military look, built sometime between 1263 and 1287 when the community outgrew the earlier church outside the village. The nave was rebuilt and enlarged in 1345, and again between 1460 and 1485. The constant amendments are only too clear at the west end, a model of asymmetry: the belfry (1369–74) on the north side, square at the base and octagonal above, with open bays, doubled as belfry and look-out post; it is supported by a relieving arch containing a rose window and filling the rest of the façade is a walled-up Flamboyant portal suspended high and dry above the present level of the small *place*. The present entrance on the south side has a charming polychrome wooden sculpture of the Virgin. The flat-ended apse and rectangular chapels are all that remain of the 13C building and the aisleless nave, lit only by the off-centre rose window, has chapels between the buttresses. The organ came from Notre-Dame in Paris in 1849 and is used frequently for concerts.

Back on **Grande Rue** is the **Maison du Grand Veneur** named after the huntsman in the narrative frieze running across the façade. It is the only house with the third floor still intact and bears a close resemblance to the Grand Fauconnier but without the rhythmical arrangement of the bays. Its special charm resides in the anecdotal nature of the high relief carvings. The first floor windows are a reconstruction using the second floor as a model. Birds perch on the apex of the hood moulds, dogs play and crouching figures inhabit the drop stones and the horizontal mouldings. The figures of the huntsmen, their hounds and their prey fills the spandrels on the second floor.

On the corner opposite, housing the **Information Centre** and a Cultural Centre, the **Maison Gaugiran**, heavily restored, is built around a large courtyard with a wooden staircase and galleries serving the floors.

The **Maison du Grand Ecuyer** (great equerry), now synonymous with Yves Thuriès' restaurant, is a most accomplished façade, with simpler tracery, heavily foliate capitals, and discreet carvings in the deep recesses of the window mouldings. Among the sculptures on the stringcourses, and at the level of the springing of the arches are a bird of prey devouring a rabbit, a woman with a bare breast eating an apple and a bagpipe player and some strange chimeric creatures, and on the second floor at the far right the seated horse after which the house is named. Descend one or other of the two narrow cobbled streets which meet at the **Porte des Ormeaux** to the west. Two semi-circular bastions flank the gate but the upper parts of the archway and towers were rebuilt at a very early stage. Turn right to **Porte de la Jane**, also between two semi-circular towers, but badly damaged during the Wars of Religion. There is more to explore on the lower levels and from here it is an easy route to the lower town.

By Car. Take the D91 following the Cérou valley at the foot of the *Ségala*, a generic name applied to regions where the soil was poor and only *siegle* (rye) and chestnuts would grow until lime was brought to the region by the newly built railway in the 19C. On the right of the D91 is the very pretty village of **Salles**, famous for its quarries in the Middle Ages, with a part Romanesque, part Gothic church containing four 16C painted wooden statues.

Continue another 6km to **Monestiés** (pop. 1303), a village which was put on the map in 1992 by the publicity generated when the group of late-Gothic sculptures that have been here for two centuries were restored and re-presented. Usually known as the **Mise en Tombeau**, they comprise a Crucifixion, an Entombment and a Pietà. Park in the main square and you will see it signposted (tel: 63 76 19 17/63 76 11 86). This exquisite and deeply moving work resides in the little Chapel of St-James, also the object of renovation. The chapel is a perfect foil for this unique group of polychromed stone statues, the colours now very delicate, even faded following a restoration which, in the opinion of some, was rather too vigorous. The work was commissioned by the Bishop of Albi, Louis I of Amboise, for the chapel of the Bishops' residence, the 13C Château of Combefa, 3km south of Monestiés.

This monumental work of c 1490 represents three episodes of the Passion in a vast triangular composition. It was designed, unusually, as the retable of the main altar. The plastic and expressive qualities of the carving compare with the finest produced in France at the end of the 15C, marking the transition between Gothic spirituality and humanist naturalism.

At the apex of the triangle is the **Crucifixion**. The Christ of this Crucifixion is a figure that has passed through suffering to a state of compassion. Below is the **Pietà**, in an extremely rare iconography including six extra figures, the five Maries and St John. The same figures, amplified by four more, appear again in the wide open **Entombment** scene forming the base of the triangle, also a unique arrangement, spread out to either side in a very theatrical manner. Each of the lifesize figures, five male, five female, is a masterpiece and conveys a remarkable sense of tenderness and grief. And every attention is paid to the minutest detail. The donor prelate, Louis I of Amboise, holds the shroud at the head of Christ thus displacing Joseph of Arimathaea. Next to him is St James, not usually found in an Entombment.

Also in the chapel are the stalls and some floor tiles recovered from Combefa. The glass in the chapel is recent. Monestiés is a pretty village and merits a stroll around the centre past the medieval houses, the old market place, the Church of St-Pierre and particularly the old bridge.

Stay on the D91 to Carmaux, a former mining town, and cross it rapidly to join the N88 to **Tanus** (27km).

Detour. If you feel like a walk of about a half hour to a magical place in the woods above the Viaur Gorges, turn left on the D53 just before Tanus and after about 2km park at the beginning of the un-made road leading to **Las Planques** (key at the Mairie, Tanus). There was once a village in this remote spot, but all that remains is the stark and dramatic 11C church built in dark gneiss. After Tanus the D88 dips right down to the Viaur, the boundary between the Tarn and the Aveyron. This ravine was spanned by the elegant **Viaduc de Viaur** in 1902, a railway bridge on the Carmaux–Rodez line. It comes into view on the right as you climb out of the valley. (Car park.) No mean feat at the time, it is still one of the most impressive constructions of its kind in France, built by a local engineer, Bodin, who won the competition held in 1887. The central arch has a span of 220m.

Continue to Naucelle on the N88 and turn right on to the D10, and follow the signs to the **Château du Bosc** (tel: 65 69 20 83), 15km, one of the properties still belonging to descendants of the family of Toulouse-Lautrec and where the painter spent much of his childhood. Quite apart from this connection, it is a salutary hour or so spent in a property that has not been sold since the 12C and in a setting that epitomises *la France profonde*. The visit is accompanied and takes you through the library, dining room, private chapel and drawing room as well as the bedroom of Adèle, Countess Toulouse-Lautrec, the painter's mother, with the English books, the crayons and the Punch and Judy that belonged to little Henri. A visit to the Bosc offers an important insight to Toulouse-Lautrec's background and the family's attitude to him, and complements a visit to the museum in Albi.

Detour. D10, D83, D617, 10km, to the **Château de Taurines** (tel: 65 69 24 59) mainly because it is being restored with such enthusiasm by local people and holds interesting exhibitions of contemporary art.

From the Bosc take the D10 across the N88 5km to **Naucelle** (Tourist Information, tel: 65 47 04 32), a busy little town with a tiny arcaded square and a restored church with a Flamboyant decoration inside the porch. Continue to **Sauveterre-de-Rouergue** (11.5km) (pop. 1929, Tourist Information, tel: 65 47 05 32), an excellent *bastide* with a rectangular plan founded in 1281. The large central *place* is overlooked by well-restored 15C and 16C houses shoulder to shoulder extended out over the street to form continous *couverts* (or arcades), each with its particular characteristics. There are the remains of a tower, two of the old gates, and the city ditch, and the small 14C church is set back to the east. Between 1362 and 1369

Rouergue was under English domination and Sauveterre was one of their most resistant strongholds. The hotel-restaurant, the *Auberge de Sénéchal* (tel: 65 47 02 65), is recommended. (See also Routes 26, 27, 28, Rodez, Villefranche-de-Rouergue and the Lévézou.)

Forest and Vine: between Cordes and Gaillac

Total distance: 90km (56 miles).

This is a short circuit through the vineyards of Gaillac on the *coteaux* above the right bank of the Tarn. It is often referred to as the *route des bastides*, but although it includes some picturesque villages on hills, only Cordes and Castelnau-de-Montmiral are bona fide *bastides*.

By Road. From Cordes go west on the D600 to **Vindrac** (5km) and the **Musée de l'Outil** (tel: 63 56 02 17/63 56 05 77, 15.00–19.00), where in part of a beautifully restored house is a fascinating collection of 18C and 19C domestic and agricultural implements.

Turn left under the railway bridge in the direction of Vaour on the D91 which winds up along the perimeter of the vineyards and the Forêt de Grésigne. After 15km ignore the first turning left to Vaour because a further 1.5km brings you to a dolmen and panoramic views of the Quercy. Return to the D33 (4km) to reach the ruins of a Templar Commandery.

Vaour comes to life for two weeks in August during the international laughter spectacular, *Festival du rire*, held in the open air. Stay on the D33, 8.5km, to **Penne**, a village strung out along a narrow promontory with the precariously fragile ruins of a 13C château overhanging the Aveyron valley. It has a small square and a church which has been reoriented, and beside the church an archway with a bell. Penne lights up in the summer with a *son et lumière* extravaganza (tel: 63 56 36 68, Wed and Fri, June–mid Sept), one of the few in the region.

Wiggle along the D9 and D87, 11km, and turn left on the D964 below **Bruniquel** (see Route 27, Villefranche). You willl pass *L'Auberge du Lac* (tel: 63 33 15 58) with hearty food, and **Larroque**, a mainly 17C village built into the cliffs below the Grésigne Forest.

After 11km is a left turn to **Puycelci**, an impressive sight as you drive up to the plateau; there is parking by the war memorial on the site of the old château. The village is still contained within the boundaries of its 15C walls. The tiny Baroque Chapel of St-Roch north of the square (now used by the Tourist Information, tel: 63 33 19 25) was built in 1703 and has a vine entwined gilded retable. There is a fortified gate, Porte d'Irrissou, the 15C Château du Petit St-Roch, and various other fortifications, including a 17C tower and the prison tower. In Place de la Mairie are the old Maison Commune and good 15C and 16C façades. The Church of St-Corneille, part 14C, part 15C with a 18C belfry, is a simple structure with one or two amusing carvings around the porch. There are a few craftsmen working in Puycelsi and just one café.

Stay on the D964 and 10km on is **Castelnau-de-Montmiral**, a veritable *bastide* in miniature, also on a hill, founded at the same time as Cordes. There is a car park at the top. In the tiny arcaded square where you will find the Tourist Information Office (tel: 63 33 15 11) (note the plaque commemorating a visit by Jean-Paul Sartre and Simone de Beauvoir outside), the pillory, and a café-restaurant that does a good line in *sanglier* (wild boar) stew, and another restaurant. This must be the only hilltop village that still has a cowshed in use—your nose will lead you to it. The church contains a remarkable wooden **reliquary cross** (behind bars in the north-east, with light), 96cm tall, covered in silver and gilt, decorated with filigree and studded with semi-precious stones, containing a relic of the True Cross.

Take the D964 then the D115a, 9km, to **Cahuzac-sur-Vère**. Nearby (D1 then turn right) the **Château du Caylar** (tel: 63 33 90 30), a 14C and 18C house, was the birthplace of the writers Eugénie de Guérin (1805–48) and her poet brother Maurice (1810–39).

From Cahuzac go 2km south-east on the D21 to the **Château du Mauriac** (tel: 63 41 71 18, 15.00–18.00), a severe military fortress domesticated during the Renaissance, the house of the painter Bistes. Many years of dedicated renovation, including several murals and ceiling paintings by the present owners, have turned it into a beautiful setting for Bistes' works.

13km to Cordes on the D922.

35

Gaillac, the Vineyards, Lisle-sur-Tarn, Rabastens, Lavaur

Land of Wine and Plenty

Total distance: 100km (75 miles).

This itinerary starts out from Gaillac and heads through towns built in rustic pink brick on the banks of the Tarn and the Agout, and a landscape that has been patchworked with vineyards for about a thousand years. In the 14C and 15C, particularly towards the south-east of this region, the vineyards gave way to fields of *pastel* or woad which produced a very high-quality blue or indigo dye. The dried leaves were compressed into balls for storage and transport, called *coques*, and gave rise to the expression *le pays de cocagne* (Cockaigne), the land of plenty. *Pastel* gave way to imported indigo at the end of the 16C. The third important crop is garlic, grown to the east of this region, around Lautrec and Réalmont.

GAILLAC (pop. 11,742, Tourist Information, 81600-Place de la Libération, tel: 63 57 14 65) has a busy market on Fridays. Promoted as one of the oldest wine producing areas in France, the cultivation of vines on the banks of the Tarn is thought to go back to the 6C BC. The Benedictine monks of the Abbey of St-Michel were the prime movers in the development and perfection of viticulture and vinification and as early as 1271 a charter was granted guaranteeing the quality of Gaillac wine. The wine was carried via the Tarn and the Garonne to Bordeaux, and shipped to northern Europe. The vineyards were badly hit, as elsewhere, by phylloxera in 1879, but in the 1920s there was a strong revival and by 1938 the Gaillac whites received an *appellation contrôlée* label, followed in 1970 by the reds. There are 400 producers and three cooperatives over an area of more than 2000 hectares between Cordes, Rabastens, Graulhet and Castelnau-de-Levis on the banks of the parallel valleys of the Tarn and the Vère where there is a microclimate and soils suited to vines. The local grape varieties are Mauzac and, Len de l'El plus Sauvignon and Muscadelle for whites, and Duras and Braucol the basis of the red appellation complemented by Syrah, Gamay, Merlot and Cabernet. The cooperatives are at Labastide-de-Levis, Rabastens and Técou, the latter producing an excellent and typical red provocatively named *Passion*. The characteristic of the Gaillac reds is a flavour of blackcurrants or raspberries, and the whites are slightly appley. Most of the 400 producers and the cooperatives are happy to give a tasting and the town is at its liveliest at the beginning of August during La Fête des Vins de Gaillac.

On Foot. From the shady **Place de la Libération** take Rue Portal past the old Church of St-Pierre with a 13C doorway. **Hôtel de Brens**, just off Rue Portal on the right, is a pretty 13C–15C building in timber and brick with two overhanging turrets and a pentagonal gallery, home to the Museum of Vine and Wine (afternoons except Tues). At the end of Rue Portal is **Place Thiers** with arcades and le Griffoul fountain in the middle. This is at the heart of the old town.

Leave the square by the south-east corner to arrive in **Place St-Michel**, in front of the sheer brick face of the old abbey **church of St-Michel** facing Place St-Michel. The gabled west end is flanked by a tower (13C and 14C) and the portal was added in 1847. The single vessel of the nave, typical of the Midi, is huge, 47.5m long and 17m wide, painted in *trompe l'oeil* in the 19C. The oldest part of the church is the 13C east end, profoundly modified in 1869 when pillars and arcades were substituted for a semi-circular wall around the choir. Between the interior buttresses are chapels, except on the third and fourth bays south where the abbey abuts the church. The chapel in the second bay on the north, with decorated capitals, was built in the late 14C, possibly as a funerary chapel by Abbot Roger de Latour whose coat of arms is on the boss. There are some fittings and furnishings of note, including an early 14C polychromed wooden statue of the Virgin and Child wearing crowns; a holy water stoup (13C?) on the left of the entrance decorated with birds and flowers; a Baroque retable with a painting by Antoine Rivalz (1667–1735) and on the wall of the south-east chapel a 15C high-relief panel of the Resurrected Christ appearing to Mary Magdalene. The main altar is of 1785–90 and the elaborate pulpit was made in 1883–85. The organ above the west door was made by Dominique Cavaillé-Col, from a dynasty of organ-builders who originated from Gaillac.

Beside the bridge is the Maison des Vins, in the former abbey buildings, headquarters of the Gaillac wine producers association (C.I.V.G. Information, tel: 63 57 15 40).

East of the church is the **parc** and **Château de Foucaud**, built in 1647 on the edge of the Tarn. The building shows its most elegant face to the river, with double flights of steps leading to a formal garden and terraces to the river bank. In the château is the Fine Arts Museum (tel: 63 57 18 25, 14.00–18.00, Apr–Oct, except Tues), with works by regional artists, and the Gaillac wine festival is held in the park.

By Road. Cross the Tarn and take the D87 for 5km to **Montans**. A tiny community today of about 200 inhabitants, it was the site of a huge

Gallo-Roman pottery works and has a fascinating little museum of local finds (tel: 63 57 19 68, 14.00–18.00, mid-Jun–mid-Sept, plus 12.00–18.00 Sun). Occupied since the Iron Age (c 700 BC), the village developed on the edge of a small ravine above the confluence of the Rieutort and the Tarn. With all the raw materials on hand, pots were produced here before the arrival of Romans, but they introduced skilled potters from Arezzo with more sophisticated techniques and decoration. The best and most creative period was AD 20–75, then production became more utilitarian. Much of the work is signed. The display of the techniques, tools and periods of production from 100 BC to the early 4C is very comprehensive. In 1992 an important find of 40 gold pieces was made, but this is not (yet) on display. At the height of production there could have been as many as 40 or 50 kilns at one time and only a part of the huge area used by the potteries has been excavated. The museum is expanding, a documentation centre is underway, and an *archéodrome* will recreate a Gallo-Roman street and winery.

From Montans either take the D13 (7km) direct to Lisle-sur-Tarn, in which case you approach it across the Tarn—a fine approach—or, if you are considering a wine tasting, return to the junction with the D964, and turn right to the Cooperative at Técou; alternatively, turn left and left again on to the N88 and about 3.5km turn off down a tree-lined avenue to the Château de Lastours, a friendly family-run winery.

Lisle-sur-Tarn (Tourist Information, tel: 63 33 35 18) is a beautiful, warm, sleepy brick *bastide* founded in the 13C with the largest square in the south-west, surrounded by *corniers* and *couverts* and a variety of façades, some half-timbered, some rebuilt from the 17C–19C entirely in brick.

The narrow streets behind the square are lined with brick and timber houses in different states of repair, six with *pountets*. The **Church of Notre-Dame de la Jonquière** is a 14C southern Gothic aisleless brick building with a 13C Romanesque-style porch on the north with sculpted capitals and carved archivolts. The porch at the west supports a two-tier octagonal belfry. Most of the interior furnishings are 17C and 18C. The **Musée Raymond Lafage** (open Jun–Sept, and Thur & Fri out of season, check times with Tourist Information) has drawings and engravings by the local artist, Lafage (1656–85), who spent time in Rome, and local archaeology.

Midway between Lisle-sur-Tarn and Rabastens is the **Château de St-Géry** (N88), so close to the Tarn river that the terrace collapsed twenty years ago and had to be rebuilt (open Sun afternoon, Easter–Oct, every day Jul–Aug). On three sides of a courtyard, part of the east wing is 13C–14C, and the rest is 17C and 18C. There is a superb 18C chapel and the château has kept its original furnishings. It is a surprise to find the dining room decorated in a blue and white Wedgewood motif, introduced by the owner who fled to England during the Revolution. The château has been owned by the O'Byrne family since 1829.

RABASTENS (pop. 3834, Tourist Information, tel: 63 40 65 65/63 33 70 18), 8km from Lisle-sur-Tarn on the N88, also overlooks the Tarn. Towards the middle of the 12C Moissac founded a priory here where the old Roman road crossed the river and it became an important stage for medieval pilgrims between Rodez and Toulouse, partly because Rabastens possessed numerous relics, including relics of St James, until the end of the 18C. The priory church of **Notre-Dame du Bourg** is at the west of the town, on the D12. At the end of the Albigensian period the church was rebuilt. Eight capitals (1190–1200) were re-used with their slender marble columns in the recessed west porch (recently restored). The capitals have scenes from the birth and childhood of Christ and the Temptation in the Wilderness. The new church conceived in the Gothic style of the south-west has a cliff-like, angular west end pierced by a small rose window and two turrets flanking a rectangular gable belfry, the upper part completed in the 19C.

The interior of Notre-Dame du Bourg is rather gloomy and heavily ornate, reminiscent of Albi and it is absolutely essential to have 5 Fr pieces to feed the light meter. It is arranged in the traditional southern Gothic way, with an unaisled nave. The 13C church was built with a flat east end, but in the 14C this was opened and extended to make a large choir and polygonal chevet with chapels between the buttresses and an unusual Romanesque style arcaded triforium was built above. The remodelled east end was consecrated in 1318. The vaults, walls and most of the chapels have **painted decoration** from different periods which disappeared under plaster after the Reformation. With one exception they were rediscovered c 1859 and almost entirely repainted 1860–63 by Joseph Engalières.

The murals on the **vaults of the nave** are thought to originate from the second half of the 13C, and include St James on the first crossing arch and St Christopher on the second, and knights, possibly participating in a pilgrimage or in a crusade. On the walls of the nave are two cycles: on the south scenes from the Childhood of Christ, but in the 4th bay the original mural was replaced by the Expulsion of Adam and Eve in the 15C; on the north the Resurrection, Crucifixion and Ascension.

Five chapels were built between the buttresses between 1374 and the end of the 15C. The **chapel St Roch** on the north was painted in 1520–30, and only discovered in 1972. On a red background on the walls are St Peter, St Michael with the scales and sword, and Christ. The choir vaults up to the triforium were painted with a geometric design and quadrilobe medallions with Christ, the Virgin, Apostles and saints, c 1320. Only the **chapels of St-Martin** and **St-Jacques** on the north, and **St-Augustin** on the south, have conserved their 14C paintings, with episodes of the life of the respective saint on alternate blue and red backgrounds. Late in the 14C or early in the 15C, another cycle of the Childhood of Christ was painted in the spandrels on the high walls of the **choir**. St James appears again on the transverse rib of the chancel arch (14C) and on the east side of the arch are Christ and the four Evangelists.

In a narrow street opposite the church is the **Musée du Pays Rabastinois** (tel: 63 40 65 65, May–Oct, check times), in Hôtel de la Fite, a fine end-17C–18C mansion. The museum has a collection ranging from a Gallo-Roman mosaic to haute-couture embroidery.

Overlooking the Promenades is the former 15C/16C priory building, significantly altered in 1830 but retaining the elegant 16C tower giving access to the church. The Hôtel de Rolland de Combettes, further west, is a 15C building that was entirely renovated and embellished in the 19C. The view from the bridge over the Tarn is impressive.

Giroussens, on the D12, 8km south-east of Rabastens, started in the 12C as a fort defending the castle of the Viscounts of Albi in a strategic position overlooking the Agout. It was granted the privileges of a *bastide* in the 13C, and was a pottery town until the 18C. The 15C church was repaired and amended in the 17C, and contains sumptuous decoration. As well as two 17C retables, the main retable in wood, gilded in 1734, has a painting of the Crucifixion and three pedimented aedicules containing statues of St Joseph, the Virgin and Child, and the saint-bishop Salvy.

An outing for children at **St-Lieux-lès-Lavaur**, just south of Giroussens on the D38, is the **Petit Train Touristique**, a steam train which makes a journey of 7km on an old line across the Agout (tel: 61 47 44 52, Sun & BH all year; Sat, Sun & Mon, Jul–Aug).

The D12/D87 brings you to (10km) **LAVAUR** (pop. 8147, Tourist Information, tel: 63 58 02 00/63 58 06 71), notable for the Gothic brick **Cathedral of St-Alain** on a sheer cliff above the Agout, set in pleasant gardens. Simon de Montfort all but destroyed the first church, and in 1255 the city fathers undertook, in the presence of the Inquisitors, to build a new one. Five bays of the new church had been completed in 1317 when the town was elevated to episcopal see. The exterior walls between the buttresses were added in the 14C, and the two south-east chapels in 1450. The massive west end closely resembles Albi Cathedral, enclosed in square buttresses, with a truncated octagonal tower added at the end of the 15C. The rather too small east end, sheer above the river, has two little turrets. The Jacquemart, who hits his bell with a hatchet every hour, is on the small belfry on the south flank of the church and is unique in the south-west. There has been one since 1604, but the present oak figurine dates from 1922 and the bell from 1523.

The simple **interior**, aisleless with shallow chapels on the north and extended on the south in the 15C, was damaged at the Revolution and restored 1843–47, and painted with coloured and grisaille *trompe l'oeil* by Italian painters, the Ceroni. To light the interior there is a 1Fr meter near the candles. The cathedral has reacquired the 12C **altar table**, a relic of the first church, sculpted with a eucharistic theme on the chamfer with stylistic similarities to the altar table at St-Sernin, Toulouse, and the capitals of Moissac. Also salvaged from the first church is the **Romanesque porch** in the first chapel on the right; the carved capitals have scenes from the childhood of Christ (the first and last are 19C plaster replicas). An organ was installed in 1523 and the magnificent **organ case** was recently restored. When the instrument was remade by Aristide Cavaillé-Col in 1874, certain elements, notably the volutes, vases and balustrade, were added as well as a coating of dark varnish. The varnish has been removed to reveal the original 16C colours. Other fittings include the mausoleum of Bishop Simon de Beausoleil (d. 1531), a wooden painted and gilded Pietà (17C), six paintings of Scenes of the Passsion (18C), attributed to Pierre Subleyras (1699–1749), the main altar in polychrome marble, the wrought-iron lectern signed by Bernard Ortet (1778), who worked at the Cathedral of St-Etienne in Toulouse, and the 19C pulpit. The stained glass of the choir is dated 1853–54.

The **Musée des Pays Vaurais**, in the old chapel of the Doctrinaires, has religious art and archaeology (to visit tel: 63 58 00 31).

Leave on the D112 for **St-Paul-Cap-de-Joux**, 15km. 6km south-west of St-Paul is the Renaissance **Château de Magrin**, at the heart of the Pays de Cocagne, with a museum of the history of *pastel*, its cultivation, production and use (tel: 63 70 63 82, Museum, Easter–Oct, château Sun, Jul–Aug).

For somewhere to stay, 5km south from Lavaur at **Bosc Lebat** is an English-owned *chambres d'hôte*, tel: 63 58 04 89.

On Sundays in August you can visit the **Château de Roquevidal** (D12 from Magrin, tel: 63 41 32 32), a medieval château transformed in the late-16C or 17C, after the Wars of Religion, and owned in the 17C and 18C by Protestant families.

The fame of **Puylaurens**, 9km south-west of Magrin on the D12, rests on the fact that one of her daughters was immortalised as Marianne, symbol of the French Republic. It also has a recommended restaurant at the *Hôtel Pages* (tel: 63 75 00 09).

11km east of **St-Paul** on the D112 turn left on to the D92, 10km, and you get a good view of **Lautrec** (Tourist Information, tel: 63 75 31 40) as you approach and views on all sides when you get there, including the Black Mountains to the south. Is there also a hint of garlic on the air? The region around produces pink garlic with an *appellation contrôlée* qualification, at the rate of 4000 tonnes a year from 1000 ha (380 producers), one-tenth of the production of France. Friday morning from 20 July to 31 March you can buy the garlic at market, and kept in a cool place it will last up to a year.

Lautrec itself is a charming medieval village on a hill with some well-maintained 16C and 17C timber-framed houses with jetties or arcades. Still intact on the east side of the town is part of the old ramparts and one of the eight original gateways, Porte de la Caussade. The Church of St-Rémy, was begun in the 15C, vaulted in 1769, and has lots of 19C *trompe l'oeil* and false marbling. Behind the church in Rue de St-Esprit, off the Grande Rue, are the steps up to the greatest attraction of Lautrec, the still-turning 17C **Moulin de la Salette** (tel: 63 75 96 78, 14.00–19.00 Jul–Aug).

*Detail of the Maison du Grand Fauconnier, 13C, Cordes-sur-Ciel.
Photograph by Pierre Blanc*

BLUE GUIDES

The Blue Guide series was founded in 1915 by Muirhead Guide-Books Limited. In 1918 the first Blue Guide, London and its Environs, was published. Findlay and James Muirhead already had extensive experience of guide-book publishing: before the First World War they had been the editors of the English editions of the German Baedekers, and by 1915 they had acquired the copyright of most of the famous 'Red' Handbooks from John Murray.

An agreement made with the French publishing house Hachette et Cie in 1917 led to the translation of Muirhead's London guide, which became the first 'Guide Bleu', Hachette had previously published the blue-covered 'Guides Joanne'. Subsequently, Hachette's Guide Blue 'Paris et ses Environs' was adapted and published in London by Muirhead.

In 1931 Ernest Benn Limited took over the Blue Guides, appointing Russell Muirhead, Findlay Muirhead's son, editor in 1934. The Muirheads' connection with the Blue Guides ended in 1963, when Stuart Rossiter, who had been working on the Guides since 1954, became house editor, revising and compiling several of the books himself.

The Blue Guides are now published by A & C Black, who acquired Ernest Benn in 1984, so continuing the tradition of guide-book publishing which began in 1826 with 'Black's Economical Tourist of Scotland'. The series continues to grow: there are now more than 60 titles in print, with revised editions appearing regularly, and many new titles in preparation.

INDEX

The index lists all of the places described in the text. Châteaux, gorges, cols, etc are entered under their individual names.

BLUE GUIDES ORDER FORM

Blue Guides are available through all bookshops or can be obtained directly from A & C Black by writing to: **A & C Black, PO Box 19, Huntingdon, Cambs PE19 3SF** or telephone (01480) 212666, fax: (01480) 212666. Access and Visa are accepted. Availability and published prices are correct at the time of going to press, but are subject to change without notice. For information on our other travel guide series, please contact our sales department.

BLUE GUIDES ISBN prefix: 0-7136

Albania 3785-4	£12.99
Amsterdam 3228-3	£8.99
Athens 3rd ed 3506-1	£12.99
Austria 3rd ed 3383-2	£12.99
Barcelona 3229-1	£8.99
Belgium & Luxembourg 8th ed 3732-3	£13.99
Berlin and Eastern Germany 3871-0	£13.99
Boston and Cambridge 2nd ed 3170-8	£14.99
Burgundy 3384-0	£8.99
Channel Islands 2nd ed 2835-9	£6.95
China 3027-2	£16.99
Churches & Chapels of:	
Northern England 3171-6	£14.95
Southern England 3029-9	£14.95
Corsica 2nd ed 3589-4	£9.99
Country houses of England 3780-3	£15.99
Crete 6th ed 3588-6	£11.99
Cyprus 3rd ed 3274-7	£9.99
Czechoslovakia 3230-5	£13.99
Denmark 3474-X	£10.99
Egypt 3rd ed 3590-8	£17.99
England 11th ed 3874-5	£14.99
Florence 6th ed 4073-1	£10.99
France 3rd ed 3386-7	£16.99
Gardens of England 3389-1	£14.99
Greece 6th ed 3250-X	£16.99
Holland 5th ed 3654-8	£11.99
Hungary 3030-2	£12.95
Ireland 7th ed 3870-2	£13.99
Istanbul 3rd ed 3275-5	£12.99

Jerusalem 2944-4	£11.95
Literary Britain & Ireland 2nd ed 3152-X	£12.95
The Loire Valley 3872-9	£10.99
London 15th ed 3972-5	£12.99
Madrid 4106-1	£9.99
Malta & Gozo 4th ed 3954-7	£9.99
Midi-Pyrénées 3853-2	£10.99
Morocco 2nd ed 3592-4	£9.99
Moscow & Leningrad 2nd ed 3387-5	£12.99
Museums & galleries of London 3rd ed 3168-6	£12.95
New York 2nd ed 3169-4	£17.99
Normandy 3730-7	£9.99
Northern Italy 9th ed 3276-3	£14.99
Oxford & Cambridge 4th ed 3904-0	£9.99
Paris & Versailles 8th ed 3581-9	£10.99
Portugal 3rd ed 2966-5	£8.95
Rome & environs 5th ed 3939-3	£13.99
Scotland 10th ed 3426-X	£16.99
Sicily 4th ed 3784-6	£11.99
Southern Italy 7th ed 3141-4	£12.95
South-west France 3910-5	£9.99
Spain 6th ed 3731-5	£14.99
Sweden 3935-0	£12.99
Switzerland 5th ed 3559-2	£11.99
Turkey 2nd ed 3829-X	£16.99
Tuscany 3388-3	£12.99
Umbria 3705-6	£9.99
Venice 5th ed 3873-7	£9.99
Victorian architecture in Britain 2842-1	£14.95
Wales 8th ed 4074-X	£12.99
Western Germany 2nd ed 3278-X	£14.99

Please send me the following *Blue Guides*:_____

_____

_____

____ I enclose a cheque for: £_____ made payable to A & C Black *(please add £1.50 for p&p)*

____ Please debit my credit card Access/Visa ⬚⬚⬚⬚⬚⬚⬚⬚⬚⬚⬚⬚⬚⬚

Expiry Date: ⬚⬚⬚⬚⬚⬚

Name: _____

Address: _____

_____

⬚ *I do not wish to receive information about **Blue Guides** in the future.*